RETURN TO THE MIDDLE ★KINGDOM★

Also by Yuan-tsung Chen

The Dragon's Village

RETURN <small>TO THE</small> MIDDLE ★KINGDOM★

ONE FAMILY, THREE REVOLUTIONARIES, AND THE BIRTH OF MODERN CHINA

YUAN-TSUNG CHEN

UNION SQUARE PRESS
An imprint of Sterling Publishing Co., Inc.

New York / London
www.sterlingpublishing.com

STERLING and the distinctive Sterling logo are registered trademarks of
Sterling Publishing Co., Inc.

Library of Congress Cataloging-in-Publication Data Available

2   4   6   8   10   9   7   5   3   1

Published by Sterling Publishing Co., Inc.
387 Park Avenue South, New York, NY 10016
© 2008 by Yuan-tsung Chen
Map Illustration © 2008 Jeffrey L. Ward
Distributed in Canada by Sterling Publishing
c/o Canadian Manda Group, 165 Dufferin Street,
Toronto, Ontario, Canada M6K 3H6
Distributed in the United Kingdom by GMC Distribution Services
Castle Place, 166 High Street, East Sussex, England, BN7 1XU
Distributed in Australia by Capricorn Link (Australia) Pty. Ltd.
P.O. Box 704, Windsor, NSW 2756, Australia

Manufactured in the United States of America
All Rights Reserved

Sterling ISBN 978-1-4027-5697-9

For information about custom editions, special sales, premium and
corporate purchases, please contact Sterling Special Sales
Department at 800-805-5489 or specialsales@sterlingpublishing.com.

DEDICATION

To my son Jay Acham and his family with love

Contents

UNION OF SOVIET
SOCIALIST REPUBLICS

XINJIANG

0 Miles 250 500

0 Kilometers 500

QINGHAI

GREAT WALL

XIZANG

C H I

NEPAL

SICHUAN

INDIA

BHUTAN

YUNNAN

BURMA

★

➤–➤ THE TAIPING REBELLION,
1850–1864
(GRANDFATHER CHEN)

➤— THE NORTHERN EXPEDITION,
JULY 1926–APRIL 1927
(EUGENE CHEN)

➤···· JACK CHEN'S ESCAPE ROUTE,
JULY 1927–OCTOBER 1927

★

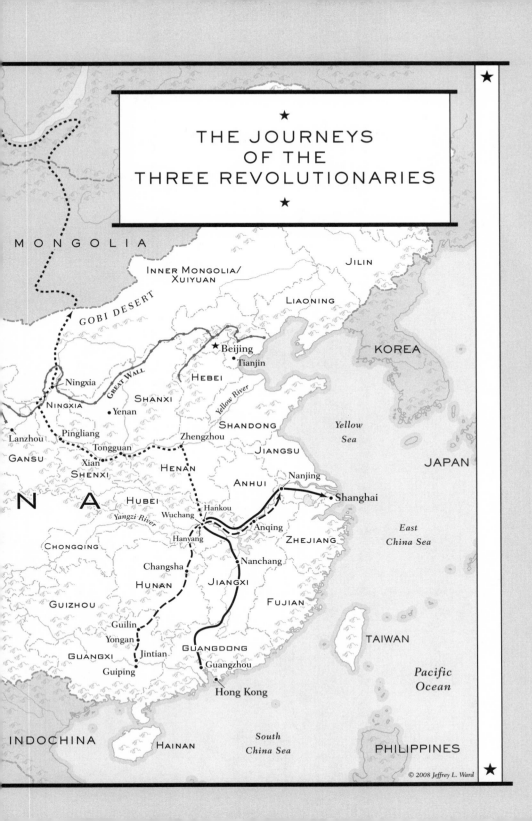

★

THE JOURNEYS
OF THE
THREE REVOLUTIONARIES

★

MONGOLIA

INNER MONGOLIA/
XUIYUAN

JILIN

LIAONING

GOBI DESERT

KOREA

★Beijing
• Tianjin

Ningxia

HEBEI

GREAT WALL

SHANXI

Yellow River

NINGXIA

• Yenan

SHANDONG

Yellow
Sea

JAPAN

Lanzhou

Pingliang

Zhengzhou

GANSU

Tongguan

JIANGSU

Xian

HENAN

SHENXI

ANHUI

Nanjing

N A

HUBEI

• Shanghai

Yangzi River

Wuchang

Hankou

Hanyang

Anqing

East
China
Sea

CHONGQING

Changsha

Nanchang

ZHEJIANG

HUNAN

JIANGXI

FUJIAN

GUIZHOU

Guilin

Yongan

GUANGXI

Jintian

GUANGDONG

Guiping

Guangzhou

TAIWAN

Pacific
Ocean

Hong Kong

INDOCHINA

HAINAN

South
China Sea

PHILIPPINES

★

CAST OF CHARACTERS

Key to abbreviations: CCP, Chinese Communist Party; KMT, Kuomintang; PRC, People's Republic of China

Western-Style Names

Borah, William E. (1865–1940), a Republican senator from Idaho who helped Eugene expose President Wilson's secret pact with Japan, double-crossing China

Borodin, Mikhail (Mikhail Markovich Gruzenberg) (1884–1951), Comintern agent who was sent by Lenin to help the KMT (nationalist party led by the bourgeois Sun Yatsen)

Bukharin, Nikolai Ivanovich (1888–1938), editor of *Pravda*, Stalin's right-hand man who partied with the teenaged Jack in 1927–1928

Chen, Eugene (1878–1944), Jack's father, the second revolutionary of the Chen family, the architect of the Russia-oriented policy that brought Mao Zedong, Zhou Enlai, and other communist leaders into the KMT

Chen, Jack (1908–1995), author's husband, the third revolutionary of the Chen family. He served the revolution with his art and journalism

Chen, Joseph (1830–1891), Jack's grandfather, a Taiping rebel, the first revolutionary of the Chen family, who fought for God's Kingdom of equality, fraternity, and liberty on Earth

Chen family: Percy (1901–1986), Jack's brother; **Silan** (1905–1996) and **Yolanda** (1913–), his sisters

Doriot, Jacques (1898–1945), a French socialist before WWII, joined Vichy after France fell

Gantheaume, Alphonsine Agatha ("Aisy") (1878–1926), Jack's mother

Gruzenberg, Mikhail Markovich, (1884–1951), *see* Borodin, Mikhail

Joffe, Adolph A. (1883–1927), communist revolutionary, Soviet diplomat. In early 1923, he signed a joint statement with Sun Yatsen, publicly declaring cooperation between the KMT government and the Soviet Union, which shocked the Western powers out of their complacency

Karakhan, Lev (1889–1937), Soviet deputy commissar for foreign affairs, wrote the Manifesto that answered Eugene's questions raised in the Paris Peace Conference, giving the first signal of possible alliance; ambassador to China, 1923–1926

Koo, Wellington (1888–1985), Chinese diplomat whose success depended on the goodwill of the United States. When President Wilson double-crossed China in the Treaty of Versailles, Eugene came into conflict with Koo

Leyda, Jay (1910–1988), Silan Chen's American husband, who arranged Jack's lecture tour to Canada and the United States while Jack was still being held in captivity by the Cultural Revolution's Red Guards

Longchallon (Leong), Marie (later Mary) (1855–1951), Jack's grandmother, Joseph Chen's wife

Mann, Tom (1856–1941), British trade unionist who helped Eugene get in touch with the Soviet Russians in Paris, 1919

Maring, *see* Sneevliet, Hendricus

O'Malley, Owen St. Clair (1887–1974), British diplomat in China who signed the agreement with Eugene to return the British concessions in Hankou and Jiujiang, 1927

Roots, Logan H. (1870–1945), Episcopal Church bishop who sheltered Zhou Enlai when Jack brought his new communist friend to the home of this church dignitary

Shi, Alfred (Shi Zhaoji) (1877–1958), minister of communications and acting minister of finance under Yuan Shikai, later minister to the Court of St. James. Eugene Chen's mentor; at the Paris Peace Conference, he backed up Eugene when he walked out on the Allied powers

Sneevliet, Hendricus (Henk aka Maring) (1883–1942), Dutch communist who delivered the infant CCP on July 1, 1921

Soong, Tse-ven (T. V.) (1894–1971), between 1923 and 1927 worked closely with Eugene; premier of China, 1930

Soong family: father **Charlie**; daughters **Ailing, Chingling, Mayling**; son **Tse-Ven**

Stalin, Joseph Vissarionovich Jugashvili (1878–1953), changed Lenin's China policy and rejected Eugene's proposal to revive the United Front between the Left KMT and CCP after the split in early 1927

Trotsky, Leon (1879–1940), the Peter Pan of the world revolution, had the fantasy that he could remake the world in his image. His followers attacked Eugene savagely when Eugene arrived in Moscow in 1927

Voitinsky, Gregory (1893–1953), Comintern agent who set up the Peking and Shanghai cells in 1920–1921. In 1925, he replaced Maring and accepted a new task from Moscow: to usurp the KMT's leadership in the Chinese revolution; a series of disasters ensued

Wang, Thomas C. T. (1882–1961), vice speaker of Chinese National Assembly who worked with Eugene to smash Yuan Shikai's dynastic dream and thwart Duan Qirui's secret deal with Japan, and later, at the Versailles Peace Conference, to refuse to sign the humiliating Peace Treaty

Wu, C. C. (Wu Zhaoshu) (1886–1934), member of National Assembly, later foreign minister, worked with Eugene against the Peking warlords and also at the Paris Peace Conference battling the Allied powers

Xu, George Qian, a member of the Episcopal Church, a sort of intermediary between the Christian community and the KMT government at Wuhan

Chinese-Style Names

Cai Er (1882–1916), military governor of Yunnan Province who called on the military governors to fight Yuan Shikai's dream of donning the royal yellow. Eugene published the manifesto of Cai's teacher/ally Liang Qicao

Chen Boda (1904–1989), director of the Cultural Revolution Unit, once Mao Zedong's chief secretary

Chen Duxiu (1879–1942), co-founder of the CCP and editor of *New Youth*, a Marxist magazine that inspired a whole generation of revolutionaries, including Mao Zedong and Zhou Enlai

Chen Guixin, Jack's grandfather's Chinese name, *see* Joseph Chen

Chen Jiongming (1878–1933), Cantonese warlord; at various times military governor of Guangdong and Guangxi and civil governor of Guangdong, competed with Sun Yatsen for the Soviets' favor. The Soviets flirted with him for a while

Chen Lianbo (1884–1941), leader of Canton Chamber of Commerce and of the Merchants' Volunteer Force who plotted to overthrow Sun Yatsen and became the merchant president with Britain's blessing

Chen Yi (1901–1972), foreign minister 1958–1972, Zhou Enlai's right-hand man who encouraged Jack to launch a lecture tour in the West, especially in the United States

Chen Youren (Chen Yujen) Jack's father Eugene, *see* Eugene Chen

Chiang Kaishek (1887–1975), admired Eugene's diplomatic talents but failed to win Eugene over after he split with the CCP

Deng Xiaoping (1904–1997), leader of Baise Uprising against the KMT government; Zhou Enlai's successor as premier. He met Zhou in Paris. The two worked together so closely that Deng became Zhou's "kid brother"

Duan Qirui (the "Righteous Buddhist") (1864–1936), minister of war under Yuan Shikai, then minister of war and premier under Li Yuanhong. The power struggle between Duan and Li was a favorite topic of gossip. To Li's pleasure, Eugene's writings in the *Peking Gazette* contributed to dislodging Duan in June 1917

Feng Yuxiang (1882–1948), a Judas-like "Christian General," Chinese warlord, first allied with the Left KMT, then betrayed them to become the sworn brother of Chiang Kaishek

Guo Songling, garrison general who rebelled against Zhang Zuolin, the "Manchurian Tiger," and enabled Eugene to escape from Zhang Zuolin's death row in 1925

Guo Taiqi (1888–1952), Eugene's friend since the *Peking Gazette* days, briefly minister of foreign affairs in the early 1940s

Hong Xiuquan (1814–1864), leader of the Taiping Rebellion, inspired by a Western Christian missionary

Kong Xiangxi ("Daddy Kong") Ailing Soong's husband, minister of finance

Liang Qicao (1873–1929), leading intellectual and journalist, briefly minister of finance under Li Yuanhong in 1917. He was one of Eugene's sources of inside information

Liao Zhongkai (1877–1925), Sun Yatsen's close aide and Eugene's close colleague

Li Dazhao (1888–1927), co-founder of the CCP who worked closely with Eugene in 1925 to prepare the Northern Expedition to defeat the warlords

Li Lisan (1899–1967), firebrand of the CCP who, guided by the fast-moving Comintern agent Gregory Voitinsky, rushed to follow Moscow's instructions to seize power from the KMT. He failed and received his punishment in Moscow: he was detained there for nearly 20 years and came back to China only after his party's victory in 1949

Lin Biao (1907–1971), became Mao's hand-picked successor during the Cultural Revolution. He was the only marshal on Mao's side, while the other eight marshals were behind Zhou Enlai

Liu Shaoqi (1898–1969), a Hong Kong–Canton strike leader who helped Eugene bring the strike to a successful conclusion and followed Eugene marching into the repossessed British concession in Hankou in 1927; second president of PRC, 1959–1968

Li Yuanhong (1864–1928), Yuan Shikai's vice president and his rival, who partly funded Eugene's *Peking Gazette* attacking Yuan; president after Yuan's death

Mao Zedong (1893–1976). His relationship with the Chen family began in 1924. Eugene was the only KMT leader who apologized for Mao's radical experiment in the famous Hunan peasant movement

Shi Zhaoji, *see* Shi, Alfred

Soong Chingling (Madame Sun Yatsen) (1893–1981), supported Eugene's vision of the Russia-oriented policy from the beginning, later developed an intimate friendship with Eugene

Soong Mayling (Madame Chiang Kaishek) (1898–2003), used to tease Eugene and called him "Uncle Eugene." Between 1923 and 1927, they became close friends

Sun Ke (aka Sun Fo) (1891–1973), Sun Yatsen's son

Sun Yatsen (1866–1925), the first president of the Chinese Republic, who adopted, with Eugene's help, the Russia-oriented policy, that later developed into the policy of allying with the Soviet Union, accepting the communists into the KMT, and supporting the labor and peasant movements

Wang Jingwei (the "Chinese Byron") (1883–1944), member of the left wing of the KMT, close associate of Sun; president of China, 1925–1926; premier, 1932–1935; leader of the puppet government under the Japanese Occupation Army, from 1940–1944

Wang Ming (1904–1974), mastermind of the "28 Bolsheviks," rival of Mao, Stalin's man in the CCP

Wu Hao, *see* Zhou Enlai

Wu Tingfang (1842–1922), Wu Zhaoshu's father; foreign minister under Li Yuanhong

Wu Zhaoshu (often spelled Chaoshu), *see* C. C. Wu

Yuan Shikai (1860–1916), provisional president after Sun Yatsen resigned in 1912, dreamed of becoming emperor

Zhang Jingjiang ("Curio Zhang") (1877–1950), senior conservative member of KMT, political broker, supporter of Sun Yatsen in 1911 revolution, mentor of Chiang Kaishek, father of the second Mrs. Eugene Chen

Zhang Zuolin (the "Manchurian Tiger") (1873–1928), Chinese warlord who put Eugene before the firing squad in 1925

Zhou Enlai (aka Wu Hao) (1898–1976), leader of the moderate faction in the CCP, versus the more radical and sometimes extreme Mao Zedong. Zhou tried to reach some understanding with, and open the door to, the West

Zhu De (often spelled Chu Teh) (1886–1976), a KMT police chief of Nanchang in 1928, the Father of the Chinese Red Army, a lifelong opponent of Mao Zedong's extreme measures and lifelong friend of Zhou Enlai

TIMELINE

YEAR	CHEN	CHINA	WORLD
1830	Joseph Chen is born		
1839		Nov 3: Opium War begins	
1842		Aug 29: Opium War ends	
1850		Late Dec: Taiping Rebellion begins	
1855	Jack's grandmother Marie Longchallon (later Mary Chen) is born		
1861			Apr 12: U.S. Civil War begins
1864		July: Taiping Rebellion ends for all practical purposes	
1865			Apr 9: U.S. Civil War ends (Lee's surrender)
1868			Meiji Restoration in Japan
1871		Aug: Last fighting of Taiping Rebellion	
1876	Joseph Chen and Marie Longchallon marry		
c. 1877	Ah Chen arrives in Trinidad with his wife		
1878	Eugene Chen is born		
ca. 1878	Aisy Gantheaume is born		
1891	Joseph Chen dies		
1894		Aug 1: First Sino-Japanese War begins	
1895		Apr 17: First Sino-Japanese War ends	
1898			Apr 25–Aug 12: Spanish-American War
1899	Eugene and Aisy marry	Nov 2: Boxer Rebellion begins	
1901		Sep 7: Formal end to Boxer Rebellion	
1903–06	Eugene's first trip to London, exact date not known, but likely before beginning of Russo-Japanese War		
1904			Feb 10: Russo-Japanese War begins
1905			Jan 22–Dec 31: First Russian Revolution. Sep 5: Russo-Japanese War ends
1908	Jack Chen is born		
1911	Early: Eugene moves to London	Chinese Revolution	
1912	Jan: Eugene goes to Peking; eventually goes to work at *Peking Gazette*	Feb 1: Sun Yatsen resigns in favor of Yuan Shikai	

YEAR	CHEN	CHINA	WORLD
1914	Summer: Eugene becomes temporary editor of *Peking Gazette*		July 28: World War I begins
1915		May 25: Yuan Shikai accedes to Japan's 21 Demands. Aug-Dec: effectively becomes emperor	
1916		Mar 22: Yuan steps down. June 6: Yuan dies. June 7: VP Li Yuanhong becomes president. June 29: Sec'y of War Duan Qirui becomes PM	
1917	May 19: Eugene arrested by Duan. June: released after Duan's fall, he arrives in Shanghai	Apr 25: Duan dissolves Nat'l Assembly. May 23: Li fires Duan; Wu Tingfang becomes acting PM. July 14: Duan resumes premiership. Aug 14: China declares war on Germany. Nov 30: Duan out as PM	Feb 22 (O.S.*): February Russian Revolution. Apr 6: U.S. joins World War I. Oct 25 (O.S.*): Bolshevik (or October) Revolution, leading directly into Russian Civil War
1918	Eugene begins to formulate the Russia-oriented policy: allying with the Soviet Union, accepting the Chinese communists, supporting the labor and peasant movements	Mar 23: Duan becomes PM again. Oct 10: Duan out again	Nov 11: World War I ends
1919	Eugene at Paris Peace Conference, then home to London	May 4: May Fourth Movement	Jan 18: Paris Peace Conference begins
1920	Spring: Eugene returns to China		Jan 21: Paris Peace Conference ends
1921		Early June: Maring arrives Shanghai. Mid-July: First congress of the Communist Party of China (party had been officially founded on July 1)	
1922		Chen Jiongming's revolt	Oct 25: Official end of Russian Civil War. Dec 22: Creation of Soviet Union
1923		Jan: Adolph Joffe arrives Shanghai. Oct 23: Borodin arrives Canton. Chen Jiongming is defeated	Jun 17: Final surrender of Russian Civil War
1924	Mid-Sept: Eugene meets Zhou Enlai	Jan 20: First National Congress of KMT. Sept: Zhou Enlai returns from Paris. Oct 14: KMT attacks Chamber of Commerce private army (the Merchants' Volunteer Force) to consolidate its base in Canton. Nov 21: Sun makes his last trip to Peking to negotiate with the warlords then in power	
1925	Aug 26: Eugene is arrested and imprisoned by Zhang Zuolin	Mar 12: Sun Yatsen dies. Jun 19: Hong Kong–Canton strike	
			*As per old-style calendar

YEAR	CHEN	CHINA	WORLD
1926	May: Aisy dies. Eugene becomes acting foreign minister; made permanent in Oct	Mar: Zhongshan Gunboat Incident. Nov 16: KMT moves capital from Canton to Wuhan. Dec 10: Beginning of Wuhan regime	
1927	Eugene negotiates for return of concessions from British. Feb 19: signs Chen-O'Malley Agreement. Feb: Jack and Yolanda join Eugene in Wuhan. Mar 12: Jack's first cartoon published. July 27: Eugene's foreign ministry position vanishes along with the rest of the Wuhan government	Jan 3: Anti-British riot in Wuhan. Apr 3: Japanese Incident in Nanjing. July 27: End of Wuhan regime; Jack/Borodin party leaves for Moscow via Gobi Desert and Trans-Siberian RR; reaches Moscow early Oct. Aug 22: Eugene's party leaves for Moscow via ship to Vladivostok and Trans-Siberian; reaches Moscow Sep 6. Aug 1: Nanchang Uprising, first major KMT-communist battle of Chinese Civil War. Dec 11: Guangzhou Uprising	Approx. this year, perhaps 1928: Stalin effectively becomes Soviet dictator
1928	Eugene goes into exile in Paris, until 1931	Chiang Kaishek takes power	
1931	June 1: Eugene becomes foreign minister in Nanjing government	Sep 18: Mukden Incident; Japan seizes Manchuria	
1932	Eugene resigns as foreign minister in Nanjing government	Jan 28: Japan invades Shanghai	
1933	Nov 22: Eugene is appointed foreign minister in the Fujian government	Nov 22: Fujian People's Government is formed in opposition to Chiang Kaishek	
1934	Jan 13: Eugene's foreign ministry position vanishes along with the rest of the Fujian government	Jan 13: Defeat of the Fujian government by Chiang. Oct: The Long March of the communists	
1936	Spring: Jack arrives in Shanghai		
1937	Jack on world tour with his art	July 7: Second Sino-Japanese War starts (Marco Polo Bridge Incident). Aug 13: Japan launches all-out attack on China. Sep 25: Battle of Pingxinguan Pass, first Red Chinese Army victory over the Imperial Japanese Army (IJA)	
1938	Jack on world tour with his art. His first visit to Yanan in the summer		
1939	Jack goes to London, is trapped there by outbreak of WWII, has to stay there for duration		Sep 1: World War II in Europe begins
1941			Jun 22: Germany invades Soviet Union. Dec 7: Japan attacks U.S.
1942	Early in the year: Japanese arrest Eugene in Hong Kong		
1944	May: Eugene dies in captivity in Shanghai		
1945		Post-WWII phase of Chinese Civil War begins	Sep 2: World War II officially ends (Japanese surrender ceremony)

YEAR	CHEN	CHINA	WORLD
1946	Jack returns to China, his second visit to Yanan		
1947	Jack returns to London from Yanan, establishes first New China News Agency in the West		
1949		Chinese Civil War ends	
1950	Jack returns to Beijing. Yuan-tsung also arrives in Beijing		June 25: Korean War begins
1953			July 27: Korean War ends with armistice
1957	Jack tours on the Silk Road and collects material for his book *The Sinkiang Story* while the Anti-Rightists' purge is raging		
1958	Apr: Jack and Yuan-tsung marry	Great Leap Forward 5-year plan	
1959		Famine	
1964			Aug 2: Gulf of Tonkin Incident; major U.S. involvement in Vietnam begins
1966		Cultural Revolution begins	
1968	Jack arrested by Cultural Revolution Red Guards		
1971	May 1: Jack and Yuan-tsung, with personal permission of Zhou Enlai, go to Hong Kong. Jack begins lecture tours in U.S. and Canada		
1972	Jack continues lecture tours, then becomes consultant to New York State Education Dept.		Feb 21: President Nixon visits China, the first step in normalizing relations between the two countries
1973			Jan 27: Paris Peace Accord signed, formally ending U.S. involvement in Vietnam
1973–77	Jack lectures, researches, and writes at Cornell		
1976		Jan 8: Zhou Enlai dies. Sep 9: Mao Zedong dies	
1978–81	Jack works on the "Chinese of America" exhibit and book at Chinese Cultural Center, San Francisco		
1982–94	Jack founds The Pear Garden in the West, a Chinese American performing arts group		
1985	Jack is appointed senior vice-chairman of the Soong Chingling (Madame Sun Yatsen) Foundation of the U.S.		
1995	Jack dies		

PROLOGUE

There was nothing in my early life to indicate that I would write a family saga of three generations of Chinese revolutionaries intent on establishing an independent China. I was born in Shanghai, the greatest metropolis of China, a port city that ranked with London, New York, and Amsterdam. My family lived in a very special district of the city, the "Foreign Devil's Vanity Fair" (Shi Li Yang Chang), a satirical label for the French concession combined with the British- and American-dominated International Settlement. Although its circumference was only three to five miles, the small number of its inhabitants, Chinese and foreign, possessed, it was said, more than 95 percent of China's wealth. My middle-class family was not rich, but we were well connected. Our proper niche in the social hierarchy was on the fringe of this Foreign Devil's Vanity Fair.

My mother was a worldly and clever woman. She knew that my father, an engineer, would not be able to provide much of a dowry for me. If she wanted me to move upward, to reach for the money tree, she had to groom me to be a player who could compete with other young ladies for the eligible bachelors. She sent me to study at the fashionable St. Mary's Hall, a sort of finishing school, well known in China for its English class. Before the communists' takeover, English was the second language of the elite and "high" intellectuals, just as French had been for the Russians during the time of the later czars. Conversing in fluent English did wonders for one's social ambitions.

My favorite class was English composition, and I often got good marks for my writing. A few compositions became party pieces I was asked to recite at gatherings of my family and friends. One lady in the

A bourgeois young lady in Shanghai's French Park, 1949.

audience, whom I called Aunt Zeng, was more than worldly and clever; she was a bluestocking with a degree or two in English literature, either from Cambridge or Oxford. I confided to her that I wanted to be more than a social butterfly; some day I wanted to become a writer and write something that would make a difference. Aunt Zeng approved heartily.

But I kept my secret aspiration from my mother. To all appearances, I was her obedient, dutiful daughter. It seemed that I would go far under her guidance. Then came 1949, the communists came to power, and down fell the corrupt bourgeoisie! So much for Mother's trouble. So much for my training befitting a young lady.

The year 1949 was, in China, a time of swift and radical change in every sphere of life, just as I was growing up. I was almost ready to graduate from St. Mary's Hall when the Kuomintang government headed by Chiang Kaishek was defeated by the insurgent communist army. Chiang and his troops fled to the offshore island of Taiwan.

My parents chose to stay on when many of their friends left for Taiwan, Hong Kong, or the United States. Anxious to free myself from my domineering mother, I took the risk of entering the unknown realm. Through a former schoolmate, I got a job working in the Department of Film Scenario Writing in Beijing, also known as Peking, the new capital of the communist-led coalition government. In 1950 when I came to Beijing, Jack Chen, my future husband, also arrived there from London. We were introduced by our mutual friend, Dora Zhang, who became our go-between. In 1958 she succeeded in urging us to tie the knot.

Actually, I first learned about Jack's family before I met him, from a few lines in a history textbook in my fifth-grade classroom in Chongqing (Chungking). They told me that Eugene Chen, Jack's father, whose Chinese name was Chen Youren (also known as Chen Yujen), was the first foreign minister of modern China to have taken back land from the colonial powers, land that China had ceded to Britain after the Opium War of the early 1840s. In 1927, in the name of the Chinese people, Eugene reclaimed two tiny strips of land—the British concession in the port city of Hankou (Hankow) and another British concession in the port city of Jiujiang (Kiukiang). Eugene was hailed as a hero when he marched into Hankou's newly freed British concession surrounded by supporters, among them the future Chinese head of state Liu Shaoqi (1959–1967).

Arriving in Beijing in 1950: A new cadre dreaming of writing something that would make a difference.

The two strips of land Eugene reclaimed were a great symbol of liberation for people, not only in colonized China but also elsewhere in colonized Asia. The myth of the invincibility of the colonialists was shattered. The response of revolutionary Asians was best reflected in a statement of the first prime minister of independent Malaya, Tunku Abdul Rahman. "In 1931 on the liner to Malaya, I met the ex–Foreign Minister of China, Eugene Chen.... It was this man who really led me into politics. Not by what he said, but the great feeling that he communicated. I was able to breathe and feel what he was talking about.... The enthusiasm that Eugene Chen kindled in me continued to burn fiercely."[1]

What I learned about Eugene outside my history class came from friends of my mother, as well as from the mothers of my friends. Eugene Chen, in their eyes, was a great lover. His romance with Soong Chingling, the widow of Sun Yatsen, father of the Chinese Republic and founder of the Kuomintang (the Nationalist Party), was a favorite topic of conversation in the ladies' parlors. Most of them were Soong Chingling's younger contemporaries, and more than a few were her friends.

Naturally, I was curious about Eugene's love affair and asked Jack, but I could not extract a word from him. Later when I met his older sister, Silan, she, with an elfish smile, titillated me with her observations from close quarters.

Anyway, Jack was not a name-dropper. He seldom talked about his illustrious father or his own friendships with political leaders such as Zhou Enlai (prime minister between 1949 and 1976). But this changed in 1966 with the onset of the Cultural Revolution. Despite its attractive name, the Cultural Revolution was a violent purge that lasted ten years—from 1966 to 1976. It was Mao Zedong's version of the Great Terror that Stalin had launched in the 1930s. Jack, who worked in the Foreign Language Bureau as expert (in English language matters), adviser, and editor, became the prime target in the whole bureau for several reasons. For one, he was more Westernized than anyone else in his office, and therefore more suspicious in the eyes of the Red Guards, the hit men of the Cultural Revolution.

Because he spoke very little Chinese, Jack insisted that I accompany him when he was interrogated. Only then did he begin to tell me about his family history. What he told me formed the embryo of this book.

One of the things Mao Zedong was determined to do was to destroy history. The Red Guards did his bidding and ransacked public and private libraries, burning many books and documents and generally clearing the way for Mao to promote his version of events. During one interrogation session, the ringleader of the Red Guard said to Jack: "You must go back three generations to see what crimes your family has committed against the revolution, and write them down. By the way, give more detail about the Wuhan period." The scar above the Red Guard's right eye turned darker. "You mean my father's taking back the two British concessions was a crime?" Jack asked, outraged.

"It's not your father, but the Communist Party under Chairman Mao's leadership, that was solely responsible for such an act of heroism," the Red Guard answered without blushing.

Both Jack and I treasured our family heritage, and we were determined to save as much as we could of what we knew about China's struggle for independence during the last century and a half. We embarked on this quest without knowing that such a long, tortuous, bumpy road lay ahead. Together we sought to trace the three generations of men in the Chen family. Ah Chen, Jack's grandfather, a landless peasant, fought in the Taiping Rebellion of 1850–1864. Eugene Chen, Ah Chen's oldest son, worked as a close aide to Sun Yatsen, the man who led the 1911 Revolution, overthrowing the last dynasty, and played a leading role in preserving the Republic of China. Jack Chen, Eugene's younger son (and my husband), through his art and journalism, represented and explained the Chinese Marxist revolution to the outside world; by countering Chiang Kaishek's propaganda in the world's media,

Jack helped Mao Zedong and Zhou Enlai defeat Chiang and create the People's Republic of China.

By reviewing the family history, we also reviewed the historical events in which the three men were actively involved. Many of the events described in this book have been recorded in numerous books and articles, and I have read a lot of them, both in Chinese and English, in the course of my research on three continents: Asia, America, and Europe. Such reading and research helps me form a big picture, and through the family history Jack recounted to me, I place each of the three Chens in this big picture. Thus, from a special vantage point, I am able to fill a few gaps in this most vital period of modern Chinese history.

By the time we were ready to start the actual writing, Jack had passed away, in April 1995. I lost half of my will to continue the project, and, putting it on hold, I went on a tour of Greece. Jack had wanted to take me to visit there. He loved Renaissance art and longed to see the country that had inspired it. When he was ill and knew that he would not make the trip, he said: "See Greece for both of us—have a good time."

The centerpiece of the Olympia museum was Praxiteles's statue of Hermes. It was appropriate to display it there. When Praxiteles decided to create a perfect composite of male beauty, he found it in the young, handsome, masculine athletes gathered at Olympia every four years to compete in the nude. Hermes was a runner, a messenger, and also a sort of intermediary between this world and Hades. I wondered why Praxiteles did not name his masterpiece Apollo, the Sun God; instead, he gave so much seductive virility to the god who guided human souls into the realm of death. I had never seen a work of art with a death subtheme so bright, so full of light and life. Was death the beginning of a new life? The artist seemed to say that if we lived with passion, we would die without fear.

Yes, Praxiteles was telling me something through Hermes, his messenger, which reminded me of what Aunt Zeng, an admirer of ancient Greek art, drama, and mythology, had once said to me: "The ancient Greeks accepted the tragic in life. They grieved over their loss and dealt, with endurance, with what was left to them."

I emerged from grief, and, on my return home, I plunged into work on this history with a vengeance. I knew I needed to do more research to flesh out certain episodes. For example, according to the family lore, Eugene attended the Paris Peace Conference in 1919 as the legal adviser to the Chinese delegation, and there he got hold of a copy of the secret pact signed by Robert Lansing, the secretary of state in Woodrow Wilson's administration, and the Japanese diplomat Baron Ishii, in which they decided to transfer the defeated Germany's colonial interests in Shandong Province to Japan. Eugene sent a copy to Sun Yatsen and another to the Republican senator William Borah. The exposure "was the undoing of Wilson," Percy, Jack's older brother, told me with pride.

In Greece in 1996. If Chinese culture is my mother, Western culture is my wet nurse.

This was a real-life story of David versus Goliath. But it required more documentation to sound believable. I have a bad habit: when invited to a party, I often slip into the host's library and browse the bookshelves. Doing so, I got lucky one day, chancing on John B. Powell's *My Twenty-five Years in China*. The book gave me two pieces of important information: One, the "Rape of Shandong" did cost the Democrats some votes during the election year, although it was not the major reason for their losing the presidency; two, in 1917 the Soviet Russians confiscated the czar's archive with all its secret documents, among them the Lansing-Ishii agreement, and it was brought to Paris by some Soviets eager to make trouble for President Wilson and the Allied powers.

Then on a pleasure tour to Hong Kong, I spent most of my time sightseeing in bookshops. At one bookshop located in a back alley, with a narrow, dim staircase leading to its small display room, I discovered a used book, Ye Yonglie's *The Beginning of the Chinese Communist Party*, which gave a full account as to how the exposure of the Lansing-Ishii agreement roused the whole nation to stand up for their rights in the May Fourth Movement. For the first time in China's modern history, the diplomats refused to sign an "unequal treaty"—the Treaty of Versailles—dictated by the foreign powers. Meanwhile, my research enabled me to see the May Fourth Movement in a light different from that of the Maoist historians. They claimed that the Russian proletarian revolution inspired the movement, but actually it was the Chinese middle class who had initiated and led it.

In the 1980s and 1990s, I had access to more recorded documents, because China began the gradual liberalization of its intellectual policy and published a great number of history books. From *The Biography of Chen Youren* by Qian Yuli, I learned more about the impact that exposing the Lansing-Ishii agreement had on Washington after Eugene sent a copy to Republican Senator William Borah. This was an important contributing cause, although not the major reason, for the Senate's refusal to endorse President Wilson's plan for the League of Nations.

From a few torn pages of the *World's Great Men of Color*, written by the historian J. A. Rogers, and a gift book given by a friend, *Nationalist China's "Revolutionary Diplomacy," 1925–1931*, written by Professor Enhan Lee and published by the Institute of Modern History of Taiwan's Academia Sinica, I learned that it was also at Versailles that Eugene first mapped out the "Revolutionary Policy," which he launched in 1926 and which culminated in the repossessing of the two British concessions, a fact the Maoist historians denied.

Playing detective, I found shreds of evidence scattered here and there, and, by piecing them together, I was able to paint a fuller portrait of Eugene Chen.

As I immersed myself in the work, time flew by. In 2003, the Iraq War broke out. It was painful to watch the news, seeing innocent people suffering and dying, children in particular. As I sat in front of the television and listened to politicians and experts analyzing the situation and offering strategies, I could not help saying to myself, as an immigrant, I had a different perspective and therefore a different story to tell. After the Second World War, the United States bet on the wrong horse, Chiang Kaishek, in their game of deciding what regime China should have. American dollars poured in to support Chiang and his six to eight million soldiers. Within three years, it all melted down to nothing. The Chen family saga is a testimony to the time-proved fact that a huge wallet and military might do not necessarily warrant victory.

Having said that, the most important reason for telling this family story is personal. During the Cultural Revolution, Jack's bedtime story for our son, Jay, was about the adventures of *A Man with a Free Spirit*, in which the protagonist was the combined alter ego of the three Chen men. Years later, when Jay searched for this storybook in campus libraries, he couldn't find it. But now I can tell him: "Here is the book you have been looking for."

FIGHT FOR GOD'S KINGDOM ON EARTH

There are things I hear about in the Chen family and accept as facts, as family lore; but when I try to check them out and get firm proof, they turn elusive. Such was the case with Ah Chen, Jack's grandfather. The Chen offspring always knew that their patriarch was special. He was a revolutionary, a soldier in the rebel Taiping armies. This was why, after the defeat of the Taiping Rebellion, he emigrated from China to Trinidad in the 1870s.

Jack and his siblings were born in a mansion in Port-of-Spain. They spoke of their grandfather in general terms—he was a poor peasant kid who started working with his hands almost as soon as he could walk on his legs. They did not have much idea of the old man's early life in China, but by a quirk of fate I have. So, as I dig into the family lore, collect the findings, and fit them to one another, I can imagine the old man's boyhood and adolescence.

This is not to say I was a peasant girl. Actually I was a rather privileged, middle-class city girl, born in Shanghai. In 1950 I went to Beijing, working in the Department of Film Scenario Writing as an assistant editor. My office adhered to the Communist Party's cultural policy, which encouraged city workers in literature and art to "experience life" in farm villages. Such experience was supposed to give us more background knowledge, which would prove useful when we selected and edited stories about peasants.

1952, working with peasants in the land reform in Dragon's Village, Gansu Province.

From that year on, I went to the countryside almost every year, most of the time for a short stay of a month or so, but at other times for longer sojourns of six months or more. I was familiar with the life of the peasants, for I had gone through trials with them—famine, flood, drought, an epidemic of hepatitis—as Grandfather Chen must have. Although Grandfather Chen was born a hundred years before me, the awful conditions in the countryside had not changed much in my day. When Jack told me about incidents in his grandfather's early life, I not only knew what it meant but also what it felt like.

Every village I went to had only a few old beasts of burden that no one expected to work hard. Most of the land had to be plowed by hand with a spade. Believe me, it was not a fool's job, as I, a smart city dweller, had thought. It required the skill of moving my limbs and body rhythmically, a skill I did not have. My legs seemed to move of their own accord and paid no heed to what my arms were doing. Nevertheless, I plodded on. Soon I was all in a sweat. Sweat slid down my spine. Sweat trickled into my eyes. I lost track of time. The next thing I knew, I was lying flat on my back. I had caught my heel

Great Famine in 1960. Me (bottom left), with my colleagues working in the Red Flag Commune near Pi County in Jiangsu Province.

on something and, through sheer fatigue, had tripped. This was a usual ending to my first few hours of field labor.

The peasants took pity on me and let me do the lighter work along with the children. I was grateful, but to be honest, there was no work in the field that was not backbreaking. After a while, my back was stiff from bending over and picking up stones. It ached if I stayed bent, and it ached if I straightened up. I marveled at the children who worked tirelessly alongside me.

When I cast my mind back to that time, I realize that that was when I first crossed the path of Grandfather Chen. In his boyhood, he must have worked like one of these children.

According to family legend, he was a slightly built boy, and his legs were long for his body. Their land was poor and covered with stones and weeds. Father and son worked together, father plowing, the small boy picking up stones and pulling up weeds, just like the children I knew in many farm villages. The Chen boy, with quick and darting eyes, was good at spotting and getting the small stones hidden in the earth. Many times his hands got scratched or bruised, but he did not cry in pain even if his hands bled. He would be rewarded for his hard work and, during the lunch break, allowed to be a child for half an hour or so.

He had one favorite game—flying kites with other children. Holding the strings to colorful kites, they ran about as the kites twirled crazily in the air. Some slipped from the hands of the younger children and rose high into the sky. They chased after them and one another, laughing and crying at the same time. Once the chase caused the Chen boy to stumble onto a horrendous scene. "A scene like this one," Jack said while showing me an old clipping, a picture of peasant addicts strewn over a hillside, a scene that was ubiquitous in impoverished areas in those days. The Chen boy saw men lying in the midst of gravestones and weeds. He could not tell, by their ashen faces, emaciated bodies, and bony limbs, whether they were dead or alive. Scared, he turned around sharply and ran back to his father, who told him that these miserable souls were opium addicts. They were poor peasants and had no money to go to an opium den, his father continued; instead, each rented a narrow dirt lot from the owner of the hillside, where he was provided with cheap opium, a pipe, and other trappings for smoking the drug. Their addiction would strip their families down to the last cent, but they couldn't help it because they were possessed by the "foreign devils."

One day, the Chen boy was told that more foreign devils were coming to destroy the villagers. It was, in fact, the beginning of the Opium War in

1839. The British, who had already colonized India, discovered that China could be the largest market for the opium the East India Company grew. For this newfound opportunity, they declared war on China.

The Chen family ran with the other villagers; and in the mad stampede they headed, without realizing what they were doing, toward the river. Halfway across a narrow bridge, the boy's right foot slipped, and he cried out. His father spun around and caught him, but the surge of human bodies broke the father's grip on the bridge's handrail, and he plunged over the edge. The small boy watched with horror as the dark waters below sucked his father down.

The foreign devils—the British soldiers—knocked down doors and windows and looted the village. Chinese brigands followed, plundering what was left. Then came the Chinese soldiers of the Manchu Court, ostensibly to save the villagers from the brigands. The brigands were gone, but the Chinese soldiers were in and it was their turn to pillage.

Family lore has it that the boy's mother was not able to support him and so farmed him out to an uncle. The boy worked the land with his uncle and grew up with little time for frolicking in the field. Harsh reality sharpened his wits. During one drought, his aunt had just miscarried and bled too much to toil in the field, and his uncle was not well. The youngster, now in his midteens, was left alone to save the harvest. He plucked the weeds that consumed the precious moisture the crops needed. At times clouds appeared and a few drops of rain fell. His wheat and corn plants benefited from his labors, because the rain, though scarce, revived the roots of the plants, not those of the weeds.

The youngster had known cruel mockery from men and now endured the same from nature. The drought ended when the rains came, but they came when they were not needed. Rain pelted down, hammering the crops yet to be cut. The leveled crops rotted in the field. Then the land was lost too; it had to be sold in order to get medical care for his uncle and aunt.

Young Chen was now homeless. He wandered around, looking for odd jobs. He worked as a farmhand. On his lucky days, someone would give him some chores to do, earning him a meal. On his bad days, when he had not found anyone willing to give him work, he starved. Adversity steeled him. He became a champion for village underdogs. He spoke out while others complained in whispers. In his native village, he was labeled a troublemaker by the rich landowners, whom he ran afoul of and had to flee.

Young Chen was not a regular peasant, because he worked alternately as an itinerant carpenter and a barber. With a toolbox on his back, he roamed through the fields and streets, from village to village. I ran into such men in my forays into rural China. They were usually shrewd and articulate. To sell their crafts, they depended a lot on an engaging smile and a smooth tongue. As an itinerant carpenter, young Chen would do a lot of repairs around a house and at the end of the day be invited to the dining table, sometimes his only payment. As an itinerant barber, he had to entertain his customers, so they would not get bored sitting on a hard bench while he was shaving them.

One day a customer mentioned the name of a Hakka weirdo, Hong Xiuquan, during their chitchat. Hong was said to have seen strange visions in which a foreign god told him to cleanse the city of Canton (Guangzhou) of sins. One of the sins was opium smoking.

The story of Hong Xiuquan riveted young Chen's attention. Like Hong, he hated opium, the cause of such misery. As a Hakka himself, he felt a strong affinity for a fellow Hakka. The Hakka—or Kejia—are one of the nationalities of South China. They are, it is said, originally Hans, the largest nationality, who were driven from their homes during the twelfth century by Northern Hans pressing into South Central China. The Hakka in turn migrated further south. Finding the best lands already occupied, these Strangers, or Guest People—which is what the word "Hakka" means—were forced to settle on hilly and barren lands. They eked out a living, and their hard life made them rebellious.

When young Chen learned that there were poor peasants like himself who had banded together in the neighboring province of Guangxi to fight the rich and predatory, he traveled there to look for them.

This Taiping Rebellion, which started in 1850, was inspired by the Christian missionaries sent from the West. When the missionaries spread the Word—that all men are created equal in the eyes of God—they inadvertently touched the right chord in these potential revolutionaries. Their words had struck the heart of the young Cantonese Hakka man—Hong Xiuquan—who would become the leader of the Taiping Rebellion.

Hong was of peasant descent. Unhappy about their smartest son's bleak prospects, his family had endured much hardship to save for his education. They hoped he would pass the imperial examinations, gain entry into the Manchu government, work his way up, and bring glory to his family. But he took the exam three times and failed each time. He brooded over his failures and came to the conclusion that he had been discriminated against because he was Hakka, a race regarded as inferior to the Manchu and Han races. Worse still, during the twilight years of the Manchu Court, it was an open secret that imperial degrees were for sale. Intelligent though Hong was, he could not shine without money.

He suffered a nervous breakdown after his third failure, and as he lay in his sickbed with a high fever, he had hallucinations, which he later recounted as visions. In one, he was admitted to a heavenly palace and received by an old man with a foreigner's golden beard but wearing a black Chinese robe embroidered with the traditionally kingly dragon. This was Jehovah. According to Hong Xiuquan, God adopted him and gave him the divine power of attorney, enabling him to speak and act in God's name, as Hong's older brother Jesus Christ had done. When God commanded him to destroy all unbelievers and idolaters, Hong had no doubt that He meant the heathen Manchu rulers.

Hong recovered from his illness, and, after thinking things over in a calmer mood, he took the imperial examination for one last time. He failed once again. Now Hong's eagerness to make his career through the Manchu bureaucratic system turned into resentment and then hatred for everything the Manchu Court stood for. He made up his mind. Rebellion was his only way out of obscurity. He knew that nobody would follow a man of humble origins, so he spoke of his visions, which assured the audiences of his God-sent mandate. With an extraordinary political acumen, Hong fused his dream of kingship with the dream shared by all of the common people. He told them that if they followed him, he would lead the revolt to overthrow the Manchu emperor and build a Kingdom of Heavenly Peace (Taiping Tian Guo) on Earth. He would replace the autocratic empire of the Manchu intruders, who had reigned over the peasants for more than two hundred years.

Grandfather Chen, owning nothing to be abolished, embraced the rebellion wholeheartedly in 1850, when he was about twenty years old. The Taiping soldiers gave what little they owned to the "Sacred Treasury," sharing their possessions like the early Christians. Men and women lived in separate camps. For the first time in Chinese history, combat forces admitted women. A revolutionary army arose, and the barracks became Grandfather Chen's substitute for family and home. It was an exhilarating moment when he and his comrades—in rags and armed with spears, bows, arrows, spades, hoes, scythes, and other tools—gathered in Jintian Village at the foot of Purple Thistle Mountain in Guangxi. They marched into a square surrounded by mud huts with thatched roofs. The heat made their faces glisten with sweat, their tattered red turbans grimy from dirt and perspiration, as Hong Xiuquan, the Prince of Heaven, and his lieutenants passed them in review.

Family lore did not give a clue as to what Grandfather Chen achieved as a warrior. I read piles of books concerning the Taiping Rebellion, but I could not find Grandfather Chen anywhere. He was but a foot soldier, and to find him, as an old Chinese saying went, was like looking for a needle in the sea. He was not important to history, but he was important to my family story, so I dived again and again, looking for the tiny needle in the sea, but with no luck.

One day when I was cleaning up my basement, a yellowing page fell beside the short stool I sat on. From the corner of my eye I saw the title of an article: *Chen Youren (Eugene Chen), Diplomat of the Early Republic*. I picked it up. Lo and behold, the last line was half torn, but I still could read the remaining part: "Chen Youren's father Chen Guixin—." I could not believe my eyes. The information I had spent years searching for was actually at my feet. I scribbled down the author's name: Wang Binyi; the magazine's name: *Biographical Literature*, volume 67, number 2, published in Taiwan. I ran to the campus library at UC Berkeley, checked out the magazine, and photocopied the whole text.

From this article I got a summary of Grandfather Chen's military feats, and from the other research materials I got the bigger picture. Setting his activities against the historical backdrop of that time, I could see more clearly what kind of a man he was. His speedy transformation from an aimless drifter to a fighter with a purpose was remarkable. He must have had the qualities requisite for such quick promotion, and he also must have known how to strut his stuff.

Though a new recruit in 1852, Grandfather Chen was elected to the post of bodyguard for a former charcoal burner who now became the Prince of the East, a title that gave him second-in-line access to the Heavenly Father, behind the Prince of Heaven. The Prince of the East had a gaunt, stern face and piercing black eyes. He was illiterate, but dynamic and charismatic. It was indeed an honor to serve such an important personage. However, Grandfather, young and restless, yearned to do battle and to win glory, but if he did not come up with a good reason to leave his post, he would incur the Prince's displeasure.

That did not deter Grandfather Chen from trying. Being close to the Prince of the East, he knew the Taiping army would fight down the Yangzi River into a region where many tributaries converged, and they would need makeshift bridges. He had done carpentry, and, because this skill would be very useful to the army, he appealed to his commander. The Prince of the

East, moved by his enthusiasm and impressed by his persuasion, gave his young bodyguard more than he had bargained for. He "appointed him [Chen] the deputy commander of the carpentry battalion, responsible for pitching tents, building floating bridges and repairing military vehicles."[1] The battalion was destined for decisive battles around Wuhan, a strategic area in Central China. They could not win without taking Wuhan first.

The army found Grandfather Chen's skills handy. He was credited for having done important work in the drive to conquer Wuhan, the merged name of three cities—Wuchang, Hankou, and Hanyang. When the Taipings marched into the cities of Hanyang and Hankon, they found their advance stymied by the Yangzi River. They did not have enough boats to ferry themselves across to capture the important city of Wuchang, capital of Hubei Province. At this juncture, Grandfather Chen's comrades made use of his carpentry skills. He oversaw the building of two floating bridges, linking the two cities, Hankou and Hanyang, which were less guarded and served as the strategic springboards to Wuchang with the provincial capital. Then after combining and reinforcing their forces, they crossed over from Hankou to attack Wuchang. The work was done under the cover of darkness to prevent their enemies from discovering them. With incredible efficiency they finished "at daybreak on January 12, 1853."[2]

After having crossed the Yangzi River, the Taiping soldiers blew up the thick, tall walls of Wuchang and conquered the city on the same day, January 12, 1853. The capture of the Wuhan area was of great significance for the Taiping rebels. They were able to set up a more substantial "Sacred Treasury" in Wuchang with war booty and "contributions" from rich landlords and wealthy merchants. With funds to pay for an army of half a million—fifty times the size of the original—and a navy, the rebels launched an eastward campaign by land and water. The land forces marched down both banks of the Yangzi while the navy sailed down the river. The army with their colorful banners and the navy with the white sails of their boats formed a magnificent column that stretched for miles under blue skies.

They defeated enemies on the way and, within a month, by March of the same year, they were at the gates of Nanjing, the ancient Southern Capital. The rebels killed the Manchu commander, routed his soldiers, and took control of the city. They made a grand entrance into the city, twenty-five to a column, clad in tidy army uniforms with bright red turbans, holding shining swords or spears in their hands. The triumphal parade was highlighted by Hong Xiuquan's arrival: Sixteen men carried the Prince of Heaven, who was wearing royal yellow robes and shoes and sitting on a massive golden palanquin.

The rebels were at the peak of their power. But, over time, power corrupted the leaders and discipline failed. Disturbing rumors circulated. It was said that there was a growing rivalry between the Prince of Heaven and the Prince of the East, not only politically but also romantically. A war exploded between the two over attractive female courtiers. Each prince considered himself more equal than the other. Both liked pretty women, and both had plenty of them.

The Prince of Heaven, incensed by his chief lieutenant's insubordination, secretly summoned another commander, the Prince of the North, to the capital in a plot against the Prince of the East. On a September night in 1856, the Prince of the North did his boss's bidding. With three thousand loyal men, he surrounded the palace of the Prince of the East, blocked off all exits, and entered before dawn, killing the Prince of the East, his family, his staff, and his retainers. By sunrise, corpses littered the palace grounds.

The Manchu government, taking advantage of the internecine conflict and the ensuing chaos, launched a ferocious offensive that recaptured many cities and towns. The tide had turned against the Taiping rebels.

Grandfather Chen was then a naval officer assigned to defend the port of Pukou, gateway to the Heavenly Capital. He fought to the last minute both on water and on land. When the Heavenly Capital fell, his superior commander, Prince Shi, was besieged by enemy fire. Grandfather Chen "broke through, enabling Prince Shi to beat a fighting retreat from Huzhou."[3] In 1864, the rebels were finally crushed, with fearful loss of life. According to Jack and his older brother, Percy, Grandfather Chen managed to escape with a bullet in his leg. Constantly on the run, his wounded leg became gangrenous and had to be amputated. With a new leg made of cork, he fled to Hong Kong, a British colony. Since this was so close to Mainland China, he planned to fight his way back home with other refugee-comrades. They pooled their resources and opened a small jewelry shop as a front, but "the Hong Kong British authorities somehow found out the secret plot. Martial law was declared... [and] the police raided the shop.... Chen Guixin escaped annihilation by selling himself as an indentured laborer and with the cash he bought his passage... and emigrated to Jamaica."[4]

Jack once said there was documentary evidence in the immigration files that Grandfather Chen was an indentured laborer. An indentured laborer was a man too poor to afford the passage who had to work for years to pay off the debt borrowed at usurious interest rates. Jack traced his grandfather's origin back to Shunde County in the south of Guangdong Province, but he had not been able to document this. Given the circumstances, it would not be surprising if Grandfather Chen had covered his tracks to prevent implicating relatives and friends who remained in China.

But this Chen family does have an ancestral village, sort of. When Jack became old enough to be interested in such matters, he asked his father about their ancestral village. Eugene told him that it was in Zhongshan County on the coast, south of Canton and north of Aomen (Macao). It took Jack another five years before he found out that this too was only possibly true. It happened that Sun Yatsen had one day asked Eugene where he came from. When Eugene replied that he did not know for sure, Sun paused. Lack of a native place, a place your ancestors had lived, was a serious matter for a Chinese at that time. That prompted Sun to declare with great finality: "Then you came from Xiangshan County." And so it was. Xiangshan—the Fragrant Hill—was later given its new name, Zhongshan, in honor of its most famous son, Sun Yatsen, whose honorific title in Chinese is Zhongshan. So let us say that the Chen family came from Zhongshan by personal decree of the Chinese Republic's first president, the Chinese version of George Washington.

I had better luck piecing together Grandfather Chen's early life in China than I did with Grandmother Chen's. When I turned my attention to her early years, I found them a blank. It was not until 1987 that the Chen family matriarch emerged out of the emptiness as a small girl. In 1987, Jack's cousin, Angela Cheyne (Chen Anglicized), learned that Jack and I were doing research on his family, and she sent us what she knew of Grandmother Chen. Based on her information, Jack and I made a draft of Grandmother Chen's childhood in her home country.[5]

Grandmother Chen's maiden name was Leong. The Leong family originated in Shenzhen in Guangdong Province. It is located on the present border between Hong Kong's New Territories and Canton on the mainland, where the railway crossed the boundary. Although Hakka in ancestry, Jack's grandmother was born in Peking. Her father and grandfather were dressmakers. The Leong family lived in an area outside Qianmen, the Front Gate to the Tartar City. Their courtyard was behind a tall wall on a small, unpaved lane. Roofed verandahs enclosed three sides of the courtyard, and there was a wicker chair in the center of the yard next to a willow tree. It was in this house that the Leong family had lived for as long as the oldest member of the family, Grandfather Leong, could recall. There in the district of Tianqiao—the Bridge of Heaven—many artisans like the Leongs lived along the small crisscrossing lanes. Many, like the Leongs, were skilled enough to serve the Court of the Manchu rulers and the noble families. They were known for their needlework and fine stitching. The women of the Leong family did the most resplendent embroidery, including the emblems of the dragon and phoenix, which were the exclusive hallmarks of the emperors and empresses respectively. The Leongs were traditional artists; the craft was passed on from father to son and mother to daughter. In this enclave, the Leongs had lived and died generation upon generation, cutting and sewing for the Manchu Court.

Sometime late in the 1850s, Father Leong had a talk with his father. Times were changing, Father Leong said, and the respect that the family had held over the years for the Court was being replaced with anxiety. Monies due to the family had been unpaid for months, and there was talk of corruption at the Court; some had even said that the Court was showing signs of decadence. All this would not concern Father Leong if he had been paid for his services, but he was worried for his family and his livelihood. He had spoken to some friends, also Hakka descendants from Guangdong Province, who were planning on going overseas to make new lives for themselves. He was thinking about it himself. The old patriarch shook his head. Going overseas, that had never entered his mind. There was much heart-searching, as these were indeed troubled times and the future was uncertain. The country had been engaged in internal strife, which later became known as the Taiping Rebellion.

The yearning for a new life had begun. The quiet conversations in the house became more frequent. The oldest grandson, Leong Shing, found out more about the voyage, and soon it was a secret no more and was openly discussed. Then a decision was made in a family meeting. Father Leong would remain in China with his two younger unmarried sons and Grandfather Leong. Leong Shing and his wife and their four children would make the journey overseas.

Father Leong gave Leong Shing a good part of his life savings, contained in a silk bag cinched at the top with a metal fastener. As the time approached for their departure, the children, who had been left out of the discussions, knew that something important was afoot. New clothing was sewn and much packing done.

After tearful good-byes, Leong Shing and his wife started the journey southward to the Port of Canton. They traveled by road in a covered wagon, assisted by a porter, to the port of Tianjin, then down the Grand Canal to the Yangzi River, to the city of Changsha in Hunan Province, and then overland again to the port of Hankou in the Wuhan area. From Wuhan, the Leongs took another river trip to Canton. Their journey was fraught with danger, due to the fighting between the Taiping rebels and the soldiers of the Manchu rulers.

In Canton, the new arrivals found that there were droves of people everywhere, jostling and pushing, a heaving mass of humanity. The cries of the sampan vendors on the Pearl River vied with the screech of gulls. Rickshas darted here and there. The stench of rotting fish in the sweltering heat contrasted with the aroma of fried noodles.

Leong Shing's wife, hobbling on bound feet, carried the younger son, a mere baby of less than one year, on her back while holding the older son, a small lively lad of four years old, by his hand. The older daughter, five, and her younger sister, three, were held by Leong Shing. During embarkation in this teeming port, there was a fight to get on the ship, and in the ensuing melee, the mother lost her grip on her older son. He was separated and lost in the tide of human bodies surging, pushing, and shoving aboard. Leong Shing's wife wanted to go back to look for her son, but seeing the sea of faces behind him, Leong Shing realized there was no possibility of turning back. They were thrust forward by wave after wave of human bodies. That was the last they ever saw of their older boy. Leong Shing's wife cried, and there was no comforting her. It was a cruel blow and did not bode well for their new life. Leong Shing took his wife's hand and stroked it gently. He too was saddened by the loss, but he could not afford to let his grief take hold. It was true that it was not an auspicious beginning, but he tried to console his wife by saying that their older son was their "sacrifice" for leaving the motherland. They had paid their price and their future was assured.

The Leong family continued their journey, setting sail from the port of Canton sometime between the end of the 1850s and the early 1860s. They crossed the China Sea and the swirling Pacific to Panama, then to Havana. From there they went to Martinique, the French island two hundred and fifty miles north of Trinidad. Under the French law, immigrants had to be baptized into the Catholic faith, and their Chinese name had to be replaced with a French one before they would be allowed to stay. Thus Leong Shing became Longchallon, and the whole family became Roman Catholics.

Mother Longchallon reared three daughters and two sons in Martinique. The two older daughters and son had been born in China and after baptism were known respectively as Marie, Angele, and Alexander Louis; the two younger children, Lucie and Joseph George, were born in Martinique.

Time passed, and young Marie was growing up. She was about twenty when her parents arranged her marriage with Grandfather Chen. It was an excellent match for him. His bride was young, pretty, and of a family whose social and financial status was higher than his own. Fifteen years after they had come to Martinique, the Leong family was well established in the Chinese community and owned a few shops.

Grandfather Chen was at the time a barber and had worked in Jamaica and then moved to Martinique. All he possessed was a small bank account and a toolbox. He and Marie married in Fort-de-France, Martinique, sometime around 1875, and he renamed his bride Mary to match his own Anglicized, baptized name, Joseph. Shortly afterward, they moved to the British colony of Trinidad and settled in the town of San Fernando, the chief city of the southern part of the island.

The two refugees from China had found each other in the New World and were now set to start a new life together.

A Celestial Empire Lost, a Paradise Regained

Uneducated and illiterate, Jack's grandfather and grandmother had used thumbprints as signatures upon entering Trinidad. Even if they had used the correct Chinese characters, it probably would have made no difference. Some immigrants did so, but their names were still corrupted.

Grandfather Chen was known to his friends as Ah-Chan. The Ah had no real meaning, except for conveying a sense of camaraderie and good-natured respect. "Chan" was how "Chen" is pronounced in the Cantonese dialect. When Grandfather Chen registered in Trinidad in the mid-1870s, the immigration clerk, unused to Chinese sounds, wrote this as Ahchan, and this was further corrupted to Ahcham, and then Anglicized to Acham. Later his oldest son, Eugene, changed his name back to the original when he went to China for the first time and discovered his true family name, Chen.

Grandfather Chen had probably served out his indenture in Jamaica and somehow managed to save a little money. To cope with a new life and to support a growing family, he and his wife squirreled away every cent they could. They bought a minuscule plot of land above a crossroads on Mount Moriah Road just outside San Fernando. They planted a few cocoa trees and, more importantly, coconut palms, mango, sugarcane, guava, and avocado. They cultivated a ragged vegetable plot on which they raised yams, sweet potatoes, corn, peppers, and okra. A few ducks and chickens completed the farm.

In the space between the unpainted wooden frame cottage and the covered concrete cistern that held fresh rainwater runoff from the galvanized iron roof, they planted an orange tree. Three generations of men were required to urinate under it to make the fruit sweet. As the years went by, the family expanded to include five sons and one daughter. Eugene was the oldest, born in 1878; then came Joseph Leon, Lionel David, Bernardine, Ronald, and Alfred Bruno. All the children lived to adulthood except the fifth child and fourth son, Ronald. Alfred, the youngest child, was born after the death of his father.

This was how I first concluded Grandfather Chen's story. He seemed to have lived a rather humdrum life in Trinidad. It was so unlike the old warrior. Granted, he was fading, but surely he could not fade without any traces of his former self. I asked Jack, but he only shrugged.

I told Jack that I was puzzled by yet another question. There was nothing in the family lore that hinted at Grandfather's relationship with women in China; it was as if he had lived like a monk during his sexually most active years, which I found impossible to believe. He was what I called a rustic dandy; I had run into such men in rural villages. They just could not keep their hands off women.

Jack admonished me for making such a generalization about individuals. Grandfather Chen was different, Jack argued; he might have had a wife in China, but as a dedicated revolutionary fighter he had no time for womanizing. As far as he knew, Grandfather Chen had seven children and that was all. Jack was so carried away with his argument that he had made a slip of the tongue. I immediately pounced on the word "seven." Grandmother Chen bore only six children. Who gave him the seventh child? I went on prying and ferreted out more of the family secrets. I thought I had a more colorful ending to the patriarch's story.

I wrote in a light, prankish vein: "Grandfather Chen, after the defeat of the Taiping Rebellion, escaped death but lost a leg. He wore an artificial leg made of cork and walked with difficulty. But that did not slow his running after women. He would tease them by jabbing pins into his cork leg covered by a trouser. Pretending to make little of the pain, he would move his bushy, fierce eyebrows up and down, imitating a warrior played by a Cantonese opera actor. The women would swoon, more out of coyness than fright. It's not surprising that Grandfather Chen sired a large brood—five sons and one daughter in holy matrimony and one love child, on record, on the side."

Grandmother Chen lived much longer. Jack visited her regularly after he had returned to Trinidad from London in 1923 with his mother and three siblings. She was a font of family lore, and Jack tapped it with earnestness. Widowed, Grandma Chen's spirit was as tough as her small, resilient body. Single-handedly, she had raised the whole family. She never stopped moving, trotting about with bare feet just as she might have done in the Hakka village back in Guangdong Province. Her wispy hair was forever falling out from under the tattered brim of a man's Panama hat she wore. Her Victorian petticoats were gray from much washing. Working by herself, with some help from her young children, the tiny farm provided subsistence. Cash came from the vegetable stall she erected at the crossroads below the house. Under an old sheet awning, she displayed her goods on a rough plank table. She sold corn and other farm produce, but her best-selling commodity was coconut cakes. Her young boys would climb the coconut trees to cut down the nuts. She shredded the white meat, boiled it in white or brown sugar, and let the irregular blobs dry into hard patties.

She liked to give her children surprising treats when they behaved well and worked hard. On a sudden impulse, she would go out with a cutlass and return dragging several lengths of sugar cane. She would cut them from the cane brake at the top of the garden where they got the most sun and grew sweet. With one slash of the cutlass she could hack these into short lengths for them to chew on. Her greatest pride and source of satisfaction was the heavy, Chinese-style coffin she kept ready under her bed. She had bought it at the same time she had bought one for her deceased husband.

Grandma Chen never left her farm. Indeed, both she and Grandpa Chen are buried there. Eugene and his children never contemplated moving their remains to the old country. They thought the old couple were finally at home on this West Indies island. The warm weather, the blue waters, and the green fields are much like the Guangdong villages along the seacoast.

It is easy to imagine why Grandpa and Grandma Chen chose to settle down in Trinidad. It is beautiful. The vegetation looked familiar, but more lush than that in their native land. At first glance Grandfather Chen, a weary fugitive, probably wondered if this was paradise regained. This thought would have been some comfort to one who had left behind the Celestial Empire. But in reality, the seeming paradise was a slave mill. Those who followed Columbus to this island saw Caribbean gold—it was not yellow but green gold. A century and a half later, all those handsome, graceful natives, the Caribs, had been worked to death reaping the cocoa, coconuts, and sugarcane. Trinidad, like the original Eden, had become a paradise without work hands, so new hands were kidnapped from West Africa and shipped to Trinidad in chains. Since the working life of a slave in the Spanish colony was short, the supply of labor had to be constantly replenished.

The island changed hands when the British seized it from the Spaniards in 1797, but slavery continued. Once it became clear that the slave trade would be prohibited by the growing middle class and democratic governments of Europe and America, colonial administrators began to consider alternatives.

They turned to the East Indians and the Chinese. The newcomers were not treated as slaves, but were considered inferior to the white people.

Grandfather Chen probably did not try to right the wrongs here as he had in China. Old and tired, he had to fend for his family first. Even in that he was thwarted, as he died before he could see his children grow into adulthood. Eugene, Grandma Chen's oldest son and great comfort, was still in his teens. Eugene's early upbringing was austere, but it proved to be good training for him. In his childhood he helped around the farm, but when he began school, he was told that he would be excused from farm work to concentrate on homework. But while learning about the world beyond this patch of land, Eugene worked even harder with his hands on the family farm. He knew that to get out of an obscure existence and live a life with a higher purpose, like the Taiping heroes of his father's conversations, he needed a strong constitution and mind.

Eugene was a diligent student, raw village youth though he was. He attended the San Fernando borough school and was bright enough to win a scholarship to Port-of-Spain's St. Mary's College, run by the Holy Ghost Fathers, an Irish Catholic order. There is no doubt that as the oldest son of a large family without a father, he embraced the family philosophy of the typical Chinese immigrant: righteousness and learning. Learning a skill was the only way for an immigrant family to get ahead. And righteousness—Li—summed up a multitude of virtues: diligence, honesty, frugality, filial piety...the precepts

St. Mary's College in Port-of-Spain, Trinidad, where Eugene studied.

of the Confucianism of the people. *Li* was "the Way," for a Chinese, the way to do the right things.

Eugene graduated from St. Mary's College at the early age of sixteen and began to look for a job. He attracted the attention of Edgar Maress Smith, a local solicitor, and entered his law office as an apprentice-clerk in 1894. Maress Smith was reputed to have "radical ideas"—or, more simply put, he was horrified by the condition of the masses living in the Crown colony. He wanted to do something about it. A member of the privileged ruling class, he was a man with an uneasy social conscience and sympathy for the poor. Eugene completed his apprenticeship in four years and passed the law examinations qualifying him as a solicitor before the turn of the century. He then helped his two brothers Joseph and David through school and their law training as solicitors. Finally he set up his own law practice, and it grew quickly. His brothers joined him in the firm, named Acham and Acham Solicitors, Notaries Public and Conveyances. The office was a modest, narrow, one-floor stucco structure. It was painted pink, and its side wall ran a quarter block along the road facing the Red House, where the local government was. When

Eugene Chen (1878–1944), a successful lawyer in Trinidad.

Jack's mother, Alphonsine Agatha Gantheaume, who married Eugene in 1899.

a client entered, the clerks' desks were lined up on his left behind a wooden railing. To the right was a wall decorated with certificates and licenses to practice. A swing gate ahead allowed one to enter the office through the railing. A length of coconut matting over the polished floor led to the inner offices of the three partners. It was a solemn place.

In 1899, it was time for Eugene, according to Chinese ideas of what was proper, to get married, and in that year Eugene married Aisy, Jack's mother.

Aisy was born around 1878. Her full name was Alphonsine Agatha Gantheaume. She was good-looking, about five feet tall, petite, and small-boned with light brown skin. She had lively features. Her nose and mouth were delicate. Her black hair, though somewhat kinky, was manageable when shampooed and oiled. A vivacious, elegantly sculpted French Creole, she was one of her father's favorite daughters, and he sent her to get a first-class education as a boarder at St. Joseph's Convent.

Eugene was handsome. His intense facial expression contrasted with the unhurried elegance in his movements. Jack's father was always a neat dresser. He became quite dapper as he fell in love. He wore a fine, soft Panama hat conservatively tilted, comfortable shirts with ample neck room, and tasteful, subdued ties. Every day, he put on a fresh cream or white linen suit and well-shined brown shoes. Eugene did not ever appear untidily dressed or even sweaty in the humid Trinidad rainy season. And that was his style throughout his life.

It was not surprising that these two young people were attracted to each other. The unusual part was how an alliance formed between them. In those days, it was nearly impossible for a Creole girl of good family to meet with a boy unchaperoned, much less a Chinese one. But she got around that somehow, to know him well enough for affection to blossom, leading to a proposal of marriage.

The difficulties facing this marriage were on the Chinese side. The Chinese, and particularly the Hakka, were clannish, even if they lived overseas. For self-preservation they tended to keep within their clan associations and marry within their own communities. Arranged marriages were the norm. Most of the young Hakka women were uneducated, or educated little, trained only to do domestic work. But Eugene wanted to marry a well-educated, modern young woman who would be a helpmate in every sense of the word.

Grandmother Chen was horrified. A wife, she pleaded, was a hen whose sole duty was to lay eggs. It would bring terrible misfortune on the family, she continued between sobs, if a hen crowed like a rooster.

Relatives, friends, and neighbors were stunned by the bad news, and all pressured Eugene to be a filial eldest son, to set a good example for his younger siblings and obey his widowed mother's wish. He was a pure-blooded Chinese, they soberly reminded him, and was under the obligation to keep the blood pure in his family as well as in his community.

Eugene did not yield. A marriage like Eugene's and Aisy's—between a Chinese Hakka and a French, British, or Spanish Creole—was unheard of at that time in Trinidad. Love, however, found a way.

This was basically Jack's version of his parents' romance. But I suspected that there was more than love that led them to the altar. Eugene's career took off in an auspicious start after he got married. He was a poor Chinese lad struggling in a white-controlled colony. Would a rich white father-in-law be helpful? Jack bristled and called that an insult to his parents. He felt it his filial duly to match insult with insult.

"There it goes again, your Shanghai cynicism. Why do you have to read something commercial into a pure love affair? You are infected with your mother's decadent thinking. I know such Shanghai ladies, cynical, artful, manipulating, scheming. . . ."

With no evidence contradicting Jack, I gave the benefit of the doubt to his claim that his parents' marriage was based on pure love. Not until a few years ago did his claim come into question. My son, Jay, returned from a trip to Trinidad in the late 1990s, and brought back anecdotes and pictures of relatives, close and distant. I was particularly pleased with his findings in regard to the Gantheaume family. There had been pitifully little information about them. I supposed that the Chens were too proud to associate themselves with their colonialist in-laws. Fastidiousness, however, is not one of my vices. I incorporate whatever I can get hold of. Jay told me that Aisy's father was a very religious man and was very generous in his charity. He owned one of the largest estates in Trinidad, with plenty of money to donate. So my hunch was correct. Monsieur Gantheaume was rich. After a pause, Jay added that he was also a ladies' man.

That did not surprise me. The Noble Part of Monsieur Gantheaume was in a sort of autonomous region of a man's body, and it did not always take orders from his pious head. I fastened my eyes on a picture of him with his wife. He looked stony, and she looked frigid. It must have been awfully cold in his mansion. No wonder he hopped into the bed of a slave maid with warm dark skin that the Sun God loved to kiss.

A few days later, Jay sent me an e-mail, telling me he had found out the name of his great-grandfather Chen's natural daughter, Amelia, whose mother was a Creole. The next thing he disclosed came as a mild shock. He said that his grandfather, Eugene, had a second family in Trinidad, though nobody knows their whereabouts or their names. Eugene had conveniently set his Creole mistress up in San Fernando, Jay revealed, where he had opened a branch office of his law firm. He was the natural father to twin daughters who were a year or two younger than Percy, his second child by Aisy.

A little philandering certainly would not have made too much of a dent in Eugene's reputation as a lawyer in Trinidad. Infidelity in a man, especially a man of Eugene's status, would not have caused much problem in China either. But later, as a leader in the nationalist revolution, his mixed marriage, mixed affair, and mixed progeny would have been scrutinized. Foreign blood was deemed barbarous and slave blood, inferior. Jack's anger at my prying into his father's private life veiled a much more severe trauma than I had thought. But I mustn't jump ahead of the story.

Aisy was the natural daughter of François Alphonse Gantheaume, who preferred to be called Louis, a nephew or grand-nephew of Admiral Honore Joseph Antoine Gantheaume of Napoleon's navy. The name Gantheaume, a well-known French maritime family originating in Aix-en-Provence, goes back to 1721. Joseph Gantheaume was restless and a bit of a buccaneer. He was engaged, it seems, in every war that France had championed during his lifetime. After he had shed enough blood for France, he was made Count de Gantheaume in 1810 and had his name inscribed on the south side of the Arc de Triomphe. On the waters of Trafalgar, he fought until his vessel was blasted into pieces, shattering the surrounding vessels and nearly burying them all under sharp, burning fragments.

After that debacle, Admiral Joseph Gantheaume continued to serve the government. When Napoleon was finally overthrown in 1815, he and his two brothers fled to Martinique where, it seems, their paterfamilias, a Pierre Gantheaume, had emigrated at the end of the seventeenth century. Later some of the Gantheaumes, including Aisy's father, moved from Martinique to the British colony Trinidad.

Aisy's mother—Mama Goring, as Jack and his siblings called her—had once been a Creole slave. Later she was a servant and cook in the household of François Alphonse Gantheaume. Among the easygoing French, a liaison between the master and his former slave raised no eyebrows and rated not much more than a short comment, usually not even disdainful or disapproving. Gantheaume was a well-known womanizer, somewhat envied by his male friends. He was easily captivated by a swish of the skirt, and the result of his skirt chasing was fruitful. His offspring ranged from milk chocolate brown to blond. All of them, without exception, were good-looking, and some among the women were beautiful, particularly in the second generation. It was an interesting fact that in those early years while Eugene and

Aisy started raising a family, friendly relations existed among all the many branches of the extended Gantheaume family.

Both Aisy and Eugene had their schooling at about the same time in Port-of-Spain. The proximity of their respective schools might explain how they crossed each other's paths in the first place. The boys at St. Mary's College usually arrived and left their building by the back door on Prince Street, ten yards down the street, on the opposite side of the road, from the entrance to St. Joseph's Convent run by the Sisters of Mary, also an Irish Catholic order.

My son Jay, his wife, Chui-Inn, and their daughter, Erita, in front of the Arch of Triumph and under the name "Gantheaume" in 2006.

This was the female counterpart of St. Mary's. The wisdom of having these two gates so close together was a topic that cropped up perennially in discussions between the good fathers and sisters. But nothing had been done about it. Any worldly solution would have involved expensive structural changes. Eugene and Aisy thus had opportunities to meet. But in the atmosphere of strong racial prejudices, it was still a mystery how a Chinese and a French Creole were finally affianced and married, even allowing for the fact that Aisy was a young girl of great resource and that Eugene had even then shown a talent for diplomacy. The key to the mystery was in Monsieur Gantheaume's hand.

The marriage might have been a love match, but it would not have been too far from the truth to say it was initiated to some extent by Monsieur Gantheaume himself. Anxious to find a suitable husband for his high-spirited natural daughter, he might have requested the aid of the good sisters of St. Joseph and the good fathers of St. Mary's. The good fathers of St. Mary's recommended Eugene to the good sisters of St. Joseph, and both presented the candidate to Monsieur Gantheaume for inspection. Eugene, as human as any young enterprising lover, was more than ready to marry a wife with a dowry, considerable by the standard of the Chinese community, and an influential father.

The marriage also set a pattern for Eugene to follow in the future. At every critical stage of his life, he had an eye for the extraordinary opportunity and for taking an unusual course.

<h1 align="center">★ 3 ★</h1>

<h1 align="center">THE RETURN OF THE NATIVE</h1>

At the age of twenty, Eugene had the blessings of two men, both of the ruling class. Maress Smith, Eugene's former boss in the law firm, was campaigning to broaden the representation of the elected members of the Legislative Council. He wanted to see Eugene rise in the world. The other man was Monsieur Gantheaume, Eugene's new father-in-law. Monsieur Gantheaume's interest was purely personal: He had entrusted his daughter's future to Eugene. With these two promoting his budding law firm, plus his hard work and astute business sense, Eugene's career took off.

Events proved this marriage of Jack's parents a most advantageous match for all concerned. The Chinese community naturally flocked to the first young Chinese to open a solicitor's office in Port-of-Spain, and so did the Creoles, delighted to help a local girl make good even if it involved helping a Chinese boy. The two communities together made up a sizable part of the city's population. Eugene, clever and keen, extended his practice to San Fernando in the south and to Arima in the middle of the island, where few whites practiced. The Trinidadians loved the drama of the courtrooms. Litigation was then as popular a pastime in the colony as football, racing, and politics are today. Aisy helped Eugene's career by her social activities and by cultivating their natural links with their communities.

Eugene's reputation attracted a good-sized white clientele as well. One of them was English journalist H. Noble Hall, of the local newspaper, *Pioneer*. Twenty-five years later, at the height of Eugene's fame as China's foreign minister, Hall was asked by the British Foreign Office to provide information about the Trinidad-born revolutionary. Hall wrote a note, dated February 18, 1927, testifying about Eugene's early career and character. "He [Eugene] was a most painstaking student. This trait distinguished his work as a solicitor. He was admitted to practice, if my memory is correct, about 1897: In any case he had only been practicing three or four years when I first met him and he had already won the reputation of being about the best conveyancer in the Colony, always searching titles with great care and drawing up flawless instruments.... When I knew Acham, he was a quiet studious young man of about 25 who believed in work as the way to get on in life.... Like all Chinamen of his class, Acham was most scrupulously honest."[1]

"Honest" was the key to Eugene's success. He was an unusual solicitor. Like his father, he was a champion of the underprivileged. He steadfastly refused to outwit justice. If you had a good case, if you believed that Right and Justice were on your side, if you had broken the law unwittingly, or under great provocation and extenuating circumstances, then you took your case to him. If you were trying to cover up wrongdoing or merely trying to get yourself out of a tight corner in which your shady manipulations had landed you, then you kept out of his office. If he found out your case was not just, he would advise you to take it elsewhere. Magistrates and juries learned of this eccentric attitude. When his clients' cases came to court, the scales of justice were heavily weighted in their favor. Eugene's one-story office, at the corner by the Red House and its courtrooms, was one of the busiest law offices on the island.

Eugene was long remembered by the common people of Trinidad, who knew him not as China's foreign minister but as a bright scholar, successful professional, and a good man. In 1925, many years after he had left Trinidad, Jack found himself near Manzanilla Bay on the east coast of the island. He was with a white estate manager who knew the district and its people well. They met an old barefoot East Indian in white turban and dhoti. When Jack's companion told the old man that this was Eugene's son, the old man looked Jack over with renewed interest and approval. Then the old man bowed down, took a pinch of dust from the road in his thumb and forefinger, raised it to the sky, and touched it to his forehead. He said not a word. By this ritual gesture, so solemn and dignified, he had conveyed his appraisal: the salt of the earth.

Ambitious for himself and his family, Eugene worked hard to build his legal practice. He saw this as the foundation for the advancement of his future, and he succeeded in this brilliantly. Acham and Acham flourished. Eugene invested in land like everyone else in Trinidad who had money. By the end of the first decade of the century, as a result of a little more than ten years' practice, the family had achieved a solid economic position, even a measure of wealth and an envied social status. He owned several cocoa estates. The largest was St. Isadore, inland from Manzanilla Beach on the almost uninhabited east coast of the island. La Mascotte was a nearby smaller property. He owned land at La Brea and Cedros that later proved oil-rich. He owned Acham's Bay, a little private cove on one of the larger islands near the Dragon's Mouth, the strait at the northwestern tip of the island. On the rocky cliff above this cove was an airy house, basically an all-covered verandah. In the tiny bay beneath it, reached by curving rocky steps, was a sheltered jetty. It was at Acham's Bay that Jack learned to swim and fish.

Eugene also owned several houses: Kim Lin, the Chen family's main residence, a few vacation homes, and a couple more small places for Aisy's mother, Mama Goring, and her lethargic brother.

Eight children in all were born to the couple, but only four survived. The first, a girl, the never-forgotten Kim Lin, died early. The second child was a boy named Percy, who became a lawyer. The next, a boy, Alain, died. The fourth, a daughter, Silan, lived. The fifth, a boy, Jack, died. The sixth, born in 1908, was my future husband, who inherited his immediate predecessor's name. The seventh, another girl, died. The eighth, Yolanda, was born in 1913 in England. What caused this rhythm of life and death nobody has found out. There was no common cause of death, and all who survived childhood were long-lived. In addition to the children, there were always extra people in the house. Relatives, close or distant, or friends of the family, Creole or white. When the family was in Port-of-Spain, Mama Goring was usually around to help Aisy look after the children.

Eugene's family grew. They moved into his new house on Broom Street in St. Clair, the most opulent district in Port-of-Spain and hitherto exclusively inhabited by whites, English, French, and old Spanish families. This was a white, two-story mansion, a Victorian colonial with a wide verandah running around three sides. It had a carriage yard, a stable, outbuildings, and lots of fretwork on its balconies. Chinese, Creoles, East Indians, and blacks gaped at the temerity of Eugene and his wife invading "white" St. Clair, but they loved it. The white establishment commented, some paternalistically, some condescendingly, some scathingly.

Aisy cut quite a figure in island society. She bought a carriage, a Cadillac of its class, and a magnificent chestnut named Prince. Many Sunday afternoons, her coachman drove Prince around the Savannah, the large grass-covered space between the downtown district and the hills back of the city. Prince paced grandly. The black coachman wore a shiny top hat and a dark suit, sitting, with Jack beside him, on the high box. In the carriage, Jack's mother and her lovely white cousin Stella wore the large picture hats made fashionable at that time by the Gaiety Girls. Holding their little ruffled parasols over their heads, their voluminous skirts and flounces were set off by the shining black leather seats of the carriage and its glinting panels. Jack's older sister, Silan, completed the picture. She had an elfin smile and long, naturally curly hair. She wore a sailor blouse to match Jack's.

The Sunday afternoon ritual was to circle the Savannah once, and then join the line of carriages drawn up in front of the governor's mansion. There a band performed sedate music in the bandstand of the botanical garden. It was an occasion to see and be seen; to beam a smile at a friend and administer a cut to an enemy; to snub the presumptuous; to show the whites that Chinese and Creoles knew what a real carriage turnout should be.

Life was affluent and fun. On holidays, the family went to their vacation homes. Jack's mother took the children on the long drive to St. Isadore. The house stood high on concrete pillars on the windward side of a hill. Below was a blue sea, shimmering through the tops of the green palm trees. On the top of the hill were the two cocoa-drying sheds, their gabled roofs fitted with small wheels running on iron rails. They could be slid away to uncover the drying floors. Here the air was always redolent of the sweet smell of the cocoa beans. After being scooped out of the pods, the beans were spread out on the polished boards of the drying shed. They were covered with the sweet white mush of fine filaments, like sticky cotton wool, that anchored them inside the pods. The Chen children liked to be there when the pods were broken open, to suck this sweet mush off.

At St. Isadore, the children had the run of a domain whose boundaries they had never seen. They took long walks beneath the rows of cocoa trees, through dim leafy tunnels dappled with sunlight. Sometimes they followed the estate manager carrying his hunting rifle, seeking out a wild pig for a barbecue party at the estate house. Sometimes the Chen children rode mules or ponies on the trails on an inspection tour. These tours would somehow always wind up on the sands at Manzanilla Beach. There they rode races or body-surfed or came sailing into shore on the tops of makeshift surfboards. When the rains came, they played in the swollen drainage ditches that crisscrossed the estate, searching for fish or freshwater clams torn loose from their moorings by the flood waters.

This early part of Jack's life was veiled in the glow of a happy childhood. Everything was going well for the family. Britain was at the height of her power. The Chen family enjoyed the Pax Britannica symbolized by the lordly British warships, which now and then dropped anchor in the harbor at Port-of-Spain, or by the red, white, and black liners of the Royal Mail. The Chen family was among the chosen rich in this island paradise that was Trinidad. They were proud of being British.

Eugene enjoyed the fresh breezes of success. He liked material comforts, but that was not all he wanted from life. He yearned for something beyond the confines of his small island. For him to look beyond its horizon, he had to read, and he read voraciously. His was one of the best private libraries in the colony at the time. It came into Jack's possession in 1924 and showed that Eugene had honed his later famous writing skills on a study of the best of English literature. He had volumes of Chaucer, Shakespeare, Milton, Fielding, Byron, Shelley, Thackeray, Dickens, and George Eliot, as well as writers and essayists of belles lettres such as Lamb, Hazlitt, Carlyle, Emerson, Walter Savage Landor, Max Beerbohm, and George Bernard Shaw. English authors made up the bulk of the collection. Among the French were Voltaire, Rousseau, and Montesquieu. Not many American writers were in evidence.

But he did not have a single volume by radical socialist, communist, or anarchist thinkers such as Marx or Mikhail Bakunin. William Morris was the sole representative of socialism in his library.

There was curiously little about Asia and China. His was the library of a cultured, liberal Englishman of his day, very much focused on England and Europe. One reason was that he did not have a Chinese education as some overseas Chinese had, and thus could not read Chinese. Books about China, written in English, were almost nonexistent in Trinidad in those days. At that time, things Chinese seemingly played a small part in his thoughts.

While feeling his way forward as a writer, Eugene, in addition to drawing up briefs, began to contribute letters and articles to the press. Knowing how important the skill of public speaking was to a man of law, he took part in the debates organized by the public library. Later he attended the meetings, discussions, and debates at the Victoria Institute, a gathering place for intellectuals in Port-of-Spain. These debates made quite a stir in the small island society. They were well-argued, well-styled expositions of his liberal views.

The English journalist H. Noble Hall, who had participated in the same debates, wrote: "He [Eugene] not only looked after my legal affairs, but we used to attend the debates at the Victoria Institute together and got to be close friends. I remember Hugh Clifford, who was then Colonial Secretary, complimenting Acham on his delightfully harmonious English after a debate, in which I led and he supported me, on the side of Wentworth, Earl of Strafford. Acham was greatly interested in history.... He used often to say that the condition in which rulers left their country after their death was a sure test of their greatness or otherwise.... He was very keen on the French Revolution and never tired of talking about a subject with which at the time I was well acquainted."[2]

But the intellectual life in Port-of-Spain was too constricted for Jack's father. As early as 1903, he witnessed how people's narrow thinking had led to bigotry and calamity. In that year, the government attempted to enact a law raising water rates, which would affect the livelihood of the poor. Teamed with Maress Smith, Eugene opposed it. Despite protests, the law was passed. Feelings ran high, and a riot broke out, which was brutally crushed. Maress Smith was thrown into prison for rabble-rousing, and Eugene had to lay low. Accompanied by Aisy and their two children, he stayed in his vacation home at St. Isadore.

It happened that one wounded fugitive from the Water Riot hid in the laborers' barracks on his estate. Eugene visited the wounded man and got him medical care. When the man asked if Eugene could help him make a case, suing the government for damages, Eugene wistfully shook his head. If he came out of hiding now, Eugene explained, he would get himself arrested.

With heavy heart, Eugene came out of the barracks. He saw a woman sitting there on the stoop, surrounded by the sighing stillness of the plantation groves, with kerosene lanterns twinkling dimly on the hillsides. Several black children had gathered at their mother's knee, nestling in her wide skirts, singing the ditty:

"Mama, are there any angels black like me?"

And they would get the answer: "No, you sweet little bastard. When you dies, the good Lord will turn yo' soul white." As the voices would trail off, the hoarse croaking of the frogs would take over: "Calakala, calakala..."

Eugene simmered with indignation. Years later, he recalled the sad ditty to Jack when Jack began to be aware of the racial discrimination around him. Compelled by this experience, Eugene struggled to understand the broader and deeper meaning of social injustice. Sometime between 1903 and 1906, he took his first trip to London and got in touch with the Chinese community there. From 1906 on, Eugene made an annual pilgrimage to London and its Chinese community. He came at the right time: London was cosmopolitan, and China was making headlines in all the newspapers. The unfolding drama of the Chinese Revolution was the central topic among the Chinese expatriates in London. Eugene mingled with other like-minded wandering sons there. At one Chinese New Year party, he happened on two fellow

Cantonese men, Dr. Wu Liande and Dr. Philip Tyau. Both said that they had plans to go to China. Eugene was interested in knowing more, but on such a public occasion their conversations were constantly interrupted. Eugene thought of circling around a bit and then inviting them to dinner; but when he came back, he found them gone. If he had had any idea of what their friendship would later mean to him, Eugene would have kicked himself for letting the chance slip by.

Such encounters gave him food for thought and planted in Eugene a desire to learn more about his home country and read more about its history. It was probably at this time that his father's stories of the Taiping Rebellion, which had been at the back of his mind, came to the fore.

At the age of thirty-two and after spending twelve years practicing law, Eugene considered entering politics, but could not yet decide where he would start, Trinidad or China.

His first move was to London in early 1911. He and his family lived in a well-furnished flat in a ten-story residential block named Clarence Gate Mansions, at the back of Baker Street. This was a convenient distance from downtown London. As new arrivals, the flat suited the Chen family well for a short while. Then they moved from the area of Regent's Park farther north-west to St. John's Wood, which was precisely their proper niche in the social hierarchy of London. It was a quiet, genteel, upper-middle-class neighborhood of lawyers, bankers, and directors of city companies, with a smattering of well-to-do artists, musicians, actors, and a few fashionable mistresses of upper-class gentlemen.

Eugene and Aisy took a ninety-nine-year lease on number eleven Clifton Hill, and hired a cook, nicknamed Cookie. She was a large-bosomed, motherly soul. Because of her cooking, the Chens developed an abiding love for good English roast lamb with a dash of mint sauce made with mint fresh from the garden. Cookie saw to it that they ate well. They also had an eager little maid. She cleaned and answered the door and spoke with a Cockney accent. When they entertained, she served meals in a black dress with a white frilly apron and little lace cap. She taught the Chen children, in a garbled sort of way, how babies were made and born.

After they had settled in, Eugene took courses in philosophy, economics, and political science at London University. Before he had time to decide if he wanted to enroll and study in a law school, China beckoned her wandering son to return home and take part in building a new nation. The tottering Manchu Court had finally collapsed. This was not exactly a sudden turn of events. The Manchu Court had been in its death throes for quite a while. The bell first started tolling for them during their defeat in the Opium War in 1842. After that, China was invaded and vanquished in war after war. By the end of the nineteenth century, China was divided into spheres of influence by Britain, Russia, Japan, Germany, France, and so on, who forced, not negotiated, their terms on China, in what the Chinese called "Unequal Treaties." Imperial China was at her last gasp, the colonialists predicted.

The ineffectual and moribund Manchu rulers finally did die, but China did not. On October 10, 1911, the uprising led primarily by Sun Yatsen's comrades erupted in the city of Wuchang situated in the Wuhan area on the middle Yangzi River. The revolutionaries held the city. In the following days, city after city and province after province declared for the republicans. Within six weeks, two thirds of all China had abandoned the Manchu rulers of the Qing dynasty.

Eugene read the sensational reports of these events in the London press. Then came a brief meeting between him and the leading revolutionary, Sun Yatsen, which proved to be a turning point in Eugene's life.

Sun Yatsen was in Denver in the middle of a propaganda and organizing tour in the United States when he received news of the revolutionary victory and an urgent call to return immediately to China. But instead of returning by the shortest route, he turned in his tracks and journeyed through Europe, the long way home. He reached London in late October and held a meeting for the Chinese expatriates. Eugene was among those in the audience. In his speech, Sun urged them to go home and serve the new republic. The overseas Chinese in the assembly understood the message; Sun himself was an overseas Chinese from Hawaii. What he had made out of his life, they could too.

Right then and there, Eugene realized that he could play a part on a stage much, much larger than Trinidad. There is no doubt that Eugene decided to travel to China because of Sun Yatsen. He used to insist on this point whenever he mentioned Sun later in life. And for many years it was assumed that he arranged for his journey to China to coincide with Sun's. But this was not exactly so.

When Eugene began preparing for his China trip, he probably realized he faced difficulties ahead. But he knew that in entering the modern world, the new Chinese republic needed able men, including Chinese émigrés from abroad. He could put to good use his knowledge of English law and history and his ability to write in English.

The difficult part of his preparation was telling his wife of his intended venture. She blinked at it and asked to have a little time to take it in. Her brain turned his words back and forth, seeking their meaning. He wanted to go to China, a place she knew practically nothing about. Letting him go was like watching him vanish into a mysterious, bottomless void. She shuddered. And yet she did not want to prevent Eugene from going.

Aisy had known inequality since the day she was born. Her mother was a former slave, a colored woman. She herself, a favorite natural daughter of her aristocratic father, was brought up as a young lady and was not allowed to call a servant her mother. She had a mother, and yet she had no mother. She lived with her father in the main house, a mansion filled with sunlight. Beyond that was a small cool cobblestoned courtyard shaded by miniature palm trees, and at their back were a couple of dark rooms, one a kitchen. There her mother, Mama Goring, lived with Aisy's younger half-sister Augustine. Sometimes Aisy scuttled in and out of their room for a stealthy kiss or hug.

Mixtures were discriminated against from all sides, and her children were of mixed blood. The inequality Eugene wanted to fight was for the sake of their children as well as for his homeland.

Then came the time to part. Jack's mother was adequately provided for and busy with the education of the children, so she consented to let her husband go to China and try to do what he hoped.

In January 1912, Eugene left the middle-class comforts of St. John's Wood and bought his ticket for the Trans-Siberian Express to the unknown world of Peking. Aisy and the three children came down to Liverpool Street Station to say their good-byes. They were sad, but it was not a tearful departure. Eugene promised to return soon.

When Eugene stepped aboard the train in early 1912, all he took with him was the remarkable courage—some might say foolhardiness—that led him to set off for Peking, despite not knowing anyone in China, not speaking a word of Chinese, and having no knowledge of the maelstrom of Chinese politics he was about to plunge into.

The journey was long and slow. Comfortable in his first-class, two-berth compartment, Eugene did not find the wintry days as boring as one might imagine. The scenery was charming, as the train passed through the prosperous Western European countryside with numerous fine towns and villages. There was a lengthy stop in Berlin. While waiting on the platform at Friedrichstrasse Station, Eugene accidentally ran into a nodding acquaintance and immediately recognized the warm smiling eyes behind the round-lensed glasses.

At the Elms in London. Jack and Silan in the middle of the front row with their classmates, circa 1912.

Dr. Wu Liande (also known as Wu Lienteh), like Eugene, was immaculately dressed in Western style and, again like Eugene and other fashionable gentlemen in those days, wore a Panama hat and fawn-colored spats over his highly polished shoes. Dr. Wu was an overseas Chinese born in 1879 in Penang, Malaya. His father was a Cantonese goldsmith who had enough savings to give him a good education. After being graduated from Queen's College as the first Chinese to study medicine at Cambridge University, Dr. Wu went back to Penang to practice. He was horrified to find the number of Chinese smoking opium had increased dramatically, and he campaigned hard against the drug. Inevitably, he clashed with those who had a vested interest in an addicted populace, and they plotted to get rid of him. They managed to stop his medical practice. He cast about for an opportunity to work elsewhere in his field of epidemiology. His search was resolved when he visited relatives in China, where he witnessed the periodic devastation wreaked by various plagues. Since then, he had been working ceaselessly to bring the pneumonic plague under control. Now he was on his way to Manchuria in northeast China to continue work on an internationally sponsored anti-plague campaign based in the city of Harbin.

From the moment Dr. Wu Liande finished his self-introduction, Eugene knew he had found a sympathetic friend in this man. In turn, Eugene told his new friend of his plans to serve the motherland. Dr. Wu assured him that he would get a job to his satisfaction.

For the rest of the trip, Dr. Wu told Eugene as much as he could about China. As a native son returning home, Eugene should have a Chinese name, he advised. Then he suggested the Chinese transliteration of Youren, for which the Chinese characters mean "Possessor of Benevolence." Eugene liked the significance of his new Chinese name. From this time on he also reverted to Chen as his surname. In China he is known as Chen Youren (or Chen Yujen).

The meeting between Eugene and Dr. Wu was accidental, but not the congeniality that came afterward. They were like many other wandering sons of China. Discriminated against in their adopted countries, they saw China as their Promised Land. It is not difficult to imagine the instant kinship that arose between the two.

When Eugene and Dr. Wu arrived in Peking in early 1912, the city, under a coat of snow, looked its best. As the train crept into the station, the snow romanticized the city and hid the squalor of the slums. It was too cold even for the usual horde of beggars, sick, tattered, and clamorous, to pester the arriving travelers. Dr. Wu took Eugene to the best hotel in town. The Peking

The Hour: the Front Gate of Peking.

Hotel was owned and run by the British, and the lobby was decorated in British style with a slightly oriental flavor, like the electric bulbs hidden in lanterns sculpted into exotic flowers, dragons, phoenix, fish, and lovely women in ancient Chinese costumes. Most of the guests chatted in English and French, the two languages in which Eugene was fluent, and he did not feel out of place.

From the upper windows of the Peking Hotel, Eugene could see the huge rectangle of the great city wall. It was forty feet high with battlements, bastions, and stone towers over its several gateways. Beyond that were the curving eaves and amber tiled roofs of the Forbidden City, bathed in the glorious winter light. This was the ancient capital of a brand-new government, Eugene told himself in euphoria. Here he was, back home at long last, to serve the revolution, which Sun Yatsen had claimed to be a continuation of the Taiping Rebellion. Eugene was now committed to the same task as his father, the Taiping rebel, and he was determined to accomplish what his father had left unfinished.

★ 4 ★

THE MAELSTROM OF PEKING POLITICS

Eugene, a newcomer in a strange land, had no idea how precarious Sun Yatsen's position was. When Sun was inaugurated on January 1, 1912, in Nanjing, the Southern Capital, the last emperor of the Manchu Court was still perched on his Dragon Throne in Peking. The last emperor's fate was in the hands of the archwarlord Yuan Shikai. In its last days, the Manchu Court had lost its grip on its military governors, and these regional militarists became powerful warlords and ruled their respective territories like independent fiefdoms. The strongest was Yuan Shikai.

Yuan, seeing that the flood of revolution could not be stopped, switched sides. He proposed to the republicans that he would arrange the abdication of the last emperor in return for the presidency. All through this period, he was in close contact with ministers of the foreign powers in Peking, and they backed his proposal. The colonialist envoys decided Yuan Shikai could stabilize the situation and would let them do business as usual.

Sun Yatsen was faced with the prospect of civil war in which the scattered forces of the infant republic would be pitted against a trained modern army under Yuan Shikai. Sun was pressured by both domestic opponents and the foreign powers to accept Yuan Shikai's pledge to support the republic. They pointed out that Sun had no governing experience whatsoever. If he refused to resign, they warned, he would make a terrible mess of state affairs. On the other hand, Yuan Shikai had had a successful career as a military commander and civil administrator.

No sooner had Eugene unpacked his suitcase than Wu Liande came in with the bad news. He had just read about Sun's formal message addressed to the National Assembly (the Chinese equivalent of Parliament) while submitting his resignation on February 13, 1912. It went as follows:

"Today I present you my resignation and request you to elect a good and talented man as the new president. . . . Mr. Yuan [Shikai] is a man of political experience, upon whose constructive ability our united nation looks forward to the consolidation of its interests. . . ."[1]

Sun Yatsen gave Yuan Shikai the benefit of the doubt, as did many people. Eugene should do the same, Dr. Wu Liande advised, and stay in Peking.

Eugene said matter-of-factly: "I need a job to pay for food and board."

It was fortunate that Dr. Wu had accompanied him to Peking. Wu was well connected and a member of a powerful political group. Quite a few, but not all, of them were Cantonese from Guangdong Province, so the whole group, Cantonese and non-Cantonese, was nicknamed the "Cantonese Clique." But it is more appropriate to call it the Cantonese Club, because these Western-educated or Western-influenced liberals did not all belong to the same faction in the government. They got together when they wanted to work for some common task, usually liberal in nature.

The first member of the Cantonese Club whom Dr. Wu Liande took Eugene to meet was Alfred Shi (1877–1958), also known as Shi Zhaoji. Although Shi was not Cantonese, he had a Cornell master's in economics and had acquired enough liberal ideas to be welcomed into the Cantonese Club. He was minister of communications and acting minister of finance in the Peking government. He had great credentials, and he had even greater in-laws. His wife, Alice, was the niece of the current prime minister, Tang Shaoyi, and the cousin of the first Mrs. Wellington Koo, wife of the future prime minister.

Alfred Shi's private residence was one of Peking's old mansions, which had been fixed up with modern conveniences without losing its old-world charm. It boasted a drawing room resplendent with Chinese silks and brocades, antiques and scrolls, and redwood furniture. Into this scene came the host, dignified, handsome, and impassive of expression, as befitted a well-bred modernized Chinese mandarin.

Shi had a high opinion of Eugene and hired him to act as his secretary after their first meeting. Eugene advised him on contracts and foreign concessions, and on other legal matters involving foreign railway interests. For Eugene, this was a valuable apprenticeship in state affairs. What he saw was a horrendous picture of a China chained in a servile condition. At the beginning of the twentieth century, China had about 9,618 kilometers of railway, and over 91 percent of that was controlled by the colonialists. Controlling the railways, the foreign powers controlled the arteries of China and the resources along them. China had lost its sovereignty on land and also on water. By 1911, the colonial powers had brought in their marines and forced open

Eugene liked to stroll on the Old Peking street with the famous arches.

eighty-two port cities. They were free to sail wherever they chose. China's seas and rivers were choked with these warships. The foreigners felt justified in opening fire indiscriminately on the unarmed Chinese whenever they decided that their own citizens' lives, properties, and interests were in danger.

Numerous questions arose from the control of the railways by the foreign powers to the number of foreign staff employed on those railways. Although Shi was the minister of communications of the new Chinese Republic, he worked not so much to protect China's interests as those of the foreign powers. This was not what Eugene had returned to his home country for, and he set about looking for a more meaningful job.

He was in a sort of midlife crisis. Because he was a latecomer, he did not have seniority in the government and worked under men of his own age or younger, men who had family ties and connections and were alumni in a broad sense, since most of them had attended the Ivy League universities in the United States. If he did not make a breakthrough, he could end up being a perennially subordinate official. Anxious to get ahead, Eugene began to move into a different direction, where he could excel.

Eugene had one chief asset that others fell short of: his ability to write English. English was their second language and there was a certain awkwardness to their expressions. To them, English was a tool; to him, it was an extension of his mind and personality. Therefore he chose journalism.

He discussed it with Philip Tyau, another acquaintance he had made back in London. Philip Tyau was an overseas Cantonese from Hawaii and a member of the Cantonese Club. He was at the moment editing the English edition of the *Peking Daily News*. The paper was publicly unofficial, but it was actually the mouthpiece of the ministry of foreign affairs. Like the ministry of communications, the ministry of foreign affairs in a country as poor and weak as China was tilted toward the interests of foreigners rather than its own foreign interests. While the Chinese officially swallowed their pride, they unleashed, though mildly, their resentment against the colonialist overlords through the "unofficial" *Peking Daily News*.

Its primary targets were the British-owned *Peking and Tientsin [Tianjin] Times* and the *North China Daily News*, as both were unabashedly imperialistic. Philip Tyau was aware of his huge task, and he needed good writers. At his urging, Eugene began to contribute articles to the *Peking Daily News*. By defending the Chinese government, Eugene had to defend the president, Yuan Shikai, against the rumors of Yuan's dreams of starting a new dynasty, and he did quite a bit of apologizing for the former feudal warlord. But he did not dwell on Yuan. He put special emphasis on the strength and will of the people. The Chinese people, he said, had reversed the teachings of forty centuries and were dedicating themselves to the mighty work of adapting their civilization—which had witnessed the rise and fall of empires in the valleys of the Nile and Euphrates—to the aims and needs of the new republic.

Ironically, by doing what he deemed the duty of a Chinese journalist, Eugene got involved in things that he later preferred to forget. In 1912 or 1913, Alfred Shi asked Eugene to look into the matter of the so-called Reorganization Loan and to find some way to facilitate the process of obtaining it. Nobody knew better than Alfred Shi, the once–acting minister of finance and since late 1912 the chief of protocol in the president's office, how hard the government was pressed for cash. The new republic had inherited an empty treasury without any sources of revenue. In its twilight years, the Manchu Court's treasury had shrunk nearly to zero. After the Boxer Uprising was officially concluded by the signing of the Boxer Protocol on September 7, 1901, China was further burdened with the payment of the enormous restitution to the foreign powers. To make sure that they would get the money, the powers required that the important post of inspector-general of customs should go to an Englishman. The Manchu rulers had mortgaged practically everything they could come up with. No matter who was the president of the new republic, he must get a new loan; both Yuan Shikai and Sun Yatsen agreed on that course.

Sun made a statement in the summer of 1912 in which he said that he and Yuan Shikai "discussed at length the Six-Power loan [later renamed the Reorganization Loan]. . . . Almost to the last word of that statement my own views were in accord with those of the President."[2]

A new collateral was required to secure this loan. In the past, the customs service had furnished security for loans, but the exorbitant demand made upon it for the Boxer indemnity had drained their coffers. The Five-Power Banking Consortium (after the Americans dropped out), representing Banks of Britain, Germany, France, Russia, and Japan, made it known to President Yuan Shikai that the national salt taxes, commonly referred to as the Salt Gabelle, would be satisfactory security, provided it was brought under the administration of the British-controlled Customs Service. Yuan yielded.

Anticipating that the news would cause much controversy, Alfred Shi invited Eugene in for a chat. Eugene was more than glad to oblige. He always found it a delight to sit in one of the courtyards, surrounded by vermilion-pillared verandahs and windows with their exquisite paper-covered lattices, listening to the tips his friend gave.

Eugene was privy to much information his friend leaked to him. His articles attracted considerable attention, and their author soon established a reputation as the most forceful and accomplished writer in the English-language Chinese press. Moreover, he clearly had inside information on government affairs and understood the official viewpoint on current affairs. The foreign community was curious, and a British journalist named H. G. W. Woodhead was especially piqued.

In 1913 Woodhead was the editor of a popular newspaper, the *Peking Gazette*. Published in English, it was the brainchild of a man named Eggeling, a German born in Edinburgh. He worked as vice manager at the German (Deutsch Asiatic) Bank, a member of the international banking consortium in Peking. He started the *Peking Gazette* to reflect the ideas of the consortium of British, German, American, French, Russian, and Japanese interests. With plenty of funding, the newspaper was a success under Woodhead's direction. Impressed by Eugene's distinctive writing style and obvious access to officials in high places, Woodhead tried to entice

Eugene to the *Peking Gazette*. Eugene was seeking a wider readership and was encouraged by his friends in the Cantonese Club, among them a portly young man by the name of Guo Taiqi, who was the English secretary of Vice President Li Yuanhong.

Guo was a graduate of the University of Pennsylvania, where he had majored in political science. His boss, Li Yuanhong, was more a rival than a partner to Yuan Shikai. Naturally he would like to see Eugene more critical of the administration.

"My paper, the *Peking Daily News*, is funded by the government. It won't carry any articles to embarrass the president," Eugene apologized mopingly.

"That's why you need a new paper. Why don't you acquire the *Peking Gazette?*" Guo Taiqi asked, in his sedate, bookish manner.

The tension between Britain and Germany was mounting. War could break out at any time. Although Britain and Germany were still on speaking terms at the moment, the affairs of the international banking consortium were running less smoothly than in previous years. The possible outbreak of war would turn the two countries into adversaries and drive Woodhead and Eggeling to each other's throats. At that time, Eugene could make an offer, and Eggeling would jump at it.

"Where is the money?" Eugene asked.

"You don't need to worry about this," Guo Taiqi said with a deadpan expression.

In his first months and years in Peking, Eugene depended a great deal on the Cantonese Club for his reading of the tangled situation in China. He and Alfred Shi became bosom friends. When Eugene needed advice, Alfred Shi was always there for him. Shi said he could think more clearly when he felt closer to nature, so they walked up a footpath toward a small pavilion. As they strolled, Shi gave his analysis of the rumors of Yuan Shikai's intention of donning the yellow dragon robe.

If Yuan Shikai, a relic from the feudal Manchu Court, fancied that he could transform himself overnight into a republican, Alfred Shi said, he had given up any attempt to make this come true. He was used to an autocratic way of solving problems. The endless debate and clamoring for change, which was carried on in the National Assembly, was a nuisance to him. All it did, Yuan grumbled, was prevent him from efficiently running the government. He had concluded negotiations on the Reorganization Loan with the

Five-Power consortium. But the National Assembly, in which Sun Yatsen's Kuomintang was the strongest party, suddenly went back on their word and would not let him implement it. They accused him of wanting to use the loan to usurp their republican rights; and he counter-charged them with intending to grab the loan to consolidate their party's power. Well, there was some truth in both allegations. The National Assembly was a new institution imported from the West, but its members, unlike their Western counterparts, were not elected by the people: the seats were divided between various political parties. The members naturally represented the interests of their respective parties, not the people.

"I don't see that any side is completely blameless," Alfred Shi sighed again when they reached the small pavilion.

After a pause, Shi confided to Eugene that he had been stymied in his efforts to enact reform from within. Yuan Shikai employed him, but distrusted him and detested his liberal views. Yuan staffed his ministries with an ill-assorted combination of modern-trained bureaucrats and trusted, old-fashioned mandarins, while he and his generals, such as the minister of war, Duan Qirui, so tightly controlled the channels of government that Alfred Shi and his like-minded colleagues could make little headway. Frustrated, Shi sought to serve his country in a different capacity. He had been appointed minister to the Court of St. James and would leave for London in the coming summer.

"Eugene, you can go with me and find work in our Legation," he offered. "You can come back here later if you wish, when the situation is improved."

Shi did not say so in so many words, but he made it clear to Eugene that he intended to keep as far away as he could from the monarchical intrigues.

"I am thinking of freelance journalism," Eugene said. "My fear is that perhaps I cannot afford to give up the salary."

"I'll get you a sinecure in the ministry of communications," Alfred Shi said.

With a solid, stable income, Eugene devoted more time to writing for the *Peking Gazette* and in the natural course of events got to know its publisher, Eggeling. Eggeling and Woodhead found Eugene charming and brilliant. Eugene was on friendly terms with both, adroitly keeping away from any flashpoints between them. When Woodhead became ill in the summer of 1914, his doctor advised him to go to the seaside for a rest cure. He had no one on his staff to whom he could entrust the editorship, so he wanted to recruit Eugene for the post. Eggeling readily approved. Eugene accepted and began to write editorials and to supervise the contents of the paper.

During Eugene's first visit to his new boss's home, his host was keen to know how he would run the paper. Knowing what was on Eggeling's mind, Eugene gave him the answer he wanted.

"China is neutral in the European war, and the *Peking Gazette* should be neutral too," Eugene said.

Eggeling's eyes looked up sharply. "If I have to sell the paper, I'll sell it to the buyer who will reduce the British influence in China." He spoke fluent English with a slight German accent.

Eugene relayed the conversation to Guo Taiqi, the English secretary of Vice President Li Yuanhong. Eggeling's was not a difficult condition for Eugene and Guo Taiqi to accept. For the moment, both the Peking warlord government and its Kuomintang opposition supported neither the British and their allies nor the Germans. As far as China was concerned, all the foreign powers were imperialists, holding territory or rights filched from China. As for the feudal militarist cliques that vied for control of the Peking government, they could not care less about the European conflict. China's middle class, which the Kuomintang represented, was faring well because of the impending war. With their European and Japanese competitors distracted, Chinese traders and manufacturers, like their American counterparts, were expanding their share of the markets both at home and abroad.

A deal was in the making. By the time Woodhead recovered and returned to Peking, the First World War was well under way, forcing a confrontation between the editor, Woodhead, a Brit, and Eggeling, the paper's British-born but German publisher. Their feud peaked when Woodhead had a shouting match with his publisher. There was a bulldog ferocity on the Englishman's wide face as he cut short Eggeling's tirade against Reuters for its frequent lies, unworthy of publication. A day or two later, Eggeling sent his editor a pamphlet, titled *The Truth About Great Britain*, which he thought worthy of publication. But Woodhead found it scurrilous. He published it, nevertheless, as an example of German propaganda, and in the same issue printed his editorial, titled *The Truth About Germany*, tongue-lashing his enemy. Eggeling, furious, warned that he was not going to have Germany attacked in the paper he funded. Woodhead retorted that he had his obligations as a patriotic British journalist. As Eggeling became increasingly pro-German and anti-British, Woodhead became more pro-British and anti-German. There was no possibility of resolving the feud.

"He thinks he holds the purse strings, but I have the British Legation at my back," Woodhead declared with pride.

As the shouting matches grew more frequent, Eugene approached Eggeling and gave a dispassionate appraisal of the feud. Yes, Eggeling had the power to halt publication, cutting off the monthly subsidy to the paper and letting it wither on the vine. But it would be a pity to close down such a popular, influential newspaper. Before Eggeling made the final decision, would he consider a proposal to buy it? Still suppressing his excitement, Eugene said:

"We are not particularly fond of Britain."

"Done," Eggeling said.

No sooner had Eugene stepped out of Eggeling's residence than he dashed to Guo Taiqi's.

"I need the money as soon as possible, before Eggeling changes his mind," Eugene said, still panting.

"You can have it tomorrow," Guo Taiqi promised without batting an eyelid.

"It is a huge amount," Eugene cautioned. "The lender will ask for a large collateral."

"Larger than the Salt Gabelle?"

Eugene stiffened. He cast down his eyes as though sinking into thought. Was this a crude joke? Was Guo mocking his role in getting the Reorganization Loan for Yuan Shikai? The revenues of the salt tax were collected by the British-controlled Customs Service and disbursed to the Chinese government as they saw fit. The British naturally doled out revenues to support the warlords favorable to them, at that particular moment Yuan Shikai. Could this same salt tax, used in the previous year to secure the Reorganization Loan, which had helped propel Yuan toward realizing his monarchical dream, now be used to buy the *Peking Gazette*? There were only two men in Peking or even in the whole country who had the authority to tap into that fund: the president and the vice president, two reluctant teammates. Could it be the vice president who was directing Guo Taiqi's hands to seize the *Peking Gazette* so he could use it in his wrestling match with the president? Eugene refrained from asking. Guo Taiqi, a prudent man, would not discuss such matters.

Now the question was how to ease Woodhead out of the editor's office. In late September, Woodhead showed Eugene a letter of congratulation from President Yuan Shikai. Thinking he had established good faith with the most powerful Chinese in the capital, Woodhead felt that he was invincible and was confident of knocking down Eggeling.

Woodhead's victory lasted for a few days. One morning when he came to his editorial sanctum, he found the door locked. His staff was working inside, and they ignored his knock. The lockout, which was well timed, occurred when the Germans were on the river Marne, close to Paris, and the Allied powers were in serious difficulties. Britain had its hands full and could not bother with helping Woodhead and such a small business as the *Peking Gazette*. The time was conducive to Eugene's taking drastic measures, and despite the backing of the British Legation, Woodhead was forced out.

It must have further surprised Woodhead when he learned that Eugene was his replacement. But Eugene's ownership of the newspaper was a secret so well guarded that Woodhead was kept in the dark until "a day or two later Mr. Eugene Chen called upon me to tell me that he was acquiring the controlling interest in the *Peking Gazette*."[3] He was incensed and blamed Eggeling, attacking the German in the pages of the *Peking* and *Tientsin [Tianjin] Times*. Eggeling shrugged off the diatribes. The whole episode read like a satire in a novel, but it was a classic denouement in typical Peking style: Eggeling continued to pay Woodhead a salary in German marks while Woodhead vilified him in a rival newspaper, and Eugene exposed and railed against the scandalous intrigues of Yuan Shikai's administration while still on the government's payroll as an "employee" of the ministry of communications.

Understanding Peking politics, Eugene once said, was like opening Chinese boxes, one inside another, each containing layers of intricacy.

★ 5 ★

BATTLING THE WARLORDS

The office of the *Peking Gazette* was in a semi-Western-style house in Chuanban Hutong. Eugene moved to the apartment above the office. He was an amateur interior decorator, and since Peking's antique markets, flea markets, and temple fairs were held every day in one part or another of the city, they provided him with materials to indulge in his hobby. Aristocrats, who had lost their sinecures and pensions after the 1911 Revolution, sold their belongings cheap. The most attractive piece of furniture in Eugene's living room was a beautifully carved side table, and on top of it was a large, shallow rectangular bowl half-filled with water. In its center was an island, a miniature rocky hill covered with moss and lichens and one tiny, twisted tree. Flower petals floated on the water. Eugene, enamored with Chinese culture, pretended to fancy that flowers, like humans, had a spiritual essence. He hated to toss a bunch of withering but still living flowers into the garbage. Instead, he picked up petals and blossoms and kept them in bowls, vases, or jars. The loveliest ones he let sail on the miniature lake on his long side table. The island in the same bowl was surrounded with sand, and here he had scattered choice little shells that he had collected at resort beaches.

The so-called scenery in a bowl (*pengching*) exuded tranquility like a classical Chinese scroll. It soothed Eugene's nerves. He needed the calm to work out what to do with his newly acquired political clout. He would turn the *Peking Gazette* into a fighting paper and aim at his first target, who was none other than the reigning president. Taking on this enormous task, he must raise more funds to pay for the best staff and writers. That posed no problem, for he had a secret financial source right under the president's nose.

It's not clear exactly what role the reigning vice president, Li Yuanhong, played in the takeover of the *Peking Gazette*, but there was little doubt that he had given the green light to Guo Taiqi, his trusted English secretary, to make it happen. Li Yuanhong bore an old grudge against Yuan Shikai. When Yuan was elected provisional president in 1912, he knew better than anyone else that his presidency depended on the number of his troops, most of which were controlled by other warlords. As soon as he assumed the presidency, he worked to reduce the power of the regional militarists and bring them under his thumb. He closed in on Li Yuanhong first, because Li posed the greatest threat to his authority, offering Li the vice presidency to lure him away from his power base in Hubei Province. Aware of Yuan's intention, Li evinced no enthusiasm for the position and repeatedly postponed his journey to Peking. Yuan finally decided to use force. In December 1913, Yuan's minister of war, Duan Qirui, the self-styled Righteous Buddhist, suddenly barged into Li's official residence. He read Yuan's summons and escorted Li at gunpoint onto a train bound for Peking. Nearly two years after he had been chosen vice president, Li Yuanhong took office. In fact, he was a captive. He adopted an attitude of passive noncooperation and waited for his revenge. It was understandable why he used Guo Taiqi as a pipeline to supply the *Peking Gazette* with cash.

One of Guo's duties, as the vice president's English secretary, was briefing Li Yuanhong on what was being published in the English-language presses. He was a staunch friend of Eugene's and did not forget to make special mention of the *Peking Gazette*. So Li Yuanhong was well informed about the role Eugene's paper was playing to bring about the downfall of Yuan Shikai. On one occasion, Guo mentioned that the *Peking Gazette* was on the verge of foundering for lack of funds. Li asked blandly why Guo didn't help Eugene tide things over. Guo took the cue and funneled $50,000 to the paper from the private funds controlled by the vice president.

As an established journalist on a widely circulating English newspaper, Eugene frequented the International Club, which was the haunt of foreign journalists and an ideal place to mingle and keep updated on the plots and counterplots in the Legation Quarters. His frequent appearances in the club and in the company of foreign journalists served another purpose: they confused Yuan Shikai's spies as to who he really was.

The International Club was inside the Legation Quarters, an area of about three quarters of a square mile. There was a gray brick wall enclosing the area and the empty glacis before it. More than a half dozen legations were clustered there—the British, American, Japanese, Russian, French, German, Italian, Belgian, and so on. The wall had gun slits, and there were corner watchtowers, giving their soldiers an unobstructed field of fire behind the

The wall surrounding the Legation Quarters, inside which is an independent kingdom of foreign powers whose marines can aim their weapons at the Forbidden City, the symbol of China's sovereignty.

wall and making the Forbidden City—the symbol of China's sovereignty—on the opposite side of the Eternal Peace Avenue vulnerable to their guns.

As Eugene sauntered into the Legation Quarters, he entered yet another world of Peking. It was a quiet haven of asphalt streets, flanked by sidewalks, street lamps, and shade trees. There were a handful of shops, one or two European banks, as well as Roman Catholic, Protestant, and Eastern Orthodox churches. Each of the legations—they did not become embassies until the 1930s—was built according to their national taste, and they kept house as at home, with few concessions to their Chinese environment.

There was a French bakery on the corner of the main street near the French Legation. Eugene, a world-class gourmet, never missed going there for a slice of cream cake whenever he found himself in the Legation Quarters. On one occasion, a man scurried by the shop's front door, stopped, and stood in the middle of the pavement. He seemed to be waiting for somebody. When he saw Eugene, he hesitated for a second and then walked on, very slowly, so slowly that Eugene caught up with him.

"Eugene." The voice was familiar. Under the shade of his hat, a pair of dark glasses glinted over a thin ridge of nose that broadened into a slightly aquiline tip.

It was Wellington Koo, the English secretary of the president. Within the Cantonese Club, Koo was known for being more status conscious than the others. How come he was sneaking around?

Wellington Koo had been trained at Columbia University and had acquired a naïve faith in the country of his alma mater. The success or failure of his diplomatic strategy depended entirely on what the United States would do in each case. He was always running around in the Legation Quarters, begging the American Legation to intercede for China, and then hinting at American intervention to Britain, Russia, and Japan if they tried to exact excessive demands from China. Eugene knew all this. What puzzled him was why Koo was incognito.

Koo beckoned Eugene on. They left the Legation Quarters and walked toward the East Peace Shopping Plaza and vanished into the anonymity of the crowd. At a small café, tucked away behind the shops, Koo paused for a minute, turned to look at Eugene, and nodded. Inside, it was like a cozy family room in a well-run household.

The tip of Wellington Koo's nose turned blue when he recounted his errand. He was on the Japanese blacklist because he had been leaking their notorious Twenty-One Demands to the Western legations.

Peking was filled with rumors of Japanese aggressiveness. Eugene had gotten wind of them, but he seized the chance to hear the whole thing from the horse's mouth. "Well," he said, "I am a journalist. You can leak something to me."

These Twenty-One Demands, divided into five groups, would turn China into a Japanese colony if they were all granted, Koo said bitterly. The first four groups were for Japanese control of Shandong (Shantung) Province, Manchuria (the three northeastern provinces), Inner Mongolia, the southeast coast, and the central Yangzi Valley. The fifth stipulated that Japanese advisers be employed in the Chinese political, financial, military, and police administrations, and that China purchase at least fifty percent of its munitions from Japan. Even Yuan Shikai hesitated to comply.

"Will our president accept them?" Eugene asked.

Wellington Koo acknowledged it with a vague shrug.

Knowing Wellington Koo well enough, Eugene sensed that he was holding back something that Guo Taiqi might be able to elucidate. Guo lifted the veil from Koo's account and astounded Eugene. To realize his monarchical ambitions, Guo said, Yuan Shikai needed to gain the backing of the foreign powers, among them Japan, geographically close to China. Yuan Shikai, in exchange for its support, on May 25, 1915, secretly acceded to Japan's Twenty-One Demands except for the fifth group of demands, involving the employment of Japanese advisers in the Chinese government as well as the purchase of half its armaments from Japan.

Yuan Shikai had been advised by Wellington Koo to rely upon other foreign powers to check the aggression of Japan. But Britain and Russia, knowing that Yuan's government was bargaining from a position of weakness, raised their stakes to match Japan's. They forced Yuan to sign agreements recognizing the special interests of Russia in Outer Mongolia (now known as the People's Republic of Mongolia) and of Britain in Tibet.

The assistance Wellington Koo had solicited from the United States, on behalf of Yuan Shikai, materialized in an American, Frank J. Goodnow, who had been Koo's professor in Columbia University and, in 1914, was chosen to be the head of Johns Hopkins University. As a scholar, Goodnow's prestige had rivaled Woodrow Wilson's, head of Princeton University. Obviously Goodnow was a very political scholar. His accepting the job of adviser to Yuan Shikai could not be without political implications.

Goodnow, a constitutional expert, first came to China in 1913 and then again in 1915, as Yuan Shikai's adviser. Throughout Yuan's monarchical campaign, he manipulated public opinion, as his adherents floated trial balloons in newspapers and speeches, proposing a dynastic system as the best solution for China. The thoroughly censored Chinese press offered little resistance. At this juncture, Goodnow provided the timely finishing touch to the campaign. He submitted a report to Yuan Shikai, reiterating the argument that a monarchy rather than a republican system was a more suitable form of government for China. Yuan used this report to justify his obsession for donning the imperial yellow.

By mid-1915, Yuan Shikai believed that by satisfying the foreign powers' demands, he had covered his external flanks, and he then moved his monarchist campaign into top gear. In August 1915, his men organized a supposedly citizen body, the Society for Planning Stability, and flooded the Political Council with petitions begging Yuan to become emperor. In October, Yuan's supporters hastily formed a rubber-stamp National Congress of Representatives. On November 20, Yuan's handpicked representatives voted overwhelmingly for a monarchy. On December 12, Yuan consented to "obey the will of the people" and set January 1, 1916, as the start of the new dynastic reign.

The foreign-owned press in China, Hong Kong, and elsewhere echoed the views of their owners, who much preferred the manageable Yuan Shikai to the more recalcitrant republicans, and created a false impression among European and American readers that the Chinese people wanted a return to the monarchy. The republicans, particularly Sun Yatsen's followers and sympathizers, felt they had to expose Yuan's plot and the international community's complicity in it. The exposé had to be conducted by someone who had command of the English language and who was an established journalist on a widely circulated newspaper in English. That someone was Eugene Chen.

Using inside information leaked to him by highly placed friends, Eugene wrote articles that shocked and enraged an ever-growing nationalistic population who could read English and therefore read what was forbidden in the tightly controlled and thoroughly censored Chinese press. Eugene could write these articles without the interference of Chinese censors because the censors feared that the real owner behind the editor of the English-language press might be a foreigner who could claim extraterritorial rights.

To his astonishment, Eugene's attack on the monarchical conspiracy attracted a most unlikely ally: the most influential promoter of the conspiracy, Professor Frank Goodnow. He complained to Eugene that he had no intention of meddling in Chinese affairs, but unfortunately what he had written in that English report to Yuan Shikai was misinterpreted by the Chinese translators. He did not mean to say that the monarchy system was most suitable for China; what he meant was that if the republican system did not work well, the monarchy system was an alternative. "On August 17 [1915] Goodnow held a press conference to give his version of facts... and asked the *Peking Gazette* to publish his original English report."[1]

Eugene thought Goodnow must have been tipped off by Wellington Koo that Yuan Shikai's monarchical dream might turn into a nightmare and that the American scholar had better take steps to protect himself. That was Koo's style, very smooth, pleasing everyone and offending no one. Whatever the intention of Frank Goodnow, the publication of his protest would to some extent repudiate Yuan Shikai's claim that he had the United States behind him. So Eugene was more than glad to oblige Frank Goodnow.

Then followed another strange turn of events that brought Eugene an even bigger surprise. It was brought about by Liang Qicao. Liang and Eugene knew each other through common friends in the Cantonese Club. They were both journalists, and they knew the power a renowned journalist could wield. Liang was the foremost intellectual of the first two decades of twentieth-century China. The young Mao Zedong and Zhou Enlai were among his many admirers. Mao admitted that before he knew Marxism, he was fundamentally under the influence of Liang Qicao, who embodied for him all that was modern and progressive.

Liang Qicao was not a revolutionary. Before 1911, he had preached reformist ideas and a constitutional monarchy. When the Manchu Court was overthrown and the republic was established, Liang took part in Peking politics. He and his Progressive Party often sided with the administration of Yuan Shikai. A few days after Eugene's interview with Professor Frank Goodnow and in the midst of the pro- and anti-monarchy furor, Liang asked to see Eugene. Eugene wondered if Liang wanted him to go easy on Yuan. Liang was an eloquent speaker, but Eugene was determined not to be persuaded.

On September 4, Liang received Eugene in his Tianjin residence. The reason he had asked Eugene to take tea was that he needed Eugene's opinion on a matter concerning the fate of the nation. He had written an article entitled "Strange, This So-Called Question of the Form of State," condemning Yuan Shikai. This would be used by his former pupil, General Cai Er, as a manifesto to draw other military governors around him and prepare an armed campaign against Yuan Shikai.

Eugene was struck dumb. Only when he met Liang's eyes, wide open with expectation, did Eugene find his voice. He said that he could not puzzle out why Liang, a constitutional monarchist, would break from Yuan Shikai, an aspiring constitutional monarch. And where did General Cai Er come in?

Liang confessed that he had had a change of heart, partly due to his soul-searching and partly due to General Cai Er's persuasion.

General Cai Er was the military governor of Yunnan, a province on the southwestern border, which was not within Yuan Shikai's easy reach. But somehow, in 1913 Yuan had lured General Cai to Peking and later put him under house arrest. Secretly General Cai kept in touch with his former teacher, Liang Qicao, and they agreed to dislodge Yuan Shikai. So it was of the utmost importance to get the manifesto out in English, to get the message across to the foreign powers. Without their financial and military aid, Yuan would break down instantly. But no foreign-owned English newspapers would publish Liang's article. Liang would like to know if Eugene could publish this interview, in which he would emphasize the two main points of what he had written in "Strange, This So-Called Question of the Form of State": one, that Yuan Shikai's plot to change the form of government "was not good for the nation"; two, that any "cheap cliché that came out of the mouth of a foreign holder of a doctoral degree is studied as a magical totem."[2]

Liang was a confirmed constitutional monarchist and Yuan Shikai's former ally. Liang was fully aware of the impact his words would produce on Eugene, as well as on the general population and the foreigners. Then Liang explained his misplaced trust in Yuan Shikai. He was not in favor of the 1911 Revolution led by Sun Yatsen, Liang admitted. He advocated reform, which he believed was less violent, so the people would suffer less. But the revolution won, and the wish of the people had to be respected. He had supported Yuan Shikai's presidency because he thought, as did many others, that Yuan would maintain law and order. But he was sadly mistaken. It turned out that Yuan was the one who was wreaking havoc and making people suffer. Yuan must go, Liang declared.

Now Eugene responded quickly. There was nothing that would give him more pleasure than revealing Yuan Shikai's true colors. He couldn't help feeling a certain pride that Liang, the dean of the intelligentsia, had come to him for aid at this moment of great urgency.

However, as Eugene's exultation subsided, he thought about the consequences his action might have. Liang's manifesto was a clarion call to rally the military governors in an armed revolt. The publication of its contents would surely have severe consequences. Eugene worried about the effect it would have on his wife and their small children if Yuan decided to put him out of the way. He kept imagining the sorrow and despair it would inflict on his family. In these moments, alone in the empty apartment, he was tempted to pack up and go into hiding. Maybe he should accept Alfred Shi's offer and tag along to London. Instead, he gave himself the necessary time to regain control of himself. He had to prepare for the worst. He sat for hours until he felt tired and got up to put out the light. Then he heard a sound downstairs in the office. He knew it was his loyal assistant, Lee Choy. Lee Choy was married to their newspaper and lived with it. His home was his editorial office and the printing shop. He worked most of the night and slept on his desk during the day.

Lee Choy had known Eugene back in Trinidad. As a classmate of David, Eugene's younger brother, in the third and fourth grades, he had met Eugene, who, as a college student and then an articled clerk, paid little attention to a mere kid. Lee Choy had later heard of Eugene's return to China and thought he too would try his luck in the old home country. Arriving in Canton, he got in touch with Eugene, who invited him to come and join the staff of the *Peking Gazette*. Lee Choy reached Peking at the beginning of 1915 and immediately became Eugene's faithful colleague. Their association was especially close, because they were both Cantonese Trinidadians, probably the only two in Peking.

Lee Choy was the only man who had known Eugene's family and the only one to whom Eugene could talk about them. Eugene went downstairs. With no obvious emotion, he confided his decision to Lee Choy and asked the latter to contact his family if anything happened to him.

A curious mixture of East and West, like the China of his day, Lee Choy adopted a style of dress common among students in 1915. He wore Chinese-style black cloth shoes with white soles, gray flannel trousers, their crease long gone and baggy at the knees, and over these a Chinese long gown. A tobacco pouch of suede, blackened and shiny from long use, hung on its cord twisted around his left wrist. He smoked not cigarettes but an old-style long-stemmed, small copper-bowled Chinese pipe.

Inclining his head to his left shoulder, Lee Choy adjusted his heavy horn-rimmed spectacles, framing his small eyes that grew moist. He earnestly promised that he would do as Eugene wished.

Eugene published Liang's manifesto. Not long after, he heard that General Cai Er had escaped and reached a safe place. The news was broken to him by a British journalist in the International Club inside the Legation Quarters. The club, where they all gathered for casual socializing with their own kind, was dominated by the British and was run in British style. The wall behind the bartender was adorned with beveled glass mirrors and trophies of the chase around Peking, deer heads and antlers. The wine cellar was good. Downstairs was a bowling alley. Its pride was the oak-paneled club reading room, suitably gloomy like a London club, with walls of bookcases and reading tables, heavy with week-old copies of the *London Times*, the illustrated *London News*, and *Punch*.

With a cup of coffee by his side, Eugene sat down to read when an Englishman named B. Lenox Simpson, better known by his pen name, Putnam Weale, came in. Weale, a regular contributor to the *Peking Gazette*, was a flamboyant character and liked to be thought a man about town who knew everybody in the capital. He was, in fact, quite knowledgeable about Peking society and Peking politics. His father worked in the British-controlled Customs, and he had been born in Peking. He spoke Mandarin, and he dropped Chinese names with an enunciation that other expatriates envied.

No gossip, especially racy gossip, ever eluded him. The latest was General Cai Er's elopement with his new love. When Yuan Shikai put General Cai under house arrest, the president had resorted to an old trick to reduce a powerful man to a weakling: he found someone from the world's most ancient profession, a beautiful courtesan by the name of Xiao Feng Xian (Petite Garden Balsam). General Cai played along with Yuan's ploy, making the president believe he was completely enamored of the courtesan. Feigning lovesickness, the general appeared as if he could not stand a minute's separation from her. Finally, he begged Yuan's permission to hold a "brothel wedding," something like a real wedding with tawdry garnishes that was a commonplace practice among courtesans and their besotted patrons in those days.

Yuan Shikai granted the request but was not entirely without suspicion. He had a spy attend the "wedding." The spy, along with the other guests, participated in the "bridal chamber orgy" and later hid himself under the bridal bed. What the spy saw and heard put President Yuan's apprehensions to rest: the vociferous opponent to his monarchical plots was entirely at the mercy of his "bride." But actually the contrary was true. General Cai Er was the converter and not the converted. He had made passionate pleas, night after night in bed, for the republican cause. The courtesan, it was said, was not a Delilah and had a heart of gold. Succumbing to his moral strength as well as his sexual prowess, she helped him escape. The general then called on his troops to destroy the usurper of the republic. In December 1915, Yunnan Province, General Cai Er's power base, declared its independence of Yuan Shikai's rule. Guizhou, a neighboring province, followed suit.

Up to now, Eugene had been left more or less alone by Yuan Shikai and his minions, who were not sure who the real backers of Eugene's paper were. Eugene was editor in name, but no one could believe that he alone would dare do what he was doing. There had to be powerful forces backing him and directing his pen. Speculation abounded.

Eugene hoped that before Yuan Shikai's police could figure him out, the game would be over for them. Meanwhile, he took precautions to avoid trouble, like choosing a quieter road to or from home. Peking at that time was like a huge village: some *hutongs*—narrow alleys—were placed back to back with farming fields. One evening as Eugene strolled into a part of the fields that lay hidden in the shadows of trees, he had the feeling that he was not alone. The silhouette of a human figure leaned motionless against a tree. Both fear and curiosity drew Eugene closer. It was too late to run, and he might as well see who that person was. He could see a pipe glowing red in the dark and a man looking upward, as if he was making a wish on a star.

The silhouette was familiar to Eugene, and he thought he knew who it was as he stopped before the man. Lee Choy sensed Eugene's presence and came out of his reverie. He told Eugene that there had been several dubious characters visiting their office, asking funny questions. He urged Eugene to spend the night somewhere else. The safest place was probably the residence of C. C. Wu, also known as Wu Zhaoshu, a friend from the Cantonese Club.

Wu was the scion of a wealthy mandarin family of bureaucrats. Because of his family ties and his own ability, he rose to prominence immediately after he had earned his law degree from the University of London. Yuan Shikai's police would not be so bold as to break into the mansion belonging to Wu's illustrious father, Wu Tingfang, the renowned diplomat who had been Yuan's colleague in the Manchu Court. The surrounding walls of Wu's dwelling looked higher, wider, and longer than its neighbors'. Two ferocious white stone lions, perched on pedestals on either side of the large red door, guarded against intruders. To increase the impression of affluence, several stone steps led to the high lintel of the front doorway.

Stepping up, Eugene saw the door open and two men, the host and his guest in a civilian gown, bowing each other out. When the guest turned to walk down the steps, Eugene saw his face and was flabbergasted: stepping back and holding himself rigidly upright, he stared at General Duan Qirui, Yuan Shikai's right-hand man and the minister of war, who controlled the troops as well as the police.

Two soulful eyes looked out from a cold, hollow-cheeked face. The strangely contrasting features of Duan, at once a bully and a devout Buddhist, were hard to miss. He and Eugene both nodded perfunctorily at, and then passed by each other.

"Surprised?" C. C. Wu asked, a grin appearing on his angular face.

"I hope he did not come with a warrant to search the house?" Eugene asked dryly.

On the contrary, C. C. Wu said, Duan Qirui had come to express regret over his past behavior as Yuan Shikai's ally. It seemed that opposition to Yuan had spread swiftly, even among his most trusted officers. Duan, who had browbeaten the National Assembly on Yuan's orders and who was the most powerful man under him, now decided to sit on the fence and wait for an opportunity in the wake of the political storm.

"Did he look the other way when General Cai Er escaped?"

"General Duan has reached some understanding with your manifesto writer, Liang Qichao, who will be Duan's minister of finance in his future cabinet.

Duan also had at least one secret meeting with Liang's former pupil, General Cai Er, before or right after Cai's rumored elopement with the courtesan."

While still vowing loyalty to Yuan, Duan was trying to replace him. Abandoned by the foreign powers and his military clique, Yuan Shikai was doomed. In a last-minute effort to stem the tide, Yuan postponed his January 1, 1916, enthronement. On March 22, he backed down totally and promised to recall the National Assembly and reestablish the republic. But it was too late. His field commanders, led by Duan Qirui, declined to lead a punitive campaign against the intractable southwestern provinces, led by General Cai Er. Province after province declared against Yuan. Broken in health and dejected, Yuan had a relapse of uremia and died on June 6, 1916, at the age of fifty-six.

The *Peking Gazette* gloated over Yuan Shikai's defeat. Eugene claimed that the paper had procured the abortion of the empire and killed Yuan too. This perhaps was a little exaggerated, but the *Peking Gazette* had certainly hastened Yuan to his grave.

In the end, Eugene survived, but he had taken a perilous risk nevertheless. Even his detractor, the English journalist W. Sheldon Ridge, marveled at his intrepidity. Ridge wrote in the *Far Eastern Times* of June 16: ". . . half-way through 1915 a still greater opportunity was offered [to Eugene]. Yuan's friends whispered in Yuan's ear sweet words about the possibility of Imperial dignities and Yuan listened. So did [Eugene] Chen. He saw a chance for a bigger fight, and, cautiously at first, he approached the battleground. Before long he was in the battle slashing round bravely. He fought Yuan's schemes with amazing courage, even with foolhardiness, for Yuan was not over scrupulous with those who thwarted his designs."[3]

With the death of Yuan Shikai, the vice president, Li Yuanhong, took over the presidency in June 1916, as prescribed by law. Li was also a warlord, though a warlord without an army. His military power had been stripped by the now-dead Yuan Shikai and Yuan's aide, Duan Qirui. The minister of war, who called himself the peace-loving "Righteous Buddhist," in the last months of Yuan's presidency, had resigned to distance himself from his embattled boss, but he did not give up his troops. Now with troops at his command, Duan appointed himself both premier and minister of war.

It was not unexpected that the two men, Li Yuanhong and Duan Qirui, would come to blows. President Li resented his prime minister who regarded him, in turn, as little more than a figurehead. Duan despised his new boss as a toothless and clawless lion king.

However, they agreed on one thing: their new administration needed a façade to cover up the old stains Yuan Shikai had left. They restored the National Assembly. They invited the staunch republican Sun Yatsen to visit Peking and discuss affairs of the state. Sun did not come, but his close aide, Liao Zhongkai, came with a Kuomintang delegation three months after Yuan Shikai's demise.

Liao Zhongkai was also an overseas Cantonese. He was born in 1877 in San Francisco's Chinatown. His family was financially better off than many residents there. Before he was sixteen, Liao studied, spoke, and ate Chinese. Like many youth of Chinatown then, Liao was not admitted to the English-speaking schools outside Chinatown. He got his higher education in Tokyo's Waseda University and majored in political economy. In 1903, he met Sun Yatsen at a Chinese students' gathering, and several days later a mutual friend took him to visit Sun in a small, narrow, cheap room. They had a long, lively talk that decided Liao's future path. He was to overthrow the Manchu dynasty with Sun.

From all appearances, Liao, representing Sun Yatsen, came to seek unity with the Peking government. Behind closed doors, he felt the pulse of some firm republicans, including Eugene, Guo Taiqi, and C. C. Wu, counselor to his father, Foreign Minister Wu Tingfang.

The presidents of the early republic had a special treat for their special guests: they would open part of the old palace, where the last ex–empress dowager and emperor were still allowed to reside in the Forbidden City, for the honored visitors' amusement.

Chrysanthemum and Chinese laurel scented the air in the royal garden. Beyond the flowering blossoms, eunuchs, still in the uniforms of the Manchu Court and under the supervision of the ex–empress dowager, padded across the courtyard and glided in and out of rooms. Liao Zhongkai, a fragile man with vigilant eyes, wondered aloud when the residue of feudalism could be cleaned off. Then he asked his friends for their appraisal of the current Peking government.

Eugene, Guo Taiqi, and C. C. Wu all expressed doubt. The fact was, no sooner had Duan Qirui taken control of the government than he began negotiations with Japan. Although he conducted these meetings secretly, his opponents in the cabinet and in the National Assembly found out. It was clear to them that Peking had simply exchanged one military dictatorship for another, one no less autocratic, corrupt, and inept.

At this point, Liao Zhongkai weighed in. He said that a considerable number of Duan's opponents had been in secret contact with Sun Yatsen. Then Liao delivered a message to these republican-leaning political players: Sun was planning to form a rival government in Canton in the south and welcomed them to join him.

Sun Yatsen knew the importance of propaganda, Liao continued. Sun had once said that the firepower of one newspaper was equal to the firepower of a hundred thousand soldiers.

Eugene fully understood what Sun Yatsen was asking him to do. Sun had had no English-language forum that could talk back to the foreign journalists who distorted his ideas; this had been a weak link in the machinery of the Chinese Revolution. But now Eugene's *Peking Gazette* fortified it. Sun would like to see this well-established large-circulation newspaper continue to further the republican cause among foreigners (key players in Chinese politics), well-educated Chinese intellectuals, and students, who were growing more and more influential in the nationalist movement. In other words, Sun Yatsen was asking Eugene to bring down Duan Qirui's cabinet as he had helped end Yuan Shikai's reign.

Eugene's friends were fed up with the warlord government in Peking and were prepared to resign. But they were not men who would go quietly, and they knew exactly how to expose Premier Duan Qirui's scheme, since they were all insiders. They complimented Eugene on his articles denouncing Yuan Shikai's monarchical plots, which were still discussed among his readers. Using the idiom of the day, Eugene had become, by general consent of friend and foe, China's leading polemicist in the English language.

If the *Peking Gazette* was a muckraker, Peking was an Augean stable. The paper went on to expose skulduggery in high places, and in no time Eugene found himself embroiled in another maelstrom of intrigue involving the foreign powers and warlord factions.

In the beginning of 1917, Eugene was frequently closeted with Guo Taiqi and C. C. Wu to work out a course of action. On April 6, the United States ended its neutrality and entered the Great War. President Wilson called on all neutral nations to join forces with the Allies. With that, all the Allied legations in Peking exerted pressure on the Peking government. President Li Yuanhong, who was pro-American and pro-British, favored declaring war on Germany. In the meantime Japan, which fought on the Allied side, bet on the Allies' eventual victory and Germany's ultimate defeat, and so began to maneuver into a position to take over Germany's colonial interests in China's Shandong Province. Japan secretly promised the pro-Japan prime minister, Duan Qirui, enormous bribes and encouraged him to declare war. When the American Legation heard of this, it urged President Li Yuanhong to use the National Assembly, where the opposition to Duan Qirui was led by the American-educated vice-speaker, Thomas C. T. Wang, who was also associated with the Cantonese Club. Thus urged, President Li insisted that Duan observe the constitution, which required the National Assembly to approve any declaration of war. Duan knew that once this issue reached the National Assembly, the opposition would lead an inquiry into his dealings with Japan. Duan could not afford that, and so he ignored the legal restraints on his power and dissolved the National Assembly on April 25, 1917, a week after Eugene's first probing article had been published.

"We have been dismissed," Thomas C. T. Wang muttered bitterly, rolling his eyes upward as if asking for divine intervention, a trace of his past profession as a sort of priest. He had often translated for visiting church dignitaries from America when they gave sermons; he actually looked like a priest with a clean-shaven, gentle face and his hair combed back austerely.

Eugene and his friends decided it was time to strike. One evening in early May, he came home to find that his apartment over the office was lit. Suspicion flashed through his mind. He knew he was under the surveillance of Duan Qirui's police. He peered into the office and saw his assistant, Lee Choy, hunched over a small pile of papers. He tapped on the door. Lee Choy came out and told him that he had three visitors: Guo Taiqi, C. C. Wu, and Thomas C. T. Wang. Relieved, Eugene went upstairs.

The three friends wanted to kindle a great conflagration to burn down Duan Qirui's cabinet. They asked if Eugene would light the match. At the same time, C. C. Wu warned that there was danger. His square face and prematurely receding hairline made him look older and sterner. Eugene must know the risk he would take, C. C. Wu said: he himself might be engulfed in the flames. Eugene did not withdraw. Whenever it came for him to decide what to do, the right thing or the safe thing, he invariably chose the former.

Eugene had another provider of inside information, Liang Qicao. Liang had been awarded the post of minister of finance in the current cabinet for his contribution to preventing the monarchical restoration. Now, as minister of finance, he was in on the premier's secret dealings with Japan. A man with a keen eye for his place in history, Liang decided to quit, but not before he leaked these secret dealings to Eugene.

Eugene chose this moment to throw a bombshell. On April 17, the *Peking Gazette* published an exposé of the Japanese manipulations designed to get China into the war on the Allied side. This article was the first to reveal the activities of the Japanese agent Nishihara and the millions in loans that he was dangling before the mesmerized eyes of Duan Qirui and his generals.

The next day, the *Peking Gazette* appeared with a half-inch banner headline above the lead editorial article: SELLING CHINA, A SECRET COMPACT. It revealed Duan Qirui's secret negotiations with Japan to give that country's rulers control over Chinese resources in the northeast (Manchuria) and Mongolia, as well as various privileges in Shandong Province, and, in addition, control over the Chinese armed forces, in return for hard cash—100 million yen.

Eugene's paper was gaining a new type of readership. By this time, Peking had become not just a cultural center but a place of intellectual ferment, with thousands of students learning modern ideas in its new universities and middle schools. Debating and propounding ideas and schemes for the salvation of the country, the students were becoming a major force in Chinese politics. These eager, literate, patriotic youths were avid readers of the *Peking Gazette*. The scandalous facts exposed in "Selling China" shocked and incensed them. In meetings and demonstrations, they and the republican parliamentarians led by Thomas C. T. Wang demanded that Duan Qirui admit or deny the allegations of the *Peking Gazette*.

Duan Qirui decided that he had had enough from Eugene Chen. No matter who stood behind him, Duan had to stop his articles. He sent police to interrogate the staff of the *Peking Gazette*. While Eugene sat in the upstairs apartment typing his next editorial, his loyal assistant, Lee Choy, and the rest of the staff tried all the delaying tactics they could think of to stall their editor's arrest and to play for time to rally help from Eugene's friends. But on May 19 at 2:30 A.M., Duan's police moved in. Eugene was hauled off in a dilapidated van with half a roof. It slowly went down Hatamen Street. On reaching the Hatamen Gate, the police van turned across the eastern section of the city, toward the Front Gate. It drove through the arch-like gateway and entered the part of Peking crowded with mud huts, paltry brothels, tawdry stalls, and tumbledown playhouses. Then they went across the district of Heavenly Bridge—Tianqiao—and passed the city's execution ground.

Where are they taking me? Eugene wondered uneasily.

The van deposited Eugene at a police station in the midst of this squalor, and, after a summary hearing on a charge of "spreading rumors," he was thrown into a cell.

The small room, dim and dingy, had no windows. Five ghostlike prisoners crouched on a mud floor, their feet steeped in urine and excrement, scratching madly at their lice-covered bodies. The jailer warned Eugene to watch out for himself; his five cellmates had committed the most heinous murders, he muttered darkly. Eugene feared for his life, a fear so strong that it was somehow conveyed to his wife in an uncanny way. Aisy had a strange dream about this time, in late spring of 1917. One night, a shriek from her room woke Jack up. He rushed to her bedside with his sister Silan and found the lights on and Germaine, his mother's cousin and companion, trying to calm her down. With horror in her eyes, his mother told the two children that she had had a nightmare in which their father's skeleton lay beside her. With the certainty of a clairvoyant, she knew that he had either met with a violent death or was in mortal danger. Her frantic anxiety astounded Jack. Nothing like this had ever happened before. His mother was not one to lose her head in an emergency. When Silan's little friend Cathy Ewen dislocated her arm while playing in their garden, he saw their mother seize the dangling arm and wrench the bone back into its socket so quickly that Cathy did not even realize what had happened. But now their mother was distraught.

"Something has happened to Ben"—her pet name for Eugene—"something terrible. He is in danger, oh God, he is in danger."

This was not a night Jack could forget easily. Holding his mother's trembling hand, he had his first glimpse into the pain and anguish under her cheerful appearance.

The next morning, the jailer came to fetch Eugene and told him that a great lord wanted to see him.

The great lord was Xu Shuzheng, police chief and Duan Qirui's deputy in the ministry of war. Seeing Eugene's disheveled state, the visitor shammed sympathy. Deploring the situation, he promised to help Eugene get out of prison if Eugene promised to recant the "groundless accusation" he had made against the prime minister. Eugene refused and insisted on having an open trial. In that case, Xu warned, Eugene should be aware of the grim choice he had made.

A few hours later, another visitor was announced. Judging from the jailer's malicious grin, Eugene speculated that he might be transferred to a "better place." "Better place" was a euphemism for the execution ground. Only with an utmost effort did he quell his trembling, and he nearly fell over when he saw his visitor. Eugene could not believe his eyes. But the man was unmistakably Lee Choy, his faithful comrade. Lee Choy brought news: he had contacted Eugene's friends, and they were planning to rescue him. In Peking, ways could be found to foil the moves of even such powerful figures as the prime minister with his thousands of troops. The rescue plan exposed not only the complexity of Peking politics but also the dominance of the foreign powers. Eugene's friends, all familiar with the rules of the game, played it with dexterity. The quickest way to get Eugene out of jail was to get the British Legation to intervene, they said, since Eugene was a British subject. Lee Choy, the front man, was going to approach the British Legation for help.

But there was a hitch, Eugene said, as he shook his head. He explained why the plan wouldn't work. On first arriving in Peking, Eugene, as a British subject accustomed to obeying the law, had made a formal call at the British Legation and had his name recorded in the list of British residents in the Chinese capital. However on January 1, 1914, when he received the usual notification of the annual renewal of this registration, Eugene sent his compliments to His Britannic Majesty's vice-consul and begged to inform him that he should from then on be considered a Chinese citizen and would neither expect British solicitude for his welfare, seek British protection, nor acknowledge British jurisdiction.

Lee Choy relayed this information to Eugene's friends and returned with their ideas. Whether this "renunciation" of British citizenship was legally valid was a matter for lawyers, they said, and, if circumstances required, they would hire the best English lawyers in Peking, Shanghai, Hong Kong, or London to defend him.

Eugene paused for a long moment before he responded. As far as he was concerned, the meaning of his renunciation was clear. Even with a noose around his neck, he would not renounce his Chinese citizenship and beg the British to save him.

Lee Choy assured Eugene that he did not have to do anything, and then divulged more information. Both sides, Eugene's friends and his enemies, were mobilizing their forces. Eugene uttered no more objections as he increasingly realized what this skirmish was all about. His friends were waiting for the right time to make a grand exit. Then came this skirmish, which was not just over Eugene Chen: it was also a showcase for how much political muscle each side could flex. To topple Duan Qirui's cabinet was to cross their Rubicon. Eugene and his allies were to go south and to reinforce Sun Yatsen's campaign against the warlord-dominated Peking government. They must leave with a bang.

In a hushed voice, Lee Choy told Eugene that hefty bribes had been paid to the jailers and Eugene would be moved into a better cell. It turned out he was the sole occupant and was left in quiet to read the books, newspapers, and a small box of old and recent letters from his wife, Aisy. Rereading these letters made him feel closer to his family in this lonely ordeal.

Since Eugene's last visit to London in early 1913, more than four years had elapsed. During that period, the family had a new addition, Yolanda. Aisy educated the children according to the plans that she and Eugene had agreed upon. Their oldest son, Percy, was entered at University College School up on Hampstead Hill. Their older daughter, Silan, and younger son, Jack, were enrolled at the Elms. It was a school for the daughters of gentlemen. Jack followed Silan into it because of his attachment to his older sister. Miss Dothie, the headmistress of the school, made allowances for him. Silan, the performer of the family, showed off her new talents for dancing and singing. Jack, in his mother's doting eyes, had shown definite signs of "artistic talent." He liked to draw and color pictures, and to make paper models of houses and buildings.

The letters were cheerful. Aisy had kept a stiff upper lip. The household without Father was not shrouded in sorrow and despair, but filled with sunshine and laughter, as Aisy would have it. But there were occasional hints about the difficulties in taking care of her brood by herself. Eugene was grateful. Bolstered by her love, he felt more confident in facing down his enemies.

A muffled groan brought him back to this human dump yard. He looked up, straining his ears to catch any unusual sound, and when he heard none, turned his eyes back to the bedside table. The small table light shone directly on the box of letters, and it suddenly occurred to him what an easy target it was for theft, spotlighted there in the dimness. He hid it under the blanket and then went to sleep with it in his arms.

Unfortunately, Lee Choy's first visit to the British Legation was met with complete indifference. So Eugene's friends instructed him to contact the English journalist Putnam Weale. Weale had been writing for the *Peking*

Gazette and had supported Eugene when he had attacked Yuan Shikai's monarchical conspiracy. Flamboyant, Weale was the sort to relish a cause célèbre. Now he jumped onto his high horse and set out to rescue a fellow journalist with good old English professional ethics. In a lead article in the *Peking Gazette* of May 23, he decried the hands-off policy of the British Legation. "Unless his [Eugene's] release is secured and he is handed over to the competent authorities, the writer proposes telegraphically to invoke the aid of the British government. That Mr. Lloyd George's government, when the facts are known in England, will not desert a British subject is as certain as that the sun rises."

No sooner had Putnam Weale raised such a great hue and cry than other Western journalists began questioning the Chinese prime minister's motives. They presumed that the Japanese were the ones behind Eugene's arrest and that other arrests and summary executions would soon follow. Who would be the next target? the journalists demanded.

The outcry was loud. The American Legation weighed in to make their stand clear to the British. In 1917, the First World War was still raging, but both the United States and Japan were far from the European theater and much less exhausted by the war. Anticipating the diminishing influence of their war-ravaged European allies, each aspired to replace them. The competition between the two countries over China was growing. Well aware of Duan Qirui's pro-Japanese leanings, the Americans preferred to side with the prime minister's opponents.

The British Legation could no longer ignore the storm growing over the arrest of Eugene Chen. They cabled London for advice. The Foreign Office under the Liberal Lloyd George took the long view. It tolerated Eugene's friends better than his enemies—they were either English- or American-educated, and were all pro-West. Whitehall advised the Peking Legation to do what it could to effect Eugene Chen's release, while not treating him as a British subject, and to avoid bringing up the question of the paper's ownership.

The British inquiry into Eugene's case increased the pressure for his release. It also strengthened the hand of the Chinese foreign minister, Wu Tingfang. He was an overseas Cantonese born in Singapore, and thus a British citizen. In his youth, he went to London to read law. Called to the bar in England in 1876, he became the first Chinese to practice law in the British colony of Hong Kong. For all his dissatisfaction with Britain's China policy, he was more than a bit of an Anglophile. And so was his son C. C. Wu. No doubt the older Wu had all the information his son provided and was well aware of what the uproar was about. Eugene was fortunate to have such a man as Wu Tingfang in charge of China's foreign office and willing to work for his release.

Eugene survived his opponents again. Duan Qirui had climbed to the top by making more than a few enemies. The time had come for them to surface. The *Peking Gazette* gleefully reported telegrams, letters, and statements attacking Duan. At this juncture, Thomas C. T. Wang and C. C. Wu, a member of the National Assembly, together plunged into the fray with a vengeance. Led by Wang, the parliamentarians called on President Li Yuanhong to dismiss the prime minister. Li was more than glad to oblige, for he had a score to settle with Duan Qirui, who had helped Yuan Shikai bring him to his knees more than three years earlier. Li hated Duan's arrogance and moved quickly to break his monopoly of power. He fired his Prime Minister Duan on May 23. C. C. Wu's father, Wu Tingfang, as foreign minister and ranking elder statesman, countersigned the order and assumed the post of acting prime minister. Duan Qirui fled to Tianjin's British concession, news that the brash *Peking Gazette* reported the moment he left Peking. Thus it came about that five days after Eugene's arrest, the cards stacked against him were reshuffled and redealt and were now in his favor.

A week or so later, Eugene was released. He came out in pretty good shape. But it was considered too risky for him to return to the apartment above the office of the *Peking Gazette*. The Peking situation was too volatile. So Eugene's friends booked him into a room in the Wagon Lit Hotel inside the Legation Quarters until he could leave Peking by train for Tianjin, where he would get on a British ship bound for the greater safety of the International Settlement in Shanghai.

★ 6 ★

FROM SHANGHAI TO VERSAILLES

Before the Opium War, Shanghai was a fishing village and a haunt of smugglers. It grew into a metropolis after the Manchu Court opened its doors to the British and other colonialist powers in 1843. It soon became a major port, where industry and commerce flourished. By the second decade of the twentieth century, it had gained parity with the giant ports of the world: New York, Amsterdam, London, and Hamburg.

Shanghai's International Settlement—which the colonialists proudly billed as the model concession of the world—was a perfect illustration of the extra-territorial rights the foreign powers enjoyed. It was governed by a municipal council whose members were elected by the ratepayers: to be more accurate, by the Western ratepayers. The council was chaired either by an Englishman or an American. It had its own police force, court of justice, and military defenses. Western offenders were supposed to be sent to their own court to receive punishment. Needless to say, they were most leniently dealt with. If the Chinese relatives and friends of the victims did not like the verdict, the marines were at hand and could rush into action at any minute to keep them quiet.

Eugene went ashore in Shanghai in the first half of June 1917. He took a taxi westward, away from Avenue Edward VII, and entered a city-state where the streets were named after French heroes. The French concession was ruled by aloof and proud Frenchmen who still thought like the courtiers of Louis XIV and often turned their noses up at the English shopkeepers and American Yankees. The rest of Shanghai was divided into two different districts. The Chinese City was nominally governed by Chinese authorities, but subject to the ever-changing whims of the foreign powers. Hongkou was the unofficial concession of the Japanese, where men could dine and wine while geishas played sensual music and sang erotic songs. The desirable residential area was in the French concession, where Eugene rented an apartment on Rue Foch.

International boundary stone, Shanghai, in the mid-nineteenth century.

It was to the French concession that Sun Yatsen sojourned in the first part of 1917. The foreign rulers of these concessions sometimes let in revolutionaries like Sun Yatsen and Eugene Chen as a way of taking out an insurance policy to protect their future, just in case the revolutionaries won.

Like Eugene, Sun was a farmboy. He was born in November 1866 in Cuiheng Village of Guangdong Province, about fifty miles northwest of Hong Kong. His family was poor and could not afford to give him a regular education. It was not until he was ten years old that he began to learn to read a little by attending an old-fashioned class, with a teacher paid by the better-off parents of his classmates. Three years later, his life took a sudden new turn. His older brother, who had migrated to Hawaii and owned a small store, took Sun there and enrolled him in the Iolani School, a Hawaiian institution run by Anglican missionaries. The teachers were British, and the training they gave Sun was English-oriented. From 1879 to 1882, he learned the same language and practically the same ideas and ideals that Eugene was to learn

ten years later. Their mutual congeniality sprang from their quite similar backgrounds.

In 1883, Sun went back to his
native village. For the next eight
years, he studied off and on in Hong
Kong, and by 1892 graduated from
the College of Medicine for the
Chinese, and then practiced in
Macao and Canton for a brief period.
During these twelve years, he started
his revolutionary career—for the
most part by developing a large
network of comrades and sympathizers, mainly among the overseas
Chinese and Western missionaries.
Sun credited the missionaries for
transforming Hawaii into a modern
place. He thought he could do the
same with China. He toyed with
the idea of becoming a missionary
himself. He never did, but he used

Soong Chingling and Sun Yatsen, circa 1915.

his preaching talents to help instigate the greatest revolutionary storm in
modern Chinese history. In fact, his major contribution to the revolution was
fund-raising on lecture tours, so as to finance the numerous uprisings
against the Manchu Court, which finally ended four thousand years of
dynastic rule.

But Sun's strength was also his weakness. Once the 1911 Revolution was
won, his talents could not help him govern. His talk of salvaging the republic from the warlords was sneered at as empty rigmarole. He was satirically
nicknamed the "Loose Cannon Sun." Very few people now listened to him.
Eugene was one of them.

In 1917, Sun's house was at 63 Route Vallon. It was not large, but by
Shanghai standards it was spacious. Most of the houses in the small and
dense French concession were huddled together, some with tiny yards about
the size of a car.

Sun came out in the yard to greet his guest. He was of medium height with regular features, a graying mustache in the Japanese style, and a Western manner. Beside him stood his young second wife. Madame Sun was then twenty-four years old. By nature, she was shy; by education and upbringing, she was trained to be feminine in the old-world sense. Both her parents were Christians and had reared their children with strict Christian morals. She began her education at McTyeire, an American missionary school in Shanghai where all the textbooks were in English. When she was fifteen, she was sent to study in America. Graduating from Wesleyan College in Georgia in 1913, she spoke English with the slight lilt of a southern accent. And she looked like a southern belle. She had led a sheltered life, and would have continued to live a sheltered life had she chosen a different path.

Eugene reunited with Sun, and the two men immediately fell into a discussion about the current state of affairs. The archwarlord Yuan Shikai was gone, Sun complained, but not all the smaller warlords. They took charge of Peking by turns, like playing round after round of musical chairs. In the eyes of Sun, who was not known to be self-effacing, the northern warlords were the root of his problems and therefore of China's. Republican China, Sun declared, was his child, and he alone had the right to guide it to maturity. He decided it was imperative to lead a Northern Expedition to defeat the warlord government in Peking. He asked the Western powers, mainly Britain and the United States, to help him, but they dismissed him as just another politician who aspired to become a warlord, with nothing to offer in return. Sun had no territory, no troops, no bureaucratic apparatus. Naturally they preferred to collaborate with the warlords and the de facto government in Peking.

In June 1917, when Eugene arrived in Shanghai, Sun Yatsen was ready to leave for Canton, to establish a rival government there. Eugene did not go to Canton with Sun, but, as Sun's new adviser on international affairs, he visited Canton now and then. About this time, Eugene joined the Kuomintang. During Sun's absence, Eugene was mostly in Shanghai and prepared to start a new paper, the *Shanghai Gazette*. In order to coexist with the British and Americans in the International Settlement, the *Shanghai Gazette* would be liberal leaning, but not be as radical as the *Peking Gazette*.

The journalistic work offered Eugene many occasions to socialize with his Western counterparts, hearing and reading about the events of the outside world long before his countrymen. Next to London and New York, Shanghai was reputed to be the third major center for gathering world news. If you had access, you could read all the important news from London, New York, Paris,

Berlin, Moscow, Tokyo, and so on. In November 1917, less than four months after Eugene had seen Sun Yatsen off, the news of the Bolshevik Revolution came from Russia. It stirred wide interest among the foreign journalists in Shanghai and became their most discussed and debated topic. Nearly all of them called the new Soviet Russia a pariah of the international community. It would not last, they declared with vehemence.

Shanghai was called the "Paradise of Adventurers," and Astor House, an American-owned hotel, was its hub. Sitting in the ornate but old-fashioned lobby, Eugene had the perfect vantage point to observe the collection of crooks who came to wheel and deal. Everything was for sale. Logically, the hotel became one of the favorite haunts of the Western journalists, who could buy news scoops with cash or favors. Most weekdays and weekends, they took their seats in waiting rickshas and rattled down the Bund to the hotel, just across the Garden Bridge over Suzhou Creek. Most of the time that was as far as they went, but sometimes they ventured farther to do fieldwork.

On the opposite side of the street, and on a choice site overlooking both the Suzhou Creek with its boat people and the busy panorama of the Huangpu River, was the large Russian Consulate. One day Eugene went there with several Western journalists.

The consulate was a mansion, imposing on the outside in its heavy czarist style, but, after years of neglect during the First World War and then domestic upheavals, the entrance hall was as dusty as a third-rate boarding-house. On the second floor, up a grand but uncarpeted staircase, the visitors entered a large office, sparsely furnished with ancient brocaded chairs. In this stuffy atmosphere of faded elegance sat a bureaucrat, the sort of "Superfluous Man" who lovers of Russian literature often met in the pages of the great nineteenth-century novels. The Russian said that he had nothing new to tell them. Revolution was cliché. The poor versus the rich. The poor demanded bread, he summed up; the rich told them bread was in short supply and to eat cream cake instead.

However, Eugene did not waste time listening. He looked about and spotted a book titled *Russia, on the Eve of War and Revolution,* authored by Sir Donald Mackenzie Wallace, which he borrowed and read. The book presented a panorama of society and life under the czarist reign. There were similarities between China and Russia, Eugene found, such as the prevailing poverty among the peasants, a powerful and ruthless landed class, the backwardness of an agricultural state, the lack of modern industry, an inept and corrupt government, and so on. The fact that both Sun Yatsen's Kuomintang and Lenin's Bolshevik Party were outcasts from the world community caught Eugene's immediate attention. A new idea began to germinate in his mind. Because his most important task lay in advising Sun on international affairs, he constantly thought of repairing China's foreign policy. Now he saw a chance. This was the humble beginning of the Russia-oriented policy that would eventually change China and the world.

He wanted to know more about Russia and its recent revolution. As a journalist, he had abundant opportunities to collect information about it from the foreign journalists stationed at Shanghai. But he was not satisfied, because it was all negative. He would hunt for more information abroad, specifically from London where he had a friend.

Arthur Ransome was a journalist, writing for the *Manchester Guardian*. He was related to Ramsay MacDonald, leader of the Labour Party, and a friend to some leading members of the Labour movement. Eugene had known him during his first visit home in 1913. One evening they had gotten on a boat, sailing past the edifying sights of London: Houses of Parliament, London Bridge, and other immortal monuments. Moved, Ransome recalled how his parents had believed it was important to let him see these great sights, not only the emblem of the strength of the empire but also the glory of its people. When Eugene asked him how he would react if uninvited foreign warships intruded into the Thames, Ransome's face blanched. When Eugene said China's Yangzi River was choked with foreign gunboats, most of them British, Ransome's face turned red with indignation and embarrassment.

Ransome was not a radical. He was an Englishman with a fair-mindedness that represented the best side of England. When his letters described the Soviet Union as a government that had its mandate more from the vast majority of the poor than the Romanov dynasty, Eugene knew it was worthwhile probing into the new workers' state. He would take it up with Sun Yatsen.

Sun had complained to Eugene many times about China's troubled relations with the Western powers and Japan. His pleas for reform were met with jeers from them. Now this Russian Revolution might present a straw of opportunity for the Kuomintang to form an alliance with the new Soviet Union, which was also threatened by Japan and the Western powers. Your enemy's enemy might be your friend. Why not give it a try? In the diplomatic field, there was no set rule or permanent partnership. Eugene believed attempting such an alliance would force Britain, the United States, and other Western nations to reconsider their positions. As Eugene saw it, they would be more amenable to foreign policy changes in order to prevent the

Kuomintang from becoming aligned with the Soviet Union. The so-called Russia-oriented policy was actually crafted with the Western powers in mind, intending to induce them into a better relationship with the Kuomintang.

This strategy was what Eugene presented to Sun Yatsen in early 1918 when the latter came back to Shanghai. Sun was surprised. In all his years of revolutionary activities he had been looking to the West for ideas and assistance. Now Eugene advised him to look to the north, to a Russia strange and mercurial. It was too sharp a turnaround for Sun to quickly reconcile himself to. Nevertheless, he was willing to look into the possibility.

Eugene was a frequent visitor to Sun's new residence, a larger house at 29 Rue Molière, a gift from his followers in Canada. Sun moved into this new place in mid-1918. It had a garden. When the weather was neither too cold nor too hot, Madame Sun, who later preferred to use her maiden name Soong Chingling, served tea in the garden. They conversed in English, the second language of China's upper crust.

The three friends often took tea together. The small gathering, which Madame Sun hosted in her Western dress and Westernized manner, was from all appearances a charming picture of bourgeois affluence; nothing seemed more distant than the Communists' Proletarian Revolution that had recently shaken Russia. But that was precisely the topic of their conversation. Their discussions reminded Sun of his exiled days in Europe. He recalled a particular Russian revolutionary, a man named Chicherin who was now commissar of foreign affairs. Eugene persuaded him to renew the friendship. Madame Sun expressed approval. Her response was quicker than her husband's. She was much younger than Sun Yatsen and more susceptible to new ideas.

Perhaps partly due to her urging, Sun was galvanized into action. All three were aware of the danger of clutching at this thin Russian straw. Historically, the worst invaders had always swooped down from the north; the Great Wall had been erected to stop them. To befriend the Bolsheviks north of the Chinese border was a gamble, because Russia had been an aggressive neighbor.

There was another apprehension. The backbone of the Kuomintang was the middle class and the landed gentry. To them, Marxism was anathema. Any approach to Soviet Russia had to be conducted in strict secrecy. Moreover, they could anticipate a hostile reaction from the middle-class democracies: Britain, the United States, and France.

Thin though this Russian straw was, it was better than nothing, Eugene persisted. Sun was finally persuaded and asked Eugene to draft a letter to refresh Chicherin's memory of their meeting in Paris. The letter was ready to go, but to reach the Soviet Union it had to slip through the censorship of the colonialist powers and bypass spies of various brands. The post office had eager readers who did not hesitate to open and intercept such letters. Sun had to send confidential letters by faithful messengers through clandestine channels. The letter to Chicherin was smuggled out of the French concession by Lee Choy, Eugene's assistant at the *Peking Gazette* who was now on the staff of the *Shanghai Gazette*. In a Chinese long gown that was not neatly kept and with an old-style long-stemmed, small copper-bowl Chinese pipe, Lee Choy easily blended into the crowd in the Chinese city of Shanghai. Lee Choy handed the letter to a friendly print-shop worker.

The letter, which was sent in early 1918, never got an answer from the recipient. Perhaps it never reached the desk of the commissar of foreign affairs, or had just been ignored. Chicherin must have been swamped by such letters wishing him well.

The Russian Revolution did not stir up much interest in China. There were a few articles in a radical magazine, *New Youth*, hailing the event, but there was no substantive analysis, assessment, or discussion. According to Arthur Ransome's letters, London reacted totally differently. The intellectuals, the politicians, members of the Labour movement, and many others were all absorbed in heated debate. The most obvious debate was between the Conservatives, led by Stanley Baldwin with Winston Churchill by his side, and the Labour Party, led by Ramsay MacDonald. Churchill advocated the restoration of the Romanov dynasty through armed intervention. MacDonald was against that. Eugene told Sun Yatsen that he was thinking of visiting his family in London to try to unravel the Russia puzzle.

But the trip to London had to wait. In August 1917, the Peking government, encouraged by the United States, declared war on Germany, and that forced the neutral Canton government to pronounce their alliance with the United States as well. As a gesture of cooperation, it offered to send Chinese labor battalions, as the Peking government had done. In May 1918, the Canton government sent a delegation to Washington, D.C., to discuss the matter with the Americans. Eugene was named by Sun Yatsen to the Canton delegation, but was unable to leave with the other delegates. His new paper, the *Shanghai Gazette*, had some cash problems. Eugene had been ill earlier in the year and had neglected the financial affairs of the paper. To tide things over, he had taken out a loan from a group of moneylenders, the Ezra Brothers. Goaded on by the International Settlement's police who had gotten wind of Eugene's travel plan, the moneylenders demanded that Eugene pay off the debt immediately.

This simple business transaction soon became a pretext for Eugene's enemies to prevent him from going to Washington. A warrant was issued against the *Shanghai Gazette*, with Eugene Chen named in it. But Eugene was warned by his friends that he was about to be detained. Pursued by process-servers, Eugene went into hiding in the Chinese City and arranged through Lee Choy to go from there to the liner that would take him to the United States.

On the day of departure, Eugene waited in a hovel for Lee Choy to fetch him. The monotonous sound of rain, the bleak landscape, and the empty, tumbledown shack made a bad day worse. He waited silently, gloomily, for Lee Choy and the guide who would lead the way. As the afternoon wore on, his impatience grew, and he began to fidget. He could neither sit nor stand still. He walked from one end of the room to the other and back again, just to make some noise. The sound of his own footsteps filled the empty silence. He threw his raincoat over his head and shoulders and went to the gate of the small courtyard. He looked up and down the road. A few minutes later, fretting and growing even more restless, he turned and went back inside. He fell into a rickety chair and laid his head back. As soon as he closed his eyes for a rest, he saw a vision of pandemonium. The police had arrested Lee Choy and they were coming to get him. They were rummaging about among his papers and found the letter of congratulations that he had drafted on behalf of Sun Yatsen to Lenin, and therefore discovered Sun's proposal to forge friendly ties with the Soviet Union.

Startled by the terrible vision, Eugene opened his eyes. He jumped up. He paced the room. He couldn't help glancing at the broken mirror hanging on the wall and seeing his reflection. He had the look of a stricken dog, and he hated it. As if getting out of the room would get him out of this quagmire, he took his briefcase and walked out.

It was pouring outside. The road was muddy, slippery, barely a path to make out. He didn't walk: he slithered and fell. A man passing by saw him and leaped toward him, helping him to his feet. When he got up, he saw Lee Choy's short, tubby arms around his waist.

Led by Lee Choy and a guide, Eugene leaped onto a swift launch that took him down the Huangpu River under the cover of night to the liner where Guo Taiqi waved welcome. The man escorting the process-servers had received an expensive gift from Eugene's friends, Guo said with a chuckle, and he somehow managed to lead his charges a merry dance. The whole lot of them got stuck on a mud bank in the Yangzi River estuary, and Eugene had time to slip onto the ship.

Funds were short for the Canton delegation, as always in revolutionary circles, but they were to be made up by contributions from overseas Chinese in the United States. Speeches were made to the branches of the Kuomintang in the cities that Eugene, Thomas C. T. Wang, and Guo Taiqi visited. In one such meeting, Eugene asked a Chinese American participant to find a safe channel to forward Sun Yatsen's congratulatory letter to Moscow.[1] Eugene never disclosed the identity of this man.

No sooner had the talks between Canton and Washington started than the war was over. Sun Yatsen then authorized the delegation, led by Thomas C. T. Wang, with Eugene Chen as the legal expert, to attend the Paris Peace Conference.

The Canton delegation, however, was not the only delegation China sent to France. The Peking government sent a delegation of which the two senior members were Wellington Koo and Alfred Shi. Since the Allied powers only recognized the Peking delegation, it was obvious that if the Canton delegation hoped to play any role at Versailles, they had to work with the Peking delegation. But Wellington Koo, who had a penchant for monopolizing the spotlight, was not willing to share it. Furthermore, his bosses in Peking looked askance at the Canton government. One of them, Duan Qirui, was an old nemesis of Eugene's. Duan's memory of his defeat at Eugene's hands in 1917 was still very fresh.

Thomas C. T. Wang, a former YMCA official, had a powerful friend by the name of Morde (Chinese transliteration) in the YMCA's national headquarters. Morde angled for the Canton delegation through the American minister to Peking, Dr. Reinsch, who, in turn, pressured the Peking government to invite the Canton delegates into the Peking delegation in order to maintain an appearance of unity at Versailles. Thus arranged, the Canton delegates became members of the Peking delegation. But they had their own agenda: first and foremost, they would not acknowledge that the Allied powers had the right to encroach upon China's sovereignty.

China had declared war on Germany in 1917 at the request of the United States. It had sent labor brigades at different times, a total of seven hundred fifty thousand Chinese,[2] to work along the front lines for the Allied powers;

other sources claimed it was two hundred thousand altogether.[3] More than three thousand had died when their ships had been sunk by Germans, and more than two thousand died in battles. But when the war ended and the Allied powers planned to divide the spoils, they showed extraordinary generosity at the expense of China. They did not object to the transfer of Germany's colonial interests in the province of Shandong to Japan. The Peking government acquiesced, since it was controlled by the pro-Japan warlord Duan Qirui, the man who had taken bribes from Japan and then been exposed by Eugene earlier in 1917.

On January 27, nine days after the Paris Peace Conference had opened, the Chinese delegates were suddenly called to an urgent meeting. The Allied powers played double roles, as arbiters and judges. They told the Chinese delegates to accept the transfer of Germany's colonial interests in Shandong Province to Japan. The chief Japanese delegate, Baron Muye (Chinese transliteration), emphatically said that a secret understanding had been reached between his government and the Peking government the year before.

The Chinese delegates from the Canton government knew Duan Qirui too well to be surprised by such a revelation. Later, they asked the Peking delegates to clarify this matter. Wellington Koo sidestepped their question by giving a vague answer. He had taken steps to circumvent Japan, Koo said. He had visited President Woodrow Wilson at the White House last November. Wilson had given his word that the United States would support China's claim of sovereignty at the Paris Peace Conference. As far as Koo knew, the Japanese envoy, Baron Ishii, had only exchanged documents with Wilson's administration, each side explaining their respective views on China.

Wellington Koo relied solely on Wilson's promise of intervention. What if Wilson went back on his word, or what if Wilson had lied, Eugene asked. A rumor had been bandied about ever since the visit of Baron Ishii to Washington in November 1917 that a secret pact had been signed by Japan and the United States. Under its terms, the United States acknowledged Japan's special interests in China while Japan acknowledged the United States' Open Door policy, stipulating that every foreign nation trading in China should have the same opportunities. Behind the highfalutin words was America's disaffection with other Western nations, in particular Britain, who had come to the China market earlier and thereby occupied a dominant position. The American merchants had resented the English dominance all along, but only raised their hopes of changing the status quo after the outbreak of the First World War. Both the United States and Japan were much less exhausted by the war. Anticipating the diminishing influence of their war-ravaged European allies, they decided that they should formalize their shared view of the postwar situation in this alleged secret pact.

Wellington Koo was evasive and dismissed the Canton delegates as watchdogs whose sole mission was to spy on him. Eugene turned to talk with Alfred Shi, the other senior member of the Peking delegation. In private, Shi was Eugene's bosom friend and former mentor. After their first meeting in Peking in 1912, Shi and Eugene kept in touch. Although their paths diverged and they did not agree on many points, they agreed on enough to help one another during crucial circumstances. Shi told Eugene that he would never agree to sign the peace treaty at the cost of Shandong Province, and that did not please his Peking bosses. They placed their trust in Wellington Koo, who knew much more about what had been going on between the Peking government and the Allied powers.

What Shi said alarmed Eugene. He took it that the Peking government would submit to Japan. To prevent such a move, Eugene felt it imperative to draw a line between the Canton and Peking delegates. With the backup of Thomas C. T. Wang and other Canton delegates, he prepared documents articulating demands that they believed China was entitled to make. These were that China would not agree to place any part of its territory under the control of the League of Nations; that China would not cede its territory to any foreign country; that China would take back, step by step, all the concessions; that China would recant the extraterritorial rights of foreigners and improve its own justice system; and that China would assume the customs services. Thomas C. T. Wang was deputed to read the documents in the conference.

In *World's Great Men of Color*, the historian J. A. Rogers wrote: "In 1919, [Eugene Chen] was a delegate to the Versailles Conference where he formulated China's demands in clear, unmistakable terms. He demanded, among other things, the abolition of concession territories, insisting that all such be placed under a mixed Chinese and foreign administration with Chinese predominant. This demand later paved the way for China's victory over the extra-territorial power formerly held by the White Governments."[4] All in all, China wanted to nullify all the unequal treaties forced on it.

Wellington Koo flinched, either because of the strong wording or because of his reluctance to let Thomas C. T. Wang enjoy the spotlight ahead of himself. Or both. His warlord bosses allowed him to speak in general about asserting China's sovereignty, showing that they had China's interests at heart. But they had no intention of defying the Allied powers. In the end, they would force the Peking delegates to sign the peace treaty the Allied Powers had drafted for China, including giving Japan the former concessions of Germany in Shandong Province. Koo felt that he had to take the orders from the Peking government into consideration, as he had always done. Thomas C. T. Wang, as the leader of the Canton government's delegation, could do without such scruples.

Eugene had no doubt that the revelation at Versailles was but the tip of an iceberg of a much deeper conspiracy. The Canton delegates by themselves would not be able to prevent the Peking delegates from signing the peace treaty. He must look for allies outside Versailles. There was one channel that might be open to him. After all, he was in Paris, the birthplace of European revolutions.

The political climate in Paris made Eugene's search for direct contact with the Marxist revolutionaries easier. Agents of the Comintern—the Communist International—were there. The French Socialist Party had a strong position in the National Assembly (French House of Deputies). Left-wing writers and journalists could be found sipping coffee in sidewalk cafés. With them, Eugene assumed the identity of a correspondent attached to the Chinese delegation. He moved freely among them. By way of café talk, he collected and gave information.

The Canton delegates held quite a few press conferences, and Eugene never missed an opportunity to attack colonialism. There were sympathetic listeners in the audience, and one day in March, at the end of a press conference, a French journalist went up to Eugene and suggested that he see a part of Paris where many momentous events of the French Revolution had taken place. The name of the district, Saint-Germain-des-Prés, instantly aroused Eugene's interest. Walking through a seemingly endless maze of dusty, poorly kept entrances, courtyards, corridors, and back doors, Eugene entered a stuffy hall on which a layer of dust had settled. There was so much dust that particles seemed to leap into the rays of the sunshine that came through the glass-topped door, whirling like little demons. Pushing open a door, there appeared a small garden with a delicate, soothing fragrance in the air.

A pointed, intense face with a pair of eyes magnified by rather thick lenses turned toward Eugene. The man leaped off the bench and introduced himself: Jacques Doriot, a French Marxist and a member of the French House of Deputies. Beside him was a man whose face Eugene found vaguely familiar. Tom Mann, standing beside the bouncing Doriot, was conspicuously serene, with his arms crossing over a potbelly that had grown over the years, Eugene suspected, by consuming an incredible number of bottles of beer. Once praised by Lenin as the wonder boy of the British Labour movement, Mann had had a brief encounter with Eugene in 1913 when Arthur Ransome had brought them together. Mann visited Paris intending to discredit Britain's policy on its colonies, in particular India. Doriot, for his part, followed the line of the French Marxists, attacking France's colonial policy on Annam (Vietnam). They too were questioning the hidden agendas of the Paris Peace Conference. Naturally, Eugene looked on them as potential allies. He invited them to meet again to continue the exchange of ideas.

When Eugene appeared as a journalist, he stayed away from the Canton delegates who were headquartered in the Hotel Lunette. He had a room in a small hotel on the Rue Vaugirard. Eugene and his new friends Doriot and Mann spent long hours talking. Their discussions ended only when Eugene and Doriot had drained the large tea urns dry and Mann had had his fill of beer. One night, Mann seemed drunk and reclined in the chair with his eyes half-closed. Eugene asked if he wanted to rest for a while in bed. Mann stood up and gulped down what was left in the last beer bottle. He was not drunk, he said; he was thinking if there was any way to expose Woodrow Wilson's new imperialism. English or French colonialism was an old story, not very exciting. But many people believed Wilson's promise to champion the cause of the colonized countries.

Mann's words spurred Eugene into reflection. From the information he had collected, Eugene mused aloud, the thing that bothered him most was the rumor that Japan had probably convinced American financiers of their mutual interests in postwar China. If that was the case, prospects at Versailles looked dim for China. He wanted to convey his concern to them, and he hastened to take out his scrapbook from the *Peking Gazette* and put it on the table. He watched his two friends reading it, Jacques Doriot alternately humming the "Marseillaise" and the "Internationale." Tom Mann tossed his lion's mane of white hair in indignation. They were deeply disturbed by the injustice China had suffered and said they would bring a few Russians with them next evening to hear Eugene speak in more detail on how he had had a hand in overturning two warlord regimes.

Eugene understood the significance of his presentation. He must show them that he knew his stuff, he had done his part, and he would have no difficulty doing it again. He could easily find a few reputable newspapers in China to publish whatever he muckraked at Versailles. He made his presentation with a passion that had been seldom seen in him. Neither the British-trained gentleman nor the Chinese intellectual of the day was supposed to give vent to his emotions. Eugene was usually outwardly impassive, but when he thought about China's fate, his blood boiled. His sense of righteousness, fair play, and decency was assaulted. All those emotions were revealed in his presentation.

With the words flowing and soaring, there came to him a sense of power and a feeling that he had touched his audience. He was anxious to know how they would respond. Doriot shrugged and advised patience so as to let the Russians get to know the Chinese stranger better.

But Eugene's patience stretched thinner as the divide between the Canton and Peking delegates grew deeper. Then came a weird twist in the conflict: the head of the Peking delegation and its foreign office, Lu Zhengxiang, suddenly disappeared. In his hotel suite his wife was weeping. Her husband, Madame Lu murmured between sobs, had checked into a hospital in Switzerland. The internal friction combined with the external duplicity of the Allied powers had proved too much for Lu's nerves.

Lu's dramatic withdrawal caused another bombshell for the Canton delegates. Lu had the habit of escaping into self-pity, suicide attempts, and hospital rooms when a crisis seemed impossible to resolve. Everybody knew what the current crisis was: the imminent signing of the Treaty of Versailles. His retreat gave the Peking government the excuse to place Wellington Koo at the head of the delegation. Koo was inclined to sign the peace treaty, but suggested that China must reserve the right to bring up the Shandong issue in the future.

An emergency meeting of the Canton delegates was called by Thomas C. T. Wang. It ended on a sullen note. They could walk out, hold a press conference, and protest, but they were not able to stop the betrayal. It was the small hours of the morning by the time Eugene got back to his hotel. He could not go to sleep, listening to a distant church bell ringing out slowly and gloomily, two strokes, three strokes, four strokes.

A wrenching homesickness drained him of any other emotions. He had not seen his wife and children since 1913. The children must have grown, but they remained small in his memory. In utter loneliness and driven by a burning yearning, he reached out for his family. He jumped off the bed, went to the desk, starting to write a letter telling his wife that he would soon be home. He mailed the letter first thing in the morning. When he returned, he found Jacques Doriot sitting in his room.

"I think you can use some diversion and relaxation," the Frenchman said.

He wanted to take Eugene to his friend's country house that afternoon. In a light vein, he gave a brief description of the host. The friend was an armchair socialist. "Very amusing," Doriot assured.

"I am in no mood for such entertainment," Eugene begged off. This was the first time in months that Eugene preferred to retreat into himself.

"You should go," Doriot said abruptly. "My friend keeps an open house. You never know whom you may stumble into."

Eugene discerned a hint of equivocal hope. "Do you have some inkling of who I may run into?"

"Not at all. You'll find that out yourself."

The guests who had arrived before them were strolling on the tree-lined path in a garden complete with fountain, arbor, and flowering bushes. The host, an elderly, gray-haired gentleman, came out to greet Eugene and sat him down in an arbor. Waiting for the host to bring drinks, Eugene picked up a copy of *Le Monde* and was glancing through it when suddenly two bullets, in rapid succession, pierced the paper and buried themselves in the log wall behind him, just an inch or two above his head. Russian playfulness was not familiar to the English-trained Eugene, and he was annoyed, but he went on reading calmly. Doriot was at the marksman's heels and introduced him as Igor, a political writer. Eugene doubted that was the Russian's real name. Igor wore black riding breeches with wide bugles on each thigh tapering into black top boots, a white Russian blouse caught at the waist with a thin Caucasian leather belt, and gold pince-nez on his lean face to complete the picture of an intellectual, more czarist than Bolshevik. He laughed when Eugene, playing cool, exclaimed: "Bravo!" Igor bowed graciously to the giggling ladies walking by and then to Eugene, acknowledging the applause.

Igor spoke excellent French, without any accent. He could have easily passed for a Frenchman if he hadn't been in a Russian costume. Igor showed extraordinary interest in Eugene's journalistic experiences in rallying the opposition to Yuan Shikai's monarchical plot and to Duan Qirui's selling out to Japan. But, the Russian said, the opposition seemed to have come mainly from the upper classes, the elite intelligentsia, the military governors, the parliamentarians, and so on. Not quite so, Eugene demurred politely but firmly. Many students from the lower classes had figured prominently in the campaigns against the warlords, Eugene explained.

"They are petit bourgeois," Igor said.

"They are patriots," Eugene snapped back.

Igor remained silent. An eloquent silence loudly spoke his disapproval. The silence kept pounding through Eugene's head, and he was only half-conscious that Doriot put an envelope on his knees after they got into a car, returning to the city.

"What is this?" Eugene asked without much interest.

"This is what you came here for."

Eugene sat straighter and lifted the envelope from his lap to open it.

"Wait until you are alone in your hotel room," Doriot said ponderously. "And take your time sorting it out."

"Sorting what out?"

"The secret pact."

That was way beyond what Eugene had anticipated. The most he had hoped for was that some Soviet Russian journalists might join him in denouncing the imperialists' conspiracy. When the car stopped at his hotel on the Rue Vaugirard, he got out hastily, as though breaking away from his fellow passenger. It was not until he climbed up the narrow, uncarpeted staircase into the dimness of his small room that he realized the full import of what he was trying to do. All of a sudden, he gasped for breath. He opened the window and gazed at the city, which had an air, a character, an aura that enchanted him. There was a unique light bathing the whole city, softening its lines. It even made magic out of some not-too-attractive streets, lanes, and corners. Eugene wondered if this was one reason why Paris was called the City of Light.

Somewhere beyond the rooftops and treetops was Versailles, the most grandiose palace in the Western world. Versailles was the Olympus of its time, and at the moment the gods were holding court there and deciding the fate of nations. He, Eugene Chen, was going to steal their thunder, to undo what they had done, to turn their Holy Mount upside down. At this unbelievably bold thought, a shudder of excitement, akin to fear, crept down his spine.

Pulling out papers from the large envelope, he started to read the copies of the secret treaties made by the Western powers and Japan regarding the "Rape of China" or the "Shandong Question," among them a copy of the Lansing-Ishii secret agreement. These secret documents had fallen into the

Bolsheviks' hands after the Russian communist revolution in 1917, when they had gotten hold of the czarist files and archives. Eager to make trouble at Versailles, the Russians were more than glad to give Eugene the evidence of the betrayal of China. They could not have found anyone better equipped than Eugene to make full use of it.

Eugene sent one copy to Republican senator William E. Borah, chairman of the committee of foreign affairs, who at that time was leading a campaign against Democratic president Woodrow Wilson's project, the League of Nations. Eugene was a scholar of English history and an admirer of the parliamentary system. He knew what power an opposition leader held. When the Canton delegation had arrived in Washington, his fellow delegates had sought interviews with officials inside the Wilson administration. But Eugene had done more than that, and obtained an interview with Senator Borah. With forethought, he had brought up the Shandong issue. Borah was impressed by Eugene's sharply analyzed and well-reasoned speech, alerting him to the fact that the Americans would never realize the Open Door policy in China if Japan was not contained. At the end of the interview, Borah told Eugene to keep in touch.

Eugene sent another copy to Sun Yatsen, who would arrange to get it translated for Chinese newspapers.

Supported by this secret agreement, Japan pressured President Wilson to concede to its terms. On April 22, 1919, the United States government announced that it, along with Britain, France, and Italy, was backing Japan's demands on China, and that Japan, in return, was voting for Wilson's project, the League of Nations. China was sacrificed for the sake of preserving everlasting peace, spreading democracy, and upholding the self-determination of nations. The Peking government, controlled by the warlord Duan Qirui even though he was not a member of the government at that time, complied and ordered the Peking delegation to sign the Treaty of Versailles.

But Eugene's disclosure of the secret pact posed a huge hurdle for the implementation of Peking's policy. On May 2, the *Morning Bell* of Peking— *Chen Zhong Bao*, a progressive paper popular among intellectuals and students—reported the Allied powers' decision to yield to Japan's aggressive designs on China.[5] Within days, the news of the Versailles conspiracy reached many other Chinese cities. It touched off one of the greatest events in China's modern history, the May Fourth Movement.

The May Fourth Movement was a political and also a cultural event. Its primary organizers were student-activists and intellectuals. Politically it rallied the people from all walks of Chinese life, from poor to rich, from lower

May Fourth Movement demonstration, 1919, Shanghai.

classes to upper classes, to defy the warlords and their foreign backers. In Peking, the rioting students threatened the presidential residence and disrupted the president's lunch party. They burned down the mansion of the pro-Japan minister of communications. They roughed up the pro-Japanese minister to Japan and injured him. In other cities, students held similar angry demonstrations. In Tianjin, Zhou Enlai, then a student at Nankai School, and his comrades were challenging the city authorities. In Changsha, Mao Zedong was organizing a campaign to cleanse the city of its most tyrannical warlord.

Culturally, the May Fourth Movement was a wakeup call for Chinese intellectuals. Like Dante and Boccaccio, who used the Italian vernacular instead of Latin, the Chinese writers of the May Fourth generation called for a stop to the use of a dying elite language, Wenyan, intelligible only to the well educated. They advocated Paihua, the spoken language, which would make new ideas, new knowledge, and new learning accessible to the common people. This language revolution helped the Chinese mind cross the threshold from the Middle Ages into the modern era. It was no less than the emancipation of the modern Chinese mind, which now, instead of being awed by and obedient to authorities, confronted and questioned them.

Two witnesses, of diametrically different beliefs, came to the same conclusion about the May Fourth Movement: that it was the rebirth of the Chinese nation.

In the English translation of Mao Zedong's essay "On New Democracy," published in 1965, Mao wrote: "The May 4 Movement was an anti-imperialist as well as an anti-feudal movement. Its outstanding historical significance is to be seen in a feature which was absent from the Revolution of 1911, namely, its thorough and uncompromising opposition to imperialism as well as to feudalism. The May 4 Movement possessed this quality because capitalism had developed a step further in China and because new hopes had arisen for the liberation of the Chinese nation. . . ."[6]

Mao was not exaggerating. Long before he wrote this political essay in the forties, Professor John Dewey, lecturing in Peking in 1919, had seen first-hand the patriotic Chinese students flexing their growing political muscle. The American scholar wrote: "To say that life in Peking is exciting is to put it mildly. We are witnessing the birth of a nation and birth always comes hard."[7]

Although the storm of protest scared the Peking government, it was more afraid of the Western powers and Japan, and kept pressuring the Peking delegates to bow to demands of the Allied powers. But when the Peking warlords discovered that the Canton delegation was determined not to go along, they paused. It is of note that during the Paris Peace Conference, the warlord Duan Qirui's right-hand man, Xu Shuzheng, who had incarcerated Eugene in 1917, received a secret cable from his man in the Peking delegation at Versailles, alerting him to "the presence of Chen Youren, Guo Taiqi and Wu Zhaoshu in France."[8] Duan was no stranger to Eugene's talent for wreaking havoc through the press. He probably knew that if he commanded the Peking delegation to sign the peace treaty, Eugene would do more to sway public opinion against him.

Dr. Philip Tyau, editor of the English edition of the *Peking Daily News* and a counselor of Peking's foreign office, commented on the situation with the authority of an insider. "Despite the fact that the Northern [Peking] delegation was appointed by the Waichiapu [foreign office] in Peking, they were helpless in the face of the strong national feeling expressed throughout China against the U.S.-Japan secret agreement, popularly known as the Lansing–Ishii agreement."[9]

Silan wrote: "In Paris Father had somehow obtained a copy of the secret agreement and had sent it to Dr. Sun Yat-sen. Dr. Sun used it as the evidence of the Allies' perfidy and heightened Chinese national emotions not only among students, but also bankers, merchants and even officials. Another copy was sent to Senator Borah, who then led a campaign against President Wilson whose secretary of state, Mr. Lansing, had so flagrantly double-crossed China."[10]

This clearly spelled out Eugene's role at Versailles as a catalyst in defeating the Allies' plot and in igniting the passion that swept the nation in the May Fourth Movement.

After Eugene sent a copy of the Lansing-Ishii secret agreement to Senator William Borah, he was asked to write a letter appealing directly to the Senate, which would soon vote either for or against joining the League of Nations. Eugene's long letter stated two reasons why the United States should not give in to Japan's expansionism: first, it would hurt the United States' policy of trading with China; second, "it is unfair to China, it endangers world peace, and damages the dignity and interests of the American government."[11] The letter, eloquent, impassioned, and convincing, made a splash and merited newspaper headlines. His plea for justice resonated through and beyond the capitol. Suddenly, the Shandong issue became a hot potato for Wilson. When the Senate votes were counted, the president was defeated. The United States Senate rejected the Treaty of Versailles and refused to join the League of Nations.

The American journalist John B. Powell, editor of the *China Weekly Review* published in Shanghai, confirmed the matter in his memoir, *My Twenty-five Years in China*. "A few days later I happened to meet William J. H. Cochran of Missouri, who had been publicity director of the Democratic National Committee during the Wilson incumbency. I asked Cochran what he thought of Harding's action in calling the Arms Limitation Conference (which forced Japan to promise to return the former German interests in Shandong to China). His reply was characteristic of the prevailing sentiment among the hard-boiled Washington correspondents. Cochran said, 'Harding owes his election to the Shantung [Shandong] Question, more than any other single issue.' I asked him what he meant by the statement. He replied 'Of all the issues in the campaign, the best vote-getter the Republicans had was the Shantung [Shandong] Question. Harding himself frequently used the term "rape of Shantung (Shandong)" in his pre-election addresses.' We verified this by referring to the *New York Times* index covering speeches

*Eugene (first row, second from right) was one of Sun Yatsen's representatives on the Chinese delega-
tion to the first meeting of the League of Nations in Geneva in 1920, following the Paris Peace
Conference in 1919. Wellington Koo, future ambassador to the United States, sits to his right.*

delivered by the various candidates during the campaign. Every candidate on
the Republican side from Harding down had repeatedly mentioned the
Shantung [Shandong] case and the 'rape of China,' in endeavoring to discredit the Versailles Treaty and the League of Nations Covenant."[12]

Facing insurmountable opposition, the warlords permitted their Peking
delegates to come home without signing the Treaty of Versailles. While
Eugene's colleagues still used the timeworn methods of diplomacy to assert
China's demands, Eugene had other ideas. As a diplomat, he counted on the
moral support of his own people rather than on any politician, Chinese or
foreign. At Versailles, for the first time in modern Chinese history, the
Chinese diplomats refused to sign a humiliating "Unequal Treaty," refused to
acknowledge that the foreign powers had the right to carve out any parts of
Chinese territory. This resulted in extracting a promise from the Western
nations and Japan, in the Washington Conference held in 1921, to eventually return their colonial interests to China.

★ 7 ★

BLENDING CONFUCIUS, LINCOLN, AND MARX

After Eugene concluded his mission in Versailles, he returned to London and obtained his wife's agreement to sell part of their lands in Trinidad to pay the debts of the *Shanghai Gazette*. He could not go back to Shanghai without the proceeds, because the moneylenders were waiting, still holding the warrant to arrest him. But the selling of a real property was a process that took a little time, so Eugene stayed home for a while.

Jack was ten years old when his father came home the second time in mid-1919. The semi-enforced stay in London was not wasted. Eugene had a long list of books he wanted to read, including works by Marxist thinkers. His old study had become the room of his younger daughter, Yolanda, who had been born in 1913. Eugene redecorated the living room and turned it into his new study, moving in a huge desk and a swivel chair. He took Jack along to do the shopping. It was always with a sense of adventure that Jack went out with his father. Eugene loved to stroll and took his time to see the sights along the way. They turned off the corner at Baker Street and Marylebone Road and went through the high and beautiful gates. Somehow, in Jack's imagination, he always thought that Paradise and its Pearly Gates must look like those at Regent's Park, except, of course, that the iron would be gold.

Father and son bought a large bookcase and filled it with books Eugene had brought from Paris or bought in London. The bookcase could be turned on its casters to reveal a hidden bed, soft, warm, and secure. Usually Jack was not allowed into this room. But on certain nights, he found himself waking up in it, an indulgence he had won because of his temper.

Every time Jack heard that his mother was going to see a show with her friends, he would throw a tantrum and demand to go with them. The noise brought Eugene out of his study. To quiet the boy, they said that all the seats for that particular show were sold out, but that he could go to the last performance with his father at ten o'clock. Mollified, he would don his coat and wait for his father and the appointed hour. Eugene would then continue his writing or reading under the green-glass-covered desk light in the darkened study while Jack waited on the sofa beside the desk. When Jack fell asleep, he had only himself to blame for missing out on the "last house." This stratagem was repeated several times, but Jack never doubted nor complained about it. He only wondered why his father was so absorbed in reading.

"They may tell me how to find a way back to Peking," Eugene answered.

"Why Peking?" Jack asked.

Eugene thought for a moment and answered: "Because Peking is beautiful. Do you like to fly kites?"

Jack nodded enthusiastically. Eugene smiled and told the child about the famous pastime of the Northern Capital. In the breezy spring, the cloudless sky could suddenly be filled with kites of all shapes and sizes, gaudy and pretty, soaring and bobbing in that special quality of light peculiar to Peking. Then, as suddenly as they had appeared, the kites disappeared in the engulfing twilight, and in their place were flocks of pigeons wheeling in the sky, the whistles attached to their feet shrilling as they flew.

"You'll like Peking," Eugene said, patting Jack's head. "When I settle down there, I'll come to bring your mother and all of you to be with me."

Jack mumbled: "Mother doesn't like it." Then, embarrassed by his indirect retort, he tried to justify it and blurted out the nightmare his mother had had when his father was in the prison of the warlord Duan Qirui in 1917.

Eugene remained silent for a long moment, looking distressed. Jack cursed himself for his lapse in judgment.

"I am sorry to cause your mother so much pain," Eugene sighed and went back to reading and writing.

A lot of spade work had to be done before formally opening a dialogue with Soviet Russia, and Eugene started his preparatory work as soon as his new study in his London home was ready. In 1919, the books on Marxism and the Russian Revolution he had bought in London and Paris came in handy. These books were hard to get in China. In those days, the few intellectuals who had any knowledge of Marxism were students returning from abroad. They had access to the great libraries of the universities while they studied there, but they did not have the money to buy a comprehensive collection of books by Marxist and Bolshevik writers as Eugene did. Eugene had another plus: he read German well, so he had three major European languages at his disposal.

Meanwhile Eugene studied the history of the Labour movement in England. The Labour Party depended on the ballot for getting seats in the Commons. They succeeded, because England had a long history of parliamentary democracy. Eugene considered that preferable to the violent seizure of power in Russia, in which the common people suffered terribly. But the parliamentary system had not worked in China, Eugene thought, as he recalled the fate of the National Assembly in Peking.

The question of whether Western democratic principles were feasible in China was the subject of discussion between Eugene and his friends sympathetic with or in the Labour movement. The tide of history worldwide was toward the underdogs having their share of power, and the poor peasants and laborers of China were in the same flow of history. Eugene had no problem with this conclusion. The question of democracy, however, remained unanswered. Would the underdogs be represented in the governing structure, or would the revolutionaries monopolize all power, as had happened in the Soviet Union? Eugene much preferred the former to the latter.

Arthur Ransome suggested that he visit Sir Gilbert Murray, an authority on Western democracy. The great classical scholar of Oxford was bookish and long-winded, but he did give Eugene some food for thought. The word "dictator" had not sounded as bad among ancient Greeks or Romans as it sounded now, Murray said. In a time of great upheaval, he continued, a dictatorship, not noisy parliamentarians, might be more effective in stabilizing a chaotic society. Maybe, at the moment, it was plausible in China to have an enlightened dictator who placed the nation's interest above his own and who was willing to strive toward the eventual democratic goal.

On a day in mid-August, Tom Mann showed Eugene an article in the Soviet party organ *Pravda* of July 25, 1919, less than three months after the outbreak of the May Fourth Movement. It was titled "Declaration to the Chinese People" and was signed by Lev Karakhan, deputy commissar of the foreign ministry. The Soviet Union, Karakhan wrote, was a true friend to China. "If the Chinese people wish, like the Russian people, to become free and to avoid the fate which the Allies prepared for them at Versailles, a fate designed to turn China into a second Korea or a second India, they must understand that their only allies and brothers in the struggle for freedom are the Russian workers and peasants and their Red Army."[1]

Eugene read the English translation of Karakhan's declaration carefully. It held promise for mutual cooperation between Sun Yatsen's Kuomintang and Lenin's party. This overture was immediately forwarded to Sun.

★

When Eugene left his London home for China in the spring of 1920, he had a bagful of notebooks to take with him. He spent long hours reporting his findings to Sun Yatsen. Both men realized that they had a problem. The Kuomintang wanted the Russians' material, but not their ideological, assistance. This posed a conflict, which they had to get around. Combing through his notebooks, looking for what he could lift from Marxism and apply to China, was a major part of Eugene's work.

"The Marxists' ultimate goal is a Utopia, and the means they use to achieve that goal is class war. But destroying the old order will only solve part of our problem. China was poor before the colonialists and warlords came on the scene. Can Marxist theory help us reconstruct? I don't think so. Under Russian communism, even a monkey will be labeled a capitalist for setting aside a few nuts for a rainy day," Eugene chuckled. "Those nuts will be considered stored wealth and therefore capital in Marxist terminology. For this reason alone, Marxists' methods should not be used to solve the economic problems in China. China's problem is not to get rid of capital, but to get more in and use it to benefit all the people. Both in agriculture and in industry, China needs capital. And as a matter of fact, Russia is not much richer than we are, so we have to get most of the capital from the West."

"This part of Marxism is not for China," Sun agreed, perfunctorily glancing through a page which Eugene handed over.

"Not for Russia either. . . . Well, maybe it will take them at least twenty thousand years for Marxism to elevate mankind to a higher level of being, so that he can qualify for citizenship in the Marxist Utopia. That is, if Marxism will not be outdated by then." Eugene paused. He paced up and down the room ruminatively.

"Marx's theory of achieving economic equality is naïve, to put it mildly. The Marxist tenet that 'To each, according to his need; from each, according to his abilities' sounds wonderful, but it goes against human nature. It is not in human nature to take only what one needs. Man always desires more. Nor is it in human nature to work to the best of his abilities without asking for the highest incentive possible."

At this moment, Sun did not seem to hear Eugene. He looked absent, and his thought was somewhere else. He gave a slight jump when Eugene halted suddenly, and a hush fell over the room.

"What did you say?" he asked.

Eugene repeated. This time, Sun Yatsen listened carefully, and his amused smile showed that he had discovered what he had been seeking.

He took a volume from a bookshelf and waved it. "This is the ancient *Book of Rites.* Listen to this passage.

"'All men everywhere will live for the common good. . . . They will provide sustenance to the aged as long as they live, employment to the able-bodied, opportunity for development to the young, friendly care to widows, orphans, childless men and the disabled. . . . Not wishing to be wasteful of their possessions, they will nevertheless not keep them for purely personal use; not wishing to be inactive in the application of their strength, they will at the same time not exert it merely in their own behalf. . . .' "[2]

The Confucian utopia depicted in this classic portrayed the earliest society before men were corrupted by greed. The book was much revered by the Chinese intelligentsia and much quoted by respectable reformers, and therefore, by quoting it, Sun Yatsen would not be accused of adopting the Russians' communist Utopia; at the same time, it would make sharing some ideological common ground with them possible.

Sun had written a number of political essays in Chinese, but if he aimed to win the international audience, he had to put his ideas into English. Sun could speak and read English proficiently, but he had never been able to write good English. He was supposed to have penned a slim volume titled *Kidnapped in London,* but actually it was ghost-written in his name.[3] Now, with Eugene's cooperation, he began several projects in English: *The International Development of China, China's Revolution,* and *The Organization of Nationalist Government,* as well as revising his old book *Three Principles of the People.* From that day forward, Eugene had a hand in composing and editing all of Sun's documents written in English. The exchange of official and semi-official correspondence and the conducting of negotiations with the Soviet Russians were all in English, because this was the only language through which all parties were able to communicate directly.

A typical example of the two men's co-production is manifested in the revising of Sun's work *Three Principles of the People,* which was a compilation of political essays and speeches. The original *Three Principles* was an attempt to model his republican government on Lincoln's ideal of "a government of the people, by the people, and for the people," which was rendered into Chinese as "nationalism, democracy, and people's livelihood." It was in the third principle, People's Livelihood, that Sun showed his early inclination toward socialism, for example, equalizing land ownership, restraining private capitalism, and nationalizing communications and heavy industries. A lot of the heavy revising of the book was done in this section. Eugene helped Sun embellish the Principle of the People's Livelihood with Marxist terminology, which, however, was not made public until early 1924:

> our Principle of Livelihood is a form of communism. It is not a form originated with Marx. . . . The first society formed by man was a communistic society and the primitive age was a communistic age. . . . Where there are inequalities of wealth, Marx's methods can, of course, be applied; a class war can be started to destroy the inequalities. But in China, where industry is not yet developed, class war and the dictatorship of the proletariat are unnecessary. So today we can take Marx's ideas as a guide, but we cannot make use of his methods. . . . We cannot say, then, that the theory of communism is different from our Min-sheng Principle (Principle of the People's Livelihood). Our Three Principles of the People mean government "of the people, by the people, for the people"—that is, a state belonging to all the people, a government controlled by all the people, and rights and benefits for the enjoyment of all the people. If this is true, the people will not only have a communistic share in state production, but they will have a share in everything.[4]

Having made that wordy detour, Sun drove home the final point. The ultimate goal of the Principle of the People's Livelihood was for people to share everything they possessed with each other. Great Harmony would follow, and Confucius's utopian dream would come true.

Eugene was aware that what he helped Sun develop would be criticized as a hodgepodge of contrary ideologies. For practical reasons, while drafting such a document he had to take into consideration the sensitivity of the Kuomintang backbone—the middle classes and landed gentry—as well as the potential alliance with Soviet Russia and the apprehension of the Western powers. A document of such a nature must perforce be a controversial mixture. Hodgepodge or not, it would serve a high purpose in a certain historical period. That was the point. China had its own socialism and communism, so there was no need to import them from Russia.

Thus equipped ideologically, Eugene looked forward to escorting the envoy from the Comintern to meet with Sun Yatsen.

One day at the beginning of June 1921, a tall Dutchman with the gait of a Prussian officer walked off an Italian ship from Venice. He took a taxi to Nanjing Road. On Nanjing Road, the poorest of the poor mingled with the wealthiest of the rich. The contrast between old and new, rich and poor was dramatically apparent. Human beasts of burden pushed wheelbarrows or pulled carts with harnesses strapped to their backs. This awful sight confirmed the Dutchman's belief in turning Asia into an arena of World Revolution. His taxi driver deposited him at the newest grand hotel of Shanghai, the Great East.

The Dutchman's real name was Hendricus (Henk) Sneevliet, but he had used so many aliases that he could not remember them all. In China he was best known as Maring. He was a member of the Far Eastern Section of the Comintern, and he had come to combine the small, scattered communist cells in China into a party. In his first meeting with two Chinese comrades, Li Hanjun and Li Da, he left a bad impression. Maring was not a good listener. He did not like to hear opinions different from his own. Maybe he had unwittingly acquired the mannerisms of the Dutch colonialists by working too long among the natives in Indonesia, where he had founded the Social Democratic Alliance of the East Indies, the forerunner of the Indonesian Communist Party. Li Hanjun and Li Da found Maring rude and arrogant. They were not eager to work with him; however, they duly sent out the notice for the first congress.

In mid-July 1921, nine "tourists" gathered in an inconspicuous row house on Pubai Road in the French concession. This was the Bowen Girls School, one of the many nondescript, rather commercialized institutes there. It was the summer vacation, and the faculty, staff, and students were gone, and there were rooms for rent. Mao Zedong was among the nine "tourists" and was given a rather dark room with a narrow trestle bed, while others shared larger and brighter rooms. He was left to himself, it was said, because the others snubbed him and questioned his qualifications as a delegate.

The congress was held in the dining room of Li Hanjun's residence, a street or two away. There were thirteen Chinese, representing the communist units of Shanghai, Peking, Canton, Wuhan, Changsha, Jinan, and Japan; and two agents from the Comintern, Maring and Nekolsky (Chinese transliteration). Mao Zedong took notes for the meeting and sat close to the rectangular dining table, covered with a white tablecloth and decorated with a vase of fresh flowers. Usually a note taker was not considered a representative participant in a conference. Mao spoke little and, busy with his pen, was probably glad to avoid the heated arguments that flared up between Maring and the Chinese. Maring wasted no time letting them know that the Comintern was not only an alliance of the communist parties of nations, but also was their leader, their superior. Each party was a branch of the Comintern.

The Chinese delegates, led by the outspoken Li Hanjun, objected vehemently. They had become revolutionaries because they hated the foreign devils who reduced them to second-class citizens. Now again, in their own land they were to be given status as second-class comrades. No, no way. The debate went on and on, and it got on everybody's nerves. Unexpectedly, it was broken by an uninvited guest on the seventh day. A suspicious stranger sneaked into the dining room from the back door. He looked around and then apologized: "I am sorry. I came to the wrong address." And he hurried out, bowing.

Maring, more experienced in underground activities, sensed trouble. He brought his fist heavily down on the table and demanded adjournment of the meeting immediately.

It was not safe to continue the meeting in Shanghai. The Chinese delegates traveled to Jiaxing, an old small town to the south of Shanghai. The two Comintern envoys were advised not to come along, because foreign devils would attract hostile glances in a place changed little by the passage of time, perhaps for centuries. Without Maring around to bully them, the Chinese delegates wrote into the bylaws that their newborn party was an ally of, but not a subordinate to, the Comintern. When the document was translated and read to Maring, he hit the ceiling. But what had been done had been done. It was not until the second congress, held the next year, that Maring got his way: the clause was rewritten to specify that the Chinese Communist Party was a branch of the Comintern. The official birthday of the Party was July 1, 1921.

His first mission accomplished, Maring turned his mind to his second mission, to persuade the Kuomintang to treat the newborn Communist Party as an equal partner. This precluded any chance that he would have a smooth-sailing meeting with Sun Yatsen. The first thing on Sun's mind was to get financial and military assistance. Through his experiences of the past ten years, Sun knew that as long as he did not have his own army, he would be at the mercy of one warlord or another. To raise an army, he needed cash, and he wanted cash from Moscow to launch the Northern Expedition to end the warlords' regime in Peking.

Maring, on the other hand, had his own priorities. He had just witnessed the birth of the infant Chinese Communist Party. Nobody knew better than he how weak and undersized the baby was. Altogether, it could boast of fewer than fifty members with, in his eyes, as much knowledge of Marxism as adolescents, so someone had to provide a lot of nourishment to help it grow. He decided that that someone had to be the Kuomintang, which was comparatively much better established.

Escorted by Eugene, Maring visited Sun Yatsen in December 1921 in the city of Guilin, the provincial capital of Guangxi. Maring offered two proposals for discussion: to build a military academy, and to form an alliance between the infant Communist Party and the Kuomintang.

Sun turned down the second proposal outright. He told Maring bluntly that his own revolutionary program was inclusive and that he saw no need for another revolutionary party. If the Chinese communists wanted to contribute to the Chinese revolution, they should merge into his party, the Kuomintang. From the very beginning, Sun made it clear that the Chinese Communist Party could be part of the Kuomintang, but its members must observe the constitution and rules of the Kuomintang. It was something like a merger, an acquisition of a small company by a large corporation.

Staring at Sun with his stern, protruding eyes, Maring disagreed.

Then Sun bluntly delivered the statement Eugene had been helping him prepare for the past year and a half. He could see nothing new in Marxism, Sun retorted. What Marx advocated had been professed twenty-five hundred years ago by Confucius and his disciples, and had been written in the Chinese classics.

Maring shifted back and forth in his seat while Sun was speaking. His attention was flagging, as he couldn't wait to have his say.

Sun refused to let up. He interspersed his speech with quotes from Chinese classics that, judging by their language, Maring suspected had been written by very learned scholars. Precisely because he did not understand what on earth Sun was talking about, Maring was intimidated and mortified.

Delighted to see the Dutchman laboring and puzzling through the labyrinthine trains of thought in which Sun intentionally trapped him, Eugene interposed.

"Dr. Sun's writing is and will be the sole guideline of our revolution."

Sun followed with a long tirade. He admonished those young men who were actively organizing a communist party, because they did not understand what his Principle of the People's Livelihood really was: it was a form of indigenous communism modernized by him, Sun noted, a form of communism acceptable not only to the rank and file of the Kuomintang but also to the Chinese people at large.

Maring felt the sting of Sun's words and was surprised to discover such an oversized ego in the medium-sized, mild-mannered, soft-spoken doctor. Exasperated though he was, he wrote a report to the Comintern in favor of Sun's proposal, accepting the Chinese Communist Party as the Kuomintang's junior partner. The Communist Party was but a small cell, Maring noted, and it was further hindered by the fact that it was outlawed from day one. If it did not use the Kuomintang as a form of camouflage, its prospect of growing was bleak—that was Maring's prediction. His suggestions were approved by the Comintern in Moscow.

As a result of the meeting, Moscow was made to understand that they could not press the Kuomintang too hard. The next envoy they sent was a man much more pleasant and sophisticated than Maring.

In January 1923, Adolph A. Joffe, who represented Moscow in his capacity as the deputy commissar of foreign affairs, came to Shanghai. The meeting between him and Sun Yatsen would be a bombshell to the Western powers. Eugene meant it to be so, shaking them out of their complacency but not making them desperate. Therefore, in the weeks before and after the Sun-Joffe meeting, he frequently crossed over the Suzhou River Bridge, where the American and British Consulates-General were located, the two main targets of his persuasion. It was his belief that the British Empire was on the wane and the United States, with its vast size and unlimited resources, was replacing Britain as the most important world power. The diminishing British Lion was not likely to roar without the backing of its junior-turned-senior partner. Eugene started what he later called the "appeal to America's best instincts."

Acting as Sun Yatsen's secretary and spokesman, Eugene explained the Kuomintang's new policy. The drift of it was that if the Western powers continued their hostilities against the Canton government, it would have no choice but to form an alliance with Soviet Russia for the sole purpose of self-preservation. After the Sun-Joffe meeting, there would be a joint statement of friendship and, Eugene emphasized, a pledge of mutual assistance between the two governments, not the two political parties: thus no ideological issues would be involved.

After nearly four years of courtship, the marriage of convenience was near consummation. On January 26, 1923, Sun Yatsen issued the joint statement, drafted by Eugene, with Joffe, making public the Russia-oriented policy and the Kuomintang's independence of Soviet ideology.

"Dr. Sun Yatsen holds that the communistic order, or even the Soviet system, cannot actually be introduced into China because there do not exist the conditions for the successful establishment of either communism or Sovietism. This view is entirely shared by Mr. Joffe, who is further of the opinion that China's paramount and most pressing problem is to achieve national unification and attain full national independence; and regarding this great task he has assured Dr. Sun Yatsen that China has the warmest sympathy of the Russian people and can count on the support of Russia."[5]

Eugene's speeches and statements brought him to the notice of a special envoy from the State Department by the name of Nelson T. Johnson, who was on the same boat, sailing for Hong Kong, with Sun Yatsen and Eugene. As a rule, Eugene knew, American ministers and consul-generals posted in China usually followed Britain's lead. Unfortunately, the British in China existed in a golden fishbowl, away from the smelly natives and indifferent to the surging nationalism. But a visiting American official might see the Chinese situation with a fresh eye. On this supposition, Eugene actively sought the understanding and sympathy of this new arrival from the United States. The United States, Eugene said to Johnson, seemed most interested in trade, and a united, stable China would be good for business.

Nelson Johnson was concerned about how far the Canton government would go with the Soviets. Eugene did not mince words: the Canton government had plans to reconstruct China, developing industry, modernizing agriculture, and improving commerce. All these plans needed money to carry them out. Foreign trade and capital were welcomed. Soviet Russia could help to some degree, but they were facing difficulties in reconstructing their own country. Besides, Eugene added, China was establishing a system on an economic basis different from theirs. And he believed that it was sounder than any.

Meanwhile, Eugene gave a message from Sun Yatsen to Johnson. Sun said he had faith in American democracy and believed Americans had sympathy for a revolution, which struggled to realize Lincoln's ideal in the

Eastern Hemisphere. He suggested that the American government send a ranking official who understood China and could help to persuade the different Chinese factions to establish a unified China. Evidently Eugene's argument swayed Johnson, who reported it to Dr. John Van Antwerp MacMurray, head of the Far East Department of the State Department. A year or two later, MacMurray himself would come to Peking as the new American minister, and he would demonstrate some goodwill during the early stage of the Northern Expedition, launched by the Canton government in 1926.

All grounds covered, Sun and Eugene were ready to greet a Russian, sent by Lenin, whose specialty was to make revolutions.

Borodin was born in 1884 of poor Jewish parents. His real name was Mikhail Markovich Gruzenberg. He spent his early childhood in one of the small villages of the Pale. The place was smaller and more backward than Chagall's curious, cock-eyed world of the Jewish *shtetl*, he told Jack when he knew the young man's bent for drawing.

As a matter of fact, it was very close to the great painter's native village. Three years later, the family moved to Latvia. Borodin had a traditional Jewish education in his childhood. Yiddish was his first language. A rambunctious child, he had a great distaste for the rigidity of his environment and the mandatory religious teachings. When he reached adolescence, he made his first attempt to break away. He worked on riverboats, floating logs down the Divina River to Riga. He loved the openness of the river, the fluffy mist lying on the bushes and reeds, the smell of the budding leaves in the air. When he was sixteen, he got involved in the Bund, a Jewish socialist group. He joined it not only because it was Jewish, but also because it taught him that not all gentiles were Grand Inquisitors or Crusaders, and that there was brotherhood among all honest working men, regardless of race or nationality or religious belief.

Living in the lower depths of the society, suffering discrimination as a Jew, he nursed a compassion for the "scum" who wasted their lives, as he saw it, in an unjust society. He did not want to repeat their mistakes of drowning their sorrow in vodka, brothels, and gambling. He was eager to get into the mainstream. He attended night school and learned Russian. Basically, however, he was a self-educated man. When he tired of reading, he lay on the grass beside the river, gazing at the stars and listening to the folk songs floating over the water. As he grew up, he developed a taste for literature and art and music. The musician he admired most was the composer Alexander Porphyriewitch Borodin. He loved Borodin's music so much that he adopted his surname when he needed a revolutionary pseudonym. Some said that he chose a gentile name to cover his Jewish origins. Maybe or maybe not.

Borodin never spoke of his love life, but he must have loved when he was a lad, because he was very susceptible to feminine charms. He was a man who could sum up the beauty of a young woman walking by in a single line: "Her cheeks are like a bouquet of wild flowers," as recalled by his Wuhan colleague Milly Bennett, an American journalist, in her memoir *On Her Own*.

Perhaps Borodin had no time for romantic love, since he studied hard. Within three years of night school, he could sit down to chat with Lenin, and he impressed the Bolshevik leader so much that he was thought to be the best man to organize a Bolshevik branch in Latvia. Borodin started to work with the Bolsheviks when they were in the tiny minority, altogether less than a hundred members in all of Europe. During the 1905 Revolution, he successfully pushed the Bolshevik faction in Riga into the foreground. Although the revolution failed, Borodin's Bolshevik comrades discovered his gift for making revolution. In 1906, the twenty-one-year-old Borodin was chosen to represent the Bolshevik branch from Riga and attend a conference in Stockholm. He found himself brushing shoulders with top Bolsheviks, including Lenin and Stalin. He also found himself sitting next to Stalin and voting, in the eighteen recorded votes, fourteen times with Stalin and eleven times with Lenin.[6] Throughout the conference, he demonstrated his support for Bolshevik internationalism against Latvian nationalism. Borodin yearned to embrace the whole world.

Borodin's star was rising when he was abruptly arrested by the czarist police in the summer of 1906 and given the choice of going into exile in Europe or in Siberia. Not surprisingly, he chose the warmer London.

Six months later, he was deported by Scotland Yard, which suspected him of stirring up trouble among immigrants. Borodin crossed the Atlantic to the New World, first appearing in Boston in early 1907. One year later, he moved to Chicago, the center of American socialism. For the next ten years, he taught in Hull House, founded by Jane Addams.

Borodin also taught in his own school, which he moved a few times before settling down on 2058 West Division Street. He had a job and he married Fanya, a plain-faced Russian woman with a heavy jaw. She was a revolutionary in her own right and his loyal workmate. They had two sons, the older born in Chicago. During this period, he honed two skills that he later used in China: to work with people of different backgrounds, and to make ideological adjustments to suit new realities. There were numerous factions among the immigrants in Chicago's slums. Even those inclined toward socialism found the Leninist gospel hard to stomach. Ever so flexible, Borodin toned down the Bolshevik rhetoric.

He returned to Russia in 1918 following the victory of the Bolshevik Revolution. Since he had not been in Russia for ten years, his position in the hierarchy of the Party had suffered. An ambitious man, he was eager to move up and find his niche.

The opportunities came when the Comintern needed a troubleshooter to set up their local centers and communist parties in Europe and America. During the next four or five years, Borodin smuggled himself in and out of Germany, Switzerland, Holland, Jamaica, the United States, Mexico, Spain, and England.

It was Mexico, Borodin told the teenaged Jack later in Wuhan, that held his fondest memories. "Imagine, all year round there is sunshine! It is a wonder for a man from a country with long winters. And the pretty maidens, half Spanish and half native Indian. When they smiled, their dark faces blossomed like violets." After a pause, he went on to quote Wordsworth with proletarian tenderness:

> A violet by a mossy stone
>> Half-hidden from the eye!
>>> Fair as a star, when only one
>>> Is shining in the sky.

When Borodin was in a less poetic mood, he would, with a rakish wink, tell Jack how to live a high life without a cent.

Borodin's last assignment was in England. He got arrested there and spent most of his time in a British prison, reading the Holy Bible, the only book his warden gave him. In later years, Borodin often said how much he cherished reading and reflecting in solitude in the Barlinnie Prison. His familiarity with the Bible helped him make friends, both Chinese and Western, during his China years. Some people thought Borodin was just play-acting in order to curry favor with Sun Yatsen, Soong Chingling, Eugene Chen, and the Western journalists dazzled by his erudition and oratory. That was an oversimplification of a complicated Bolshevik.

In 1923, Borodin became the Comintern's top agent. He came instantly to mind when Lenin wanted someone in China. Early in his China mission, Borodin was not Stalin's man. He had worked closely with Lenin. And he had one more edge over the other potential competitors: he was an old friend of the newly appointed ambassador to China, Lev Karakhan.

Borodin's small cattle boat dropped anchor at the port of Canton on October 23, 1923. He avoided, for obvious reasons, the regular passenger vessels that stopped at the British colony of Hong Kong. Just recently, British immigration officers at ports around the world had been alerted to the coming of the troublemaker. When he landed, Borodin's suit, made of inexpensive material, looked more rumpled than usual, and his thick, dark walrus mustache drooped. His boat had nearly sunk in a typhoon near Formosa (Taiwan). A few hundred sheep had drowned. He had floated and survived. But even walking down the gangplank from the cheap cattle boat, Borodin had the presence of a royal envoy. He was not tall, about five feet ten, but he looked larger than life. His eyes were steady and direct. There was no trace of furtive business—illegal work, underground conspiracy, secret rendezvous— in his pale and distinguished face.

The welcome was not official. Eugene Chen met him. He took the Russian to see Sun Yatsen. Borodin had been briefed in Moscow and then in

Borodin, sent by Lenin in 1923 to be the Kuomintang's High Adviser, 1927.

Peking about the Chinese situation, but no briefing could have prepared him for what he encountered. He must have been shocked to learn that the president he had come to serve barely controlled the presidential residence, much less the city or the province, and that the government he had been appointed to work for was nonexistent. The Kuomintang he was supposed to develop was a political party in name only, more like a loosely organized conglomerate of bourgeois and feudal politicians. The "friendly" militarists, on whom Sun Yatsen depended, could turn against him at any minute. Their soldiers protected no one except the shopkeepers who paid protection money. The customs and salt tax were monopolized by the British, who kept the larger part of the collection for themselves and sent the rest to the warlord-controlled Peking government. Canton's local tax collectors, colluding with corrupt officials, diverted part of the money into their own wallets. Meanwhile, revenue was scanty, but expenses were huge. To keep the "friendly" militarists happy, Sun Yatsen handed out $26,000 (Chinese) every day.

To prevent the collapse of the tottering Canton government, Borodin had to act quickly, which was nearly impossible given the situation. He faced suspicion, misgivings, and resistance not only from the Right Kuomintang, but also from the Left Kuomintang (most were middle class), who had a constitutional fear of the Bolsheviks and the Chinese Communist Party. His Chinese Communist comrades resented his downgrading them and expecting them to play second fiddle to Sun Yatsen—in their eyes, an egocentric bourgeois. Sun himself, as the leader of the Kuomintang, had to be very cautious in his support of Borodin. Along with his middle-class supporters, both in China and abroad, he was not sure of the new Russian High Adviser's intention. Sun kept Borodin at arm's length and put Eugene in charge of daily interactions with him.

With everybody wondering, hesitating, and wavering inside Canton, the local warlord, Chen Jiongming, threatened to recapture Canton, which he said he had lost to the Bolsheviks. Not surprisingly, the northern warlords and the pro-British compradors inside Canton urged him onward. Borodin told Eugene there was no time to lose. To win the confidence of Sun, Borodin knew that he first had to gain Eugene's trust. He first tried by inviting Eugene to rallies and meetings, which started with his leading the Chinese participants into a remembrance of their past.

The memories were bitter. Many of them were members of various secret societies that had mushroomed during the lawless days before and after the fall of the Manchu Court. They were peasant lads who had come to the city for a better life. Ignorant, lost, frightened, they sought the brotherhood of secret societies, where they were trapped and exploited. As they recalled their pain, they wept. Weeping was like laughing. It was contagious. Soon throughout the room everyone would be seized with patriotic zeal and begin to cry. Then the Soviet instructors and their Chinese pupils advised the uninitiated to look for real brotherhood. This recruiting method was highly effective.

At the end, Borodin agitated them with his oratory. He told them that they were his comrades, and the bond between him and them was stronger than that of sworn brothers in secret societies and sometimes even than that of blood brothers. He further aroused them by paraphrasing the lyrics of the "Internationale." For centuries, Borodin started, the poor had put their hope in gods or saviors or kings and expected them to save them from their misery. That always ended in disappointment. They had to do it themselves, smashing the chains of the old world. Yes, they could do it, should they set their mind to it. They mustn't let their oppressors scoff at them as ignorant and worthless. They were not, for they would be the masters of a new world. This new world, however, wouldn't just come to them. They must strive for it. In fact, they were part of the last struggle that would end all struggles against man's inhumanity to man.

It was not Borodin the High Adviser, but the young boatman, drifting on the Divina River in Latvia, speaking of his dream of universal brotherhood. The faces of half-naked, sweaty, smelly coolies lit up and hardened with determination. Eugene was nearly moved to tears at the sight. He saw in these peasant lads his father as a youth.

Eugene reported to Sun Yatsen that as far as he knew, Borodin had not said anything that they themselves would not have said. So far, Borodin had not violated his agreement with the Kuomintang that the communists should do only propaganda work under the Kuomintang's authority and on behalf of the Kuomintang.

But Sun still hesitated to let Borodin arm his newly recruited rabble. What Borodin saw as revolutionary masses, most of the Kuomintang members saw as a mob. Borodin sought an audience with Sun Yatsen and hoped to convince him. Sun, a habitual exile, seemed interested only in one subject, his possible exile either in Moscow or Berlin. Maybe this was designed to dodge Borodin. While pondering what to do, Sun told Eugene to take care of the Russian.

Sun did not want the Russians to start a world revolution in Canton, Eugene stated to Borodin. Borodin did not counter. With a wry smile, he pointed at the night scene outside the window.

Gazing at the Pearl River, the two of them stood there for a moment lost in thought. From far off came the hum of machines from the colonialist gunboats. The palm grove below the Central Bank Building was almost invisible, lost in the shadows. Far to their right was the haze of light, a yellow aura over the city made from the thousands of lights of warships, and above, the answering twinkling lights of the stars in the ultramarine sky.

Eugene understood what Borodin meant to show him: that the Chinese revolution by itself was a world revolution; carrying it out would inevitably collide with the most powerful nations in the whole world.

What was left unsaid by Borodin made Eugene take another look at reality. He had hoped, as Sun Yatsen had, that the Chinese revolution could be modeled after the French and American ones. But time and again, the Chinese revolution had been aborted because the support from the middle classes was not enough. They were small in number and not as strong as their French and American counterparts had been. France was a major power in the Western world, and the French middle classes were in a position to decide their own fate in 1789. As for the American revolutionaries, they had only one English king to deal with, whereas the Chinese patriots had to confront a number of foreign overlords. The Chinese middle classes were under the thumbs of the colonialists. They desired independence, but they feared the cost of fighting for it. On the other hand, the peasants and laborers had nothing to lose but their lives, and many of them were tired of living on bended knees. *A great deal of power indeed*, Eugene mused, *lay in their vast population. It was imperative to organize them into a fighting force.*

Eugene accepted Borodin's argument, and he told Sun Yatsen so.

About a month after Borodin arrived in Canton, enemy troops besieged the city. The mercenary soldiers of the "friendly" militarists—paid to defend the city—had no intention of dying for Sun Yatsen or his cause. New defenses had to be organized immediately. Borodin renewed his plea for arming his ragtag followers. Sun Yatsen still avoided seeing him. Borodin was frustrated. Sun was the only man who could hold the United Front together, Borodin confided to Eugene; he, Borodin, could not betray Sun without betraying himself first.

Eugene told Sun that he was in favor of Borodin's proposals: not because he had no reservations about the Russian's motives, but simply because there was no choice. He argued that the Kuomintang had to defeat its enemies in the same way the Soviet Russians had defeated the military interventionists led by the British. It had to mobilize the revolutionary masses into a fighting force to take the place of a disloyal army. Failing that, the Kuomintang would lose Canton, their only foothold in China.

This was strong argument. Sun immediately called a small, highly confidential meeting with his two most trusted lieutenants, Eugene Chen and Liao Zhongkai, who from the very beginning had been a staunch supporter of the Russia-oriented policy.

Between Liao Zhongkai and Eugene there was a division of labor. Usually it was Eugene who did the troubleshooting when Sun had problems with the Russians, and it was Liao who mended fences with the Kuomintang dissidents.

Both Eugene and Liao chose fighting over retreat. Sun paused a minute and wrote a letter for Liao to read to the Central Executive Committee of the Kuomintang. In this letter, Sun warned Borodin that if he tried to take advantage of the situation to establish a Soviet base in Canton, Sun would not allow it. The message was neither a commitment nor a rebuke to Borodin. However, simultaneously Sun sent Eugene to deliver to Borodin, in private, another message: Borodin had his acquiescence in marshaling a fighting force.

Borodin, the Soviets who worked under him, and the Chinese communist cadres indoctrinated by them, roused their armed ragtag recruits—540 all together—with a desperate passion. They had to fight to the death, if necessary, to win a life. If they won, they and their families would have a brighter prospect. If they lost, they would not only lose their lives, but their parents' livelihood and the future of their children. For a Chinese man, there was nothing more worth fighting for than his family.

Borodin's new converts formed a network that even penetrated the troops of the currently "friendly" militarists. Quite a number of their soldiers and some of their officers joined forces with the motley collection of fearless warriors.

Eugene, waiting by the telephone in his office at the presidential residence, received conflicting reports. His anxiety grew, and his confidence diminished. He could not dismiss some information indicating that Borodin was taking advantage of the chaos and turning Canton bloody Red. Nor could he overlook the possibility that the seemingly "friendly" regional militarists, whose authority was being challenged by Borodin, might plot a coup d'état.

The soldiers of either faction might march on the presidential residence. Eugene and Madame Sun were helping Sun Yatsen hide important papers. When she went to Eugene's office, she found him carefully putting a box between the bathtub and the wall. Some important documents? She asked. No, just a few musical discs, recordings of the great operatic basso Feodor Chaliapin, that Borodin had loaned him, Eugene replied wistfully; he had a hunch that Borodin would remain an ally, and he wanted to keep the discs intact for their owner. Borodin, a calculating strategist, was not likely to do something rash to nip his China mission in the bud, Eugene explained matter-of-factly.

The turning point in the battle came as Eugene hoped. Borodin did not betray the Kuomintang, and his volunteer detachment fought bravely. They forced the "friendly" militarists to come to the realization that they would have no claim on the imminent victory if they did not get on board; so they did, in order to keep their grip on power and hard cash.

The enemy troops of General Chen Jiongming, unprepared for such a ferocious counterattack, backed off.

Eugene, when he went to Sun Yatsen's study to give the final confirmation of the victory, took Borodin's incredibly scratched discs of Chaliapin with him. Before he played them to celebrate the end of the battle, he gave Sun and his wife a compelling description of the story of *Boris Godunov*, so that when they strained they could really hear that glorious voice above the scratches, singing praises of those who fought for freedom.

★ 8 ★

THE MERGER OF THE KUOMINTANG AND THE COMMUNIST PARTY

In the first flush of victory, Sun Yatsen called Borodin—who had saved the day—his Lafayette. This anecdote was instigated by a group of American visitors. They disliked Jews as well as Bolsheviks and told Sun that Borodin was not a Jewish name. Did Sun know his High Adviser's real name? Sun answered with a smile that his real name was "Lafayette."

Sun's public affection for Borodin, however, did not correspond to his private evaluation. Borodin now had easier access to Sun, but not his ready ear. In fact, as the opening day of the planned First National Congress of the Kuomintang neared, Sun distanced himself from Borodin on the main issues. Like any skillful politician, Sun had mastered the art of elusiveness. Up to then, he had not made clear whether he would cooperate with the Bolshevik Party. He had had only a government-to-government agreement. But he could no longer dodge this tough question.

Sun knew the different factions would battle over each and every issue. Moscow wanted to steer the Kuomintang further left. The right-wingers of the Kuomintang decided that the Congress was their forum to denounce Borodin and the Chinese communists. The rest, from the center to the left, in different degrees, had some doubt about allying with Moscow, but were prepared to make concessions they could live with. It was not practical to ask the Russians to open their wallet without offering them something in return.

The Congress aimed at accomplishing two things: One, reorganize the Kuomintang into a political party not only of the middle classes and mandarins, but also of the peasants, laborers, and foot soldiers. And two, to ally with the Soviet Union, accept Chinese communists into the Kuomintang, and support the worker and peasant movements. The writing of the Declaration of the First National Congress of the Kuomintang was essential to its success. Sun Yatsen described it as the "spiritual life of the Congress," which had to reflect the spirit, principles, and political outline of the Kuomintang.

The Declaration was of course a collective work, summarizing the input of Kuomintang members across the board, the Chinese communists, and, last but not least, Borodin. Some from the right claimed it was drafted by Borodin in Russian and translated into Chinese for Sun Yatsen to rubber-stamp. But this was only a rumor; all the documents that Sun presented to the congress were definitely first written in English, and Borodin never wrote in English.

Although in public Sun never mentioned Eugene's role in drafting the English documents in order to shield his loyal aide from an attack from the right, they knew who had really wielded the pen. They leaked what they knew as insiders and started a smear campaign against Eugene, recapitulated by an English journalist, W. Sheldon Ridge, in an article, "One Who Knows Him [Eugene Chen]," published in the *Far Eastern Times* on the sixteenth of that month:

> Borodin was in Canton by this time [between 1923 and 1926], and the two men suited each other admirably. Eugene Chen could write and declaim and pour out as a flood all the grand and grandiose ideas that Borodin could merely formulate in cold blood. Since then, Borodin has been Canton's man of action, Eugene Chen his mouthpiece, trumpeter, prophet, indeed.... There is nothing placid in anything Chen writes. He fetches his stinging words and phrases from the whole range of the English polemical vocabulary.... Borodin, in these days, provides the ideas, and Chen clothes them in red-hot words.... it must have been a supremely subtle sense of irony that led him, when the time came for him to choose a Chinese name, to select the two characters transliterated "Yu-jen" for Chen Yu-jen, i.e. Eugene Chen, means Chen of the Friendly Benevolence that clothes in phrases of burning hatred the cold and calculated enmity of Borodin.[1]

And yet some people from the left made the same claim for a different purpose. They wanted to give all the credit to Borodin and the Chinese communists. But Sun Yatsen was not an idiot, and he knew that the Declaration was too important a document to leave to Borodin and his Chinese comrades. The drafting had to be entrusted to a Chinese and a Kuomintang member who had a mastery of the English language. Sun asked Eugene to pen it in English so that both Sun and Borodin could read it, and each could argue for his point directly. When the draft was finalized, Sun would give it to a translation team headed by Liao Zhongkai, a leading left-winger who was Eugene's closest colleague in supporting the Russia-oriented policy. Then the Chinese version was edited by Wang Jingwei, a centrist.

The Declaration consisted of three parts. The first part was about the current situation of China; the third part concerned foreign and domestic policies. The second part was the most important, the revised *Three Principles of the People*, of which Borodin found the Principle of the People's Livelihood most controversial. Sun, with Eugene's help, had in 1921 started revising and translating into English this huge document, which blended Confucius, Lincoln, and Marx, more than two years before Borodin came to China.

There was another reason why Sun gave this extremely important task to Eugene. While drafting the Declaration, Sun kept two other documents for possible substitution. These spare documents, written in English, basically comprised two parts. One was *The International Development of China*, which Eugene had helped Sun write in 1920–1921. This stated positively Sun's intention to "make capitalism create socialism" in China, meaning using money from trading and joint ventures with foreign capitalists to build socialism. The other, *The Organization of Nationalist Government*, evolved from the combined reading and interpretation by Sun Yatsen and Eugene Chen of the French philosopher Montesquieu.[2] Eugene had been a scholar of the French Enlightenment since his youth, and Montesquieu was one of his idols. Sun Yatsen was a fan of the Constitution of the United States of America, the classic example of the application of Montesquieu's theory.

The Chinese constitution in the making, Sun declared, would assure the division of powers as in the Constitution of the United States, but instead of a three-branch system, there would be five: executive, legislative, judicial, and two more: the Department of Examination and the Department of Censors. The two additional branches had their origins in China's past. The Department of Examination was a modernization of the Imperial Examination of the past dynasties. The censors had been appointed by the emperors and now would be assigned by the president. They were supposed to be men of great moral strength, like their dynastic predecessors, who dared to speak their mind and to criticize and impeach any misbehaving officials, including the president. Another blend of Chinese and Western political theories.

While these two spare documents indicated that the Kuomintang's ultimate goal was to build China into a constitutional democracy, the Declaration of the Congress sounded more militant. Sun Yatsen wanted Eugene to help him draft the three contradictory documents simultaneously, because he kept revising them to complement one another. Sun was not sure which one he would use to open the congress until the last minute. His final decision would depend a great deal on the result of yet another task he had deputed Eugene to tackle: Eugene was carrying on negotiations with Britain on the question of the Customs revenue.

The British had controlled the Chinese Customs Service after 1901, the year they and seven other foreign powers—Germany, Czarist Russia, the United States, France, Japan, Austria, and Italy—had crushed the peasant-led Boxer Rebellion. That was armed intervention, but they demanded that the Chinese use the Customs revenue to pay them indemnities, and what was left, called the Customs surplus, was channeled to the Peking government, which the colonial powers recognized as the de facto central government. This situation was considered unjust by the Canton government in the south, since the funds collected in its sphere went to strengthen the rival Peking government. The Kuomintang government at Canton wanted its share of the Customs surplus.

The British inspector general of the Customs Service, Sir Francis Aglen, rejected this proposal. Sun made as if to take back the Customs Service by force. The foreign consulates at Shameen, the island concession in the heart of Canton, immediately rushed into action. They deployed more than twenty gunboats, including four British, four American, three Japanese, and two French, along the rivers of the city of Canton and the province of Guangdong.

While both sides posed tough in public, they quietly tried to seek a compromise. The American minister to China, Jacob Gould Schurman, came forward to encourage the Canton government to talk with the Hong Kong governor, Sir Reginald Stubbs, who hinted at his willingness to mediate.

Sun thought the advice feasible. There had been unrest among the working class in Hong Kong. It was an international port, and the seamen had brought new, democratic ideas home before there was a Communist Party. In 1917, the Kuomintang had founded the Canton Mechanics Union. It operated beyond Canton into the British colony. The Hong Kong government knew that to stabilize Hong Kong, they must stabilize their relationship with the government in the neighboring city of Canton.

Sun Yatsen dispatched Eugene to Hong Kong to meet with the governor.[3] Eugene received a polite reception. Stubbs invited him to take tea before they started the official negotiation. During the exchange of pleasant preliminaries, Eugene prudently reminded the Englishman that Hong Kong's relationship with Canton was not confined to trading. Hong Kong, an enormous piece of rock surrounded by the salty seawater, depended on Canton for its supply of food, water, and manpower. Ninety-nine percent of Hong Kong's population was Cantonese, and they were the creators and preservers of this Crown Jewel in the Far East. It was mutually beneficial for Canton and Hong Kong to live in harmony and prosperity.

The Hong Kong governor jovially concurred. Canton was closer to Hong Kong than Peking and naturally required more of his attention. It was expedient for the Hong Kong governor to mediate between the Canton government and the British Legation at Peking. The Canton government could hope to get some of the Customs surplus from the revenue collected at Canton, the governor promised.[4]

With that potential source of cash, the Canton government would depend less on Soviet aid and be less susceptible to Russian arm-twisting. Consequently, the Declaration that Eugene was drafting should be less jarring to the capitalists' ears. Sun Yatsen even considered the possibility of withdrawing the Declaration altogether, should Britain demonstrate more goodwill than the Kuomintang expected.

Eugene's office in the presidential residence became what he jokingly called a sort of miniature debating society. Sometimes Sun sought his opinions, and sometimes Borodin took issue with him. Eugene was not shy about expressing his views. He believed that real consensus could be reached only after debate. He actually throve on debate, as he was intellectually curious.

What Sun Yatsen and Borodin differed on most vehemently was the new policy regarding the peasantry. Borodin, on instructions from Moscow, wanted a wholesale land revolution, confiscating the land from landowners and redistributing it among the poor peasants. Sun would not hear of it. A wholesale land revolution would break the backbone of the Kuomintang—the generals, officers, civil servants, merchants, mandarins, and overseas Chinese. They were nearly all landowners, big or small. It was only fair that the Declaration should be phrased in a way that would not cause them concern, Eugene argued with Borodin. When the argument grew heated, Eugene told the Soviet High Adviser that the vast majority of Chinese landowners were hardworking people who had nothing in common with the aristocratic landowners in Czarist Russia. A revolution was like an avalanche, Borodin retorted: it did not spare hardworking people in its way.

"Well said, but our revolution is not a Bolshevik revolution," Eugene asserted. "We are determined to cause as few casualties as possible."

Debate after debate resulted in no consensus. At last, Sun said in agitation that he would make a decision about the question of land after he consulted with the peasants. Borodin was mystified. He did not understand what Sun meant. Eugene, who had been closeted with Sun, puzzled it out for the Russian High Adviser by suggesting that he should talk with a peasant too. Eugene had one in mind. The young peasant was Mao Zedong, who was reputed to know more about the peasantry than anybody else in his own party or in the Kuomintang. Mao Zedong as an individual communist had joined the Kuomintang at that time.

Mao was a peasant and a self-educated intellectual. He had a famously intractable temper, but in his humble days he kept it in check and displayed a pliancy that charmed quite a few Kuomintang leaders and his Comintern boss, Maring. Maring, who had helped found the Chinese Communist Party in 1921, warned his Chinese comrades that the two-year-old Party should not wean itself from its wet nurse, the Kuomintang. He stressed the fact that the Party had to work and get strong through the Kuomintang. Not everyone agreed, but Mao Zedong did. He parroted his boss and pointed out that in China the working class was not only small in number, but also low in political consciousness. Their main concern was to get a pay raise, and it would take some time to educate them and make them understand the significance of joining the political struggle. The middle class, on the other hand, was politically active. Therefore, the Kuomintang, whose backbone was middle class, had a bright prospect. Moreover, Mao went on, the Kuomintang had a strong base in Canton, for they had mobilized and recruited the local peasants into their army. Mao's speech corroborated Sun Yatsen's claim that the Kuomintang was the recognized leader of the peasant movement.

It was noticed that whenever Maring rebuked his Chinese opponents, he quoted Mao. He got Mao, whose claim as a founding member of his party was questioned by his peers, elected to the Central Committee of the Communist Party. Maring was loud in his praise for Mao's pragmatism. Eugene was not a stranger to it. When Sun needed a peasant to speak out for the Kuomintang, Mao was the first one who came to mind.

Borodin brought Mao into a communist-only meeting. Mao had second-guessed Borodin's inclination for reaching a compromise with the Kuomintang and spoke against broaching the question of land revolution in the Declaration. Mao argued that because their "Party is not yet strong and has little influence with the masses, the time has not yet come to publish the anti-big-landowners slogans."[5] Experience had told the Party that such slogans would meet with stiff resistance from the Kuomintang officials and their allies, the merchants. Mao was certain that due to the peasants' lack of class-consciousness, they would not join the struggle for land.

Mao won the debate, which enabled Borodin to report to Moscow that he had the support of his Chinese comrades. As a follow-up, Borodin took Mao to see Eugene.

Mao was lanky, his chest hollow and his shoulders slightly stooped. He was not tidy in appearance, and he could have used a haircut. Sitting beside the always very well-groomed Eugene, Mao was ill at ease. Before he spoke, he looked at Borodin as if asking for permission. It seemed to Eugene that Borodin had rehearsed the young man. That was in the beginning. As soon as Mao warmed up to a subject, his confidence returned, and he gesticulated with his expressive hands with long, slender fingers, the hands of a peasant-turned-intellectual who hadn't done menial work for quite a while.

Mao cited an example of the peasant movement around and close to Canton. The Canton experiment was the role model. There was no use talking about Marxism or imperialism to the peasants. All these "isms" sounded too strange, too incomprehensible, and too removed. When they could not think why a peasant should join the Kuomintang army, it was explained to them in folksy terms that they could understand. There is a folktale that illustrates the point perfectly. It goes like this: A patriarch, who knows he does not have much time left, calls his sons, grandsons, and great-grandsons to his side. On the table beside his sickbed is placed a bunch of bamboo chopsticks. He picks one and breaks it easily. He picks a couple and breaks them less easily. He picks up the whole bunch, and he is not able to break a single one of them. That is the strength of unity. The listening peasants nodded their heads, but then asked what they needed the unity for. They would soon answer this question themselves.

Eugene was one of the first to appreciate Mao's talent for translating an idea into plain words. Pleased, he put in a good word for Mao when he relayed the conversation to Sun Yatsen. A few weeks later, Mao, gliding over the heads of his communist comrades higher in the Party hierarchy, was elected a candidate member to the Central Committee of the Kuomintang.

Getting around this sticky question—the land revolution—did not leave Eugene in peace to do his job. There was an assault from the right to ward off. He tried to be as objective as he could. Eugene's empathy lay with the peasantry, but it was not unmixed with political expediency. The peasants did play a luminous role in the Chinese revolution, Eugene acknowledged; but the Kuomintang was the leading light of the revolution, and the peasantry would only glow by reflection. While elevating the status of the peasants, Eugene avoided bringing up the redistribution of land, or even tax and rent reduction. To the landowners, Eugene assured, giving land to the tiller was an indigenous goal that for several thousand years the dynastic governments had set but never seriously intended to strive for. It could not be labeled a Bolshevik invention. The peasants would get their fair share of land, Eugene suggested, when the Kuomintang government had the cash to help them buy it from the landowners. The promise would be long coming, as the government could hardly pay for its own overhead.

However, Eugene still met with thunders of anger from the right-wingers. They wanted Borodin out and the Chinese communists to follow. Although the centrists and many Kuomintang leftists did not think they would go to that length at the moment, they too raised eyebrows at the draft. Never in Chinese history had peasants been brought into such prominence. They were menial laborers, fit only to be ruled, according to the Confucian teachings that had dominated Chinese thinking for nearly twenty-five hundred years. To ask the elite members of the Kuomintang to accept the illiterate peasants as their equals was as unimaginable as asking the founding fathers of the American republic to accept the black slaves as their equals. Could they have ever agreed to revise the most famous line in the Declaration of Independence to say: "All men are created equal, including our slaves"?

As the opening of the congress neared, a menacing rumor surfaced. The diehards found it unwise to directly attack their longstanding leader, Sun Yatsen, whom they had regrettably semi-deified and in whose hands they had placed unlimited power at a different time, when they had wanted him to use it for their benefit. So, instead of attacking him, they assailed his close aides. Their first targets were, of course, Eugene Chen and Borodin. Eugene Chen was an upstart who, they raved, had wormed his way into Sun's innermost circle within six short years. Borodin was the evil mastermind who provided ideas for the other one to translate into written words. The unlimited power that Sun held was endorsed by the Kuomintang constitution, and it was now exercised by the duo behind the throne, the diehards warned.

No sooner had that rumor been bandied about than another one began to circulate: Eugene Chen was not Chinese; his mother was a French Creole slut. Eugene had a warm, dark complexion like a Cantonese's, and that, they decried contemptuously, exposed him as a bastard of mixed blood and African slave origin. Eugene did not openly challenge them, because he thought it was more important to guard and protect the privacy of his family. Grandfather Chen had had a natural daughter from a French Creole woman. The rumormongers in both Trinidad and China intentionally confused Eugene's parentage with his half-sister's.

The right-wingers were intent on scaring people into a frenzy of nationalism: China's fate had fallen into the hands of a sinister Russian Bolshevik and a toady of a half-foreign devil! The rumor played on a long-standing fear of the Chinese people, who had been invaded and pillaged time and again by the barbarian foreigners from the northern border and from the sea.

Eugene, usually unflinching, did a great deal of soul-searching. He was made to look like a liability to Sun Yatsen. He was not a quitter, but hanging on seemed self-serving, as though all he cared for was his own career. He toyed with the idea of retreating; but where to and how far? Alone in his office, he felt oppressed in a closed room, and he went to the balcony. He let his eyes wander over the moving fronds of trees. The houses in the Eastern Hill were of modern Western style. Beyond was an expanse of field and a small village with cobbled streets and houses of bricks and wood and gray tiles. It was said that more than a millennium ago, this village had been the metropolis for a proud kingdom. Now it was famous only for the size of its chicken eggs. In Canton, there were new buildings, but the backdrop, the environment in which they were set, was age-old. Here Eugene was constantly reminded of the shortness of life and of the timelessness of history. At no other time had he felt the weight of the responsibility he had taken on and such an urgency to fulfill his destiny.

Eugene withstood the attacks and finished the Declaration, but he was hurt silently by the racial snipe. The long separation from his family troubled his wife deeply. Her recent letter had given vague hints at a health problem. There was a note of urgency in her suggestion to bring their three younger, unmarried children to reunite with him in Canton. But how could he let them come into an environment not only politically precarious but also racially discriminating? The thought troubled him.

The First National Congress of the Kuomintang opened on January 20, 1924, and ended ten days later. The first documents to be passed were the Declaration and its attachment, the Outline of Reconstruction. These documents left an indelible stamp on Chinese history and influenced the Chinese Communist Party's policies for years. It put what traditionally had been described as rabble on the political map and released a force unseen before in China. It deserves a reading.

We should like to say this to the farmers:

China has been and still is an agricultural nation, and of all the classes of people, the agricultural class has suffered the most from economic exploitation. According to our Doctrine of Livelihood, the state will provide land for cultivation to those farmers who have been deprived of their land or to those who have suffered from their landlords.

It is the earnest hope of the Party (Kuomintang) that everything be done to restore normal happiness to the farmers.

To the workers, the Kuomintang has also a special message.

For centuries, the Chinese government has not done anything to ensure the livelihood of the working class. According to our principles, the state should help the unemployed and pass laws to improve the conditions of the laborers. Systems for the relief of the aged, for the care of children, for providing pensions for the disabled, and for providing education for the mass of the people will also be attended to by the Party (Kuomintang) in order to better the conditions of the less fortunate classes.

Throughout the length and breadth of China, there is no place where we cannot find destitute farmers and exploited workers. Because their conditions are so difficult, their desire for emancipation is correspondingly great. So the laborers and farmers may be counted among those who will most strongly oppose imperialism, and who will help in our work toward a national revolution. On the one hand, the people's revolution can achieve victory only when the farmers and laborers of the country give it their whole-hearted support. On the other hand, the Kuomintang will do its best to help peasant and labor movements in order to strengthen the people's revolution.[6]

Admittedly these documents were a rather confusing blend of contrary ideologies. The confusion reflected Sun Yatsen's—as well as Eugene's—constantly evolving philosophy about a vast, immensely difficult revolution. Confusion was inevitable with a nation, vast in size and population, that was emerging from more than four thousand years of feudal dynastic rule and was forced instantly by the complication of circumstances to leap into semi-socialism.

Eugene would have been very gratified had he known that what was then regarded as a muddleheaded fantasy—the Chinese version of socialism with limited capitalism—would become the precedent, sixty years later, for a revolution of "socialism with Chinese characteristics" by a quarter of the world's humankind in an independent China.

★ 9 ★

FROM DRAWING ROOM
TO FIRING WALL

For all Eugene's work in promoting the United Front, Sun Yatsen, under pressure from the right-wingers, hesitated to reward him with a more substantial position than what he had in the ministry of hot air (the air force, with a grand total of three shabby planes). Eugene said that he understood and, in any case, it was an honor to serve the revolution. When his opponents heard of this exchange, they snorted cynically. Eugene Chen, they said, deposited the small award in his savings account to earn big interest, which he would collect later.

Eugene found sympathy in Madame Sun, Soong Chingling, who was attacked by the same people. All through Sun Yatsen's Russia-oriented years, she had been supportive of Eugene. When the conservatives opposed Sun's policies, they attacked her personally. They questioned her marital status, which was, to her chagrin, dubious. Sun had already had a wife when he married Chingling. It was not unusual for men at that time to acquire a second or third or fourth wife. But in Sun's case it was different.

Both Sun and Chingling were Christians. Their union openly violated the Sixth Commandment and scandalized their churches, the Kuomintang, and traditional society. They denied her status as Sun's spouse, since Sun had not legally divorced his first wife and Chingling did not have a legal marriage certificate. The only proof Chingling had of her marriage was a piece of paper signed by the bride, the bridegroom, and two friends as witnesses. Worse still, both her church and Sun's refused to give them their blessing. That was tantamount to condemning them for living in sin. That was a terrible blow to her father, a revered Methodist minister, and also to her devout mother. By some accounts, Charlie Soong's sudden death at age fifty-two was partly caused by the scandal.

Some conservatives even criticized the shape of Chingling's face. She was good-looking, but her face, with its prominent cheekbones and strong jaw, was not exactly the desirable oval shape. A woman with a face like hers, according to Chinese superstitions, would send her husband to an early grave. And Sun Yatsen's visibly declining health somehow validated the accusation.

Chingling and Eugene had become close since the formulation of the Russia-oriented policy. She took him into her family, and her siblings accepted him as one of their own. Their home became Eugene's substitute family. At that time, Chingling's siblings did not seem to have a problem with the Russia-oriented policy. They all knew that Russia was the only country that supported Sun Yatsen's call for China's reunification.

Ailing Soong was the oldest, and the first of three sisters to have enrolled in Wesleyan College of Georgia. When Chingling followed in her footsteps and finished her American education in 1913, Mayling transferred from Wesleyan to Wellesley College to be close to her brother, T. V. Soong, who was studying at Harvard, and in 1917 both graduated and came home. The three sisters were from the same stock but very different in character and looks, and this was most noticeable when they were together. Ailing was the least attractive. She was rather casual in appearance. Her loose-fitting Chinese sheath wrapped around her like a sack. From her neck up, she had a long face like a horse's. From her neck down, she looked like a moneybag, bulging here and there. She was married to Kong Xiangxi, a banker and the future minister of finance. His wife addressed him as Daddy to remind their children to speak English like Americans, thus his nickname, "Daddy Kong," stuck.

Mayling, the least known, became famous years later as the fourth Madame Chiang Kaishek. Mayling, in her late twenties at that time, was more vivacious than pretty. She wore rather heavy makeup, unusual for a young unmarried woman in those days. To give her American English a finishing touch, she playfully followed Ailing's children in welcoming "Uncle Eugene" into their family circle and diligently practiced her faultless enunciation with him. Intellectually, she was more inquisitive than her two older sisters. When she said that she liked to read books that were more than love stories, Eugene suggested George Eliot's *Middlemarch* and Elizabeth Gaskell's *Mary Barton*, as he presumed that she might prefer woman writers. No, she said, she was not finicky. She wanted to know which works, men's or women's, Eugene liked most.

Eugene suggested that she read the political novels written by Benjamin Disraeli and Anthony Trollope, although he thought George Eliot was a much better artist. From the fact that the female author had to assume a man's name in order to be published or read, Mayling wondered when China, at

The Soong sisters in the early 1940s. From left to right: Mayling, Ailing, and Chingling.

least a century behind England in most things, would lift the restriction on women's activities.

Knowing that Mayling was interested in politics, Eugene assured her that China was at the threshold of a new era. Things which had never been done before were being done. Mayling was pleased with his exultation, and was often found engrossed in conversation with Eugene.

Both the oldest and the youngest sisters lacked the intrinsic quality that gave Chingling grace. It came from within. No amount of makeup could give Mayling the kind of refinement that Chingling naturally possessed.

Their brother, T. V. Soong, was a Harvard-trained economist. He had a round face and wore spectacles with round lenses that made him look like an owl. He did not talk much around his sisters, perhaps because he was intimidated by their strong wills or because he was a gentleman who preferred to take a back seat to the ladies. He was not a revolutionary and had no penchant for radical politics. When he first returned to China, he worked in the office of the gigantic Han-Ye-Ping Conglomerate, which owned coal mines, iron mines, and the largest and oldest steel mills in China. T. V. fell in love with his boss's favorite daughter. But when her father, Sheng Xuan-huai, heard about the courtship, he put an abrupt stop to it. The Soong family, by the Shanghai standards of the time, was only comfortable and so T. V. was no financial match for Miss Sheng, who was later married with a dowry that became Shanghai legend.

Lovesick, T. V. went to Canton in October 1923 to forget his woes. He was Chingling's favorite sibling; on her recommendation, her husband, Sun Yatsen, gave him the task of straightening out Canton's financial mess.

Ailing often gave parties to entertain high-ranking Kuomintang officials. Her house was in the Eastern Hills, where there were a number of foreign pavilions, as the locals called them. Ailing's was the former residence of the chief executive of Standard Oil, and it was one of the best. It was within walking distance of Eugene's cottage. From afar, he could glimpse the corner of Ailing's house, gleaming white in a haze of red, gold, pink, blue, and purple flowers and tall green trees.

Eugene always arrived earlier than the other guests and joined Ailing's siblings in warming up the atmosphere for the reception. In the early evening, guests started to come. Ailing, house-proud, would look over at her heavy-eyed, stodgy husband and ask Eugene to take them on a house tour. It was an apparent snub at the host, although Daddy Kong was blessedly unperturbed and took a back seat without complaint. The intimate tone in which Madame Kong spoke to Eugene did not escape the notice of her guests. That impressed the young general, Chiang Kaishek, who was about thirty-eight years old in 1924. He admired Eugene's erudition and was a little envious of Eugene's engaging repartee with the Soongs in a language he himself lacked.

Chiang had intelligent, keen eyes; but his small, rather long, and prematurely balding head somehow seemed to epitomize his stubborn, narrow character. His detractors questioned his sincerity and looked askance at him as a soldier of fortune. There was very little in his background that buttressed his claim to be a left-winger. He was the son of a small salt trader in the town of Xikou in Zhejiang Province. His father had died when Kaishek was little. His mother had a hard time bringing him up, and they became very attached to each other. He made the decision at age fifteen to become a soldier and enrolled in the Baoding Military School in the north. Four years later, he went to Japan and enlisted in another military school. When he finished his training, he enlisted in the Kuomintang army and skirmished with the warlord forces around Shanghai. With few military feats to boast of, Chiang fell on hard times after he was demobilized. He became a masterless samurai and drifted into Shanghai's stock market. In the summer of 1922, he was broke when Sun Yatsen summoned him, after Sun, also a broke man, had been driven temporarily from the city onto the boat *Yongfeng* by the

Cantonese militarist Chen Jiongming. Chiang responded quickly and stayed at Sun's side throughout the ordeal on the sea, which earned him Sun's gratitude. In 1923, Sun returned to Canton and dispatched Chiang to the Soviet Union to study the Russian military system; during his brief stay there, Chiang reinvented himself as a left-winger.

Still, Chiang Kaishek was a better choice than his competitors for the top job in the Whampoa Military Academy, newly established in mid-1924 with Russian assistance. Chiang's military career started in the Kuomintang army; their past was a different story. Before they joined forces with Sun Yatsen, they either were warlords or served under warlords. Chiang was younger, more open to new ideas. At the moment, he desperately wanted to hold on to his new post, commandant of the military academy, for he knew that the commandant would be in a pivotal position to seize control of the future revolutionary army. He had sought long and hard for the friendship of the powerful Soong clan, who were closely related to the supreme leader, Sun Yatsen. Chiang made every effort to enchant Ailing into pulling strings for him.

Chiang also worked his charm on Eugene because of the latter's special friendship with Sun and the Soong clan. He sought Eugene's opinions on historical and current events, with T. V. interpreting for them. Their discussions, more often than not, revolved around the Declaration of the First National Congress of the Kuomintang. Eugene revealed that when he took part in drafting it, he had the English parliamentary system in mind. The English Parliament was a multiparty establishment; the Kuomintang comprised two parties—the Nationalists and the Communists. Whichever served the people better would grow stronger. That was what Sun Yatsen meant when he explained the policy of merging the Nationalist and Communist Parties.

In Chiang's training, there was an obvious lack of knowledge about the West, and at that stage of his life he was humble enough to learn from Eugene. Chiang was one of the very few top Kuomintang generals who read books on the French and Russian revolutions, which Eugene recommended to him. He, of course, hoped to make himself agreeable to Sun Yatsen. However, it should be noted that self-improvement was Chiang's other goal. Sun quoted the American Revolution too, but Chiang was quite indifferent to it.

On Eugene's part, like Sun Yatsen and Borodin, he had reservations about Chiang's display of revolutionary fervor. However, they thought Chiang had the kind of stuff that a near-great general was made of, if they could keep him on track. In mid-1924, they doubled their efforts to do so, for a civil war seemed imminent.

The Kuomintang's left-leaning policies shocked medieval Canton. Canton was a port city, and the merchant princes were powerful. They had close ties to the British, and lived and behaved like robber barons. In their factories, a worker earned less than thirty cents (Chinese) for a straight, uninterrupted sixteen-hour workday without a lunch break. An apprentice, who worked without compensation in their shops, waited on the master or the mistress twenty-four hours a day, slept on the floor in the shop, and could be awakened at any minute.

When the Soviet Russians appeared on the streets of the city, these merchant princes felt troubled. They had heard horror stories from the White Russians who had swarmed over Siberia into China's port cities after the Bolshevik Revolution. Now the Red Russians were here to spill their blood. The increasing instigation by the demagogues, the mounting agitation among their employees, the accelerating momentum for unionizing the workers and peasants, and, scariest of all, the swift development of a new Kuomintang army trained in Soviet Russian military tactics threatened their safety. Knowing that they had to act before it was too late, the merchant princes formed an armed resistance, with the blessing of the British colonialists.

Secretly, the British had decided on a proxy war. They would provide weapons, and the rich members of the Canton Chamber of Commerce, their protégés, would do the real fighting. At the end of 1923, the number of the Merchants' Volunteers, organized and funded by the Canton Chamber of Commerce, reached twelve thousand inside the city and fifty thousand in the whole of Guangdong Province. The leader of the Canton Chamber of Commerce was Chen Lianbo, a comprador of the British-owned Hong Kong and Shanghai Bank. He had invested in factories, banks, shops, brothels, gambling houses, and opium dens. His financial empire extended beyond the Chinese border into territories around the Pacific Rim and the Chinese communities in Europe and America. He was more dangerous than the other merchant princes because of his greater wealth and greater ambition. When the British assured him that they would support a Merchants' government if he rallied the Canton merchants into opposing the Kuomintang, Chen Lianbo could not resist the temptation of becoming the prince of the princes.

The mutual hostility first led to a skirmish. In June 1924, when a group of French residents held a banquet at Shameen Concession in honor of the visiting French governor of Annam (Vietnam), an Annamese revolutionary threw a bomb into the dining room. It missed the governor, but killed two lesser Frenchmen and wounded six. The British immediately suspected Chinese entanglement in the attempted assassination. Their spies informed them that Ho Chi Minh was often seen in Borodin's house, and others studied at the Whampoa Military Academy.

It was not clear whether Borodin chose this moment to stir up the hornets' nest, but his frequent meetings with the Annamese revolutionaries made him suspect. The Canton government could be thrown over the edge by such an international incident. Sun Yatsen feared that it was a Soviet ploy to sow more dissension in his relations with the Western powers.

The hostility escalated. The British demanded that Canton deport all dangerous aliens, obviously a swipe at the Soviet Russians, and simultaneously proclaimed a New Police Law that no Chinese could enter Shameen without an ID card issued by the concession authority. This proclamation so infuriated the usually obedient employees of the colonialists, including the police, that the unbelievable happened: they walked off their jobs. The British brought in the marines to oversee water and electricity, but the machines came to a gasping halt. The British marines had apparently inadvertently damaged the machines with their unprofessional hands. But the colonialists had no doubt that underground unionists, who had remained on the job, had sabotaged the machinery. Shameen was sinking in a dark sea of animosity.

The marines jumped the gun and aimed their cannons at Sun's presidential house. Sun sent Eugene to quiet the jittery residents of Shameen Concession.[1] The British indeed were afraid that the Kuomintang might repossess the concession without giving any notice. Their consul general at Canton, Giles Bertram, seething with anger, was in no mood to be pacified. Eugene chose to be forthright with him. He admitted frankly that he saw the concession as a problem, one that would not be resolved any time soon. It would help if each party took a step back and put the conflict in its historical perspective.

When China started trading extensively with foreign businessmen, mostly British, in the eighteenth century, it found its judicial system inadequate to cope with modern ways. China and the West had sharply different conceptions of the function of law and the place of the individual in society. In China, the basic unit of society was not the individual but the collective. If a man was alleged to have committed a crime, more often than not he would be brought to his group leader—the patriarch of his clan or the head of his guild. There, he would put his life in the group leader's hands and be forced to accept whatever judgment was passed on him. Torture was often used to extract a confession of guilt. Without commercial law and without the law protecting private property and without proper criminal procedures, the Western merchants had to submit to the pronouncements of the Manchu Court. A few blond heads had been chopped off.

After China's defeat in the Opium War, the British demanded that their traders live in specified places, which the Chinese called concessions, and be granted extraterritorial rights to manage their own affairs. As China grew weaker, the foreigners became more abusive. Over all those years, China's relations with Britain and other foreign powers were in such a tangle that it needed men trained in modern law to unravel them.

The British consul general listened with a faintly cynical grin, all his colonialist instincts contradicting what he was hearing.

Eugene pretended not to see the Englishman's negative reaction and continued: "I have repeatedly explained our government policy about the concessions and reassured your government that the future transition would be orderly and peaceful. Furthermore, the future Chinese administrators in the repossessed concessions will seek British cooperation in modernizing the justice system. This harks back to what I wrote in 1919, when I was a delegate to the Paris Peace Conference. This is the policy of our government, and no one should violate it."

Giles Bertram began to feel amused by Eugene's wishful thinking. Britain, the pillar of the civilized world, would never give in to the demands of an obscure quasi-government. Nevertheless, Eugene's speech lightened his day of stress. He agreed to rescind the New Police Law, so as to play for time for a plot that would end the reign of the Canton government once and for all.

Chen Lianbo, Giles Bertram's co-plotter, passed a resolution to launch the revolt on August 14, 1924. But the Kuomintang foiled their plan five days before it was put into effect. Chiang Kaishek and his Whampoa cadets, under the order of Sun Yatsen, impounded a Norwegian freighter loaded with more than nine thousand eight hundred rifles, pistols, and revolvers, and more than three million bullets. The Canton Chamber of Commerce had bought the ammunition through the British-owned Hong Kong and Shanghai Bank from a German-owned company.

The Kuomintang confronted the British consul general with evidence that implicated Britain in an armed insurrection aimed at destroying the Canton government, with which he was supposed to keep normal relations. Bertram retorted that the British government could not stop private companies from making business deals with the Canton Chamber of Commerce. Then with haughty candor, the consul general said more arms would arrive.

Bolstered by the British, the Canton Chamber of Commerce staged a protest and ordered the closure of all shops. The left-wing Kuomintang and Borodin urged Sun Yatsen to declare martial law and seize the properties of Chen Lianbo and his leading accomplices. Scared, many smaller shopkeepers quickly responded to the government's demand to re-open their businesses. Enraged by their desertion, the British consul general dispatched an ultimatum to Sun Yatsen, warning him of possible naval intervention if the Kuomintang government began an attack on the merchants still on strike.

The British verbal assault had the expected effect on the divided Kuomintang. The right-wingers, including the regional militarists, had been in covert dealings with the Canton merchant princes. They shared at least one agenda: to turn back the clock and to nip the Russia-oriented policy in its infancy.

Chiang Kaishek, to his credit, acted with courage and determination. He gave his vote to Eugene and Liao Zhongkai, who chose to fight back. Chiang also had a personal reason to tame the right-wingers. He was then recognized as a left-winger and a rival to those right-wing militarists. They feared his growing strength, and he hated begging them for money to run the academy. These militarists tied him hand and foot with the purse strings they held, for it was they, not the minister of finance—nor the governor of Guangdong nor the mayor of Canton—who determined the tax rates, collected the taxes, and kept the revenue. A great part of the revenue they collected was from the merchants who were dominated by the leaders of the Chamber of Commerce. Money and profit bound these right-wing militarists tighter to the merchant princes than to their supreme leader, Sun Yatsen.

In one conference, Sun meant to reconcile disputes with the leaders of the Chamber of Commerce who demanded to get back the confiscated weapons and to declare their private army lawful. At Sun's objection, the right-wing General Liao Xingzhou leaped up and harangued wildly. "The situation inside the city [Canton] is fraught with danger and can explode at any minute.... I want an answer to resolve the problems [on the terms of the merchant princes present at the meeting] within two or three days, otherwise I'll overrule the order from above and withdraw my soldiers from the front and deploy them inside the city. For security reasons I'll hit hard any troops, no matter who commands them, that disturb the markets or harass the inhabitants in the West Gate district."[2]

Sun's face paled, as he came to the painful realization that he was under siege and that the men who were laying siege to him were his own subordinates. With two formidable enemies, the British colonialists and the leaders of the Canton Chamber of Commerce, attacking from outside and opponents attacking from within, Canton would fall. Despite the fact that the general spit in his face, Sun said nothing in rebuke; but immediately after the meeting, he asked his wife, Chingling, to quietly fetch Eugene.

Sun sat in a rocking chair in the study with a light blanket wrapped around his knees and legs, in spite of the hot weather. As he dropped the mask he wore for the public, he looked poorly.

Eugene hazarded a guess: "Should we prepare for the worst?"

Scowling wearily, Sun confided to Eugene that he had lost confidence in defending Canton. He would take part of the revolutionary army with him and fight his way northward, trying to find new allies in "friendly militarists" along the road.

Listening to that hacking cough, Eugene's scalp prickled with apprehension. Could Sun's declining health be affecting his mental state, as rumor had it? Could Sun get so used to being chased into exile that he would automatically take the escape route? A great sadness overcame Eugene and plunged him into deep reflection.

He had joined Sun in 1917, when Sun had received an invitation to Canton from a group of warlords of the southwestern provinces who then controlled the city. Sun had been out of office for five years, since he had resigned from the presidency, and had no immediate prospect of returning to power. Under such dire circumstances, he accepted the not-so-sweet deal. They conferred on him the empty title "generalissimo" without giving him any military authority. Sun was not unaware of their motivation. They wanted his prestige to form a credible government to profit only themselves.

The southwestern warlords, like their northern counterparts, were also adroit at playing the game of musical chairs. They were alternately friendly and unfriendly to Sun. Sun had been "in" and "out" several times over. These bitter experiences had finally made up his mind to adopt the Russia-oriented policy and create a revolutionary army. The policy was showing good results and promising more. The Canton government had a revolutionary army now, although it was only three months old. Eugene believed that an army was like a person, in that it matured much more quickly in crises.

"Let me discuss it first with Liao Zhongkai, Chiang Kaishek, and Borodin," Eugene said, gazing at the shriveled older man.

"Borodin?" Sun sighed. Closing his eyes, he murmured, "If you don't mind, I'll rest."

"Good night," Eugene said, walking to the door.

Sun abruptly changed his mind and called Eugene back. He pointed out morosely that, after the death of Lenin, there was a war of succession going on between Trotsky and Stalin, and the Kuomintang had no clue how this would impact their relations with the Chinese Communist Party. Most likely, the Russians would press on more aggressively with their agenda. It had been Sun's—as well as the left Kuomintang's—constant concern that the Russians might transform Canton, through young and inexperienced Chinese communists, into their Soviet base in China.

Eugene said that he would be on the lookout as Sun instructed. Maybe he ought to talk with Liao and Chiang first.

Aware of the importance of having the civilian check on the military, Sun Yatsen had assigned Liao Zhongkai to the post of Party representative to oversee the work of the Whampoa Military Academy and to exert a restraining influence on Chiang Kaishek. Liao had an office in the academy on the island of Whampoa, about twenty miles from the east side of Canton. Green hills, covered with trees, bushes, and grasses, undulated toward the south, linking the island to Humen, the Tiger Gate, an ancient fortress shielding Canton from foreign gunboats reconnoitering on the Pearl River. In good weather, the island glittered like an enormous emerald set in a golden ring of water. Against the backdrop of natural beauty were the roughly patched-up barracks, inherited from an army and naval school of the Manchu Court, all newly plastered and painted. All was done by the unprofessional hands of the students. Part of the compound was still littered with debris and overgrown with tall weeds. Wild animals nested there. To Eugene's eyes, the humble place looked splendid under the glorious blue sky of August.

Sitting with Chiang Kaishek in Liao Zhongkai's office, Eugene spoke of Sun Yatsen's decision. Liao frowned. Chiang said nothing, but his silence was eloquent with alarm. Even if he had the whole army under his command, Chiang finally said to break the silence, the Kuomintang would still be outnumbered by the Merchants' Volunteer Force. He would plead with Sun from the military angle.

With just the right tone of importance, ceremony, showmanship, and servility, Chiang entreated Sun to change his mind. Chiang said he knew the

Merchants' Volunteer Force had not only a large army, but also an almost-unlimited supply of weapons from the West. The Canton government had to use innovative tactics in order to avoid defeat by such a formidable enemy. Chiang Kaishek, the former stockbroker with gambling instincts, made a bold proposal.

According to the intelligence of his scouts, Chiang continued carefully and evenly, the Merchants' Volunteers were building bamboo and wood defenses around their headquarters in the West Gate district, where traditional houses of wood and bamboo cluttered the narrow streets.

"They are hemmed in with inflammable structures." Chiang Kaishek halted as he saw Sun tense at his insinuation, but then hastened to convince his boss of the soundness of his argument. "I can finish them off quickly. A spark and few bottles of gasoline can easily grow into a conflagration. It will be all over before they figure out what is happening to them."

"How many fighters can you mobilize?" Sun asked.

"Four or five thousand," Chiang answered.

"How many have they?" Sun asked.

"About twelve thousand. Plus they have a large number of reservists, at least fifty thousand. And that's not all." At this point, Chiang assumed a superior military demeanor and sneered, "Some of our generals may go over to reinforce them."

Liao Zhongkai leaned forward to interpose: "They have quantity; we have quality. The Merchants' Volunteers are mercenaries; our soldiers are real fighters. We have constantly reminded them that they are soldiers of the people, and by their acts and behavior they will repeal the old Chinese saying 'Good iron is for making better things than nails, and good men have better work to do than bearing arms.' They are chosen, we tell them, because they are the best," Liao Zhongkai said proudly. As the Party representative in the army, he took care of indoctrinating these young men.

Sun shrugged dismissively. "Your plan sounds good, but it's not viable in practice. Burning the West Gate district will surely throw the colonialists in the Shameen Concession into a panic. With their backs to a wall of fire, they will scramble to action, returning fire for fire. And their fire is much more destructive."

The room fell into silent disappointment. After a long pause, Chiang Kaishek's voice broke into their dismal reverie. He was confident that he would win the war, provided the foreign powers did not jump into the fray and kept in the background.

All eyes turned to Eugene. Following a pensive moment, during which he fastidiously inspected the pattern on the carpet, Eugene said, with his head still lowered, that he would go to the British "Lion's lair"—the Shameen Concession—when the fire started. He could not go there one minute earlier, as he was aware that it would be a surprise attack and that any leak or any sign of it would be self-defeating. The trip carried grave risks. He might be killed in the crossfire, or he might be held hostage, or he might be assassinated by the thugs of Chen Lianbo who operated inside the Shameen Concession. But Eugene hoped to reach the British safely, to make it clear to them that the Canton government would vouch for their safety if they did not actually jump into the fray. Otherwise, Shameen would be razed to the ground, should they use their gunboats to help the Kuomintang's enemies.

"We'll have all or nothing," Eugene vowed.

Their arguments had a mixed effect on Sun. It made him all the more determined to leave Canton. If Canton burned, he would not like to take any responsibility for having set it on fire. On the other hand, he told his aides to prepare to form a Revolutionary Committee in an emergency, so as to go over the heads of the powerful right-wingers in the government.

"All the committee members should be Chinese," Sun instructed, hinting at excluding Borodin. "And tell him to keep a close watch on his young hotheads."

"Borodin will listen," Eugene said. "He knows how far he can push."

Borodin's headquarters was in the Eastern Hills, the best residential area in Canton where high-ranking Kuomintang officials and their families lived. Borodin's house was a two-story tropical mansion with verandahs and a flat roof. Inside, there were no supporting walls to separate the rooms, but only light partitions that didn't reach the ceiling, allowing the breezes from windows and doors to circulate freely around the whole floor. Across the street was where the Central Executive Committee of the Kuomintang and the Workers' and Peasants' Departments were located. Behind Borodin's house was an enormous parade ground—a place for mass meetings and for Borodin's hobby, horseback riding. The top floor was Borodin's apartment, where his two aides, a typist, and a house orderly, also lived. A large part of his staff worked downstairs and would stop unwelcome visitors.

On a morning in mid-September 1924, Eugene dropped by and discussed the impending clash with Borodin. Softly twisting the end of his walrus mustache, his host said that he would introduce a prudent young man to assist his visitor. Borodin clapped his hands, and an orderly appeared at the door. Borodin spoke in Russian, and the orderly withdrew. Several minutes later, a man in his mid-twenties entered.

Young, handsome, and debonair, Zhou Enlai did not look the least like a fire-brand. He was born in March 1898 of a mandarin family and grew up in Huaian in Jiangsu Province, a city on the Grand Canal, an ancient waterway stretching from central China to the port city of Tianjin, about a two-hour train ride from Peking. Commerce flourished in Huaian, and Grandfather Zhou, as its prefect, drew income from sources other than his official salary. Zhou Enlai's father was the second son of his grandfather, a weakling who went through life switching from one low-paying sinecure to another. Zhou Enlai did not seem particularly fond of his father. His fond memories were of his three "mothers." In his later years, he spoke with great feelings for the three women who had brought him up to be the man he was. They were his natural mother, his adoptive mother, and his wet nurse, Jiang.

Zhou's adoptive mother was a gentle, retiring creature. She spent practically all her time quietly in her room, and she lavished on him all her love after her husband died. She sheltered him from the bullying of other boys. Her adopted son's nature was so gentle that it was often misconstrued for meekness. She instilled in him a love of learning, a taste for beautiful things, and a habit of using his mind. When Zhou recalled his childhood, he gave the impression that he had greater affection for his adoptive mother than his natural one, but he was grateful to both.

After the death of Grandfather Zhou, the family fortune declined. His father, who had never been a good provider, drew a pittance. Zhou's natural mother had to depend on her parents. It was a great humiliation for a married woman, and she compensated by being an intermediary between quarreling members in the large, extended family. There were ninety rooms in her parental mansion, and one can imagine the number of relatives who sought her services. On such occasions, she suppressed her own feelings and mediated with forbearance and conscientiousness. Her oldest son, a pretty, small boy with large, bright eyes, watched her intently. He would one day use the negotiating skills he had learned from her on a scale beyond her wildest dreams.

Zhou, being the oldest son of his father and the oldest grandson of his late grandfather, shouldered the responsibilities laid upon him by his extended family. They grew heavier when the family went bankrupt and his natural mother and adoptive mother died in 1907 and 1908. His father changed jobs and moved to another city. At age ten, Zhou found himself the man of the house, expected to look after his ailing Third Uncle, his Third Aunt, and two younger brothers. Living expenses far exceeded the little money his father and First Uncle sent home. The pawnshop was another source of income. At such dire times, he sought solace in his remaining "mother." His faithful nurse, Jiang, had not been paid for years by the Zhou family, but would not leave him. She was a good storyteller and told him tales that lifted his spirits, like those about the Taiping Rebellion. Unexpectedly, his First Uncle, his father's older brother, sent for him. First Uncle had a fairly steady job, and since he was childless he took it on himself to educate his oldest nephew as his own son. Zhou was twelve years old when he left home for Manchuria. This proved to be a turning point in his life, as well as in his way of thinking. Had he not left home, he recalled years later, he probably would have ended up sadly like his brothers and cousins, accomplishing nothing in life.

The city he went to was Shenyang, the capital of Manchuria. Zhou Enlai enrolled in a modern school where the teachers used modern curricula. He learned about the great American and French revolutions and how they had made these two nations strong and prosperous. He also learned how China had been reduced to a semi-colonized nation. He vowed that he would work for China, toward its rise again to greatness.

Three years later, his First Uncle accepted a new position in Tianjin and took his favorite nephew with him. Tianjin was the most important port city in the north, a receptacle for the best and the worst in Western culture. Zhou's alma mater, Nankai, founded on the principles of the American educational system, was one of the top middle schools in the entire country. It boasted good campus libraries, which Zhou frequented, combing through shelves and reading the Chinese translations of works by Montesquieu, Rousseau, Huxley, and others. Western literature, drama, and art intrigued him in particular. His favorite book was the Chinese translation of Alexander Dumas Jr.'s *La Dame aux Camelias*.

In the summer of 1917, he graduated and was advised by the headmaster, Zhang Boling, to go to Japan for higher learning. The cost of studying in Japan was lower, and with some financial support from friends he could afford to go. But Zhou did not like Japan's militarism. It was no secret that Japan had aggressive designs on China. His two-year stay there was miserable. Without money and prospects, he was stranded in an enemy country and could only watch his homeland disintegrating with each passing day. The pain was so unbearable that he sought relief in Buddhism. Only when a person cut off all his attachments to the world, Buddha taught, would he be admitted into the realm of total detachment and freedom from pain; but that's easier said than done.

In the midst of a spiritual storm, to paraphrase his words, he saw the red rays of a rising sun shining through the pages of the Marxist magazine, *New Youth,* edited by a future founder of the Communist Party, Chen Duxiu. At what point Zhou embraced Marxism is hard to say, but he was ready "to let go of the past. From now on, I am willing to seek a 'new ideology,' 'new learning,' 'new career' and start anew."[3]

Zhou was happy to find something he might put his faith in, but he was not a man to rush into a commitment. The next stop in his search for Marxism was Paris. He went to France under a work-study program, supported by both Chinese and French authorities. The French government needed workers in their factories after so many of their own had perished in the First World War. And Chinese educators encouraged students to seek higher learning in an advanced European country. It was a mutually beneficial deal. With the money given by Headmaster Zhang and one of the founders of the Nankai School, Zhou Enlai boarded the Messageries Maritimes ship *Porthos,* which sailed for France on November 7, 1920.

Zhou did not stay in France. In his letter to his two uncles, he explained why he had instead chosen England as his destination. London was the greatest metropolis, he wrote, and the political and commercial center of the whole world. In England, he could study more than just one country; he could study the whole international community. In another letter to his cousin, he said he wanted to know if England's Fabian (reformist, rather than revolutionary) socialism suited China, and then he would go to the United States of America, studying for a year or so. He said he was seeking an answer to China's problems by traveling as widely and learning as much as he could. But it was to be an unfulfilled wish: the cost of living in London was too great, and he could not afford a ticket to America.

Zhou left London five weeks after he had arrived, not having enough time to draw a conclusion about what he had observed. It seemed to him that China had two choices: either pursuing the path of Soviet Russia and using violence to wipe out the old system, or adopting England's methods for reform and gradually pushing China into the modern world. He claimed that he had no bias toward either. However, rather than go to extremes, he thought that probably the revolutionaries should lead the Chinese people onto a road in between. Apparently the Confucian philosophy, the Way of Moderation, "Zhong Yong Zi Dao," was still a component of Zhou's mental makeup. But a great coal miners' strike in England impelled him to think things over again. Lacking political and financial clout, the coal miners remained exploited, though somewhat less so than before. After seeing this, Zhou doubted whether Fabian socialism could serve the much vaster, poorer, more subjugated, and mostly illiterate Chinese commoners.

He returned to Paris. The City of Light appealed to Zhou Enlai's inherent romanticism. At the top of Notre Dame, he marveled at the strange beauty of the gargoyles, which, "rather like the evil spirits of Chinese mythology, were crouching there. We gazed at Paris darkening in the dusk. It was a magnificent sight. The water of the River Seine flowed pale blue and the distant Fontainebleau woods were beautifully illuminated by the rays of the setting sun. We shouted 'très bien' in French."[4]

Watching from the student balcony of the Opera House, Zhou was intoxicated by the music and lyrics of *La Traviata*. He adored Paris and appreciated the beauty of its women. His taste for bourgeois art was looked on askance by his more radical friends. With their keeping an eye on him, Zhou once said, half in jest, he could not have gone wrong. Zhou did not forget the revolution. He read radical literature to re-mold his still rather bourgeois mind. His reading, however, was not confined to Marxism. He also read about other brands of socialism. He carefully compared them to Marxism and came to think that Marxism was not empty talk or a dreamer's delirium. In his copy of Beer's *Life and Teachings of Karl Marx*, he underlined sentences about class struggle and proletarian dictatorship, about the eventual elimination of all classes and the final materialization of a Marxist Utopia in which all men were brothers, no rich nor poor, no privileged nor underdogs. After years of uncertain searching, Zhou joined the Communist Party in 1921.

In January 1924, the Kuomintang and the Chinese Communist Party formally formed their alliance and needed more cadres. Zhou was recalled. In August, he sailed back to China with a letter of recommendation from the executive committee of the Young Communists in Europe. "Zhou Enlai, a Zejiang native and twenty-six years old, is a sincere, gentle and capable man. He speaks eloquently and he writes with instant inspiration. He has a profound knowledge of Marxism and a great potential to become a total proletarian. His English is better than his French and German, in which he can read books and newspapers. He was one of the founders of the Young

Communists in Europe. He has been elected three times into our executive committee. His achievements are outstanding, due to his warm heart and endurance for hardship."[5]

Zhou reached Canton in early September, in time to be enlisted into Borodin's fighting team for the showdown.

"Ah, here is our hero from Paris," Eugene said, smiling at Zhou.

Zhou found Eugene's voice cultured and his personality pleasant. Almost before Borodin finished introducing them, Zhou and Eugene discovered their mutual love for the City of Light. They had walked the same streets, hung out in the same cafés, and visited the same museums. With disarming modesty, Zhou asked Eugene why everybody thought so highly of the statue of the Winged Victory. Eugene reflected longer than Zhou and Borodin thought necessary for the simple answer he finally gave. The Winged Victory, Eugene explained, was the first piece of marble that began to move, to fly. Before it, all statues had been still and stiff.

Then Eugene steered the conversation into another aspect of France. "Did you hear about the Shameen Incident of last June when you were in Paris?" Eugene asked.

"Not much," Zhou answered.

"Then you'll hear from the man who probably knows more about the incident than anyone else in Canton," Borodin interposed after a pregnant pause. He had an inkling why Eugene had suddenly changed the subject.

Young revolutionaries were impatient with the colonialists, Eugene said; they wondered why they were not allowed to simply occupy the concession and take it back. But revolutionary enthusiasm must adjust to reality.

The reproach in Eugene's voice was mild, but its effect on Zhou was sharp. He was made to understand that his role in the coming parade was to restrain the fervid marchers from charging into the Shameen Concession.

The reality was, Eugene continued, the coming confrontation with the Merchants' Volunteer Force would be a prelude to the Northern Expedition against the warlords. Should that occur, the Kuomintang would let the colonial powers maintain law and order in their concessions, so as to prevent their armed intervention when Kuomintang troops would cross into or skirt their fields of influence and come face-to-face with their military forces.

Eugene and Zhou Enlai became further acquainted as the Kuomintang and the Canton Chamber of Commerce moved inexorably toward a colli-

In 1955, Percy (left), a Hong Kong barrister, accompanied Jack to meet Premier Zhou Enlai (right) in the Central South Palace (Zhong Nan Hai). Zhou's friendship with the Chen family started in 1924.

sion. The British, Americans, and French wanted to know what the Canton government would do about the concession in case of a civil war. Eugene was delegated to calm them. The Shameen Concession, at the center of Canton, had communists working underground. Eugene's appearance there must not be mistaken for making mischief with the colonialists. Borodin suggested that Eugene take Zhou Enlai along for protection.

Zhou, many years later, told Jack that Eugene had given him his first opportunity to learn some diplomatic skill. He noticed that Eugene's familiarity with Western history and culture eased his way into diplomatic dialogues. Eugene's genuine appreciation and interest in the American Constitution evidently pleased the consul general, Douglas Jenkins. By the time Eugene assured the American that the Canton government would not allow anyone to solve such a complex problem as the Shameen Concession by an act of heroism, Jenkins seemed inclined to take his word. Zhou was quick to learn. From that day on, he called Eugene Chen "Laoshih" (Teacher Chen), the highest respect one man could pay to another. The relationship between teacher and pupil, according to Chinese tradition, was a very special one. Had it been a Chinese who had written the Ten Commandments, there would be an eleventh: Thou shalt honor thy teachers as thou doth thy parents. Eugene was susceptible to compliments, and, in return, he praised the young man to the skies.

Thorough in his preparation for the mission given to him, Eugene got his bearings around the places he might happen upon and observed quietly the men he would coordinate with.

The most original feature of the Whampoa Military Academy was its affiliation with the peasant movement. Every peasant cadre had to undergo one month's training, and approximately ten days were devoted to marching, shooting, knife fighting, and political study in the military academy. Eugene arranged to watch them hold joint maneuvers with the student-soldiers, and he always found that Chiang Kaishek, the commandant, was the first to arrive in full uniform. No error or negligence was tiny enough to escape his stern eyes, not even a mismatched button on a cadet's uniform. He commanded respect and demanded discipline. In turn, his cadets demanded the same discipline from the peasant militia under their training.

In comparison with the Kuomintang army, the Merchants' mercenary force was incredibly undisciplined. While the Kuomintang reconnaissance squads busily gathered intelligence, the Merchants' mercenaries remained in the dark about their enemy's tactics. While the Kuomintang was bent on launching fire attacks, the Merchants' mercenaries were building thicker, larger, longer bamboo and wood barricades, barriers, and walls. While Chiang Kaishek constantly pored over the map with his officers, the head of the Merchants' force, Chen Lianbo, moved his office to the Shameen Concession and depended on the British gunboats to win the war for him.

On October 10, 1924, the Kuomintang organized a parade to celebrate the thirteenth anniversary of the 1911 Revolution. Corps of Whampoa cadets, cadres, laborers, and students marched through the city. Zhou Enlai marched among them. The participants, about thirty to forty thousand from more than thirty organizations, first gathered in a park at the foot of the Hill of the Goddess of Mercy. Zhou, as a representative of the National Liberation Association of Canton, gave a speech and concluded by shouting slogans.

Zhou's speech aroused the marchers. When they reached Taiping Road, the marchers and the armed Merchants' Volunteers, who lay in wait, crossed paths. Suddenly push came to shove, and bullets rang out. More than twenty marchers died, and another ten or more were abducted. The Merchants' Volunteers made full use of their well-equipped torture chambers, amusing themselves with their own ingenuity by killing the marchers in a variety of ways. They shared their amusement on public execution grounds by cutting open the chests and abdomens of their prisoners and pulling out their intestines and still-pulsating hearts. They speared them, and the remains of the bodies, onto poles and paraded through the streets.

Sun Yatsen received word of the grisly demonstrations and immediately created the Revolutionary Committee, consisting of Liao Zhongkai, Chiang Kaishek, and Eugene Chen, among others.[6] He gave Chiang Kaishek full command over the campaign. Eugene was told to stay close to the West Gate district, the theater of the war.

The West Gate district was the delightful remnant of old Canton, the Canton that had done business with the Roman Empire two thousand years earlier, and later with the Arabs. Small shops lined the two sides of crowded, crooked streets. Most of the district's inhabitants were law-abiding citizens. Many worked in shops selling local products, including Canton's famous handicrafts. Eugene shuddered at their fate in the imminent cataclysm.

For all his misgivings, Eugene agreed with Chiang's battle plan. Chiang's strategy was brutal yet brilliant. The first rule of war was to destroy the enemy, even if it claimed innocent victims. What war had ever been fought without collateral human cost? He himself was willing to give his life.

Walking down the street, he saw one or two junks navigate a narrow, crooked passage between sampans, the small, flat-bottomed boats where a great number of natives lived on the water and in the open air. Some of them had amazingly tattered sails that seemed to let through more wind than they caught. A question suddenly struck him, and he thought of working it out with Chiang Kaishek.

There should be unionized peasants and laborers to guard the banks of the Pearl River near the mercenaries' headquarters in the West Gate district, Eugene suggested. When the fire started, they would shovel the scuttling enemy back into the blazing inferno.

On October 14, Chiang Kaishek managed to call up eight hundred Whampoa cadets, three hundred twenty workers and peasants, seven hundred twenty cadets from other military schools, and two thousand policemen, altogether about four thousand fighters. Noticeably absent were the troops of those right-wing "friendly" militarists. Chiang's fighters struck in the late afternoon as cadres and union members drove through the West Gate district, pouring gasoline all over the Merchants' Volunteers' defenses. As flames engulfed the area, a car sped along the embankment and veered onto a bridge straddling a narrow moat. British soldiers stopped the car at the barbed wire before the front gates of Shameen. The car's driver told them that Eugene Chen was sitting in the back. They waved the car through, and it stopped at the American Consulate. Eugene figured it was better to talk with the more flexible Americans before he approached the British.

Consul General Douglas Jenkins received him with a perfunctory handshake. He grew a little warmer when Eugene asked him to inform the British Consulate that he was here to ensure Shameen's safety.

The Merchants' Volunteers, led by Chen Lianbo's deputy, surrendered unconditionally before the sun set the next day. There was no international incident, which they had so fervently prayed for. Eugene's bold stroke in handling the matter was applauded. Once again, he was the first Chinese diplomat since the humiliating Opium War to refuse to succumb to the imperialists and who had won the day with his adeptness in the art of diplomacy.

★10★

MANEUVERING AROUND SUN YATSEN'S DEATHBED

The Kuomintang government was now in a stronger position than it had ever been before. Having consolidated its base in Canton, it was a force to be reckoned with. As it happened, Peking changed hands again at that time, and its new masters invited Sun Yatsen to visit the capital for a Reunification Conference they were organizing. Among them, the most powerful warlord was Zhang Zuolin, nicknamed the "Manchurian Tiger." The two outstanding traits of Manchurian tigers are savagery and greed; they hide themselves in the dense forests and sneak out only to attack unwary passersby from behind. Zhang Zuolin had been a bandit before he became the First Man of Peking. The second warlord, Duan Qirui, the "Righteous Buddhist," was a cub to Japanese expansionists and a wolf to Eugene, who had suffered in his prison in 1917. The third, also the youngest, was Feng Yuxiang, who had been nicknamed the "Christian General" by American missionaries. He was their biggest catch until Chiang Kaishek's later conversion.

Sun wished to form a coalition government with these three warlords. Of course, he knew that that was surely a scenario too optimistic to translate into reality, but he would give it a try. His health had deteriorated visibly. As a physician himself, there was no doubt that he had a premonition of his imminent death, which explained why he did not mind cuddling the ferocious Manchurian Tiger, the murderous Righteous Buddhist, and the Judas-like Christian General.

In Peking, fortunes were made and lost with lightning speed. Even before Sun started on his Peking trip, Feng Yuxiang, the Christian General, had been exiled to a Buddhist monastery at Heavenly Platform Hills (Tian Tai Hills), not far from Peking. The news did not bode well. Then Sun learned that the other two warlords were unilaterally inviting their allies and potential allies to the Reunification Conference and declaring their willingness to stick to the unequal treaties the colonialist powers had inflicted on previous Chinese governments. Sun told Eugene that the Peking trip would be an initial step of the Northern Expedition, first defeating the warlords with political propaganda and then with a military campaign. On his journey northward, he stopped at several cities, including Shanghai and Tianjin, to speak, vowing to repeal the unequal treaties and to abolish all special privileges in order to protect China's national interests and to eradicate the imperialist influence in China.

On November 21, 1924, Sun embarked on his last trip to Peking. His retinue included his wife, Chingling, Eugene, and Borodin. In the first week of December, Sun fell very ill and could walk ashore in Tianjin only with painful effort. He canceled all appointments save one with Zhang Zuolin, the Manchurian Tiger, who came from Peking to ceremoniously welcome him. In contrast to his nickname, Zhang was a small shrunken man with the wizened face of an opium addict.

In the middle of the conversation, the pain in Sun's liver worsened, and he collapsed. Back in his hotel, he lay in bed while a nurse brought in the medicines the doctor had prescribed. Sun made a strenuous attempt to sit up, but while doing so he lost his last bit of strength and slumped heavily back on the bed.

Suddenly the well-wishers were leaving. Eugene was about to follow, when he saw Chingling motion her chin almost imperceptibly to him and then to her husband, as if to say that Sun had something to tell him alone. Eugene remained and waited for Sun to breathe a little more easily.

Sun gazed vacantly at a cup as though he was trying to puzzle out where the water had gone. There was a long, uncertain pause. His gaze wavered and came to rest on Eugene. It seemed he could not quite remember why his "closest friend" was there.

"You want Eugene to pay a quiet visit to General Feng Yuxiang," Chingling reminded her husband.

They analyzed Feng to see if he could be a potential ally. Feng's father was at times a bricklayer or hired farmhand. In Feng's teens, he enlisted in the army of a small warlord. The numerous civil wars raging played to Feng's particular talents. He was good at switching sides, and he did it so often that no one could tell for sure whose side he was on. On one fine day in 1920 or 1921, Feng had a portent. He was dazzled by the sign of the shining dollar, as Constantine the Great had been spurred by the sign of the blazing cross. He reinvented himself as a churchgoer. The American missionaries lived a middle-class life comparable to the one they had in their home country, but in poverty-stricken China, they were very upper-crust. Because warships and extraterritoriality guaranteed them special privileges, even the powerful and wealthy Chinese regarded them with awe. As their missionary organizations, especially the Young Men's Christian Association and the Young Women's Christian Association, became more influential and outdid the missionaries from other Western nations, Feng was so impressed by their political clout that he set his mind to becoming a Christian. Feng was what people at that time called a "rice Christian," a man turning to God for a bowl of rice.

For all his theatrics, the Christian General failed to receive American financial support. Although he still marched his troops to "Onward Christian Soldiers," he started thinking of paying homage to Moscow and changing his tune to the "Internationale."

Feng Yuxiang was not a reliable ally, Sun and Eugene agreed, but he disliked Zhang Zuolin and Duan Qirui, the two warlords who had driven him out of Peking, as much as Sun Yatsen did. After discussing it with Eugene, Sun decided to contact Feng.

It was a Sunday morning in early December when Eugene, accompanied by Borodin and the Soviet Russian ambassador, Karakhan, went on a hike to Heavenly Platform Hills and witnessed a burlesque that only a medieval buffoon like Feng Yuxiang could have dreamed up.

In a great hall of the Buddhist temple and with the Buddhas and Lohans glaring down, the Christian General was attending a brief Sunday service with his soldiers. A military aide called the soldiers to attention, ordered them to stand, and led them in hymns. When the singing trailed off, the minister proceeded with a short sermon. At the end of the sermon, the same military aide loudly commanded: "Kneel down and pray!"

The farce continued as the whole audience moved to the courtyard. A huge shaven head floated formidably above all the others. Feng Yuxiang was a large-boned six-footer, broad in proportion, with heavy jowls and enormous hands. He abruptly bent down, grabbed a fire hose, and thrust it into the minister's hands to douse baptismal water over the troops. After completing his devotions to God, Feng, a Methodist or Episcopalian or both, conspired with a lapsed Roman Catholic and two Bolshevik infidels to stab his former brothers-in-arms in the back.

In Feng's memoirs, *My Life,* he recalls this meeting with Eugene, Borodin, and the Soviet Russian ambassador. "Borodin and Karakhan were introduced to me and they often came to talk with me. Every time it was Mr. Chen Youren [Eugene] who interpreted for us. We covered several subjects, revolution, religion and the revoking of unequal treaties.... The more we discussed, the closer we gravitated to one another, and the greater the impact on my political views... I then extended invitations, through Borodin and Karakhan, to thirty some Soviet advisors to help train my troops.... I took this step to support Mr. Sun Yatsen's policies of allying with Soviet Russia, the Chinese Communist Party and promoting the worker-peasant movement."[1]

What Feng said was partially true but not wholly accurate. The interpreter was not Eugene; it was either Feng's wife, Li Dequan, or one of his close aides. Eugene was there representing Sun Yatsen, not as an interpreter, since he probably understood as little Chinese as Borodin and Karakhan. Even pooling their knowledge of Chinese would not have enabled them to understand Feng's negotiations for Soviet arms, which was omitted in his memoir. The neglect was intentional but excusable, because the memoir was first published in 1947 when Feng's rival, Chiang Kaishek, was in power, and Feng was virtually his captive.

Eugene proposed building a center of communications to link the revolutionary groups taking part in the coming Northern Expedition. More concretely, Eugene wanted a news agency and a newspaper to spread Kuomintang propaganda, to mobilize and organize the masses, in particular the students.[2] Peking was not an industrial city, and there were not many working-class men and women, but there were many students who could rise up against the warlords from within when the Northern Expedition soldiers attacked from without.[3]

Eugene did have a course of action in mind, and he proposed it to Feng. Eugene wanted to purchase a moribund news agency, and there just happened to be one. Six years earlier, American businessmen who were eager to trade with China had established the Sino-American News Agency to foster better understanding between the two countries. Then the Americans lost interest. The agency was in shambles and awaited a new owner. Whoever the prospective buyer, he had to be acceptable to the American Legation, because the Sino-American News Agency's incorporation papers had been filed under the laws of New Jersey, and it had been registered as an American organization with the American Legation in Peking. If Eugene could employ an American or two to run it, the whole setup would enjoy extraterritorial rights. In other words, the warlord government would think twice before raiding it. Feng Yuxiang agreed to provide both cash and a front man.

So a deal was cut without much ado, and Feng Yuxiang's front man, an American-educated banker named Farstan Song, offered to buy the Sino-American News Agency.

Sun barely made it to Peking and was diagnosed with terminal cancer. There was not much the doctors could do. The Soong clan decided to move Sun to a more comfortable place. They looked for a house, and Wellington Koo, the former minister of the Peking government to Washington, had an unoccupied house that he let them use. The whole Soong clan moved in with Sun. Three of Chingling's siblings were with her: her younger brother T. V. Soong, her younger sister Mayling Soong, and her older sister Ailing Soong, who masterminded all the Soong plots. Ailing was manipulating her siblings to monopolize the dying man. They did not allow Borodin to see Sun alone. The Russian High Adviser was practically barred from Sun's sickroom after the fateful diagnosis of Sun's illness in January. Borodin's communication with Sun, for the most part, depended on Eugene.

Anticipating trouble after his death, Sun was in constant consultation with Eugene. They had started the Russia-oriented policy together, and its success would crown both their revolutionary careers. Sun knew it was as important to Eugene as to himself, and therefore he was sure of Eugene's determination to carry it on when he himself had passed from the scene.

Eugene, for a moment, was lost in his own sorrow. Sun Yatsen had touched his life profoundly, but he could do nothing to keep the dying man from slipping away. Chingling was sobbing quietly.

In the sad silence between them, Eugene mused to himself. He quickly sized up the changing situation and his place in it. In the past, when he had an idea, he would tell Sun; if Sun agreed, they would try it out. With Sun lending his full support, Eugene had not been really bothered by partisan politics. But now he had to continue Sun's policies without Sun. That was quite a revolutionary tightrope to walk. While balancing his act, he took counsel with Chingling, who had been a supporter of the Russia-oriented policy from the very beginning. That was about all he was able to get from her. She simply did not have the political stature, authority, and acumen that her husband had possessed. She had never held any party or government office. Her husband had commanded her life and shielded her. She was indeed a political ingénue. As the intrigue surrounding Sun's deathbed thickened, Eugene began to position himself to continue the fight against the warlords and their foreign backers. He and the Soong clan had a mutual plan, and that was to keep Chingling safe and out of harm's way. In this they were his natural allies.

Sun's weary voice intruded into Eugene's reverie. Sun touched on the question of his will. He guessed correctly that he would not be able to say all he wanted to say in his will to the Kuomintang. His party was so factious that he could not please them all. Eugene was not taken by surprise. He reminded Sun that they had started the Russia-oriented policy with a personal letter to Moscow, and Sun could send another personal letter there to confirm his deathbed wish. Sun wanted Eugene to draft this letter.

Among Sun's traveling retinue, there was a man with a round, smooth, beardless face and black, pomaded hair, nicknamed the "Chinese Byron," the ever-omnipotent editor of the Kuomintang. He had the kind of obsequious mannerisms that were usually attributed to a eunuch. His name was Wang Jingwei, supposedly a centrist. In 1924, Wang was the only member of the Central Executive Committee of the Kuomintang accompanying Sun on the northward journey. When Sun grew increasingly incapacitated, he appointed five more members to the highest governing body, and Eugene was one of them. This branch of the Central Executive Committee in Peking was authorized by Sun to act on his behalf. By selecting Eugene, Sun swiftly moved him up the ladder of the Kuomintang hierarchy and endowed him with the authority to draft the English will—the letter to the Central Executive Committee of the Russian Communist Party while Wang Jingwei, the most senior member, would have the enviable job of writing Sun's Chinese will.

Wang Jingwei was well equipped for his new task. He had edited many Kuomintang Party documents, and whatever opinions Wang held were not apparent in his editing. His slant was centrist. That is, he knew how to gloss over one rough edge or another, should it prove offensive to one faction or another. Despite his talent for editing, he was more proud of his poetry, and in his own eyes he was the Chinese Byron.

At the moment, poetry was pushed aside. With Sun's death imminent, the scramble for power had started, and so had the flurry of activity in seeking allies to fight the succession war. As head of the branch of the Central Executive Committee at Peking, Wang Jingwei had access to the fading Sun Yatsen. Every day, he took Sun's temperature, felt Sun's pulse, supervised the preparation of Sun's diet, and counted the hours Sun slept. He kept a record of all that and made a daily report to his ranking colleagues in Peking and

Canton. But he did not have much time alone with Sun, and the group of contenders who stood in his way to the sickroom was the Soong clan.

Chingling was said to hold the patient's hand all the time. Ailing would have liked to hold his other hand, but it was indecorous to show such intimacy to her brother-in-law. Thereby she deputed her puppy-like, henpecked husband, Daddy Kong, to do the hand-holding. They were alternately there around the clock. Their dynastic attitude incurred jealousy and misgiving from many leading Kuomintang members. It struck them as odd, they whispered in Wang Jingwei's ear, that Sun Ke (also known as Sun Fo), Sun Yatsen's son from his first marriage and his only son, was absent. According to Chinese tradition, the son, the male heir, assumed the role of spokesman for the dying father.

This alerted the Soong clan. Sun Ke was a constant reminder of their sister's questionable marriage to his father, and, in Sun Ke's eyes, Chingling was an ever-dubious replacement for his mother. The Soongs girded for war. Under no circumstance would they let their greatest political capital—their special relations with the dying Sun—slip through their fingers. They were Christians, and so was Sun, the Soong clan declared. Eve was created from Adam's rib, and so it was the wife, not the son, who was one with the husband. Their detractors challenged that claim and harked back to the old allegation: Sun Ke's mother—also a Christian—not Chingling, held the legitimate claim on her husband's rib.

It now became imperative for the Soong clan to clear this matter of Chingling's marital status with Sun Yatsen. He had to write a private will to prove that Chingling was his one and only lawful wife. Chingling recoiled at their suggestion. She was too exquisite a creature to discuss such crass matters herself. A family meeting was immediately called. Ailing, knowing that Eugene was her younger sister's confidant, asked him to help them convince Chingling of the importance of looking after her worldly interests.

Sitting in the Soong family meeting and listening to their insinuating and callous words, Eugene felt great sorrow and sympathy when he saw Chingling's immobile profile. She was being turned into a stone icon. What a transformation from the picture of a young woman waltzing by herself to Chopin's music, her laughing face slightly thrown back.

However, Eugene said something different aloud. He understood, he said, that it was extremely painful for Chingling to discuss this matter, but there was no time to put it off. For the sake of protecting Sun's legacy, she must make sure that she had the authority to be his keeper. Sometimes one had to put a higher purpose above one's personal feelings, Eugene persisted, though, with a touch of halting melancholy.

For a long moment, Chingling hunched over as if her slim shoulders were weighed down, then she straightened her back and nodded. She had nothing to worry about, Eugene reassured her: he would see to it that everything would work out for her.

Anxious not to wake his colleague Wang Jingwei, who shared a wing in the same mansion in which the Soong clan sojourned, Eugene moved quietly through the second courtyard. Preoccupied with reviewing the meeting he had had with the Soong clan, he walked with his eyes fixed on his moving feet and bumped into someone. Lifting his eyes, he saw Wang Jingwei standing in front of him. Wang suggested that they take a short stroll in the back garden, to enjoy the lovely moonlight. Eugene nodded and seized the moment to sound out Wang's reaction to the Soongs' request for a private will from Sun Yatsen.

Wang pondered for a moment. The arrogant clan stooped to begging him to steal, with them, Sun Ke's thunder. Quickly taking stock of the two sides, he deemed that Sun Ke, a man shielded under his father's shadow, was no match for the redoubtable Soong clan. He would grant this favor to them in exchange for one from them. He harbored a secret ambition to inherit Sun Yatsen's mantle, and he wanted the Soong clan to back up his bid for the job of writing Sun's will to the Kuomintang. By writing down Sun's instructions in the will, he would be logically the best interpreter of the supreme leader's last words.

But he would play hard to get and said that there was no good reason to stop Sun Ke from performing his filial duties. If the Soong clan insisted on its way, it would offend the sensibility of the whole nation. Bringing a factional war to a head at this moment would damage the Kuomintang irreparably.

At this moment, a noise like that of shoes scraping gravel came from behind a cluster of pine trees. Eugene pricked up his ears to hear and stared at the trees. The pale moon was momentarily obscured by low scudding clouds. Silence. But even the silence felt menacing.

"Perhaps someone is eavesdropping," Eugene said in a strained voice.

Wang Jingwei squinted into a cluster of trees where the noise seemed to have come from and said that he would let Eugene know what he would do to prevent an open collision between the Soong clan and Sun Ke.

Eugene grasped the drift of Wang Jingwei's words. He responded with an eye to the future too. When Sun Yatsen at his sickbed chose five new members, two from the left, two from the right, and one in the middle, whose name was Yu Youren, to fill the Peking branch of the Central Executive Committee, he in fact was entrusting Wang Jingwei with the power to determine the outcome of any debate. The other centrist, Yu Youren, was a long-standing crony of Wang's and would cast his vote where Wang did. So, without the two centrists' support, neither the two leftists nor the two rightists were able to win. Wang Jingwei, the Chinese Byron, in the middle, was pivotal. Whichever side he tilted toward was more likely to gain the upper hand.

Having come to this conclusion, Eugene set about nudging Wang to gravitate toward the left. Eugene confided to Chingling his calculation that they should bring Wang Jingwei on board. Assured of her support, Eugene had no difficulty in convincing the rest of the Soong clan. None of them was a member of the Central Executive Committee, and they counted on Eugene to speak for them.

The decision Wang Jingwei made was a clever one. He decided not to summon Sun Ke until the last minute. Without notice, Sun Ke would have no time to think or react. That was Wang Jingwei's scheme, and it was on target.

On February 20, three weeks before Sun Yatsen's death, Wang Jingwei held a meeting of the Central Executive Committee and discussed whether they should cable Sun Ke to come. All said yes. Three days later, Sun Ke came from Shanghai with his wife and their two children. Sun Ke was a short, burly young man with a plump, sulky face, like that of a child who craved but failed to get attention. His ambition was disproportionate to his ability, so it was easy for someone like the foxy Wang Jingwei to make him blunder. On his arrival, he was immediately ushered into the sickroom and made to witness the making of his father's wills.

There were, of course, several versions of the story of how that Chinese will came to be written. Some claimed that Sun let Wang Jingwei write it and then read it to him.[4] Some said that Sun dictated it.

Wang Jingwei, in agreement with the Soong clan, had made the first draft and passed it around among the members of the Central Executive Committee. Then he approached Sun and, without mentioning the draft of the will, asked if Sun had any instruction for them.

Sun answered: "Should I live on, I would have plenty to say. But I'll soon be gone. After my death, it will be up to you people what to do. There is no point asking for my opinion."

"We hope to have your instruction and know what you wish us to do," Wang pleaded in a low, soliciting voice. T. V. Soong and H. H. "Daddy" Kong echoed the plea.

Sun closed his eyes. When he opened them again, he said: "You are all in danger. When I die, my enemies will tempt you to switch sides. If you reject them, what more do I need to say?"

"We sincerely hope that you'll leave us a will," Wang continued to plead with artificial tears in his eyes.

"What do you want me to say?"

"We have prepared a draft and I'll read it. If you approve it, please put your signature to it. If not, please change it as you wish. I'll take notes and make another draft."

In the Chinese will, Sun reminded his comrades of the work ahead:

The Revolution has not yet been successfully concluded. Let all our comrades follow my writings—the plans of National Reconstruction, the Three Principles of the People, and the Manifesto of the First Congress of Representatives—and make every effort to carry them into effect. Above all, my recent declaration in favor of holding a National Convention of the People of China and abolishing the unequal treaties should be carried into effect as soon as possible. This is my last will and testament.[5]

"It's very good and it has my full approval," Sun Yatsen concluded.

The English will was written in the form of a letter to the Central Executive Committee of Soviet Russia. Eugene Chen, Wang Jingwei, T. V. Soong, Sun Ke, and Borodin took notes while Sun dictated in English. The final draft was penned by Eugene. It was one of the very few occasions that Borodin was admitted into the sickroom.

I am leaving behind me a party which I hoped would be associated with you in the historic work of completely liberating China and other exploited countries from this imperialist system. Fate decrees that I must leave the task unfinished and pass it on to those who, by remaining true to the principles and teachings of the Party, will constitute my real followers. I have, therefore, enjoined the Kuomintang to carry on the work of the national revolutionary movement in order that China may be freed from the semicolonial status which imperialism imposed upon her. To this end I have charged the party to keep in constant touch with you. . . .[6]

When Eugene completed the draft, Chingling read it aloud to Sun. Her younger brother, T. V. Soong, finished reading for her when she was overcome with grief and burst out sobbing. Sun Yatsen nodded his approval.

The matter of a private will was brought to Sun Yatsen's attention on the same day as the Chinese will. Sun dictated one to Wang Jingwei in the presence of his son, Sun Ke, the Soong clan, and Eugene. Sun bequeathed all his possessions, his house, and his books, to his young second wife, Soong Chingling. Not a word about his first wife, who had a legal claim to everything the dying man owned. This surprise onslaught sent Sun Ke into shellshock.

Despite the manipulation of the Soong clan to monopolize the dying man, Sun Ke had his share of time alone with his father, conversing intimately. Goaded by the right-wingers, Sun Ke took a stand against the left-leaning Chingling. He revealed intimate details in his father's talks with him. His father said that he had never stopped caring for his first wife, mother of all his children, and asked for forgiveness for what he had done to her. Sun Ke intended to send a telegram to his mother, letting her be with her stray husband for the last time. That was a snipe meant to target Chingling. She was to blame for Sun's leaving his church, and now she was in his way of making peace with God. The god of the New Testament took a dim view of polygamy. When it was time for one wife to go, it was the surplus one, not the original one.

Eugene, as requested by the Soong clan, and accompanied by Wang Jingwei, gave a piece of his mind to Sun Ke. Sun Ke was made to understand the prospect of his mother and Chingling confronting each other, and how this would affect his father. At this point, Wang Jingwei chimed in and said that if their supreme leader died broken-spirited, Sun Ke would be forever labeled an unfilial son. Sun Ke pulled back.

Sun Ke shifted even farther from his original position when the wife of the left-winger Liao Zhongkai, a formidable boudoir strategist, arrived. Her husband sent her to reinforce the left Kuomintang's interest. Although Madame Liao disliked Ailing and Mayling Soong, she joined the Soong chorus of intimidation in order to bolster Chingling. She told Sun Ke's wife that the Soong siblings might soon acquire a new brother-in-law in Chiang Kaishek. Chiang's hot pursuit of Mayling Soong was an open secret. That frightened Sun Ke into full retreat.

Eugene kept Chingling apprised of the result, but he hardly looked as if he was relieved. His face grew contemplative, and, after a pause, he said that their biggest problem was awaiting them back in Canton. Chingling understood what he meant. The restless Chiang Kaishek would give them a much worse headache than Sun Ke ever could. As early as 1922, Chiang had begun to fancy her younger sister, Mayling. He even had made so bold as to ask Sun Yatsen if he could trade in his current wife for his latest intended. Sun had remained noncommittal until he had learned what Chingling thought. Chingling did not want Mayling to repeat her marital blunder, and the matter was dropped temporarily.

On March 11, 1925, Sun Yatsen signed all three wills, with Chingling guiding his hand. The next day, he died. Now, the debate on the style of the funeral occupied everybody's attention. The Soong clan and Sun Ke insisted on a Christian funeral. The former adversaries were now forging a new alignment. Chingling was not averse to this suggestion, but she refused to yield on one point: neither Sun Yatsen nor she would apologize for their unconventional marriage and go on hands and knees to beg for forgiveness from the missionary community, which had virtually ostracized them. Eugene promised to see to it that no one and nothing would compromise her dignity. For all intents and purposes, Chingling should not be the one to block a Christian funeral, Eugene told her; a Christian funeral with speeches in English was a step in a process of making it up with the Western powers. If she never wished to return to her church, Eugene said, it was her personal decision, but for the sake of the revolutionary cause she should be on affable terms with them.

Having that matter settled, there arose another flashpoint, which caused a further round of flurried realignments. The right-wing Kuomintang and the Soviet Russians, the two groups most hostile to one another, found themselves standing together and censuring the Christian funeral arrangements. The atheistic Bolsheviks were against it for obvious reasons. The right-wing Kuomintang did not desire to see the funeral being turned into a showcase for the Soong clan. They simultaneously complained to the Kuomintang centrist, Wang Jingwei, who concurred—but not disinterestedly. Wang was apprehensive that the Soong clan's funeral procession, led by Chingling, would eclipse his importance as the man who wrote Sun's last will and testament. But he was too cagey to confront them directly. The Chinese Byron whispered his suspicion about the Soongs' funeral arrangement in Sun Ke's ears. Sun Ke, agitated, threw down the gauntlet. He demanded to speak as the chief eulogist.

The Soongs themselves were not unanimous on who should be chief eulogist. Chingling's older sister, Ailing, wanted her husband, Daddy Kong, to assume the honor. Chingling wanted her favorite sibling, T. V. Soong. There was intense rivalry between the Soong sisters. The fact was that Chingling was not Sun Yatsen's first choice for a modern wife. It was Ailing, his personal secretary before Chingling came along. However, Ailing's parents arranged her marriage with Daddy Kong, and Ailing, as the oldest daughter and the oldest child, bowed to her parents' wishes, the only daughter among the three who married in full accordance with her parents' approval. But she didn't leave Sun's office without finding a successor of her own choosing. Determined to keep Sun in the family, Ailing arranged for her prettier younger sister, Chingling, to take her place. As planned, Sun Yatsen fell for Chingling. So Ailing's maneuvering to position her husband as chief eulogist was her way of repossessing Sun Yatsen. At least, that was how Chingling interpreted her older sister's actions.

Daddy Kong had his own version of Sun's last moment. Sun had confided to his older brother-in-law why he had come into this world: to start a revolution, fighting against the spirit of evil, as Christ had done long ago. It was probably true that Sun said something like this to Kong; Kong simply lacked the imagination to make up this kind of story, and Sun was good at mixing different beliefs into one pot.

However, there was one point in Kong's recounting that Eugene took more seriously. Sun had warned him not to antagonize the missionaries. Kong, who had been a high-ranking official in the Young Men's Christian Association, was a suitable person for Sun to confide this matter to. Kong knew the political clout American missionaries possessed. They were practically the only source of information regarding China for folks back home. They held sway over both the public opinion and the purse filled with the faithful's donations.

Arguing one step further, Eugene suggested that they pick someone outside the family but inside the Kuomintang to be the chief eulogist, and thus the funeral wouldn't be just a family statement, but a party and governmental statement as well. Ailing glowered, and her horse face grew longer.

"Convince her." Ailing, in hurried words, told Eugene that her younger sister was beginning to show signs of a nervous breakdown. She led him to the door of Chingling's room and left him there.

Eugene tapped at the door. A weak, sighing voice answered, and the door was opened by T. V. Soong. Chingling reclined on a couch, worn out with grief and despair. T. V. Soong, with his head lowered and his chin almost touching his chest, sat beside her. Eugene realized that what he was about

A group picture taken on the day Sun Yatsen died, in the house of Wellington Koo on loan to the Kuomintang. From left to right: a Chinese official, Borodin, Wang Jingwei (Chinese Byron), T. V. Soong, Eugene, and a servant.

to say might deepen her depression. Racked by anxiety, he sank into an exhausted silence. It was she who broke the silence and interjected, with a spurt of nervous energy, that the news that Madame Liao Zhongkai had brought from Canton was worrisome. It was about Chiang Kaishek's growing military power. In Sun Yatsen's absence, Chiang was bolder in showing his displeasure with the commissar system and the curricula that the Soviet Russians had introduced into the Whampoa Military Academy. Chiang, the academy's commandant, with his propensity for choosing cronies with links to conservative politicians and businessmen, could cause trouble. The passing of Sun Yatsen left a vacuum in the Kuomintang, and that whetted Chiang's appetite for filling it. By marrying Mayling, he would be related to Sun Yatsen and have a huge edge over the other contenders in the race to the throne.

But, to Chingling's amazement, Eugene brushed her worries aside and seemed more concerned about who should be the chief eulogist. He recommended George Qian Xu, a member of the Episcopal Church and a former ranking official of the nationwide headquarters of the YMCA in Shanghai, who kept in touch with these American Christian institutions. He had spoken in Christian forums many times on behalf of the Kuomintang, and every time, without mentioning the words "religion" or "church" or "God," he made his speech sound like a proper Sunday sermon.

In addition, Eugene noted, George Xu had other qualifications. As early as 1920, Xu had been dispatched by Sun Yatsen to solicit the support of Feng Yuxiang when the Christian warlord was giving himself a makeover. George Xu, with his YMCA connections, had done public relations work for Feng and had a hand in promoting him as the "Christian General." Feng looked on Xu as his man in the Kuomintang and would be pleased to see the latter elevated above others on the pulpit. Consequently, Feng, the pivot of the coming war on the northern front, would be more collaborative, Eugene said.

Moving his chair closer to Chingling and T. V. Soong, Eugene leaned forward with his hands clasped and his elbows resting on his knees. Thinking for a long moment, he said that by enlisting George Xu, they enlisted Feng Yuxiang, who could be used as a hold over Chiang Kaishek. Feng had been the military governor of Henan Province in the north and then of Shenxi Province in the northwest. He still maintained a stronghold there which was close to Soviet-controlled Outer Mongolia. If the Kuomintang government at Canton secured Feng, the Russians could send personnel and weapons through his stronghold—a safer and quicker route—to the northwestern part of China. And then, with Feng as the new military ally, Eugene went on, they did not have to rely entirely on Chiang Kaishek.

The dispute over the choice of the chief eulogist was thus resolved. All sides had sullenly reached a consensus. Borodin was not happy at all, but there was very little he could do against Sun Yatsen's family members. If they said that Sun wanted a Christian funeral, that was it. They were closest to the deathbed; Borodin was nowhere near it. But he did not take the hit lying down. With a swaggering air, he told people that Sun Yatsen would have liked a burial like Lenin's. Eugene put a stop to Borodin's braggadocio, warning him frankly that he could not organize a funeral without Sun's coffin, and that the remains were now in the joint custody of Sun's family and the Kuomintang.

On the morning of the funeral, Chingling briefly faltered when her sisters Ailing and Mayling put the widow's veil on her. Then, by sheer willpower, she regained her dignity and tranquility.

The Christian funeral was held at the chapel of Peking's Union Medical College, an American missionary school. Eugene stood with the Soong clan and Sun Ke to receive guests.[7] George Qian Xu, the main eulogist, used Sun's own words in a conciliatory vein. Xu selected appropriate quotes to portray Sun as a devotee working and acting in imitation of Christ, but independent of the established church he had criticized as divided and divisive.

At the end of the funeral, Chingling, with her younger sister, Mayling, and her stepson, Sun Ke, lightly holding her elbows, walked out of the chapel to acknowledge the public's condolences. Though looking frail, she carried herself erect and regal. Following her were Wang Jingwei, Eugene Chen, George Qian Xu, T. V. Soong, Daddy Kong, and Sun Ke, the lineup of the future cabinet.

★ 11 ★

FROM FIRING SQUAD TO CANTON

When his Kuomintang colleagues and Chingling returned south, Eugene stayed in Peking to set up the Kuomintang News Agency in a house at No. 2 Tai Pu Ke Shi. He took over the house from the defunct Sino-American News Agency along with its name, Zhong-Mei, meaning "Sino-American." A dry fountain stood in the middle of a square courtyard surrounded on three sides by dingy rooms, which opened onto a roofed verandah with peeling wooden rails. The fourth side faced the front gate, but because of a spirit wall—a barrier meant to keep out evil spirits—no outsiders could see in, even if the gate was open.

Eugene resumed his journalist work. Nearly every day, he went into the Legation Quarters and sat in on one or two press conferences. The Russian Embassy, boasting the largest compound in the area, was a place he frequented. A wide driveway led from the iron gate to the main white building. Beyond that were several crooked paths crisscrossing among several cottages. In one of them, on a corner screened by the tops of low-hanging trees, Li Dazhao, a founder of the Chinese Communist Party, had his office.

Throughout his career, Li showed extraordinary willingness to cooperate with people whom he disagreed with but admired. As the head librarian and a professor at Peking University, China's foremost institution of higher learning, he had a wide range of acquaintances and was well regarded by them all. He moved with ease among the many and varied political and cultural groups, including warlords and their bureaucrats. It was totally in character that Li was the first prominent communist to join the Kuomintang in 1922, while others resented submitting to the bourgeois Sun Yatsen.

Li Dazhao's reputation was a topic of debate. Some said he was slick, and others said he was credulous or bighearted. At first glance, Eugene found him bookish and his manner formal. Li spoke some English, but his sentences sounded as though they came from a textbook, which perhaps was the case, since Li had picked up his English while attending YMCA adult classes. Eugene's first impression, however, changed after the polite greetings and preliminaries were over. When Li smiled, his fierce walrus mustache and dark bushy brows gave way to a convivial and generous disposition. If he had a character flaw, Eugene reflected, it was that he did not think evil of any person until positive proof was proffered. Eugene took an instant liking to this almost saintly man.

At Sun Yatsen's sickbed, both had been simultaneously elevated to the Central Executive Committee of the Kuomintang in Peking. They were the only two leftists of the five newly elevated members, and their collaboration was indispensable to the success of the leftist agenda. There, in Li Dazhao's office at the Soviet Embassy, Eugene gathered most of the news from Canton and Moscow.

Eugene's news releases, printed in his recently established paper, *People's Tribune*, publicized two victories by the Whampoa Military Academy cadets under Chiang Kaishek's command. They had crushed the remaining troops of the militarists in March 1925, and then in June had defeated two insurgent generals who had reached a secret agreement with the warlord government at Peking to overthrow the government at Canton. In July, the Kuomintang declared that it was in control of Canton and almost the whole of Guangdong Province and its neighboring areas.

This was not good news for the warlords and the colonial powers.

The Northern Expedition seemed imminent. Then came a shocking development: Liao Zhongkai, who had implemented the Russia-oriented policy as steadfastly as Eugene, was assassinated by a British-sponsored right-Kuomintang group on August 20, 1925. The southern conspirators were in collusion with the warlord Zhang Zuolin, the Manchurian Tiger, who headed the Peking government in the north. It could not be purely coincidental that six days later, on August 26, Eugene's Peking office was raided. He was blindfolded, gagged, handcuffed, whisked onto a train, and put in a military prison in the city of Tianjin. Everything was done in one afternoon. No sooner had he been thrown off the train than he was taken in a police van, to be led, Eugene feared, to the execution ground. He heard the executioners shuffle their feet as they took aim. Then came the order to shoot and the click of the triggers. There was an explosion. He heard a piercing scream and a thump as he felt an excruciating pain in his chest.

"I am dead," Eugene muttered to himself. Momentarily numb, Eugene discovered, to his bewilderment, that he was still alive and standing on his feet. The executed one was somebody else, not him.

This was merely a rehearsal, and he would soon taste the real thing, his tormentors taunted when they escorted him to a cell. Eugene's hair turned gray overnight. Nevertheless, he was so exhausted that he fell into a troubled sleep. His head buzzed and swished with confusing noises and pounded with the sound of footsteps. He awoke with a start, believing that his executioners were coming and this time he was surely a goner.

The nightmare recurred, a prolonged torture. The best attitude he could adopt, Eugene thought, was one of amusement mingled with contempt. It was important to show that he was unafraid and considered them his inferiors. When his jailers told him he would not die if he repented, Eugene burst out laughing. He told them they were ignorant of his reputation and that they had better tread carefully, for they would not get away with this murder. His disdain had the effect he wanted. They were at once impressed and intimidated.

A warlord's reign was precarious. Nobody knew for sure who would be the master of Tianjin tomorrow. It might be someone more friendly to Eugene, and that impelled the jailers to act cautiously. Eugene was not allowed to read newspapers or go near anything that would bring him news from the outside. He did not know that his bluffing tactics matched the steps of his friends and fellow journalists, who were raising a hue and cry demanding his release. But Eugene sensed the change in his jailers' attitude and saw to it that he was regarded with respect. He could scarcely ask them to let him go, but he insisted on being accommodated as much as possible. At one point, he thought of talking his way out by using his patriotic oratory on a young captain who spoke English. It apparently had an impact, for the young man came back for more, but Eugene never discounted the possibility that his new acquaintance might have been planted there by his enemies.

One night, a barrage of gunfire startled him from sleep. Another round of executions! Then footsteps! They stopped ominously at his door. A dark figure stood behind the door. When the man took two steps forward, his face was recognizable. He was the captain Eugene had befriended. Friend or not, he would do what his superiors ordered, Eugene thought gloomily. Eugene asked for a few minutes to dress as tidily as he could before he faced the firing squad again. He was dumbfounded by the captain's reply. He said that he had come to set Eugene free. "Free from trouble," under the circumstances, could mean death. It was a euphemism for execution that jailers often used. Eugene stared at this soon-to-be executioner and thought bitterly to himself that the cruelty of man was boundless. Why lure him, who was going to die, into a false hope that he was going to live?

There was a mutiny under way, the captain explained. The garrison general, Guo Songling, in secret pact with Feng Yuxiang, the Christian General, had risen against his boss, Zhang Zuolin, the Manchurian Tiger. The chief warden, a lackey of the Tiger, was the first to flee. His officers and staff were dispersing to safety, and it was every man for himself. They had left the prisoners to their own devices. Knowing that the Christian General was a friend to Eugene, the captain said, he had come to release him.

Back in Peking, Eugene received a hero's welcome from his friends and fellow journalists. The first person he went to visit was Li Dazhao. He told Li he wanted to meet the press, thanking them and telling them about the inhuman abuse of prisoners by the secret police of the Manchurian Tiger. His public exposure of the warlord, Zhang Zuolin, stirred up more furor, and his friends again worried about his safety.

That night, from the back window, he looked out at the small, neglected garden. The branches of a large willow gracefully swayed in the slight breeze. Some touched the upturned eaves of the pavilion; others cast moving shadows on the roof. As Eugene looked at the dance of shadows, he noticed a still, darker shadow moving on its own. It broke away, leaping down. *An assassin sent by the Manchurian Tiger!* Eugene's heart skipped a beat. The imagined assassin metamorphosed into a cat, sitting poised at the foot of the rock hill. A false alarm, Eugene told Li Dazhao about the incident the next morning.

"Are you sure that you did not see anything else?" Li asked gravely, pressing Eugene's arm to emphasize his apprehension.

Eugene did not reply for some time. "What do you think I might have missed seeing?"

"A Flying Burglar, maybe," Li said, squinting at the lively crowd of students volunteering in his office. Eugene knew the source of Li's warning. The Flying Burglar was a special product of Peking. His profession required him to master the martial art of kung fu. He could leap from roof to roof like a swallow, swift and light, and break into a room without making any noise. Sometimes he hired himself out as an assassin.

Li advised Eugene to immediately leave Peking. "A Flying Burglar usually will do the reconnoitering first and then come back to do the real killing."

"How can I leave without finding my own replacement, without re-opening the news agency and the *People's Tribune?*" Eugene gazed at the teacup in his hands with an expression that betrayed his uneasiness.

Despite his fears, on the next day, December 13, Eugene walked with deceiving equanimity into a press conference. A press conference, in his experience, was an effective platform to reach out for sympathizers. In the question-and-answer session, a reporter from the *Morning Bell (Chenzhong Boo)* asked what he thought of Zhang Zuolin's future. This newspaper had a longtime working relationship with Eugene. It had once been edited by Li Dazhao, and in 1919 it had published the Lansing-Ishii Secret Pact that Eugene had gotten hold of in Paris. It had also had a positive role in causing the outbreak of the May Fourth Movement.

The question led Eugene to redouble his blast against the Manchurian Tiger, predicting his "immediate demise."[1] At the end of the press conference, Eugene noticed a woman walking toward him. It was impossible to overlook Rayna Prohme under any circumstances. Her thick red hair, like a crown, shone gloriously and framed a pale, slightly freckled face. Walking beside her was a man, her complete opposite. She was vivacious; he looked stodgy. They invited Eugene to their apartment for a cup of coffee.

This chance meeting resolved Eugene's dilemma. Rayna had come to Peking recently and become fascinated with the Chinese revolution while watching the students' activities.

Rayna was from the Midwest, a graduate of the University of Illinois. Her first husband was the playwright Samson Raphaelson, who wrote the scenario for *The Jazz Singer*, the first major sound film ever made. They were divorced in San Francisco en route to China. It was not clear whether Rayna met Bill Prohme, an editor at Hearst's *San Francisco Examiner*, before or after she became a divorcee. Anyway, Bill fell in love with her and could not live without her. He was not an extravagant type, and he meant what he said. His face, behind a pair of round spectacles, was staid and only broke into a quiet smile at the sight of her. He had come to China with and for Rayna. She was in search of a cause, and when she found one, she became more married to it than to him. She had no theory but her heart to follow and relied on him to rationalize her revolutionary passion.

Eugene asked them to take on the editorships of the *People's Tribune* and the Sino-American News Agency, but to think carefully before they accepted his offer. Working for the Kuomintang was not without danger. Despite the warning, the Prohmes, Rayna in particular, seemed exhilarated.

Now Eugene could leave Peking and return to Canton. Taking precautions against any accident, Eugene did not go home but checked into the Wagon Lit Hotel in the Legation Quarters. He closed the door, hung up the do-not-disturb sign, took a bath, and fell asleep. The next morning, he opened the door and looked out. At the same time, two doors down, another door opened and a head poked out and then quickly ducked back in. It was Eugene's erstwhile captor, the ex–chief warden. Persecutor and persecuted were hidden in the same hotel.

Eugene decided to leave as soon as he had introduced Li Dazhao to Rayna as the new editor of the *People's Tribune* and Bill Prohme as the new head of the Sino-American News Agency.

Eugene returned to Canton at the end of 1925 and found the city gripped in the succession fight between Wang Jingwei, the Chinese Byron, who claimed he'd received the mandate at Sun Yatsen's deathbed, and Chiang Kaishek, the new powerful militarist. Their fight was further complicated by a power struggle in the Moscow-controlled Comintern. After Lenin's death, Stalin and Trotsky jousted for leadership; each had his vision for the Party's future. Stalin, the more pragmatic man, wanted to proceed carefully with his strategy of world revolution in which he would conquer China and then the world. But he did not want this plan to interfere with his primary focus of consolidating power and building an imperial Bolshevik empire. Trotsky, the proletarian Peter Pan, advocated an instant world revolution, which would swiftly transform all nations in the Bolshevik image. While they pointed judgmental fingers at each other, Borodin and the Chinese Communist Party got caught in the crossfire. It was almost impossible to tell which directive was issued by the Trotskyists or the Stalinists, or whether it was a compromise between the two. Each side claimed to be more revolutionary than the other and called upon the Chinese communists to take over the bourgeois Kuomintang.

In the second half of 1924, a shift in Russian policy toward China was being implemented, and in January 1925 the Moscow-controlled Comintern fired Maring, the man who had been the midwife at the birth of the Chinese Communist Party in 1921. Maring had insisted that China was in a stage of bourgeois revolution that should be led by the bourgeois Kuomintang until the Communist Party was strong enough to assume leadership. Moscow dismissed him and put in charge Gregory Voitinsky, who had established the Peking and Shanghai communist cells back in 1920. The new deputy chief of the Comintern's Far East Bureau brought with him instructions that breached all the previous agreements on the conception and conditions of forming the alliance with the Kuomintang.

Moscow decided that the Chinese Communist Party was no longer a junior partner to the Kuomintang, but an independent entity with an independent goal, which was to turn China communistic as soon as possible. Voitinsky was to supervise the Chinese Communist Party's attempt at seizing the leadership of the nationalist revolution. The contentious Voitinsky soon collided with Borodin, the High Adviser to the Kuomintang, who knew the political landscape and the Kuomintang better. Borodin argued that hurrying the transition would alienate all Kuomintang factions, right, center, and left, at a time when the Kuomintang was still indispensable to the progress of the revolution.

Moscow's new position on China induced the Chinese Communist Party to take a perilous road. Blame, nevertheless, should not all be heaped on Moscow. They knew pitifully little about China, its history and its culture, but they fancied they would be able to direct from afar the vast and complex Chinese revolution, with confusing, conflicting, and imperialistic edicts. The Chinese Communist Party, for its part, had its share of bungling. Quite a few Party leaders were men in their late twenties or early thirties. These young men had no patience. They were impatient for power and eager to test their ideals with reckless acts of heroism. Nowhere was this more apparent than in the way they led the Hong Kong–Canton Strike.

In China, 1925 was a year remembered for its numerous strikes, demonstrations, and protests. The one that had most impact on the national scene was the Hong Kong–Canton Strike. On May 30, the British-controlled police of Shanghai's International Settlement gunned down twelve marchers in a demonstration. The whole nation was agitated into an uproar that sent shock waves outside the mainland, to Hong Kong. On June 19, about 250,000 Chinese workers walked off their posts in Hong Kong, and about 100,000 of them moved to Canton, leaving the British colony a ghost town.

A strike committee was formed. It had a force of about two thousand pickets, armed and led by the communist officers from the Whampoa Military Academy, who pushed the Kuomintang soldiers and police aside and started running Canton. They erected numerous checkpoints, halted vehicles and pedestrians, arrested suspected profiteers, and confiscated alleged contraband. Anyone who was accused of violating the boycott against British products was sent to a kangaroo court presided over by the strikers. A suspect had no recourse to appeal, since the court was considered a military tribunal. At first, the committee targeted only foreign businessmen, but they expanded their arrests to include

Chinese traders who appeared to collaborate with the enemies. While foreign businessmen had the capital to withstand the disruption, the Chinese merchants went broke. Consequently, they withdrew their sympathy—and subsidies—for the strikers. More workers lost their jobs, and more went hungry. The army of strikers expanded. Trade was disrupted, revenue kept shrinking, and Canton's economy crumbled, although the Hong Kong economy also suffered hugely.

The nebulous political situation made it easier for the strikers to get their own way. The two main contenders in the race to inherit Sun Yatsen's mantle were the Chinese Byron, Wang Jingwei, and Chiang Kaishek. After his troops had won several battles defeating local warlords in early and mid-1925, Chiang was hailed as the liberator of Canton by his supporters. Intimidated by Chiang's rising prestige and popularity, Wang leaned on Borodin and the Chinese communists to help him stay in office. He underwent a metamorphosis, tossing away his centrist label and reinventing himself as a leftist.

The strikers, buoyed by their newly acquired clout, turned the heat up on Chiang Kaishek, who was now the most powerful opponent standing in their way. For his part, Chiang was not unwilling to take them on. He had troops at his back and a coup d'état, if carried out successfully, would rid him of both the strikers and Wang Jingwei.

This was the situation Eugene faced toward the end of 1925. The minute he went ashore in Canton, he was embroiled in the Hong Kong–Canton Strike. He was met by his old friend C. C. Wu, the current foreign minister, who was negotiating with the British to conclude the strike. On their drive back to the city, the chauffer navigated through the numerous checkpoints at a snail's pace. Some strikers stopped them, but let the car pass when they were told it was an official sedan. Some strikers were less polite. They asked to see papers. At one checkpoint, their car came to a sudden halt, and their military guards jumped off the running board. A group of strikers, with bloodshot eyes and unshaven faces, swarmed the car and made attempts to drag the four guards away, banging on the windows and screaming "Get out, get out!" Both sides brandished knives and guns. A riot was close at hand. Eugene was about to get up from his seat.

"Eugene, you are not going to try to reason with them?" C. C. Wu asked in English.

"I have to do it sooner or later," Eugene said, removing Wu's hand from his knee.

He got out of the car. He looked over the crowd and said, "I am Chen Youren. Who is in charge here?" A secretary from the foreign office interpreted.

The strikers pushed Eugene aside and, pointing at C. C. Wu, demanded: "We want to talk to him. We demand our legitimate place at the negotiating table."

"I demand to talk first to your leaders of the strike committee," Eugene said, stepping back to guard the rear door of the car.

A few men in the back of the crowd put their heads together, speaking in low tones. One of them came forward and waved the potential rioters away. While retreating, one rioter thumbed his nose at C. C. Wu and shouted that the foreign minister was just like his dead father, a puppet of British imperialists. To C. C. Wu, a filial and dutiful son, there was nothing more insulting. He was livid with anger.

The strikers had gone too far, Eugene thought to himself, as he reentered the car and sat beside his friend. Eugene knew C. C. Wu too well to believe their allegation. His friend, Eugene trusted, had a strong sense of noblesse oblige and would never disgrace his country and office. C. C.'s father, Wu Tingfang, was one of the great pioneers in shaping modern Chinese diplomacy. Father and son, both patriots who had learned their liberal views from an English education, loathed militarists meddling in politics. In 1917, they had played a role in rescuing Eugene from the prison of the warlord Duan Qirui, the Righteous Buddhist, and they went south with Eugene to reinforce Sun Yatsen's Canton government.

C. C. Wu's friendship with Eugene had started in 1912, when they were associated with the Cantonese Club. From that time on, they had often worked as a team, having the same views on foreign affairs, views articulated in the documents presented at the Paris Peace Conference. Their stance was firm, but not self-righteous. They knew China and the foreign powers both needed patience and effort to untangle the problems of the past. Having said that, they were not without differences in handling the question. C. C. Wu was milder, Eugene more radical.

C. C. Wu, scion of a Hong Kong–based patrician family, was connected with the island colony's wealthy and influential families. During this strike, they were suffering financial losses along with the British banks, manufacturers, and corporations, and wanted to see it end. The Hong Kong strikers, poor and neglected, naturally distrusted a man like Wu and resented having to entrust their affairs to him. They suspected Wu of acting more like an agent of Britain than their representative. Thus C. C. Wu was pleased to welcome Eugene back from Tianjin, to help him in negotiating with the British on the settlement of the strike. Eugene had a pro-labor reputation and would make a complementary deputy.

Nothing could get done until they resolved the strike, C. C. Wu grumbled. It's no use to go after the strikers, he said; the root of trouble was in Moscow, which pulled the strings of the puppet show. Then, in an ominous voice, C. C. Wu continued: "There is a rumor that they are plotting to kidnap Chiang Kaishek."

Wu, with his Westernized liberal training, was not a man who could feel cordial toward Chiang Kaishek. But, alarmed by what he saw as the escalating of the strikers' mob rule, he began to have second thoughts. After all, Chiang was a fellow member of the Kuomintang and therefore the lesser of two evils. Chiang did not interfere in his handling of the negotiations with the British. The strikers did.

COUP D'ÉTAT AND
COUNTER-COUP D'ÉTAT

Eugene was one of the first tipped off by C. C. Wu about Chiang Kaishek's possible coup d'état. Wu was bogged down in his negotiations with the British and frustrated by the strikers' interference. Bent on giving the communists a lesson, Wu made a seemingly small remark that set in motion a series of events that finally led to the Zhongshan Gunboat Incident.

One night, C. C. Wu had the Soviet consul general over for dinner and was startled when his guest said that Chiang Kaishek was thinking of taking a vacation in Russia. Wu immediately linked this with the kidnapping rumor and jumped to the conclusion that this was a plot to get rid of Chiang.

A few days later, Wu invited Chiang Kaishek's aides to dinner and casually asked when their boss was leaving for his Russian vacation. They had no idea. Because no seemingly innocuous question could be taken at face value in intrigue-filled Canton, the aides dutifully reported their conversation to Chiang.

Wu's question heightened Chiang's suspicions. Chiang decided to take up the gauntlet. He came to see Eugene and the Soong clan.

This evening, like many others, Eugene was in the Soong living room, relaxing. Chingling held a skein of brown wool while her niece, Ailing's older daughter, rolled it into a ball. In the chair beside them sat Ailing, who took up her knitting. She had inherited some of the proselytizing fervor of her missionary parents, but she tolerated Eugene's Catholicism. She rationalized that though the Roman Catholics might be blinded by error, she and Eugene, after all, shared faith in one and the same God. She seemed to believe that she had a direct line to God because of her very proper Protestantism.

A servant came in with an envelope on a tray. He proffered it to Ailing instead of Chingling and said in a low voice that General Chiang Kaishek was asking for an audience. Ailing took her daughter's hand and signaled to Chingling to follow her into an inner room. Chingling nodded in agreement. Of all her siblings, Chingling had special regard for Ailing. According to Chinese custom, the oldest daughter in a family was a kind of substitute mother.

After the death of Sun Yatsen, Chingling had been catapulted into the Central Executive Committee of the Kuomintang. Cautioned by her siblings, in particular her older sister, Ailing, she nevertheless remained politically inactive. She seldom attended important Kuomintang meetings, but gave her brother, T. V. Soong, her voting proxy and told him to follow Eugene's lead: if things went wrong, she could say it was her brother's fault; he must have misinterpreted her intention. Thus she placed herself above controversy and reproach.

Eugene and T.V. stood up when the two sisters rose from their chairs, and by the time they sat down again, the door was closed and the two men were left to deal with Chiang Kaishek. Before they invited Chiang into the living room, they opened the envelope and saw what the general was up to. T. V. took out a small book. It was beautifully bound and neatly printed and contained a collection of quotes from Sun Yatsen's letters to Chiang, instructing the commandant on how to run the Whampoa Military Academy. In his own words, Sun clearly stated that Chiang's duty was training cadets for the Nationalist Revolution led by the Kuomintang. Chiang did not need to say a word to get his message across to the recipients of his gift. Sun Yatsen had entrusted this job to him, and he would defend the late leader's legacy at all cost.

Chiang Kaishek's face, bony and pale, showed an inner conflict that he could barely contain. He had evidence of a schism within his military: his men had picked up a circular, misplaced by the communists, attacking the Kuomintang and saying that Sun Yatsen was not as revolutionary as Marx. This was insubordination, Chiang stressed. The communists, doubling as Kuomintang members, had taken the oath to obey the Kuomintang constitution, which required loyalty to Sun Yatsen-ism. The communists sabotaged the leadership of the other Kuomintang generals as well, and lured the rank and file into their camp. The generals, incensed, would not tolerate them much longer. Chiang's black eyes turned blacker and, fixing them first on Eugene and then T. V. Soong, he said he feared a bloody internecine fight if the communists were allowed to go on with their subversive activity.

Chiang Kaishek's intention was transparent: he was preparing them for his showdown with Wang Jingwei and the communists. And yet what Chiang had said was not untrue.

With deepening misgivings, Eugene went with T. V. Soong to see Borodin. It was up to Borodin to tame Chiang Kaishek. Borodin's support had been most essential to Chiang's rise; without his support, Chiang would not have gotten the job as commandant of the Whampoa Military Academy, which had been established with Soviet sponsorship. However, Chiang Kaishek was not the only one giving them a problem: Borodin also had to tell his Chinese comrades to act with restraint.

The Soviet High Adviser was coming home from somewhere or another. He looked annoyed that one of his secretaries was waiting in the hall, holding several files. He dismissed the young man at once. He was tired, and it was late, Borodin said disagreeably. He was in no mood for more work.

Eugene thought they had come at the wrong time to admonish Borodin. As he was still reflecting, an orderly brought in a glittering samovar, a teapot on its top, and three tall glasses. The orderly poured out the tea, no milk but slices of lemon. Borodin drank tea Russian-style. Eugene lifted the glass, took a sip, and set it before Borodin with decisiveness. The Kuomintang Party constitution had given Sun Yatsen overall power. That was the right thing to do at that time because Eugene believed that Sun used it to advance a revolution that would eventually lead China to democracy. To prevent any other man from usurping this power, the Party constitution specified that it was exclusively conferred on Sun. What if a militarist like Chiang Kaishek declared that he would be the legitimate heir to Sun and all that Sun had been entitled to?

It was impossible to tame Chiang, Eugene insisted, without the cooperation of the other generals. Borodin must warn his young Chinese comrades to stop harassing them.

"Aren't they the same, the generals?" Borodin snorted.

Borodin had changed, no longer his old upbeat self. He slouched deeper into his chair, and then abruptly he rose to his feet. He paced the room, alternately shrugging his shoulders and shaking his head. He said that he had repeatedly advised caution to his Chinese comrades, but all the thanks he had gotten was a kick in his face. They had accused him of being soft on the Kuomintang. They had even aired their complaints to Moscow, through Gregory Voitinsky, his nemesis. Hamstrung by Moscow, Borodin groused, he could neither rein in his Chinese comrades nor reach a compromise with the Kuomintang.

"Is there nothing at all you can do?" Eugene asked.

Borodin turned slowly to Eugene and answered in a measured, controlled voice: "Moscow is recalling me."

Eugene stared at him as if expecting more. Borodin chain-lit another cigarette and smoked in silence.

"Who will take care of your work?" Eugene asked.

"Kuibyshev."

Eugene and T. V. Soong exchanged glances. Eugene lifted his thick eyebrows in an expression of irritation. Then he laughed softly, as if amused by a joke. "Excellent! He'll give the finishing touch to the confrontation."

N. V. Kuibyshev, known in China as Kissenka or Kisanko, was a poor substitute. While many Kuomintang members merely disliked him, Chiang Kaishek hated him with a passion. Kuibyshev talked to Chiang with condescension, as if he were already the new High Adviser. He made one suggestion that Chiang believed was a vicious design against him, urging Chiang to take the waterway in starting the Northern Expedition, so as to reinforce the army of Feng Yuxiang, the Christian General, who would fight from the northwest to Peking. This was nonsense, because in the first place, there were few ships at Chiang's disposal. Chiang could have laughed it off, but his reaction was violent. He knew the Russians had long been flirting with the Christian General. Now Moscow brazenly strong-armed him to play the supporting role to a man he despised. Meanwhile, Kuibyshev wanted Chiang to move his soldiers to Vladivostok and train them there. Kuibyshev argued that because Vladivostok was closer to both Siberia and Peking than Canton, it was a better place to carry out the military operations of the Northern Expedition. Kuibyshev's suggestions coincided with rumors that the Russians were plotting to kidnap Chiang and exile him somewhere in Siberia. To be fair to Chiang, his suspicion was well grounded—to tuck away an inconvenient person in exile was Moscow's usual practice.

"Have you heard the kidnap rumor? Any truth in it?" Eugene asked.

"I hope not," Borodin answered vaguely. "I hope no fool will give Chiang Kaishek an excuse to start a coup d'état."

Borodin avoided eye contact with Eugene, and then, to forestall further questions, he abruptly dropped the subject.

His evasiveness disquieted Eugene. Borodin knew more about what was going to happen, Eugene reflected.

Borodin left Canton on February 4, 1926, on a vacation trip, he said. But rumors of his dismissal shook the city. Concerned about Chingling's safety, Eugene, in T. V. Soong's presence, urged her to leave Canton for a while. She had a very good reason to leave the city: the cornerstones of Sun Yatsen's mausoleum would be laid on Purple Gold Hill outside the city of Nanjing. There would be a ceremony on March 12, and she should take part in it.

Chingling's eyes moistened at the mention of her husband's name. She remained silent, struggling to hold back the tears. In a black widow's robe, with her hair pulled back into a knot, her thin face looked fragile. Eugene was conscious of a sensation of nostalgia, recalling the days when Sun Yatsen, Chingling, and he had discussed the Russia-oriented policy with ardor and hope. This policy was now in danger. To salvage it, Eugene needed all his wits about him.

On March 19, 1926, the largest Kuomintang gunboat, *Zhonghan,* named after Sun Yatsen's honorific, dropped anchor at Whampoa Island, where Chiang Kaishek kept his office and where he sometimes stayed overnight. Its captain, Li Zilong, a communist and a most vociferous critic of the Kuomintang, claimed he had received an order from Chiang's office and simply obeyed it. Chiang flatly denied he had given any such order. Once Chiang believed that his opponents were closing in, he struck without hesitation. In the middle of that night, without consulting his boss, Wang Jingwei, who, as the chairman of the Military Council, had final say about any military affairs, Chiang arrested a great number of communists. He detained more than forty leftists and communist political workers—and cast out all commissars from the First Army, which was directly under his command—as suspected communists. Chiang put all the Soviet Russians under house arrest and disarmed the labor unions' militia. He seized the headquarters of the Hong Kong–Canton Strike Committee and imposed a curfew.

Two days later, Wang Jingwei called an emergency meeting of the members of the Central Executive Committee. Chiang Kaishek came, sullen and unrepentant. The meeting was held at Wang's sickbed. Wang looked haggard and turned worse when no one seriously challenged Chiang. The generals whom Wang counted on to tame Chiang only sat by and watched. They had their own problems with the communist commissars, who were using the enlarging ranks of the Hong Kong–Canton Strike and of the peasant militia to strengthen their position in the armies. Led by them, the peasants were demanding a wholesale land revolution, which the generals, landowners themselves, strongly opposed. They loathed Chiang Kaishek and goaded the Soviet Russians to get rid of their common rival, though they themselves would not fight Chiang on behalf of communism.

All the participants, right, left, and middle, unanimously voted for three proposals: limit communist activities; ask Moscow to recall Borodin's substitute, N. V. Kuibyshev; and give Eugene the power to end the Hong Kong–Canton Strike. In short, if they did not declare their support for Chiang outright, they at least acquiesced to his plan of a semi-purge of the communists.

The result demonstrated where the Central Executive Committee stood: the communists should be restrained within bounds, but Chiang Kaishek was not allowed to have his way and claim total victory. Eugene's elevation clearly spoke of their intention. Eugene read their signal correctly and responded to it accordingly. He accepted on one condition: he wanted to let the strikers take some limited part in the settlement, and he wanted to conclude the strike in a way that strengthened, not fractured, the United Front. The Kuomintang's foreign policy, Eugene went on, had to be different from that of previous governments: the policy had to be implemented in the interests of the common people, so they would understand that they had not been sold out. Eugene was speaking obliquely against Chiang Kaishek. Chiang, of course, took it as a jab, but remained silent. Eugene's words were appreciated by all who viewed Chiang's arrogance with disapproval but were afraid to say so.

The unsettling situation inside Canton looked inviting to outside meddlers. The British colonialists revived their hope of turning the clock back to the good old days before the Russia-oriented policy. Since January 1926, they had stalled negotiations to settle the strike, and now suddenly they showed great interest in reopening them. On April 9, 1926, the attorney general of the Hong Kong government, Kemp, offered a loan of $10,000,000 if the Kuomintang government disbanded the Strike Committee. C. C. Wu was tempted by the deal. He thought the British loan would give the Kuomintang some breathing space. It was time to take stock of the alliance with the communists, he argued; it did not seem to him worth the trouble to maintain it. He wanted to know what Eugene thought.

Eugene did not object to a British loan, but deemed the timing of the offer bad. The British were trying, Eugene noted, to create bad blood between the Kuomintang and the labor unionists, who he believed were indispensable to the revolution. The peasants and laborers were the new blood in the Kuomintang, and without them, Eugene predicted, the Kuomintang would degenerate into another warlord government of mandarins and landed gentry.

Having said that, Eugene did not want to reject the loan outright. He would agree to accept the loan, Eugene said, if the British would let the Kuomintang use part of it to compensate the strikers. The British responded negatively: they would never agree to strike pay for those involved in unlawful activities.

Just at this critical moment, a few suspicious coincidences occurred. The extreme right wing of the Kuomintang began stirring up trouble. After the death of Sun Yatsen, they had been banished from Canton by the combined forces of the leftists and centrists, with Wang Jingwei and Chiang Kaishek in the lead. Outnumbered, the rightists had moved their headquarters to Shanghai in 1925. Gloating over the chaos in Canton, they dreamed of recouping their lost power. They announced they would reenter Canton by force and reorganize the government with a British loan of $10,000,000, exactly the same amount that Eugene had turned down.

One evening in late March, a glum-faced T. V. Soong brought to Eugene's office a secret message from his older sister Chingling. The extreme rightists, backed by Britain and Chiang Kaishek's rival militarists who had been hounded out of Canton, were preparing to march back into Canton. When Eugene reread the message, T.V., in a subdued voice, said that the sleek political broker Zhang Jingjiang had appeared suddenly in Canton.

Eugene sank into troubled thought. Staring out the window, he saw the night sky grow murkier. The city was overrun by Chiang Kaishek's soldiers. Their omnipresence made it obvious that their commander-in-chief was now the first man in Canton. If Chiang was plotting with the extreme right-wingers, then the city was in dreadful danger.

Startled at this awful thought, Eugene was now frightened, not so much for himself as for Canton. In the past, Britain, the leading colonial power, had used their hirelings, warlords or compradors, to fight the Kuomintang; but now they were dangling their golden pounds in front of revolutionaries like C. C. Wu and Chiang Kaishek. Alarmed, Eugene's brain raced to think up a way to unravel the intricate knot. He looked for a loose thread to pull and found it in Zhang Jingjiang who, T. V. Soong said, was mysteriously visiting Canton from Shanghai.

A senior conservative member of the Kuomintang, Zhang Jingjiang, who had deep connections with the right-wing Kuomintang, was better known as Curio Zhang. The Curio had acquired this nickname because he had amassed a great fortune by selling Chinese antiques to Western clients. He had been a founding member of the Kuomintang and a patron to Chiang Kaishek. Before Chiang was summoned by Sun Yatsen in 1922, he had fallen on hard times. He drifted for a while and then went into the employ of Curio Zhang. The Curio discerned a potential strongman in Chiang Kaishek and groomed him for the role. He obtained a sinecure for Chiang in Shanghai's stock market. Next to a man's desire for food was his desire for sex, Confucius had philosophized, and men were only too happy to follow the sage's teaching. Curio Zhang made sure both of Chiang's appetites were gratified. He coaxed his

Georgette Zhang, fourth daughter of Curio Zhang, would marry Eugene in 1931 after Agatha's death in 1926.

female protégé, Miss Chen Jieru, a schoolmate of his young second wife, into becoming the third and current Madame Chiang Kaishek.

Chiang trusted the Curio not only because he was grateful. The Curio was more of a power broker than a power usurper, working to raise the market value of his stocks. He did not pose a threat to Chiang and was reputedly the only man who could curb the impetuous militarist. "Everybody knew his [Curio's] extremely close relationship with Chiang.... Chiang used his [Curio's] position, as a founder of the Kuomintang, to enhance his [Chiang's] opposition against the diehard right-wingers—the West Hills Conference faction."[1]

The Curio spoke some French and English. He was one of the few Kuomintang leaders with whom Eugene could talk easily and directly without an interpreter. Eugene knew the Curio's soft spot. Both were connoisseurs of food and art. The Curio was disabled, a cripple whose womanizing days were over, but his passion for gourmet food still burned bright, for it was the only pleasure remaining to him in his wheelchair. He never declined an invitation to Eugene's dinner parties, which were catered by the best chef in Canton. Each meal, no matter whether the style was Chinese or European, was presented to the delighted guests like a miracle.

The Curio had enjoyed a variety of cuisines, but had never yet tasted Trinidadian food. Eugene remembered a few homespun recipes, which he gave to his chef. This talented man, on short notice, somehow whipped up a delicious meal for the guest of honor. The menu comprised a dish of pilau (fried rice with chicken), salad with improvised Trinidad mayonnaise, and pigs' feet in aspic jelly.

Eugene went out of his way to please his guest. He added one decoration to the wall of his living room, a charming watercolor depicting a Parisian scene, a gift from the Curio's fourth daughter, Georgette, who had studied art in Paris. She and Eugene met once when she was home on vacation. Georgette had been born in Paris and was regarded in art circles there as a young painter of great promise. On top of all her natural endowments and acquired qualities, she was her father's princess. Georgette would become the second Mrs. Eugene Chen five years later, after the death of Aisy.

At Eugene's dining table, the Curio was further mellowed by his favorite French champagne. There was such good humor and jollity that the host and guest spoke with candor. Both knew that the small banquet of three—Eugene, T. V. Soong, and the Curio—was arranged for an intimate exchange of opinions, and in no time they broached the subject of the current upheavals.

Curio Zhang's sickly emaciated face was instantly clouded, and he sagged heavily in the wheelchair. Reflecting for a moment, he said that he would admonish Chiang Kaishek to rethink the wisdom of the peremptory arrests during the Zhongshan Gunboat Incident. By such actions, Chiang had created a quandary for himself. Now Chiang's problems lay not only with the communists but also with the rightists, especially the extreme right, who saw him as Borodin's minion, the man who had permitted the communists to indoctrinate the Whampoa cadets, and who had conspired with the Bolshevik lapdog, Wang Jingwei, to drive them out of Canton.

Eugene discreetly cleared his throat and wondered aloud if it was true that the rightists were luring Chiang into their camp.

The Curio shook his head slowly and said that if Chiang carried out a wholesale purge and ousted all the communists, he would be doing exactly what the extreme rightists wanted him to do and so would create more problems for himself, because that would be against the Central Executive Committee's decision to carry out a semi-purge by limiting only the communists' activities.

"I'll strongly advise Chiang not to rush into another quagmire. He must be made to understand that the extreme right wing won't forgive him easily," Curio Zhang said, and agreed to become Eugene's and Chiang's intermediary.

Eugene leaned forward, sitting almost face-to-face with Curio Zhang. Their eyes held each other. The Curio did not blink. He seemed to mean business because his services were not entirely altruistic. Chiang Kaishek was his largest investment. He knew he stood to collect a large payoff if Chiang stayed in power and would lose it if Chiang made a wrong move and fell.

Curio Zhang made an occasion to talk with Chiang Kaishek in private. He told his former protégé that his best course lay for now with the leftists and centrists. Before Chiang was assured of getting hold of the British pounds and American dollars, it would be foolish of him to let the Russian rubles slip through his fingers. Right after the Sun Yatsen–Joffe joint statement, the Russians had offered two million rubles as financial assistance to Sun's Kuomintang government. Then from April to October of 1925, the Russians spent 4,610,134 rubles to fund the military and political projects of the Kuomintang. Then in 1925 and 1926, the financial aid to the Kuomintang increased sharply, to 14,054,873 rubles[2]—something that Chiang could not afford to disregard. In other words, Chiang should mark time and do more groundwork before he made another move. Chiang should maintain that he was impartial. He had gotten rid of some communist troublemakers; now he should fire a few Kuomintang mischief makers. The current foreign minister, C. C. Wu, was too deeply mired in the Zhongshan Gunboat Incident to be effective; the government needed a fresher face. Many members of the Central Executive Committee favored Eugene, known as a confirmed left-wing Kuomintang, a diplomat, and a pragmatist who could balance principles with reality. The Curio advised Chiang to go along with them and support Eugene.

Chiang Kaishek, evidently convinced by the voices of moderation, was anxious to avoid an appearance of a military dictatorship. Wang Jingwei's self-exile in Paris left the three most pivotal jobs within the Kuomintang up for grabs: chairman of the Kuomintang Party, chairman of the Kuomintang government, and chairman of the Military Council. Chiang wanted to snatch all three positions, but he appointed himself only chairman of the military council. As long as he had the army behind him, he figured he could call the shots. He approved of two senior Kuomintang members to fill the other jobs: Curio Zhang as acting chairman of the party, and Tan Yankai, an old friend of Curio Zhang's, as acting chairman of the government. These two were clever choices. Both were Sun Yatsen's contemporaries and were conservatives, but mild enough to be accepted by most of the major players. However, because Wang Jingwei had only taken a sick leave and had not resigned, the two could pretend to act only on his behalf.

Chiang also sided with Eugene, turning down the British loan. He publicly denounced the extreme rightists for trying to fracture the United Front by taking Britain's money. He vowed not to let them ride back into Canton on a Trojan horse filled with British pounds and British-made fireworks. However, while Chiang in public still leaned to the political left, he quietly asked Curio Zhang to placate the hardcore conservatives.

Eugene was not naïve enough to believe Chiang totally. It was possible that some residue of revolutionary ardor was still alive in Chiang, but it was more probable that he was sitting on the fence, letting the left- and right-wingers offset one another. Chiang was positioning himself for real dictatorial power. Eugene, however, figured that even if Chiang only delayed declaring himself military dictator, that delay could also give him time to help the leftists recover from the coup d'état. Eugene and Chiang Kaishek, two men so different in background, education, mental makeup, taste, and inclination, would soon find out that for the time being they must become allies in a fight against a common opponent, the extreme right-wingers of the Kuomintang.

In the memoirs of Chiang's third wife, Chen Jieru, she wrote that before the launch of the Northern Expedition in July 1926, Chiang was definitely on amicable terms with Eugene.[3] One weekend, Chiang excitedly told Chen Jieru that Madame Kong, Ailing Soong, had invited them for dinner the following night. The Soongs' friendship was important, and so was Eugene's. Chiang, for some reason, was delayed and could not come to the party with his wife, so she arrived alone.

Nervously glancing at the unfamiliar faces, the third Madame Chiang Kaishek, at nineteen, felt rather self-conscious among the very distinguished and highly sophisticated guests. She was overjoyed to spot three friends. She went up to Eugene Chen, Mayling Soong, and Madame Liao, widow of the left-winger Liao Zhongkai. The third Madame Chiang had the feeling that Eugene wanted to put her at ease, because he turned the conversation to politics, which he knew interested her more than small talk. She recalled that he spoke with patriotic ardor, although a little too zealously for her delicate ears.

Ailing asked Eugene to show the house to the third Madame Chiang. Eugene, in his western suit of white linen, obliged gallantly. After touring the house, they strolled in the garden. It was most unusual at that time in China for a young woman to stroll in the moonlight with a handsome man without a chaperone. Chiang must have respected Eugene's integrity mightily, to have allowed his wife to be alone in Eugene's company.

On their return to the drawing room, the third Madame Chiang overheard the oldest and youngest Soong sisters plotting to steal her husband. Her fear was enhanced by Ailing's seating arrangement. Chiang Kaishek then arrived late, apologizing profusely. Ailing threw him a look of mock ill-humor. At the dinner table, the hostess placed Chiang between herself and Mayling, and placed the third Madame Chiang between Eugene and Madame Liao Zhongkai. Ailing's chef cooked French cuisine, and the last course was his masterpiece: doves baked golden and set on diamond-shaped bread dotted with emerald greens.

"Eating doves is like eating mangos; it is best to eat alone in the bathroom, tearing it with our hands," Mayling said. "But it is a pity that we don't have enough bathrooms to accommodate our guests. So here we are. Let us bow our heads over our plates, use our hands, and eat without looking up. That way we won't embarrass each other."

"What a clever sister I have," Ailing said, turning to Chiang Kaishek. He seemed so overwhelmed by her attention that he became tongue-tied.

Flirtation and repartee spiced up the gathering. Guests felt comfortable exchanging more serious ideas about the Northern Expedition. The war strategy had to be coordinated with the diplomatic tactics. Staving off the armed intervention of the foreign powers was of paramount importance. Both Eugene and Chiang Kaishek were in total agreement on this score.

Sometimes Eugene felt his conscience squirming. He was letting Chiang Kaishek exploit his name and appear loyal to Sun Yatsen's vision. He recalled with keen nostalgia the days when he had not been tormented by such burdens. Years ago, when he had an idea, he would tell Sun Yatsen. If Sun agreed, they would try it out. With Sun lending his support, Eugene had not really been bothered by partisan politics. The language barrier also protected him in a sense. Despite his long stay in China, he had never learned to speak Chinese except for a few words like "good morning" and "good-bye," and even these he sometimes mixed up. He made no apologies for his ignorance of the Chinese language; on the contrary, he was proud of it and considered it proof of his integrity as a nonpartisan revolutionary. Machiavellians could hardly entangle him in their political conspiracies when he could not speak Chinese and they could not speak English. Eugene was thus able to keep relatively free of the factional strife and to maintain the full confidence of Sun Yatsen. If any conspirators accused Eugene of saying this or that, Sun would ask who had interpreted for him. The question would end any accusation.

But Eugene was learning to dance on the political tightrope. Pressure from all sides bore down on him. Sometimes the pressure was greater from this or that side and threatened to tumble him. Concealing his fear, Eugene went on with affected ease while yearning for Borodin's return.

Ironically, Chiang Kaishek's coup d'état gave Borodin passage back to China. Moscow could find no one better qualified to clean up the mess. Rather than fire him, as they had originally decided, they sent him back to China sometime around mid or late April, two and a half months after his recall.

But he could do little about the new lineup in Canton, as the Kuomintang right, center, and left had reached a reluctant accommodation with one another.

Struggling to reassert himself, Borodin, in his capacity as the High Adviser of the Kuomintang, hoped that now that he was back at the helm, he could strongarm the Kuomintang and reverse what had been done during his absence. He called for a meeting in a Buddhist monastery in the White Cloud Hills. Everybody came as requested, except Chiang Kaishek, who was conspicuously absent. Instead, he sent a messenger, a boy of no consequence, to tell them to do some sightseeing since there were many beautiful spots around there.

Borodin's face set. He asked if that was all General Chiang had said.

"Yes, sir," the messenger answered.

Mortified, Borodin quickly walked down the steps in front of the great hall where the Buddha sat on the lotus petals. Eugene paused for a minute before he followed.

They sat down in a quiet corner and watched in silence, as the sky changed color at sunset and the horizon blended into the earth in the evening twilight. At this moment, Eugene felt a mysterious foreboding in Borodin's presence, feeling as if he had stumbled across a man subdued and lost.

Muttering bitterly, as if to himself, Borodin confessed that he could do very little to change Chiang Kaishek's mind. He had consulted his young Chinese comrades on what to do next, but they were as helpless as he. Their militiamen had been disarmed by Chiang's soldiers, and their Strike Committee was practically dissolved. The irrational exuberance of the young men had led them to overestimate their own strength. Refusing to admit their error, they blamed him for their defeat. Chiang Kaishek, they declared, was his creation. Had he not been so gullible, Chiang's coup d'état would have been exposed and stopped before it broke out.

Knitting his brows in irritation, Eugene wondered aloud why they had not asked for advice from people who knew the situation better than themselves, such as Maring, the Comintern member who had led the founding of the Chinese Communist Party.

Borodin smiled darkly and said that Maring had disagreed with Moscow on its increasingly radical China policy and for that disobedience had fallen from grace and been replaced by Voitinsky, the fast-moving new deputy chief of the Far East Bureau of the Comintern.

"He is harassing you?" Eugene asked.

"I have to stay on speaking terms with him," Borodin answered, hinting that if he acted independently he would be rendered a nonentity or worse.

Pondering the matter for a moment, he merely added, "Maring went back to Holland. Where can I go to but Russia?"

Borodin was not, of course, a man who would confide casually, without a purpose. Desperate to hang on to his job, he found Eugene, after Sun Yatsen and Liao Zhongkai, the only person in the Kuomintang leadership he still could count on. For Eugene's part, he had been working with Borodin for three years and knew him well. They were friends. Borodin was better than any other Russian as the envoy from Moscow.

But Eugene also realized that Borodin was no longer an effective vehicle for getting a message to the Comintern. He had to do it himself. After a few sleepless nights, Eugene came up with a plan to counter them. The Russians must be made to understand that they could advise the Kuomintang on how to run the show, but that they couldn't take the reins into their hands. He had used the Russia-oriented policy to induce the West into some compromise; now he would use the leverage he had earned to elicit some concession from the Russians.

The timing was perfect for Eugene to maneuver diplomatically. As it happened, the Western powers were reassessing their China policy. After nearly a century of trying to beat back surging Chinese nationalism, Britain was finally waking up to the fact that it was unstoppable. The turning point came when the Kuomintang declared the Russia-oriented policy. Following its implementation, the Kuomintang, with the assistance of the labor and peasant unions and their militiamen, had defeated the armed revolt in 1923 by a local warlord, Chen Jiongming, and by the Merchants' Volunteer Force in 1924, both egged on by Britain. The biggest and most direct blow to the Empire came between 1925 and 1926, when the Hong Kong–Canton Strike shook the British Far East powerhouse to its foundation. The attempts and subsequent failures to suppress this strike involving more than three hundred labor unions particularly irked the British Labour Party, who Eugene believed had to acknowledge the impassioned Chinese workers.

Pressed both by outside forces and domestic outcry, the British government had come to the painful realization that coercion did not work and that something had to give. They began to overhaul their outdated China policy, and in October 1925 they resuscitated a long-forgotten promissory note to return tariffs and extraterritorial rights to China. The British had signed the note at the Washington Conference of 1921–1922, but had then buried it in dust.

The United States, also galvanized, saw a chance to circumvent Britain. The Americans were latecomers to the Chinese market, and for a long time they had resented the British for being there first and controlling things. America now decided to get in first and make a gesture of goodwill. In March 1926, Washington announced that it had given up part of its extra-territorial rights, the right to send observers to Chinese courts should they feel it necessary. This was usually an excuse to interfere in the Chinese court procedure if the Chinese defendants were American cronies or hangers-on. By giving up that right, the Americans gave a signal that they were willing to rethink other extraterritorial rights. Eugene immediately extended an invitation to the American minister at Peking, John Van Antwerp MacMurry, to visit Canton.

When the American consul general, Douglas Jenkins, thanked Eugene on behalf of his boss, he said that he hoped MacMurry could come in a milder climate. Eugene interpreted the remark as a hint at the political turmoil following the breakdown of the negotiation of the Hong Kong–Canton Strike and said it was his wish too, so he would reopen the negotiation. But he was afraid that it might again deteriorate into the old argument over who had fired the first shot in the 1925 Shameen Incident, which had led to the Hong Kong–Canton Strike.

Douglas Jenkins's pale eyes assumed a puzzled expression, and he wondered who could tell. It seemed to him that the Chinese had demonstrated in an orderly way. Then, probably because of some congestion ahead, the procession had halted. A shot rang out, and more shots followed. He himself was an eyewitness, but he could not tell who had fired the first shot.

Jenkins, who usually had British words in his mouth, seemed to find his own voice. Eugene snatched at the chance to invite the Americans, as a mediating party, to the coming negotiation with Britain. Once he skipped the sticky point of who had fired the first shot, Eugene would make a proposal regarding the compensation for the families of the more than fifty victims shot dead by the British marines as well as the strikers. He would ask the Kuomintang government and the British Hong Kong government to each give a loan to resolve the strike dispute. This would be a conciliatory opening, a far cry from the original demand to hold the British totally responsible for the Shameen Incident.

Motivated by a sincere desire to arrive at a satisfactory settlement, Eugene continued, the Kuomintang would do "nothing incompatible with the real dignity and interest of Great Britain as a trading power in China. . . ."[4]

The British, however, might still reject this plan, using the excuse of the strike's so-called illegality—they had labeled the strike a political conspiracy instigated by the Bolsheviks, thus making the strikers' activities unlawful. To this, Eugene would bring a countercharge. He would challenge the legality of the extraterritorial rights. Most of all he would aim at the foreign-occupied concessions. The word "concession" (Zujie) means a rental place in Chinese. Eugene dug out the old rental agreements, dusted them off, and studied them. He found that they had been signed only by the local officials. A local official had no authority to cede any land to foreigners, so all the concessions in port cities were under Chinese sovereignty and foreigners had no right to set up their own system of administration, justice, military defense, and taxes.

If the British government turned a deaf ear to both requests, they would provoke the Kuomintang government to end the strike unilaterally and at the same time raise and collect a 2.5 percent special tax on imported items that went through the British-controlled Customs Service. Eugene stated unequivocally that the Chinese had the right to fix their own tax rate. He would use part of the cash to help the strikers relocate.

Douglas Jenkins remained silent and watchful throughout Eugene's speech. At the end, he responded ambiguously: "Give your first plan a chance."

★13★

THE STRIKE AND
THE NORTHERN EXPEDITION

When Eugene set about approaching the Strike Committee, he knew it was a formidable challenge. The British had said repeatedly and categorically that the Hong Kong government would never agree in principle to strike pay or to compensation for the laborers who were also not permitted to resume their former jobs. Compensation or no compensation, Eugene knew the strike had to be ended. It would be impossible for the Canton government to support the launching of the Northern Expedition and the ongoing strike at the same time. There was simply not enough money. The Kuomintang would publicly announce the launching of the Northern Expedition in July. Once it was done, the war effort would preempt everything else, and Chiang Kaishek would order the strikers to shut up and fold up.

Infighting had already erupted among the three hundred or so striking unions, and worsened as unemployment rose and jobs became scarcer. The propertied classes started their own counteroffensive, hiring docile, non-unionized workers. They took back concessions they had made to their employees and tenant farmers, such as higher wages and lower rents. Frustrations between factions grew and caused more rioting.

The streets echoed with the howling and cursing of the disaffected. In their midst were, without doubt, rabble-rousers, hirelings of different and even opposing political groups. One time when Eugene's car passed by them on Yuexiu Road, where the Federation of Labor Unions was located, he told his chauffer to drive off the main road to inspect the makeshift shelters of the strikers, many of whom had moved from Hong Kong to join their Canton brethren. He cared for the unionists' sacrifice and was anxious to learn more about their condition.

The place was an evil-smelling garbage dump: no trees, no bushes, not even weeds. Silence hung over the mounds and huts, and darkness enveloped them. The farther he walked into the colony, the darker the shadows became. Eugene was taken to visit several homes. What dismayed him most was the suffering of the children. When he and his bodyguard walked across a formerly wooded area, he found that there were no more trees: they had been cut down to be used as firewood or sold. Only the short, naked gray stumps remained, leafless and skeletal, with no sign of life in them. It was a terrifying sight, especially with the play of shadows created by the evening stars.

Eugene heard whimpering, but the sound was muted, hardly upsetting the darkening silence. When he was closer, he raised his head, and what he saw stunned him. There were several children, aged three to six, looking at him, their bellies visibly swollen under their clothes. The vacant stare from their emaciated faces had every symptom of mental deficiency brought on by the poverty they had suffered ever since they had been conceived in their mothers' wombs. To see such punishment inflicted on the most innocent and vulnerable was more than Eugene could bear.

Shaken by what he had seen, Eugene could not rest. For days he paced in his office, and for nights he walked around his house, worrying and thinking of what he could do to allay the misery overwhelming so many hardworking laborers.

Time was running out. With an impending war on his hands, Chiang Kaishek imposed martial law. He instructed the Canton chief of police that he would not allow the Strike Committee to interfere with the coming Hong Kong–Canton Conference that Eugene would reopen in July 1926. The strikers' anger was anticipated. They cried foul play and sent their representatives to see Eugene.

Calm and patient, Eugene was intent on showing that he respected them. He hurried out to meet them and led them to his office. He put aside his papers, and the strike leaders had his full attention. They asked him if Chiang Kaishek's statement meant the end of the strikers' participation in the settlement talk.

"Why, you are giving me advice, which is not the same as interference," Eugene answered, his gaze dwelling earnestly on the speaker. He promised to go on arguing for the strikers' cause, but he also had to prepare them for the possible result of the negotiation. He might not be able to obtain any compromise from the British. He might require the strikers to beat a retreat. A well-prepared and well-organized retreat could end the strike on a note of hope.

A young strike leader, Li Lisan, scowled, and words escaped with rapidity from his thick lips. He asked point-blank if Eugene thought their demands for compensation were reasonable and if he was with them. "Yes," Eugene answered. He was with them, because justice was on their side.

Then why should they retreat, more than one voice demanded to know. Li Lisan was notably vociferous. He was evidently a man who spoke before he thought. In all likelihood, he left the thinking to the Russian sitting next to him, Gregory Voitinsky, the deputy head of the Far East Bureau of the Comintern.

"Because justice won't prevail without patience, tact, and human and material resources," Eugene explained. "And now, more than ever, we need to work together."

Some strikers wanted to know why they would be denied representation in the negotiations.

Eugene answered with some irritation. *He* was their representative. The unions were functioning under the auspices of the Kuomintang, and he, as the foreign minister, represented the Kuomintang and therefore represented them.

"You would rather engage the Americans in negotiations. Are the Americans and British not of the same color?" an indignant voice shouted from the back row.

"There is some difference, though no big difference, between them," Eugene said, looking directly at the audience. "But the art of diplomacy is to discern such seemingly insignificant dissimilarities between two nations and exploit them to great advantage." Then he emphasized, with much significance, "That is my profession, and I have learned it the long, hard way."

Borodin, who had kept quiet, slowly and deliberately intervened. Eugene, he stressed, would counsel them regularly so that they could preserve the remaining labor force from further harm.

Voitinsky and the strike leaders felt the sting of Borodin's words. Borodin was insinuating that it was Voitinsky and his go-for-broke strategy that had been responsible for their defeat in Chiang Kaishek's coup d'état. The harm had been done. Either Voitinsky and the strike leaders got hold of themselves and let him take care of the aftermath, Borodin subtly threatened, or they would be held accountable for making a bad situation worse.

Voitinsky and the strike leaders took the beating. The strikers, who had been stripped of weapons by Chiang Kaishek and were now armed primarily with propaganda posters, could not fight real bullets.

Later that night, when Eugene was preparing for the reopening of negotiations with the British, Borodin came to call, bringing with him a young strike leader, Liu Shaoqi.

Liu Shaoqi was the youngest son of a peasant family in a village in Hunan Province, about twenty-five miles away from the birthplace of Mao Zedong. His older brothers did not have much schooling, and when they were strong enough, they worked the land. But Liu Shaoqi was special in his father's eyes. In school he did very well. His nickname was "Little Bookcase." The villagers and his schoolmates admired him as if he were a walking encyclopedia. His father had great expectations for him. On his deathbed, the old man repeatedly instructed the family to pool their scanty resources to give Liu a chance at a higher education. This family obligation weighed heavily on the child, and he took it very seriously. In 1916, when he was eighteen years old, he went to Changsha, the provincial capital of Hunan. Like many youths in those days, he was swept into the student movement. In 1921, he went to study in Moscow's University of the Toilers of the East, where he joined the Communist Party. The institute was political, specializing in training young revolutionaries from the East. In the spring of 1922, Liu came home and became a professional organizer of labor unions.

That year he put his knowledge, skill, and endurance to the test in the Anyuan Coal Miners Strike, with thirteen thousand strikers under his command. They wrested some small gains from their employers, such as increasing the more skillful miners' daily wages from twenty-four to twenty-eight cents (Chinese) and the less skillful miners' daily wages from fifteen to eighteen cents. Everybody hailed it as a great victory. In the frenzy of joy that followed, a strike of the Peking-Hankou railroad workers was staged, but without adequate preparation. The warlord government and the colonialists swiftly retaliated, surprising the unionists and nearly wiping them out. Liu later wrote about what he had learned from the defeat: "a strike would be doomed to failure"[1] if it was called at the wrong time.

When Eugene told Liu and the other strike leaders that it was time to stop the strike, Liu recalled his lesson. He agreed with Eugene on a methodically planned, orderly retreat. But there were more than three hundred unions in the strike, and preserving unity among them was a tremendous challenge. They had a collective goal, but each union also had its own agenda. The remedy, Liu Shaoqi suggested, was education. "Unity" was the operative word. Unity in spirit, unity in pooling material resources, unity in action, and unity in organizing themselves. The strike leaders would teach the workers the importance of team unity, Liu promised, if they could open a labor school.

Knitting his brows, Eugene said that he couldn't see why Chiang Kaishek would object to this proposal. The unionists should learn that their rights came with responsibilities. They had the right to strike; and, when the situation changed, they had the responsibility to bring it to a close as best they could. Eugene meant this remark to be double-edged. He would persuade Chiang to let them reorganize for and readjust to the new reality, but they ought to play their part straight. All were under the obligation to work for the launch of the Northern Expedition—and at this point his voice turned more forceful—which would be led by the Kuomintang.

Some strikers felt betrayed and clamored for war. Eugene offered to meet with them again. When the day came, the Strike Committee warned Eugene frankly that it was an unusually mixed crowd and they were not able to restrain all the strikers from rushing into random acts of violence. They advised Eugene not to go, because of rumors of a plot against him. When Eugene heard that a large number of workers was assembled for the occasion, he decided to go anyway. He did not want to let them down or to have them think he was treating them with contempt. He was, indeed, a bit of a fatalist. If he was decreed for a certain fate, there was no escape.

Absorbed in his own thoughts, Eugene was oblivious to the traffic and pedestrians outside his car. He became aware of them as the car came to a sudden halt. He glanced out and saw soldiers lined up on both sides of the driveway. Those days, Chiang Kaishek dispatched soldiers anywhere there was a large gathering of unionists. Behind them, the street was thronged with seemingly curious onlookers. Eugene alighted and walked to the hall. He heard a symphony of sounds burst forth at his entrance: applause, boos, hands clapping, feet stamping, cheering, and sniggering. He walked on and saw T. V. Soong, Borodin, Voitinsky, Li Lisan, Liu Shaoqi, and others on the stage. They were there for him, willingly or reluctantly. But when the hour came, he alone was standing at the rostrum. He had none of the glad tidings that the unionists expected.

The Kuomintang government did not have enough resources to fight two wars simultaneously, Eugene began to argue. The strike was a smaller battle, and it had to be ended so a bigger battle could be fought. The Northern Expedition had much broader scope and more urgency than the strike, Eugene continued. If it went well, the Hong Kong Chinese would surely stand to gain; but if it failed, the labor unions would be immediately liquidated. Therefore, the unionists would fare much better by cooperating with the Kuomintang government.

As he saw it, the Northern Expedition would prove successful if the foreign powers could be persuaded to sever relations with the warlords, or at least stay relatively neutral. The warlords, by themselves, were too decrepit to resist. Inducing the foreign powers to recognize the Kuomintang as the only government of China was, Eugene said unequivocally, his highest priority. To gain that recognition, the Kuomintang government, of which the labor unions were part, must show that they could govern. He requested everyone to observe discipline.

These words provoked subdued jeers and snorts. Some strikers shouted: "What about our priority?" How could they trust him, they retorted, since he knew nothing about their miserable life? Men who spoke English and made good money, they sneered, were like the hirelings paid by the British fat cats.

One striker rudely asked why Eugene spoke the imperialists' language and not Chinese. Some in the crowd took the cue and hollered at Eugene: "Bootlicker!" When they stood up and stumped angrily to the door, Eugene gestured with his hand and asked them to remain seated. He wanted to answer the question. He waited a pensive moment. Then he replied that he had finished his English education on a scholarship. There was no scholarship offered for a Chinese education on the small island colony where he was born. His family could not afford to pay for it. He was the son of a *zhuzai,* which in Cantonese dialect literally meant a hog trapped in a slaughterhouse. A *zhuzai* was an indentured laborer, and once he boarded a ship as human cargo, he was not expected to come home alive. His father had become a *zhuzai* because the old man was a Taiping rebel and was chased out of his own land.

Eugene spoke in English. His audience waited for the interpreter to render it into Chinese, but they felt the emotion of his words. He spoke as one of them. This was enough to turn the crowd. Quite a few of the participants had been *zhuzai* themselves, or had *zhuzai* in their families. They knew how it felt, slaving as a *zhuzai* in a foreign land. When they learned how Eugene's father had become a *zhuzai,* they warmed up to him. The Taiping Rebellion had started near Canton. Many of their own family members had been directly or indirectly involved. They knew the Taiping rebels had been poor and had fought for the poor. Eugene heaved a deep sigh as he saw that he had connected with the audience.

Connected with many, but not all. Some were hell-bent on breaking up the meeting.

"Turncoat!" a shout came from the back of the hall. A commotion ensued at the entrance while some bullies broke in and darted to the picket line, scuffling with Eugene's bodyguards. The bodyguards held up their rifles, and if the troublemakers surged forward, they would have to open fire to stop them. To everyone's bewilderment, Eugene ordered his bodyguards back. He told the audience that he did not fear for himself, because what he said benefited no one but them. No sooner had he uttered these words than some rioters hurled insults and benches at him, while others brandished clubs and knives. This caused a stampede toward the exits; but Eugene, ignoring the strike leaders' advice to flee, finished his speech to those who remained. He pledged to fight for their rights until his death. He asked the laborers and their representatives to trust him and gave his word that it would not be a blind trust. He would exert himself to fulfill the task at hand. With few resources, he would confront the British behemoth.

It was not until the meeting was over that Eugene felt a weakness in his limbs and an agitation in his heart. The delayed reaction kept him tensed up. He tried to sleep that night, but could not. He dozed and entered a sort of twilight zone, half sleeping and half waking. He felt someone's presence. His wife's! He could see her in the room, coming toward him. He woke up and sat up in the dark with his arms outstretched. Then he came to the slow, agonizing realization that he was dreaming.

It was an odd dream, maybe a portent. His anxiety was mixed with guilt. Two years ago, in 1924, she had started begging him to let her come to Canton with her three unmarried younger children. Silan was nineteen years old, Jack sixteen, and Yolanda eleven. They were old enough to journey halfway around the globe, and yet young enough to enter and adjust to a strange world.

Strange world indeed! Eugene thought to himself: was it wise to get his wife and children involved in this strange world, in which they would meet with violence laced with racial prejudice? He had been attacked because he had been branded a half-breed. He could imagine how they would pounce on his children. He knew he could not protect his children against life, but he could provide them a home away from the kind of unspeakable violence he had to cope with every day. Aisy had probably misconstrued his words as an excuse for refusal.

He had lived most of his married life apart from Aisy, and that gave rise to the rumor that he had abandoned her and their children. Rumor traveled fast. They had lived apart too long; they were, in fact, estranged. In 1925, Aisy shepherded her brood back to Trinidad from London and decided that she would put everything in order before joining him. Eugene detected an urgency in her arguments, which conveyed a premonition of something unsettling.

Brooding, he dawdled over his toilette. He went to the breakfast table, trying to work up an appetite, when a servant brought a letter. He put it aside, but glimpsed it from the corner of his eye as he lifted the teacup. It was not Aisy's handwriting, it was their older daughter's. Silan expressed her feelings through dancing, very seldom through words. What was up? All of a sudden, his throat tightened, and he found it difficult to swallow the tea. He put down the cup and clutched the letter in his hand.

Taking a deep breath, he opened it. What Silan told him, she later recalled in her memoir, *Footnote to History:*

> Within a week two things happened. First, we received a letter from Father telling us to come to China, and without a second thought we packed our trunks and prepared to leave Trinidad, for good this time. Father had left a house and security when he went to China, so Mother was willing to leave her house for China, too. We kids never thought of anything we were leaving, only the new experience ahead. Second, not feeling as well as usual, Mother had a physical examination. The doctor advised an operation. Even this fitted into our gay future. During our stopover in London, Mother would have her operation. . . . [2]

Aisy's doctor diagnosed her illness as terminal breast cancer. She had about six weeks or so to live. He did not tell Aisy this, but only divulged the truth to Silan and her cousin Germaine. Aisy, however, sensed that something was amiss when Silan told her that Eugene, in his latest cable, had asked them to go back to Trinidad first and then come to China. When Aisy asked for the cable, Silan said she had misplaced it. It did not take long for Aisy to realize what was happening to her. The pain worsened every day. It was almost a blessing that on a beautiful, sunny morning in May 1926, she fell into a coma and died.

The bad news devastated Eugene. He had found his true calling in China, but it had come at a price. Aisy was too young to die. She was about forty-eight years of age and in her prime. To the last minute, she lived for her husband and children, enduring the pain without a word of complaint.

There was not much time to mourn over his personal loss. He would not allow himself to forget his duty as a public servant. He concealed his grief well, and his first guest that morning, the American consul general Douglas Jenkins, did not detect anything unusual behind his smile. Jenkins came to tell him that the American minister stationed at Peking, John Van Antwerp

MacMurry, would like to visit Canton in late September, and then asked rather casually if Eugene had sounded out the British about the impending reopening of the negotiation to conclude the strike.

"Have you?" Eugene asked and saw, on Jenkins's face, what there was to see. The British had rejected all his proposals. "Then they provoked me to unilaterally raise the special 2.5 percent tax on imported items."

With a vague shrug, Jenkins merely said that if the Kuomintang would back off from the strike controversy, the British were expected to make a reciprocal gesture. Maybe the Hong Kong governor could quietly convince the inspector general of the British-controlled Customs Service of the necessity of compromise.

Eugene was quick to realize what Jenkins was hinting at. The American harked back to their mediation between the Kuomintang and the British-controlled Customs Service in 1923–1924, when the Kuomintang demanded their fair share of the Customs surplus. Eugene, of course, knew that Jenkins would not have given his advice had he not talked with the Hong Kong government first.

The British wanted to save face and would not give in to the strikers. And yet they had to reckon what stubbornness would cost them. Hong Kong was a huge rock surrounded by seas. Sea water was not drinkable. Vegetables and other agricultural produce did not grow on rocks. The strike had damaged the island colony's economy, but the British pound was strong enough to sustain the blow. But it was not possible to survive without water and food. One way or another, they would have to compensate the strikers.

At the end of the long day, Eugene still did not have time to be alone with himself and grieve: he had to go to Ailing Soong's banquet. A small delegation from Shanghai's Chinese Chamber of Commerce had come to find out how the Northern Expedition would affect them. Ailing's mansion was an ideal place to entertain these merchant princes. Her husband, Daddy Kong, was born a banker and her brother, T. V. Soong, had never hidden his predilection for capitalism. They were ideal spokesmen to lead their guests to believe that the mass actions that disrupted trade and manufacturing in Canton would not be repeated in Shanghai.

The hostess, Ailing Soong, stood chatting with a plump middle-aged man with a fleshy, oily face and a heavy-set young man. Eugene guessed that they must be her guests of honor. Knowing her as well as he did, no words were needed to conclude whom she was most eager to please. Watching her pass a glass of wine around a semicircle of her company was like watching a social and political weathervane in action. She gave the first glass of wine to the middle-aged man and the second to the heavyset young man.

"They have close ties with the Green Gang," T. V. Soong enlightened Eugene in whispers. The Green Gang of Shanghai was the equivalent of the mafia of New York, except that the Green Gang was a lawful organization. The authorities of the International Settlement and French concession were their partners-in-crime, collecting huge revenues from the opium traffic, brothels, and smuggling rings they ran. Without their protection, no businessman, Chinese or foreign, could do business in Shanghai.

Ailing Soong's attention was momentarily distracted when Zhang Jingjiang, the Curio, entered in a wheelchair, pushed by his young second wife, with Chiang Kaishek walking beside him. Mayling Soong, Ailing's younger sister, went up to greet them. When Mayling Soong and her captive passed by, she asked Eugene and her older brother to come with them. They all joined Ailing and her guests of honor. The middle-aged man was Wang Xiaolai, who had a higher position in Shanghai's Chamber of Commerce than the younger man, Yang Zhixiong. They both looked over a tray of delicacies held up by a servant, and Yang complimented the hostess in fluent English: "Did you help make all this? Nicely laid. Very artistic."

"Thank my sister. She did most of the work and supervising," Ailing said, never forgetting to show off the talents of her very marriageable younger sister.

"But like any work of art, it is transient. Come and take your share before it all vanishes," Eugene jokingly urged Mayling's admirer, Chiang Kaishek.

Chiang bent to take a closer look at the tray heaped with tasty morsels. After much theatrical deliberation, he chose and gobbled down a "dragon's eye" wrapped in a thin layer of sweet rice flour.

"You sound melancholy. You are missing your wife. When will she come?" Ailing teased Eugene.

Eugene's heart throbbed with a sudden, sharp pain. Evading an answer, he hurriedly put a piece of some refreshment into his mouth and made a muffled, noncommittal sound. The evening was still young, and he could not take his leave. As the main maker of the diplomatic policy, he was expected to calm the nerves of these merchant princes. At the dining table, with all of them sitting listening, he said the matter of the International Settlement and French concession of Shanghai should not be dealt with until after the Kuomintang accomplished the Northern Expedition, reunited China, and moved to Peking. That was the Kuomintang's policy. Shanghai was the nerve center of the colonial powers in China. Losing it would be tantamount to losing their vast investments accumulated over nearly two centuries. They would not surrender without a war. To stir up trouble in the International Settlement and French concession was like lighting a match in a tinderbox.

The senior member of the delegation, Wang Xiaolai, in his speech, joked that he did not feel threatened by Canton's communism. Anybody could see that its style of Marxism did not remotely resemble the Bolsheviks' communism. The hostess's mansion crowned the top of a hill, like a castle overlooking the beautiful scenes surrounding it. He was wondering if she was accused of hypocrisy by the proletarian rogues.

Ailing Soong jauntily rejoined that she was a practical Marxist who believed in the basic tenet of Marxism: to each according to his needs, from each according to his abilities. And what she had was what she needed and could pay for.

After the meal, the men retired to the study of the host, Daddy Kong, and had a strategy session. The merchant princes considered it possible to cooperate with the Kuomintang on the Northern Expedition. According to their plan, the Kuomintang army would enter only the Chinese City of Shanghai, the area outside the British-dominated International Settlement and French concession. There, a provisional city government would be formed, with the leaders of the Chinese Chamber of Commerce participating. Their jurisdiction would be limited to the Chinese City. They would not, for the time being, encroach upon the authorities of the International Settlement and the French concession.

Thus arranged, everyone had something to gain. The Kuomintang would use the Chinese merchant princes to put the foreign powers at ease. A strike or any sabotage would hurt the pocketbooks of the Chinese manufacturers as much as their foreign counterparts'. The Chinese merchant princes, on their part, would use the clout that the Kuomintang gave them to bargain for more gains. Actually, they had already initiated that process, and, on March 18, 1926, a few of them had been invited for the first time onto the board of the city council of the International Settlement. They were fully aware of why that door, the most exclusive one in Shanghai, had suddenly opened to them. The victories the Kuomintang had won since 1923 had shocked the foreign powers out of their complacency, and they now saw the advantage of using the natives to help them hold on to their rule. Thus power was doled out to the Shanghai men of property.

On July 9, 1926, Chiang Kaishek formally proclaimed the war of the Northern Expedition. On July 15, Eugene called on the British to restart negotiations.

The British came, went through the motions, walked out ten days afterward, and never returned. They, however, did not stop communicating. They moved the negotiations from the front room to the back room. Then they pulled back farther.

In September, barely two months after the Northern Expedition started, the revolutionary armies conquered Hanyang and Hankou, in the extremely pivotal Wuhan area. The military victory helped Eugene at the diplomatic front. It seemed inevitable that the Kuomintang would soon control central China, along with its important port cities, including Shanghai, along the Yangzi River.

The Americans and the Japanese knew, as did the British, that the lower and middle reaches of the Yangzi were areas rich with natural resources, crucial to trade and commerce. Britain, in particular, with its enormous investment in this area, had to compromise with the increasingly powerful Kuomintang. To confront the victorious revolutionary army at such a high tide of nationalism was not the wisest thing to do. While the British openly refused to resolve the Hong Kong–Canton Strike, they quietly agreed to discuss terms on ending the unequal treaties imposed on China.

His position much strengthened, Eugene informed the British on September 18 that the Strike Committee would be dissolved before October 10, the fifteenth anniversary of the Chinese Republic, and he also told them that the Kuomintang government would collect a 2.5 percent special tax on imported items. The extra cash flow filled the almost empty treasury at a time when the government desperately needed money to advance the Northern Expedition, "to recompense the strikers for their loss,"[3] and to help many who had come from Hong Kong, to go back.

The timing was perfect, as the diplomatic victory offset the languishing strike negotiation. Eugene lost no time in crediting the laborers for their part in the victory. Nor did he neglect to remind some inflexible and intractable strikers that there were many ways of striving for the same goal.

Eugene's handling of the Hong Kong–Canton Strike is cited as "one of the best models of the revolutionary diplomacy" that Eugene had initiated.[4] He had the mass movement behind him, and yet had the foresight to pull it back before it accelerated out of control.

★ 14 ★

MARCH WITH THE NORTHERN EXPEDITION ARMY

Eugene sent for his three unmarried, younger children, as Aisy had wished. Percy, their older son, was twenty-five and married with two baby boys. Percy's place, Eugene said, was with his young family. Although an absentee husband and father for half his married life, Eugene considered himself a family man. Now he would assume the role of both father and mother. Silan, the older daughter, came to Canton first, in the early autumn of 1926.

Eugene gave Silan as much time as he could from his busy schedule. They talked about getting a larger house to accommodate the whole family. There was one next to their bungalow, whose rich owner had fled to Hong Kong and abandoned the place. It had four bedrooms, just enough for them. Eugene had always been interested in interior decorating, and Silan had inherited her mother's taste. Together they daydreamed of how to furnish each room to perfection. Unfortunately, this dreaming was interrupted by a drastic change in the political situation.

On November 16, 1926, the Kuomintang government decided to move their capital from Canton to Wuhan. There were two ways to get there: one by sea and river via Shanghai; the other, traveling overland. Eugene's cabinet colleagues preferred the first one, which was much more expensive. Eugene, with his usual ingenuity, suggested that in order to show their appreciation of those who had fought so hard to get them where they were, the cabinet members and their families should travel with the rest of the government officials and their families, following in their victorious soldiers' footsteps over hills and down the valleys to Wuhan. The cabinet members balked at the prospect of such an arduous journey.

The first to withdraw was Ailing Soong. She would rather travel to Shanghai and then sail up the Yangzi River in a British ship to Wuhan. Her husband, Daddy Kong, suddenly rose to assert his manhood: he was to take his wife to safety. Eugene told him that what he ought to do was to march for two. T. V. Soong, always keen on enjoying life in comfort, thought his oldest sister had made a sensible decision. If there was an easy way to get to Wuhan, why would he choose a difficult one? But he failed to convince Chingling. She had come back to Canton from Shanghai in order to take part in the Northern Expedition. Should she march, T. V., as the man of the Soong family, had to march alongside her.

The marchers included the five most important cabinet members. Eugene was minister of foreign affairs; George Qian Xu, the chief eulogist at Sun's Christian funeral, was minister of justice; Sun Ke (Sun Fo), Sun Yatsen's son by his first marriage, was in charge of the ministry of communications; T. V. Soong was head of the ministry of finance; Daddy Kong would soon be appointed to head the ministry of industry and commerce. Last but not least was Borodin, the High Adviser to the Kuomintang.

The march, of course, was a token gesture. They would do some walking; but when they felt tired, they would have seats in trains, barges, and sedan chairs to rest in. And they would have coolies to carry their belongings. Eugene had no problem with that, but he watched with quiet exasperation at T. V. Soong's ostentation. Behind his sedan chair trudged a long file of coolies whose shoulders and backs were loaded with his imported cans of goodies. That was the Soong food, and for the Soongs only. He even excluded his brother-in-law, Daddy Kong. T. V., though a devout Christian, did not have much faith in biblical miracles: he doubted that bread or wine would multiply by itself if it was shared with the needy. Knowing that the only person who would complain to Chingling was Eugene, T. V. conciliated him with an invitation.

To Silan, the journey was a picnic: the Soong food was so much more delicious than her regular diet of hard-boiled eggs. A doting father, Eugene did not have the heart to deprive his daughter of this pleasure. His mouth was sealed by the sugar that T. V. Soong put in his teacup. For most of the journey, the Soongs' fellow travelers whispered in envy. The grumbling grew more audible when there was a short supply of coolies at a certain point. In order to carry the Soong food, the coolies had to leave behind bedding, clothing, and kitchen utensils belonging to the other marchers. Piqued though the fellow travelers were, they felt awkward complaining about T. V., because the Soong food gave his sister Chingling the energy to march on. While the men exerted control over their tongues, the lady marchers did not. Who did Chingling think she was? A sort of quasi-widow of the late "emperor-god," they scoffed. No wonder T. V. thought there was a certain imperium vested in himself as the late Sun's brother-in-law.

One day Borodin, in mock dread, whispered in Eugene's ear that they would have a mutiny on their hands if the Soongs continued to ignore their fellow travelers' needs. If they didn't have enough coolies to carry their things, the lady marchers would halt and turn back to Canton, taking their husbands with them. On hearing this through Eugene, T.V. Soong's eyes widened with indignation. As if he didn't endure enough hardship! However, he would make sacrifices for the revolution and agree to leave a large part of his hoard behind.

Eugene seemed to be the only one who had prepared to do more than token marching. He put on a pair of Chinese straw walking slippers, the kind worn by mountaineers for the last five thousand years. Feeling ill at ease in a sedan chair carried by coolies, he often induced his daughter and his secretary to walk beside him.

Eugene's compassion was handsomely rewarded. At one time, Eugene and his sedan carriers, with no burden to carry, walked quickly and arrived in a village earlier than the others, so he got to see the most inventive phenomenon of the Northern Expedition, the rallying skill of the soldier vanguard—the political propagandists. Many were communists, or had been trained by them. They had reached the village a step ahead of Eugene and were working up the villagers.

Taking his secretary/interpreter with him, Eugene followed the soldier vanguard. They fanned out among the peasants, held mass meetings, and went into people's homes to explain how the approaching soldiers were different from the mercenaries of the warlords. The revolutionary soldiers did not plunder and rob the people; they came to liberate them.

Thus these political propagandists mobilized the entire village, men and women, young and old. With the masses mobilized with whatever primitive weapons they had, they paved the way, or even took over towns before the regular army arrived. The warlord mercenaries had run away before doing battle.

Eugene's fellow travelers and the soldiers reached the gate of the county town at about the same time. They joined the grand entry ceremony. At the head of the parade trotted a mule pulling a cart decorated with red flags and streamers and loaded with painted props depicting battle scenes. A stream of townsfolk followed the cart, pushing and jostling amid the whirl of colors, applauding onlookers and jubilant children. The soldier vanguard led the crowds in revolutionary songs and tossed forth revolutionary slogans. Behind them marched Eugene and his fellow cabinet members.

As soon as he entered the gate, Eugene was overcome with emotion at the welcome. Brass bands blared, firecrackers rolled, and the main street resounded with cheers. It was a rousing political pageant, but there was discord. The slogans expressed Moscow's unhappiness with the slow progress of the peasant movement. They demanded a wholesale land revolution. On the other hand, Eugene and his colleagues abided by the Kuomintang's resolution to reduce agricultural taxes and rent. They believed that any stronger measure would result in disaster.

The debate enlivened their daily conference, usually held at the breakfast table. The most heated argument was waged by Eugene and Borodin.

Eugene did not hesitate to warn Borodin that he was playing with fire, given the fact that most of the Kuomintang generals of the Northern Expedition were big landowners and many of the lower-ranking officers were smaller landowners. Even many of the foot soldiers had relatives who owned land. An untimely full-blown land revolution to confiscate the landowners' land and redistribute it among the poor and landless peasants would cause panic among the Kuomintang army.

Borodin must have been aware of the risk, but he did not have much choice. He had to show Moscow that the peasant and labor movements were swept up in the liberating forces of the Northern Expedition and that no bourgeoisie or landed gentry was able to halt them, as if he was ignorant of the fact that his allies, the upper and middle echelons of the Kuomintang, were constituted of the people he was marking out for liquidation.

"Speeding up the mass movement is the only way to counteract Chiang Kaishek's expanding power," Borodin replied, an argument he thought Eugene and his fellow cabinet members would agree with.

Sun Ke, always suspecting that Chiang aspired to become a military emperor and dethrone him as the heir apparent, said something not so much to support as to tolerate Borodin's argument, at least for the moment.

George Qian Xu, a friend of Feng Yuxiang, the Christian General, had no love for Chiang Kaishek, Feng's rival.

Both T. V. Soong and Daddy Kong looked to Eugene for advice.

The ambitious Chiang Kaishek was another worry that preyed on Eugene's mind; but Eugene acknowledged, though reluctantly, that Chiang had taken scrupulous care to put his best foot forward since the Zhongshan Gunboat Incident, and in particular after the launching of the Northern Expedition. "He is the Supreme Commander of the Northern Expedition. Give the devil his due."

"Don't underestimate Chiang's dishonesty," Borodin warned.

"Quite, quite," Eugene agreed. "We mustn't lower our guard against Chiang's duplicity, but we ought to have the common sense to put up with that certain duplicity that is indispensable to successful politicians and accepted as political savvy. We should take steps to contain him, but not to confront him," Eugene concluded a little cynically.

As they drew near the midway stopover, Nanchang, where Chiang Kaishek's headquarters was located, Eugene and the four other Chinese leaders argued more strongly against provoking Chiang into a tantrum. Borodin seemed to relent. They took his silence for acquiescence. Reassured, they made the last part of the journey to Nanchang on December 2, 1926, in a ferryboat. When it docked at the landing stage, Eugene spotted Chiang with a group of people waiting to welcome them. Chiang seemed relaxed, with one foot on a step above the pier and one hand resting on his hip. He had put away his usually stiff, soldierly carriage for the occasion, as if looking forward to meeting old friends. The current Madame Chiang came smilingly from behind him to shake hands with the wives of the high-ranking marchers. From all appearances, Chiang was playing the part of a hospitable host.

Up from the pier and under the walls of Nanchang, a convoy of trucks and cars was ready to start. Chiang's car, with Chingling, Borodin, and T. V. Soong in it, led the motorcade. Eugene sat with George Xu and Madame Chiang in a car behind it. After a desultory exchange of pleasant generalities, they lapsed into silence, and all that could be heard was the steady roar of the engines. For a while, they sat and bumped along the rough road. At a violent bump, Eugene became aware that the engine of his car was coughing and spluttering, and then it finally stopped altogether. The driver swung out of the cabin and opened the hood. He poked about and got it going again. But something was clearly amiss: any bump bigger than the average set the horn screeching.

Startled, Chiang Kaishek stopped the motorcade and came to offer his seat to Eugene and George Xu. Both declined politely. Chiang apologized effusively for the wartime austerity and lack of funds to replace ancient vehicles. Trying to disguise his embarrassment in a joke, he said that as the car hooted through the city, the residents would know it was graced with the presence of his most honored guests.

At the dinner party, Chiang, as host, stood up and gave a speech on a subject appropriate for the occasion. He recounted the progress of the Northern Expedition and attributed its success to collective efforts. Before he sat down, he asked, with well-affected and well-rehearsed humility as required by Chinese etiquette, for Borodin's instructions. With a faint grin of uneasiness, Borodin stood up. He was expected to make a reciprocal speech, and he looked as though he were about to oblige. His hand, twitching, reached up to his chest, as if thanking the host from the bottom of his heart.

But the voice spurting from his mouth, like thunder out of the blue, flabbergasted everybody. He pointed an indignant finger at Chiang, criticizing him for imposing too heavy a tax on people, for squandering the money on officers and soldiers directly under his command, for putting off the land revolution. Then came the last and most pungent part of the speech: the Russians, who held the purse strings, had no intention of sponsoring a campaign that went in the wrong direction.

When T. V. Soong hesitatingly translated the harangue, a stunned hush fell over the dining room. No one moved, except for the servants tiptoeing soundlessly around the tables. Bewildered and annoyed, Eugene locked his eyes on the gesticulating Borodin and tried to figure out why on earth he had to pick Chiang apart at this very moment. Chiang was, after all, the Supreme Commander. Insulting him, Borodin made his colleagues, his staff, and their wives and servants feel that the snipe was also meant for them. There had been gossip that Borodin had been bragging about holding the purse strings and acting with the hauteur of an imperial viceroy, and now he himself gave credence to it.

Judging from the rigidity in his facial muscles and posture, Chiang Kaishek swallowed his pride hard. And yet throughout the rest of the evening he managed to be gracious, as if the unpleasant episode had never taken place. The next day, he took his guests to visit a few ancient historical monuments and to watch a Peking opera, and then wished them to rest well before the conference. Eugene thought it was good advice and went to bed early. He slept soundly; but before the early morning light fell on his pillows, he was startled by a tap on the door. T. V. Soong, in a dark dressing gown, entered with consternation on his usually placid face. He asked Eugene to go to his room, where Chiang Kaishek was waiting to inform Chingling, before anyone else, of a change in the locale of the conference scheduled to open the next day.

When Eugene opened his door, he saw soldiers in the hallway. They stared ahead, their faces stony, their hands clasped in back. Wondering if there was a mutiny at hand, he hastened to throw a dressing gown over his pajamas and hurried down the hall to T. V. Soong's room.

With his emotions still under control, Chiang apologized for giving such short notice, but it was imperative to move the conference to Guling, a nearby resort town. There was too much tension in the city. Borodin's wild accusations had so angered his officers and soldiers that they might, Chiang feared, erupt in loud protest, answering insult with insult.

The choice of Guling was a strange one. It was a mountain resort, nice and cool in summer, freezing in December. It seemed even odder that Chiang Kaishek pushed them into the trip with unceremonious haste, in sharp contrast with his earlier show of courteous consideration. Silan's narrative of this episode sounded as if they were in flight.

> We started up the mountainside in sedan chairs in the early evening and continued to climb for about five hours. This time I was compelled to sit in a chair, for it was pitch dark and the road was risky. Sometimes I felt the chair swing into space as we rounded a sharp corner.... Each time I imagined myself hurtling over the precipice and wondered how many victims this path had already claimed.... As we climbed higher, it became colder and colder. Soon I could hear the crunching of snow under my bearers' straw sandals, and I felt them slipping on the frozen path."[1]

One plausible excuse for such a flurry was that Chiang was anxious to begin the conference and resolve the dispute with Borodin. There would be a shouting match to watch. Chiang, however, proved that he was not easily predictable. He kept his thoughts to himself at the morning opening meeting and then vanished during a break. When the meeting resumed, his secretary came to tell the other participants to go on debating without him. Next day, he played truant again. Borodin had a temper too and angrily told Chiang's secretary to go look for his boss. The young man answered sheepishly that he did not know Chiang's whereabouts.

The answer was in a passage in Silan's memoir: "I was not the only one absent from these conferences. In my mountain-climbing expeditions to nearby peaks I was often accompanied by Chiang. Perhaps it was his politeness that allowed me always to reach the peak first. But why did he always come in third? Either a coolie or another guest would take second place."[2]

A thoroughly political animal, Chiang would not have played such antics without a political purpose. Hiking was the prelude to Madame Chiang's tea party in her little cottage, where she welcomed the hikers back, along with two guests: Eugene and T. V. Soong.

Chiang Kaishek was able to pull off his vanishing act because of the layout of the Fairy Glen Hotel. The participants of the conference were staying in the main building. In sweltering weather, it was thronged with foreign missionaries, businessmen, and diplomats escaping from the cities, but now it was almost empty. Behind it, a footpath arched over a gentle slope and stretched into a wooded area of evergreens. Small white cottages were scattered around. They were all unoccupied in the wintry season, except for one, the most secluded one, which was rented by Madame Chiang Kaishek. Blue smoke spiraled out of the chimney and exuded warmth.

Chiang had been trying to talk his guests out of going farther north. He wanted them to remain in Nanchang so as to enhance his opposition to Borodin. He worked particularly hard on Eugene. If he could persuade Eugene, he could convince the rest of the cabinet. Eugene was emerging as the brain of the group.[3]

Chiang argued in a matter-of-fact manner that Wuhan was in dire peril. It was an industrialized area, and its conquest by the Northern Expedition armies was due, in large part, to the labor unionists who attacked the citadel from the inside. The organization of the laborers, in turn, was due in large part to the communists. In October 1926, immediately after the Northern Expedition armies entered Wuhan, several famous firebrands had been dispatched by the Moscow-dominated Comintern, among them Gregory Voitinsky and Li Lisan. Within a period of two months, October and November, they staged a strike almost every other day, repeating the same tactics as the Hong Kong–Canton Strike.

Eugene frankly admitted knowing that Chiang was not exaggerating; Eugene too was concerned. Wuhan was sinking in worsening anarchy, and that was why it was all the more important for them to go there to restore law and order. The Kuomintang government had proclaimed to the whole world that Wuhan was their new capital, and Eugene had told the foreign powers that he would receive their envoys there. Any sign of disunity would put the Kuomintang government at a disadvantage when it came to negotiating for repealing the unequal treaties.

Taking the cue from Eugene, T. V. Soong interposed that he also, in his capacity as the minister of finance, had invited the members of Shanghai's Chinese Chamber of Commerce to visit Wuhan.

Pondering, Chiang gave a reluctant promise that at some stage he would visit Wuhan.

★15★

TWISTING THE TAIL OF THE BRITISH LION

Wuhan consisted of three cities. Hankou, the center of commerce, was the principal port on the right bank of the Yangzi River. The sprawling city of Wuchang, the provincial capital of Hubei and center of culture and education, was on the opposite bank. Hanyang was upriver, separated from Hankou by the Han River. Hanyang was famous for its iron and steel works, the Han-Ye-Ping, one of the first and, at that time, one of the largest modern heavy industrial plants set up in China. The city was also the site for the Hanyang Arms Factory. The three cities faced one another, and through them flowed troubled waters. The newly arrived Canton government took its new name from the joint name of these three cities—the Wuhan government.

The ship that Eugene and his colleagues had boarded came to anchor on the Hankou side. From the waterfront up to the top of the river wall was about seventy-five feet. Within this short distance they, as government officials, smoothly passed by two or three checkpoints, each guarded by a rival faction of the longshoremen's union. But other arrivals were not as lucky. The foreigners got the roughest treatment. At the first checkpoint, Eugene noticed a foreign traveler cursing and hurrying after two coolies; each had snatched one of his two small travel bags, and each had exacted an incredibly high

THE "BRAIN" OF THE WESTERNISED CANTONESE REGIME AT HANKOW; MR. EUGENE CHEN, THE FOREIGN MINISTER OF THE NATIONALIST GOVERNMENT IN CHINA.

The Daily Mail *comments on the "brain" of the Kuomintang government at Hankow.*

payment. Before the revolutionary wind blew into town, it had cost five cents for each piece of baggage; now it was more than a dollar, even as high as ten dollars (Chinese).

When they reached the street level, Eugene hopped into a waiting car, asking the chauffeur to drive slowly from the lower end of the Bund upward. He first passed by the Japanese concession and then the former German, the French, and the former Russian concession. The British concession was the last and the largest. The Bund was fronted with high and imposing buildings, all facing the river, that housed the foreign banks and corporations that kept a fatal grip on Wuhan's economy. The street closest to the river was flanked by trees and had a sidewalk used exclusively by foreigners.

The other side of the British concession, the side that was set back from the Bund, was barricaded with barbed wire and sandbags to keep out "Chinese loafers" from its immediate neighbor, the Chinese City of Hankou. The tension was palpable. Any trivial squabble could escalate into an explosive international incident. Eugene got his bearings and set his mind to prepare for whatever might come.

The anti-foreign feeling was running high, fed by a recent incident. On November 23, 1926, the British had arrested seventeen Kuomintang members in Tianjin's British concession and later handed them over to the warlord government in Peking. Seven of them were summarily executed. It was not difficult to foresee trouble.

Angry Chinese gathered at anti-British meetings held in Wuhan. The participants, it was said, numbered more than three hundred thousand. The organizers were the principal communists of the area, led by Li Lisan. They decided to launch an offensive on the third day of the New Year. On that day, more than two hundred thousand demonstrators marched to the border between the British concession and the Chinese City of Hankou. The demonstrators shouted anti-British slogans, brandished their fists, and spat at the marines. The surge of humans at the threshold of the concession panicked the marines, who fixed their bayonets, only a few feet from the demonstrators. When some demonstrators defiantly tore open their shirts, daring the marines to thrust the bayonets into their chests, some marines drew back, as they thought the demonstrators were about to hurl themselves forward; but others shot into the air, trying to frighten the crowd. The gunfire caused a stampede among the demonstrators, who scattered in different directions. Many retreated into the Chinese City, but quite a few, either in confusion or in bravado, crossed over the border into the British concession.

Bayonets and knives flashed. Blood spurted. One demonstrator was killed, five were badly wounded, more than thirty were lightly injured.

Most of the Kuomintang leadership wanted to retreat, because they believed the British might resort to drastic measures to stop further problems. As for Borodin, he was a man with a thousand faces. In the meeting with the Chinese communists on January 4, a day after the bloody rioting, he did not seem to object to their plan to break into the British concession, scheduled for the next day. Gregory Voitinsky and the Chinese communists probably had not given him much room to maneuver. Then, in a later meeting with the Kuomintang leaders, Borodin advocated prudence and restraint. He kept quiet for most of the debate. Pressed, he said the matter was complicated and that it was difficult for him to make an instant decision.

By now Eugene was familiar with the pattern by which the communists led the mass movement. He did not want to appear to dampen their revolutionary spirit by forbidding them to protest, but he was troubled that the precipitate actions of the communists could derail his coming negotiations with the British. At the end of 1926, the British minister, Sir Miles Lampson, the United States representative, Ferdinand Mayer, and Japan's envoy, Zuofenli (Chinese transliteration), would come to Wuhan to reach an understanding with the Kuomintang government before they moved their legations from Peking to Wuhan. This opportunity, exactly what the Kuomintang and Eugene had long dreamed of, was now in danger of being smashed.

It was inopportune to have a confrontation with the British, but Eugene could never disgrace himself with his countrymen by asking them to keep quiet under coercion. The Chinese demonstrators might have overstepped their bounds, but the British had conducted themselves in a manner so provocative that retaliatory action from the Chinese was predictable. Yet a disastrous incident would cripple the Kuomintang and halt its Northern Expedition. Eugene had a plan in mind, but he avoided open discussion about what he intended to do. He let only three people in on it: Chingling, T. V. Soong, and Sun Ke, whom he chose to assist him. The delicate posture of foreign affairs required secrecy.

The day after the bloody incident, the British consul general, Herbert Goffe, came to Eugene's office with an admiral in full uniform, medals on his chest befitting the commander of the mightiest naval force in the world. What they didn't say was obvious with this gesture: if the talks went awry, they would resort to force.

The contrast between the British admiral in his splendid regalia and Eugene's very modest office was striking. "It was a small single-story bungalow. . . . The gate was almost a wicket gate, with a very flimsy latch that could be opened from the outside by inserting one's hand through some thin bars."[1]

The British put on their usual lordly airs when they deigned to speak to the natives. They blamed the uncivilized Wuhan government for not being able to protect the civilized intruders. They had come to call Eugene's bluff, and they expected him to apologize. But Eugene, anticipating their questions, had worked the whole scenario out in detail.

He had the answers ready when asked how his government would guarantee the lives and property of the British in Wuhan. He told them that it was not appropriate for them to call the Chinese government uncivilized.

"As you know, when the Chinese people were wearing silk, I am afraid that the British people were running around with their bodies painted blue."[2]

This proud repartee took the colonialists by surprise. No Chinese foreign minister had ever made so bold as to defy them. Eugene made it clear to them that, from now on, the talk was between equals.

Eugene then told them flatly that he did not think they needed the protection of the Chinese government. Their marines were ready to pull the trigger. They certainly did not seem to welcome cooperation from the Chinese police. In order to avoid further misunderstanding and clashes, Eugene advised them to withdraw their marines.

Spring of 1927. Silan and Yolanda in the garden of the Foreign Office, where Eugene worked to repossess the British concessions in Hankow and Jiujiang.

The British thought that they had better play it safe, and they first evacuated their citizens onto the ships of Jardine, Matheson, and Butterfield and Swire, Ltd., and then withdrew their marines and soldiers onto the battleships while awaiting instructions from London. But the concession was not left undefended: they posted a number of Sikhs as patrolmen.

The British movements were closely monitored by Eugene's informants. As soon as he received the news, he sent for Borodin, Voitinsky, and the Chinese union leaders. Eugene knew very well that Borodin and Voitinsky had Moscow's instructions on their minds above all. It was in Moscow's interest to keep the Wuhan government in a relationship with Britain that was hostile, but short of open warfare. The more China and the Western powers developed a rapport, the less influence the Soviet Union would exert over China. Eugene decided to give them a few simple facts and nothing more.

The waterfront was congested with the foreign powers' fifty-three warships with battle-ready guns. The Union Jack, the Stars and Stripes, the Rising Sun, and other nations' flags fluttered in the wind. Even the flag of a small frigate of the Portuguese navy flew high in the face of the Wuhan government.

Under such circumstances, to use force could not help but repeat a fiasco that had occurred not long before: in June 1926, the communists had marched an army of unionists into the Japanese and British concessions of Hankou. The bluff had backfired. In no time, the entire foreign defense forces from the British, American, Japanese, French, and Italian gunboats, along with the volunteer companies from their communities, gave chase to the unionists, who barely made it back to the Chinese City. Would they again adopt this self-defeating strategy?

Eugene's plan required only a few underground unionists in the British concession to take it up. When Eugene asked them to get the Sikhs away from their posts, they responded enthusiastically: that could easily be done. They were familiar with the ways of the Sikhs. Some were even friendly with them. In the evening, they brought wine and food to comfort—as well as to warn—the colored Britons. The underground unionists said in a worried voice that the Sikhs were surrounded by angry pickets and helplessly outnumbered. Resentful that only the white British had been evacuated to safety, the Sikhs did not see why they should die for the men who had left them in the lurch. At this juncture, the underground unionists said that only the poor would help the poor. They offered to hide the Sikhs in a safe place until the British whites came back to the concession, and meanwhile volunteered to take care of the security there.

The British concession was a vacuum now. Eugene immediately sent in Chinese soldiers and policemen, on the pretext of maintaining law and order. Calm returned. The British consul general and admiral deemed it time for them to return too, to resume the management of their concession. But Eugene rejected their request and gave his reason for doing so. The situation had changed, Eugene said, and they must deal with it in a different way. The British had abandoned the concession, and so the Chinese had every right to enter it.

Then Eugene continued: "According to your own principles of common law, by evacuating all of your nationals from the area that was loaned to you by the former Chinese government, not leaving one person on the territory to show even symbolic possession, you must see that you have abandoned the area, and, according to the principles of your own common law, it thereby has come again into the possession and dominion of the Chinese people. As the de jure and de facto government of the Chinese people, my government has resumed sovereignty over this territory."[3]

The British argued that they had not surrendered the concession and in fact had left their Sikh soldiers to defend it. Eugene lifted his eyebrows and affected surprise. Not a single Sikh had been in sight, he said, when the Chinese soldiers and policemen crossed the border from the side of the Chinese City. The British could not puzzle out the mysterious disappearance of their mercenaries, until they saw them in the triumphal procession of the Chinese demonstrators. The British consul general and admiral were astounded by this twist of events.[4]

Eugene's reference to British common law was a clever stroke. The British government needed a face-saving exit for the inevitable, and Eugene, a man trained in English law, had opened the door for them and let them withdraw with a semblance of dignity. The two Englishmen left without comment. They would wait for instructions from the British Legation in Peking.

The legation in Peking decided to send a delegation headed by Owen St. Clair O'Malley to negotiate the terms of the return of the British concessions in Hankou and in Jiujiang, then known as Kiukiang, which had been seized by the Chinese two days after the Hankou incident.

The people who most wanted to sabotage these negotiations were the British merchants trading in China. They hated to see their privileges curbed, and they decried Eugene's efforts. They said it was a shame for Great Britain to surrender the two concessions. The British Chamber of Commerce at Hankou warned that it would snub O'Malley if he ever showed up. It pressured the British consul general in Wuhan to act in concert with them. Herbert Goffe succumbed, informing his legation in Peking that if he invited O'Malley to be his houseguest, he would alienate the entire British community, and he begged the legation to reconsider the matter. Faced with such formidable opposition, the British government paused.

Eugene suspected that all these behind-the-scenes maneuverings were being concocted by the British Legation in Peking and by Whitehall in London. In the past, when the British summoned an official of the Chinese foreign office, it was with only one purpose in mind—to make demands. Now the Chinese were making the demands. It was quite a turnaround. Unsure of their footing, the British proceeded slowly.

Foreseeing a fighting retreat from the British, Eugene had consistently pursued a policy that would isolate Britain, the dean of colonialism.

He gave instructions that the anti-imperialist propaganda should be aimed only at the British. Throughout this period, the Americans stood ready to jump at any opportunity, since the waning of British power offered them a chance to enhance their own. They considered themselves morally superior to the British because of their willingness to give away a little more profit. They claimed that they did not shortchange the natives—they brought commodities to China to meet its needs, and they sold them at fair prices. When they purchased China's surplus goods, they didn't rob the natives of their fair share of the profits. The American traders, puffed up by Puritanical braggadocio, made themselves believe that their work in China was responding to God's sacred call.

The local moral leader of the American community was the Young Men's Christian Association. On their board were a few rich Chinese businessmen. Besides spreading the Word of God, the YMCA was, in a discreet way, promoting trade; so, in order to win more Chinese business, they played on China's resentment toward Britain.

With the acquiescence of their legation, the YMCA was the only Christian organization that cooperated with the Wuhan government in providing relief for refugees and wounded soldiers. They were aware that the Wuhan government was not a harmonious whole: Eugene and his liberal colleagues had great difficulty in restraining Borodin and the Chinese communists from indiscriminately attacking foreigners.

Since Wuhan was the government's capital, Borodin and the communists had to concede to some extent. But incidents did happen. When American visitors from Shanghai or their home country were harassed, they borrowed Eugene's official car with its official chauffeur and four military guards riding on the running boards. When the soapbox orators grew too noisy in front of the YMCA building or on the campuses of the missionary schools, they were reported to the government, who would then send police to tell them to step down. In short, Eugene was one of the Kuomintang leaders to whom the YMCA could go to lodge a reasonable complaint and get help.

They appreciated his help and reciprocated when the chance arose. It came during this critical period while Eugene was expecting the British envoy, Owen St. Clair O'Malley, but the British Legation was putting off his visit to Wuhan indefinitely.

Eugene had an old friend who was the president of the YMCA in Wuhan. Yan Deqing was either directly or indirectly associated with the Cantonese Club. In any case, his older brother Yan Huiqing had been alternately foreign minister and prime minister in a series of Peking governments and knew Eugene well. The Yans were a devout Christian family. Father Yan was the dean of St. John's College, an American Episcopal Church institute in Shanghai. Mother Yan graduated from St. Mary's Hall of the same mission at Shanghai. The Episcopal Church of Shanghai was proud to claim that it was the direct descendant of the Church of England.

Yan Deqing had a daughter, Hilda Yan. She was about Silan's age. A comely and vivacious young woman, she had a reputation for being a little wild. She was the only woman in Wuhan driving a car. She had another unconventional hobby for a young Chinese woman in the 1920s: she enjoyed horseback riding. With Silan accompanying her and in their fashionable riding habits, they made a pretty sight for passersby to gawk at. It was said that T. V. Soong was enamored of both of them at the same time. The Chens and the Yans were friends, on easy terms. Usually it was Hilda Yan who drove her father to the Chen house. Their gatherings were informal and averted public scrutiny.

When Eugene told Yan that the British boycott against the peace talks might succeed, Yan frowned. As the president of the YMCA and a member of a powerful family, he had access to influential people who could reschedule the negotiations between Eugene and the British. A complex reception plan was worked out.[5] The president of the Indo-China Bank would put O'Malley up in his residence, on the condition that his guest would receive no Chinese or foreign visitors with views different from those of the British community. The YMCA would throw a banquet in O'Malley's honor, but the Chinese Chamber of Commerce would foot the bill. The dinner party shouldn't look like a YMCA event; it had to look like an affair of Hankou's business community. The guests included a few British businessmen who did not want to miss the money bandwagon, several American merchants eager to get down to business, and some Chinese entrepreneurs anxious to resuscitate the market. A very important personage named Eugene Barnett, who was the Senior American Secretary of the national Chinese YMCA, would come specially from Shanghai on the morning boat and leave that same night. And naturally, the representatives of the Wuhan government would be invited, and one of them was Guo Taiqi, Eugene's friend in his *Peking Gazette* days and now his assistant.

The banquet went smoothly, and pleasant exchanges led to serious talk. The first concern of the British was China's judicial system, as Eugene had learned long ago in London when he studied the history of China's relationship with Britain. China's judicial system was indeed out of date. After the fall of the Manchu dynasty fifteen years earlier, there had been endless warlords' infighting, civil wars, and revolutions. Very little time was left for any government to turn its attention to introducing or improving the commercial law or reforming legal procedures.

Eugene told O'Malley that the Wuhan government had every intention of ruling the returned concessions by law. Since China did not yet have a functional judicial system, it would select and absorb a great deal from the English common law. This description of governing the British concessions in the parts of China controlled by the Wuhan government was documented in the Chen-O'Malley Agreement. By virtue of this agreement, the concessions passed back to Chinese jurisdiction, with the administration being a joint one of Chinese and British representatives. Law courts were to be established by the Chinese government, with jurisdiction over British subjects living in the former concessions. The former British concession in Hankou became known as "Special Administration District Number 3," a law court was established, and a Chinese judge was chosen from Chinese lawyers and barristers-at-law who had been called to the bar of London's Middle Temple. Thus was ushered in the beginning of the end of extraterritoriality in China.

The document was drafted, but the road to signing it was still bumpy. There was a lot of dissension in the foreign communities. The Japanese concession, which bordered the former German concession, now under Chinese control, was worried that if Britain retreated, the Chinese might be tempted to push further into their extraterritorial privileges. The American community was not too happy either. They had enjoyed all the privileges offered to the British concession and were afraid of losing them.

Goaded on by those foreign communities, the British negotiators changed their tune and demanded written guarantees that would allow them to dictate the timing of when they would relinquish their privileges. Eugene bristled. He refused to be coerced. Britain and the other colonial powers went back to what they had been accustomed to doing. They dispatched and reinforced their troops and marines around Shanghai. There were forty-three warships, including eight British, fourteen Japanese, thirteen American, three French, one Italian, one Turkish, one Spanish, one Portuguese, and one Dutch. They had a combined force of thirty thousand men in Shanghai. And that was not all: along the seacoast and the Yangzi River, there were 171 gunboats patrolling, most of them British. They were preparing for war.[6]

The odds were not in Eugene's favor, but he told the British that he would not return to the conference room and sign any agreement under duress. The foreign powers must halt their military operations first. His stance was strengthened once again by the support of his own people. The Chinese responded to the military reinforcements of the foreign powers by demonstrating in port cities such as Chongqing (Chungking), Changsha, and Yichang. Anti-British sentiment was also rising in Hong Kong. The British government realized that it faced a far more serious situation than it had bargained for. It had placed British missionaries, merchants, and officials in great danger. It then tried to get itself out of the mess by seeking a settlement by negotiation and not by force.

Behind the imperial grandstanding, Britain was fearful of getting embroiled in a war with China. Not that they did not have the weapons to win the war: it was the peace they would not win. So they halted their military deployment in order to get Eugene back to the negotiation table.

Both sides were ready, but Moscow intervened and instructed Borodin to abort the agreement between Eugene and the British. Borodin asked Eugene several times to put off the signing, arguing that the Wuhan government had already repossessed the two British concessions and there was no need for a written agreement.[7] In addition to Moscow's pressure, a number of Chinese communists, like the firebrand Li Lisan, expressed disapproval of Eugene's diplomatic solution. The concessions had been seized by working-class men and women, led by them. They wanted all the credit and were reluctant to share it with Eugene, a bourgeois, not to mention letting him take precedence over them.

Eugene refused to leave matters hanging, thus keeping the situation unsettled between China and Britain. It was one thing to rush over the barbed-wire barricades that separated the British concession from the Chinese City, but it was quite another to keep it. What the unionists called a revolutionary act, the foreign powers deemed mob rule. Should the repossession of the concessions not be sanctioned by a legal agreement, the British could retake it at any time by force. With China's interest foremost at heart, Eugene went ahead and signed the Chen-O'Malley agreement on February 19, 1927.

The repossession of the two concessions set a precedent for the return of Hong Kong, (labeled a "Special Administrative Region," to China in 1997). During the Cultural Revolution, when Mao Zedong's Red Guards plotted to rush over the border into Hong Kong by force, Zhou Enlai stopped them. His successors carried out his policy of waiting to take back the British colony when the ninety-nine-year lease expired. Hong Kong's justice system remained basically the same as it had been under British rule, since the Chinese judicial system still needed improvement as it had in Eugene's time, particularly in commercial law and law protecting private property.

★ 16 ★

JACK SAILS INTO THE EYE
OF A REVOLUTIONARY STORM

The Northern Expedition was going well. In a sanguine mood, Eugene sent a cable telling Jack and Yolanda to come as quickly as possible, so that the whole family could follow the victorious soldiers and enter the Front Gate of Peking together. He also described their possible future home, a lovely mini-palace hidden in a *hutong*.

Jack's mother had died when he was seventeen years old. Traumatized, he expected her to appear at the head of their dining table for days and weeks. Overcome by the sense of loss, he escaped to the outdoor areas privately owned by the family. Acham's Bay was his mother's favorite spot. There Jack had learned to swim and fish. He loved to listen to the whispering silence by the sea, the lapping of the little waves against the rocks, or the *flap-flap* of the water on the boat's side. But after his mother's death, the sound of the sea was not as soothing as it had been: it carried a sorrow as endless as the ever-flowing water. As Jack trawled for fish between the islets, he saw his mother out of the corner of his eye, proud and erect, eternally youthful and beautiful.

Right after Aisy had died, when Eugene thought that it was best to bring his three younger children to China, Jack welcomed the impending change of scene, but his journey was put off. Eugene sent enough money for only the three unmarried siblings to make the trip. But Percy had his own ideas. Without consulting his father, he decided that Yolanda should not leave her school in the middle of the semester. He assured them that when she finished the school year, he himself or some friend would take her to China. As their older brother, he would go to London with Silan and Jack. Once in London, Percy abruptly told Jack that he was taking Silan all the way to China and leaving Jack behind. If Jack went, Percy would have no pretext to chaperone her. The two younger siblings argued that Percy should obey their father's instructions, but Percy would hear nothing of it.

Silan was angry. "This is your last chance to escape from your miserable marriage, right?" she cried.

Left to his own devices in London, Jack went to see his father's solicitor and told him he wanted to study law at the University of London, as his mother had planned for him. The solicitor agreed to give him the money from his father's account.

Jack was at an impressionable age and followed the fashions, vogues, and fads of the time. He continued to read voraciously, now outgrowing Dumas and Walter Scott and reading Bernard Shaw and Anatole France. He thought he understood Matisse with his odalisques and decorative arabesques of color, and Picasso with his odd and fragmented forms, though Jack's love still remained the artistic creations of the glorious Renaissance.

Jack was a regular concertgoer. He read books on music, puzzling over A and B variations. He played Chopin, Debussy, Ravel—the usual romantics and moderns—but he didn't feel at home with Stravinsky. He went to Diaghilev's Ballet Russe, a bit bedraggled from much touring but definitely chic and avant-garde. He saw Pavlova dance the "Dying Swan." No one in the theater audience moved for a full minute after her wings stopped quivering, and then they all rose as one in a thunder of applause.

While still studying law, Jack was apprenticed to a respectable law firm with offices on Piccadilly, just a few doors away from the fashionable Burlington Arcade. His allowance of eight pounds (about forty-five U.S. dollars) a week, while reasonable, was somewhat frugal for a college student in his position. Jack knew that he should make do; a Welsh coal miner in Rhondda Valley could raise a family on half or a third of that amount. But they did not have to dress well. He did, in tailored suits, wearing a bowler hat and fawn-colored spats, carrying a pair of soft leather gloves and a cane—or, if the weather was iffy, a tightly furled brolly (umbrella).

Jack's outfits, though they seemed adequate to him, drew criticism from a colleague at the law firm, a young blond Englishman who had been president of the Oxford Union debating society and knew the proper places to buy clothes and ties. He considered Austin Reed, where Jack shopped, too obviously middle-class, its cut too showy.

Once, when this colleague made yet another remark about Jack's attire, Jack switched the topic to art and literature, which he fancied he knew more about.

"That won't take you very far in your law practice," the young Englishman commented cuttingly.

"Many of our clients are cultured people, marquises, marchionesses, knights, and so forth. We must know how to talk with them," Jack asserted.

"They would rather you collect their money for them."

Jack had to concede that he lacked talent in that area.

One of Jack's errands was to deliver summonses to the people his boss wanted to haul into court. These were people who were supposedly on the wrong side of the law, meaning they were not represented by his law firm. But Jack found it embarrassing to throw papers at their feet, especially at the feet of nice and pleasant people. Sometimes it took a little time to find them, but he never once needed to throw the papers at their feet, which in legal rigmarole was the same as placing the summons in their hands. Jack disliked this kind of work, and one incident in particular confirmed that he would never make a living by hounding others with the law. He had to deliver a summons to a marquis, whom a client of his law firm had charged with fraud. The marquis's wife was none other than Jack's first love, Ena.

When Jack had been about six and Ena ten, he had fallen in love with her. Ena's father was a rich man, and he bought his daughter expensive toys. One was a mini-orchestra for her to show off her musical talents. Jack first saw her, with her long shining black hair, dark violet eyes, snow-white complexion, and rosy lips, conducting while Silan danced. Standing erect on the dais, she held in her hand the cutest baton Jack had ever seen.

His love for Ena grew. Puppy love though it was, it nevertheless had to find some tangible expression. He wrote painstakingly "Jack loves Ena" on slips of paper, which he hid under the staircase carpet, but Silan discovered his secret. She offered to help and arranged a doll's tea party for him and Ena, complete with candies and cakes, paid for by Silan, who had raided Jack's porcelain piggy bank. He had a good time and was extremely grateful for the honor, little suspecting that he himself had footed the bill. Jack was a credulous child before he grew up to be a trusting man.

Jack's self-portrait. At seventeen years old, he apprenticed with a respectable law firm on Piccadilly.

Eleven years had passed since then, but Jack remembered the tea party with fondness. Full of chivalry, he decided to pay Marchioness Ena a visit before he delivered the papers. He had the notion that he could work out a settlement between the marquis and his client in order to spare Ena the scandal of litigation.

Ena lived in an upper-class residential area near Hyde Park. On his way over, Jack pictured her sitting by a marble fireplace in a tastefully furnished drawing room, wearing a white dress with a pale blue sash around her slim waist, just as she had on that night long ago.

The first letdown was Ena's drawing room. It looked as if it had been furnished with things bought from secondhand shops. Jack waited there for quite a while, but Ena did not appear. When it became clear that she did not wish to receive him, he left.

Once outside, Jack realized he had left his gloves behind and turned back to get them. While he was telling the maid what he had come back for, he saw Ena walking down the staircase. She saw him too and stopped on the landing, and the strong sunlight coming in from the window caught her heavily made-up face, much too heavy for a young woman to wear. Jack was repulsed. She was like the female equivalent of Dorian in Oscar Wilde's *The Picture of Dorian Gray*. Jack bowed and fled without his gloves. This time he did not turn back.

After this incident, he was even more reluctant to devote his life to the law. His uncertainty about what to do next was resolved by a cable from his father. Eugene wanted Jack and Yolanda to join him and Silan, now with him in China. Eugene did not mention Percy. Eugene was a Roman Catholic, and despite his being an absentee husband, he viewed matrimony as holy and unbreakable. He had insisted that Percy leave China and go back to his wife and sons in Trinidad.

Jack cabled his younger sister to come immediately to London so they could leave together for China. When Yolanda arrived, Jack and she stayed with family friends. At eight o'clock on the morning of December 26, 1926, while the whole house was still drowsy from a night of Christmas dancing at the Kensington Hotel, Jack received a phone call from the solicitor who sent him his monthly check.

"Are you the son of Eugene Chen, the Chinese foreign minister?" the solicitor asked. Jack was still using his Trinidadian family name, Acham.

Jack answered that he was.

"Ah!" the solicitor exclaimed.

Jack could hear some muffled discussion at the other end of the line. At the time he was too naïve to guess what the mumbling was about. But two months later, when he was inadvertently embroiled in a game of cat-and-mouse with spies in Shanghai, he woke up to the fact that the solicitor must have passed on this information to agents of the British government. At the time, Jack was immediately made aware that, because of his father, he had suddenly become a person of some consequence. When his law firm was informed of who he was, those who had tended to overlook him now greeted him as if he were a potential law partner.

Jack did not dislike London life, but he was looking forward to venturing into new fields of activity. This was in the blood of his ancestors, the Guangdong seafarers, who had migrated south from Guangdong Province and gone abroad to Singapore, Indonesia, Malaya, the Philippines, Hawaii, and the west coast of the United States of America during the eighteenth and nineteenth centuries. They were also settlers in a number of the Caribbean islands, from Cuba to Trinidad. Jack's ancestors could also be found on the other side of the Atlantic, in London. Eighteen years old, Jack was retracing the route of his ancestors across the ocean to begin his journey back to China, homeward.

By 1926, Jack had already crossed the Atlantic five times, but this was his first journey to the Orient. He and Yolanda boarded a luxury liner. The journey was uneventful, remarkable only in that it opened his eyes to a side of the British Empire that he had never seen. As the liner passed through the Suez Canal, Jack had a fleeting glimpse of Port Said. On the surface, it was a very brown and arid version of the colonial towns he had seen in the Caribbean, attractive for their natural beauty rather than for anything made by man. But Bombay, his first stop in India, was something else. There he was appalled by the poverty of this Jewel in the British Crown. When Jack went ashore, he discovered the massive mound of coal dumped on the dockside under the shadow of the magnificent Arch of Triumph. Walking through the archway, a symbol to glorify the great empire on which the sun never set, he saw giant hotels next to streets teeming with homeless families, living on the sidewalks of this premier city of India. He had only glimpsed poverty in Trinidad and England. Nothing had prepared him for the horror of the slums in British India.

After that, it was a relief to see Columbo, Penang, Singapore, and Hong Kong where the poverty was discreetly hidden away. In Penang, Jack saw carriages with opulent Chinese merchants taking their families for Sunday outings. Their wives were dressed in gorgeous silk from China, their children proudly displayed like baby dolls, just like the old days when his parents had paraded him and Silan around the Savannah in their sailor suits and curls. Watching them, he thought of his smiling mother unfurling her lilac parasol as she got into their carriage for the Sunday joyride with her children.

The stopover in Hong Kong was short, only two days. In the morning of the fourth or fifth day, they turned into the yellow, turbid waters of the Yangzi estuary, the Huangpu River. With the help of his binoculars, Jack observed the strange city, Shanghai. At the farther end of the famous Bund, next to the weather station, stood a graceful winged figure of Victory. This was the International Settlement's tribute to the dead of the First World War. It was uncompromisingly Occidental and Hellenistic and did not fit in a Chinese world. Over 99 percent of Shanghai's population was Chinese, but the memorial was not meant for them. It was conspicuously placed on the border between the British-dominated International Settlement and the French concession. The statue overshadowed lines of emaciated, skeletal coolies (Chinese for bitter laborers), clothed in thin, dirty rags, with heavy boxes balanced on their shoulders, who moved along a narrow plank from a luxury liner, a sort of foreign floating palace.

Jack's liner docked. Then the strangest of all things occurred: as he and Yolanda walked down the gangplank onto the Bund, he spotted a pretty, dark young woman in a Chinese dress with a high collar reaching her chin. Their older sister, Silan, had come down from Wuhan to meet them. She rushed on board, followed by her large, broadly smiling maidservant in a black pajama-like tunic. Before he could get a word out, Silan formally introduced herself as if they had never known each other.

"My name is Chung. We've never met before, but our fathers are good friends," she said to her staring siblings.

Jack took a closer look at the familiar stranger. The impish smile behind the false name was undoubtedly Silan's.

What was she up to? Jack followed her lead as if they were playing a childhood game. He bowed and shook her hand politely. Giggling, Yolanda did the same. They were hurried through customs and whisked to Astor House. As soon as they entered their suite and closed the door, Silan laughingly threw her arms around both Jack and Yolanda. "How do you rate me as an actress?"

"What does this mean?" Jack asked, perplexed. This was the expression he would wear often when he was with Silan. He usually felt like Alice, falling through the hole, and Silan was his rabbit.

"Just playing it safe. Father's friends warned me to be careful. If I did not take precautions, I might be kidnapped and held hostage by Father's enemies. I do my best to confuse them," Silan explained.

Silan had a penchant for drama. Jack was the opposite. He had an inclination to keep things subdued. He did not take her warning seriously. He did not think she took the precautionary measures seriously herself, when she told him they were going to take tea with Mrs. Borodin at the Soviet Russian Consulate.

"Mrs. Borodin has just seen her older son off. He is going back to the Soviet Union to finish his education. She happens to be here when we are here. For the sake of politeness, we should pay her a visit."

"How can we keep ourselves anonymous when we are meeting with such a high-profile communist?" Jack said with hesitation.

Fresh off a bourgeois luxury liner, he had reservations about entering a proletarian lair. Moreover, up till then all he knew of communists came from the British press, both conservative and liberal. They presented an image of communists as inherently evil, irrational, and—worse—uncouth. These troublemakers fomented strikes, created disorder, made people disaffected. The *Daily Mirror* went so far as to carry the crusade into the canine world. It ran a comic strip titled *Pip, Squeak and Wilfred.* Pip was a dear little intelligent good dog. Squeak was an articulate penguin and Wilfred, a rabbit. They had an implacable and evil enemy who had, if Jack remembered correctly, a Russian name, Popski, and who had untidy black whiskers. Popski hurled bombs.

Jack gave another reason why he hesitated to socialize with Mrs. Borodin. "What have I got to talk about with a communist?"

"Oh, you silly boy, just mind your table manners and leave the rest to me."

The main entrance of the Soviet consulate was directly across the street from their hotel, but Silan chose to use the side door, and that meant walking in a circle for four blocks.

"Are these precautions necessary? I don't know. The Soviets warned me that if the spies saw us entering the consulate, they would suspect that we were going to visit someone we knew. Who else could that be but Mrs. Borodin? For her safety, we mustn't let anyone know where we are heading."

Fanny Borodin was waiting for them in a huge ballroom. She was a bustling, large woman with a strong square jaw. She rattled Jack at once with her intimidating composure. A Russian revolutionary in her own right, she had been active in the movement for the emancipation of women in the

Soviet Union. Fanny loved giving Russian revolutionary aphorisms which, when repeated more than once, were boring. To cite one example: "You must get rid of bourgeois ideas."

She must have sized Jack up at a glance. His upbringing was so visibly bourgeois. When she gave a call into an inner room, he expected to see a stern communist commissar darting out to help her cure his ideological disease. But, in a wonderful surprise, a bevy of the prettiest, liveliest girls Jack had ever seen breezed into the stuffy room of faded elegance. They took his breath away. These were the Duncan dancers, about thirty of them, selected by Isadora Duncan herself for their grace, good looks, and intelligence.

When the legendary Isadora Duncan arrived in Moscow, she had so charmed the country that its new rulers bestowed a small palace on her to use as a school. Irma, one of her four adopted daughters, had led this group performing in Wuhan. They were now on their way home, via Shanghai.

Before Jack could catch his breath, these girls, in short Grecian tunics that chastely showed off their limbs, started to dance. Their movements had been copied by Isadora from bas-reliefs and paintings from antique Greek vases and walls. The Hellenistic Greeks might have developed such dancing if they had had such romantic composers as Chopin and Schubert, Jack mused. Their lead dancer was about Jack's age and the most beautiful. He fell in love with her at first sight, and also with all thirty of them collectively. Suddenly he fretted that he had not given enough thought to his appearance, the color of his tie and the creases in his trousers. How did he look to them? He looked interesting. His skin was dark as a Cantonese's or that of a native from the nearby Hainan island; his hair was a little kinky, but not as kinky as that of his maternal grandmother of African ancestry; the shape of his nose was basically European, but not as high, and his nostrils were slightly distended; his lips were thick, but not too thick. His manner was that of a well-bred Edwardian gentleman.

Despite his interest in dancers, dance, and dance talk, Jack had to be off on urgent business. Silan reminded him that he needed to go to the British firm of Butterfield and Swire to buy riverboat tickets for their upstream journey to Wuhan.

Butterfield and Swire was one of the wealthiest and most reputable British firms doing business in Shanghai. They ran a line of riverboats up the Yangzi from Shanghai as far as Chongqing beyond the Three Great Gorges. Jack asked the clerk if he could book four passages, including one for the maidservant, on a boat sailing on the eighth of February. He gave his name and showed the British passports. The Englishmen at the counter seemed astonished.

The British were fleeing trouble spots like Wuhan rather than going toward them. The clerk disappeared into a back room with their papers; when he returned, he told Jack that no passengers would be carried on their next boat out of Shanghai. He then emphasized that because of the civil war (the Kuomintang's Northern Expedition against the warlords), he had no idea when another boat would be going upriver. Disappointed, Jack returned to the Soviet Consulate and consulted with Silan and Fanny Borodin.

"I am going back to Wuhan soon. I'll sail on the *Pamyat Lenina* (*In Memory of Lenin*). You can come with me." Fanny assured them that the Russian steamship was much more comfortable than a British ship.

Very British indeed, Jack felt that he, and particularly his three female companions, would be safer on a British ship. But since no British ship would carry passengers to Wuhan in the foreseeable future, he accepted Mrs. Borodin's offer for the sake of expediency.

"Since we are going to travel with Mrs. Borodin, we had better not arouse any suspicion. In China, the best trick to put your political enemies off the scent is to pretend to be indulging in merrymaking, so much so that you appear to forget everything else," Silan said after they had returned to their hotel.

"Then let's play mahjong," Yolanda suggested cleverly.

After playing the game with her hands for a little while, Silan's feet itched for action. She asked Jack to escort her to see Shanghai's night life and further mislead the ubiquitous spies. He was more than ready to oblige. Dancing was his favorite pastime.

Shanghai's nightclubs ran the gamut from the expensive and highly respectable on Nanjing Road to the sleazy in Blood Alley. Following the hotel manager's advice, Jack and Silan began with Ciro's, to which a young man could safely bring his maiden aunt. From there, they worked their way uptown. They were at their third stop at about 10:30 when a waiter came to their table and told Jack that Butterfield and Swire wished to speak to him on the phone. He was surprised that they had tracked him to this nightspot. He and Silan had picked it at random as they sauntered up the crowded Nanjing Road. Nanjing Road was a promenade where a great variety of nationalities converged, and where Jack and Silan did not look conspicuous at all. Had a tail been put on them? By whom? Anyway, there was no time to wonder. Jack took the phone message. The British firm told him it could, after all, arrange their passage to Wuhan.

Jack and Silan sped back to the hotel by taxi. Dropping Silan at the gate, Jack went on to Butterfield and Swire on the Bund. A dim light shone over the counter. This time, without much ado, the same English clerk who had bluntly turned Jack away just hours earlier took his money and made out four tickets for the next boat, leaving early the next morning. After they hurriedly informed Mrs. Borodin of their immediate departure, they boarded the river-boat a little after midnight.

The big river steamer, on which it seemed they were the only passengers, nosed out of the Huangpu River and up the Yangzi. Flat green marshlands and rice fields spread far and wide on either side of the river. They kept well in the central channel. The warlords' trigger-happy soldiers had been known to take potshots at passing Chinese vessels, although they seldom fired at foreign ships, particularly British ones. However, a heavy armor plate pro-tected the wheelhouse.

Jack and his two sisters had the privilege of dining at the captain's table, since there were no other passengers. The captain was friendly but a little too solicitous. He seemed to want to keep the Chen siblings constantly under his watchful eye.

As their ship pulled into shore at Jiujiang, Silan grew excited, anticipat-ing some adventure in the port city where the British concession had been recently returned to China. But the captain asked them to remain on board. Silan pouted in disappointment and went back to her cabin with Yolanda. Jack sat and was reading on deck when a Roman Catholic priest came on board. The stranger had on a cream-colored cassock and a large straw hat. He introduced himself politely and sat down next to Jack. His English had a heavy French accent. When Jack told him that he spoke French, the priest switched languages. Somehow he led Jack into a discourse on religion.

"I know you are a Catholic," the priest said.

This was true. Jack was so eager to have someone other than his sisters and the captain to chat with that it didn't occur to him to ask the garrulous father how he knew he was a Catholic, or the reasons for his traveling on this British ship through the heart of China.

The crux of this priest's discourse was the hope that Jack would use what-ever influence he had to protect the missionary work of Holy Mother Church in China. Jack answered that of course he would, and he meant it. Jack knew little about China, and what he knew was wholly from the view-point of an average middle-class person in England. He was ecumenically inclined, following the example of his mother. While he had attended Catholic mass on Sunday mornings, he had also gone to Protestant Sunday schools in the afternoons. He was a member of the youth organization the

Young Crusaders of the Roman Catholic Church and with his pennies supported the activities of the China Inland Mission. He saw no reason why he should not support a worthy religious cause. By the end of their conversation, the priest warned against the pervasive Tempter who had followed Jesus Christ to the high mountain. After having failed in ruining the Son of God, this Tempter had come down to the Yangzi Valley, attempting the destruction of the sons of men, the priest said with a gravity becoming a biblical prophet.

Jack expected to see his new friend at dinner. The priest didn't appear. Jack asked the captain if they should send someone to fetch him.

"He is not a passenger," the captain replied crisply without further elaboration.

The ship proceeded to Nanjing. As they entered a winter fog and drizzle, Jack, to his astonishment, saw something like a scene from a Hollywood movie. On the opposite bank, a squadron of White Russian soldiers, clad in winter furs and mounted on shaggy Mongolian ponies, was patrolling in single file. Then without warning, they charged with flashing sabers and savage battle cry. They were a terrifying sight. But there was no definite target that Jack could see. Before Jack could take in anything more, the captain hurried to his side and, in an almost peremptory tone, asked him to return to his cabin instantly.

"They are not riding full tilt at me, I am quite sure." Jack masked his uneasiness with a joke.

"Don't be so sure," the captain admonished, apparently in no joking mood.

The White Russian mercenaries, hired by a warlord named Zhang Chongchang, were the last riddle on the journey that Jack would have to puzzle out after his arrival in Hankou.

As the ship drew closer to Hankou, Jack saw a small group of people standing on the floating jetty. He discerned his father in a Chinese gown of gray silk. Next to him was Soong Chingling, whom Jack recognized from the picture he had seen. There were, of course, no customs inspections for the children of the foreign minister. Anyway, Jack and Yolanda had little baggage, just a few suitcases each. From the riverbank, they went directly to Eugene's apartment nearby on the Bund. It was on the top floor of the former Salt Gabelle (salt tax) Building in the former British concession. Now the British were out, and Eugene had moved his office here from the former German concession. The apartment had been furnished and decorated by Silan, who had created a warm domestic atmosphere, further enhanced by the excellent gourmet cooking by Eugene's miracle of a chef from Canton.

After a few days of recuperating from the trip, the family discussed Jack's future. They decided that Jack's top priority should be to learn Chinese and Chinese history: in particular, the history of the Taiping Rebellion. A young, staid-looking secretary from the foreign office, Zhang Ke, was to be his tutor. Zhang Ke was a former student of John Leighton Stuart, the president of Yenching University and later the American ambassador to China in the late 1940s. Zhang Ke was watchful and alert, and when he was with Jack, he was quick to single things out for Jack's enlightenment. Jack never asked, but he had the feeling Zhang Ke was a communist.

Besides studying, Jack was appointed to be his father's personal secretary. He was to handle correspondence addressed to his father personally but sent to the foreign office. His father was doing great things, Jack thought exuberantly; how exciting to be part of the fighting contingent! But after a few days at his revolutionary job, Jack started to suspect that this position had been invented to give him something to do to while away the long afternoons. These letters lying on his desk would be thrown into the wastepaper basket if no one had time to open them.

For example, a letter from the Duke of Bedford informed the Chinese that His Grace's estate owned a herd of spotted white deer. They had been stolen from the Imperial Hunting Park in Peking when the eight-nation force had lifted the siege of the Legation Quarters and ended the Chinese Boxer Uprising in 1901. The letter offered to return these deer at the request of the Kuomintang government in Wuhan. Jack read it and replied with the set phrase: "Minister Chen requests me to inform you that…" Then he went on to say that Minister Chen was extremely pleased to receive the Duke's letter and appreciated the offer of restitution on behalf of the Chinese people. It was not immediately possible to provide suitable quarters for the deer, but as soon as these could be found, the responsible authority would get in touch with the duke. The idea of returning the deer amused Jack. The mischievous cartoonist in him imagined the returned deer milling around the traffic-jammed Hankou streets with huge crowds of pedestrians looking on.

Another letter was written by a White Russian woman. She and her husband were refugees from the Russian Revolution. According to her, her husband had been arrested by the Chinese police at the instigation of the Red Russian advisers. She swore he was innocent of any crime and asked the foreign minister to save him. Jack learned that he should not even acknowledge receipt of such a letter, much less encroach upon the authority of the ministry of justice.

Jack endured this bureaucratic routine for a week or so until the formal signing of the Chen-O'Malley Agreement, which returned the British concessions in Hankou and Jiujiang to China. Celebratory festivities were held, and there were crowds everywhere, looking curious and excited as they pointed at things and views that had once been forbidden to them. This recent victory had removed the sandbags and barbed wire surrounding the former British concession to keep the "Chinese loiterers" out.

Then suddenly the crowds parted to make way for a huge procession. Tens of thousands of people advanced on the street, cheering and shouting slogans. When they approached the foreign office, they burst into applause as Eugene, dressed in a Chinese gown, walked down the broad, high steps to join them.

"Those who have been naught shall now be all," they sang. The hope and faith on the faces of these ill-clad people struck the Christian chord in Jack. He felt as if he were witnessing the poor, the humble, the meek inheriting the earth.

The march was a fantastic sight, unlike anything Jack had ever seen. If a revolution could inspire such passion, it must be worth fighting for! Jack wanted to be with them, more directly, more closely. At dinner, he conveyed his wish to his father. Eugene responded sympathetically.

It was a relief when one of his father's secretaries informed him that he would be transferred to another job. His father had a private talk with him and asked if he wanted to work at the soon-to-be-published *People's Tribune*. The paper, a four-page English daily, would voice the opinions of the Wuhan government. Eugene decided its general policy, giving the staff wide latitude on the details. Borodin acted as a consultant. The editor, Rayna Prohme, gave the paper her own buoyant slant.

Among those who had come to meet Jack and his sisters, when their ship waddled its way sideways to berth itself by the floating jetty at Hankou, was this young American woman, Rayna Prohme. She had been working for Eugene since they first met in Peking in 1925, as the editor of his newspaper, the *People's Tribune* of Peking. When Eugene was appointed foreign minister in 1926, he invited Rayna and her husband, Bill, to come south. Bill was slated to head the new National News Agency, while Rayna ran the newspaper, the *Canton Gazette*. When the Canton government moved to Wuhan, they followed. There Rayna set out to prepare the first Wuhan issue of the English edition of the *People's Tribune*.

Across the road from the Foreign Office Building there stood a large yellow-stone three-story mansion containing the editorial offices and printing

Jack, at this time a journalist and cartoonist working for the People's Tribune of Wuhan, examines his trusted Leika camera.

presses of the *People's Tribune*. It had a block to itself, most of it an empty, dusty playground surrounded by a six-foot-high wall. Rayna was at her desk in the inner room when Jack walked in unannounced one morning in late February. She stood up from her chair to welcome him. A ray of sunlight caught her red hair; her locks were a burst of fire; and underneath them was a most engaging smile. They became friends immediately.

Jack was attracted to Rayna's vivid personality. Rayna was an all-American girl, friendly, open, and straightforward, just as Jack imagined an American girl would be. Without wasting time on preliminaries, she explained how together they would make the *People's Tribune* the greatest newspaper in the world.

"I have done some drawing while in college, but not too well," Jack said apologetically. "I liked David Low's cartoons in the *London Star.*"

When she heard that he had tried to draw, she was immediately certain that he would make a good cartoonist. Jack's job became producing cartoons to accompany and highlight her editorials. So, at the age of eighteen, Jack became the first Chinese editorial cartoonist. And when she heard that he had taken care of the foreign minister's personal correspondence and scribbled some replies, she instantly discovered the writer and journalist in him.

"I am sure you can do it, Jack! I am sure whatever you do, you will do well," she said. Rayna then pulled several magazines from her shelf. "Have you ever seen these? They are full of cartoons."

Her stack of *New Masses* was a treasure trove. For the first time, the work of that potent group of American artists—Robert Minor, Gropper, Gellert, Fred Ellis, and many more—taught Jack how an artist could make a strong social commentary through the use of cartoons. They depicted what they saw. He wanted to do the same. Since his first assignment was to draw a cartoon about the necessity of raising the minimum wage ten cents (Chinese) a day, he felt he should know something about their work and life. A tour around a silk textile factory was arranged. It was owned by a Japanese who had promised to keep the factory running if the employees refrained from striking. But if they made trouble for him, he vowed he would close shop like so many other bosses before him, both foreign and Chinese.

The textile factory was located in the Chinese city of Hankou. The downtown area was vibrant with motion, noise, and color. The narrow streets were made narrower by the broad, long signboards hanging outside the shops. The signboards were painted in different combinations of color, black and gold, crimson and bright yellow, green and blue, and all other gaudy variations that one could fancy. When a ray of sun, filtering through the narrow strips of azure sky, fell upon them, the colors shone brilliantly and a uniquely picturesque Chinese city sprang alive.

The sparkle dimmed as soon as they left the trading and shopping arcades. Jack was brought to a halt in front of a menacing-looking building, more like a prison than a silk mill. Upon entering, Jack was immediately assaulted by the steam rising from the hot water troughs in which silk cocoons were soaked. He gasped for air, but the air was foul with the odor of sweat, urine, excrement, unwashed bodies, and garbage. It took all the stoicism he could summon not to bolt for the door.

The women worked like robots. Their hands and arms up to the elbows were covered with blisters and sores from sopping their hands and wrists in hot, dirty water sixteen hours a day. Under more than a few troughs lay their babies, bundles of misery, silent and still, not discernible from the rags and scraps around them. For a second Jack suspected they were dead, but they were not. They had been programmed to obey the rules and regulations like their mothers. The processing was simple. If they made noise, they would be put away, beside an open latrine or on the plank over a latrine. They cried until they were totally exhausted. No one, not even their mothers, would come to their aid. After a few such punishments, they learned to keep silent and still. But sometimes a baby was not so lucky. If a harried mother placed her baby too close to the latrine's edge, it could fall into the cesspool of human excrement and drown.

Jack was overpowered, but what he saw next struck him dumb. When he and his interpreter groped their way through a maze of narrow streets and even narrower alleys, they found themselves at the top of the riverbank. About fifty feet below was the wide, deep, roaring Han River. On the slopes leading down to the river were hundreds and thousands of shacks, made from straw, mud, tin, and cardboard. These were the shelters of the workers. In winter, the more frail inhabitants would freeze to death. In summer, when the waters rose, floods would wash away their ramshackle dwellings, their few belongings, and their worn-out lives. Despite such disasters, these people remained because conditions in their farming villages were even worse.

That evening at the dining table, Jack was unusually quiet, his eyes distant.

"Work hard, but don't expect instant results," Eugene advised.

Jack heeded his father's advice and redoubled his efforts at fighting the good fight. He worked wherever he was needed, drawing, reporting, photographing, editing, proofreading, printing, and so on. He worked overtime, and he noticed that he was not the only one in the building working until midnight. Borodin was too. The light in his study often burned late.

Just beyond Jack's office on the ground floor was a wide staircase leading to the second floor, which was occupied by Borodin's staff. The third floor was mainly occupied by Borodin. No attempt was made to impress anyone. There was no carpet on the stairs or floor, for there were few visitors. Borodin guarded his privacy. But one evening in March, he invited Jack over. Something unfortunate had happened to his wife, Fanny, Borodin said. Since Jack was one of the last people in Wuhan who had seen Fanny before her arrest, Borodin asked him to give a full account of their meeting.

Borodin first explained that on March 1, warlord troops had impounded the Soviet ship *Pamyat Lenina,* which was sailing from Shanghai to Wuhan. Borodin's wife, Fanny, and the whole crew were escorted to Peking. They were now left to the mercy of the warlord Zhang Zuolin, the merciless Manchurian Tiger, the same man who had held Eugene on death row a year and a half earlier in the city of Tianjin.

The name of the ship rang a bell with Jack; he remembered that it was the ship he and his sisters would have boarded with Mrs. Borodin had not the British firm decided to take them on at the last minute. Realizing how narrow their escape had been, Jack was alarmed and his memory jolted. The strange encounters in Shanghai and on his journey from there to Wuhan did not seem so inexplicable in hindsight. He recounted them to Borodin.

Borodin's face lengthened, looking grim. It was evident to him that from day one, Jack and his sisters had been followed by spies on the payrolls of the British, the French, the warlords, and even Chiang Kaishek, although the general was then still paying lip service to the Wuhan government. All the hirelings of these different groups were intermixed and in collusion. They must have coordinated the secret plot to seize the Russians and their ship, *Pamyat Lenina.* So when the British authority learned about Jack's and Silan's visit to the Soviet consulate in Shanghai, they guessed that the Chen siblings would travel to Wuhan on that Russian ship with Mrs. Borodin, since the British firm had refused to sell passenger tickets to Jack. The Chen siblings held British passports; if they were arrested along with Mrs. Borodin, it would cause the British authority a lot of inconvenience. Therefore they hastened to tell Butterfield and Swire Ltd. to arrange safe conduct for Eugene Chen's children.

Borodin saw his wife's arrest as a strategy devised by the British and their co-conspirators to widen the schism between the Kuomintang and the communists. The former they wished to woo, the latter they swore to destroy. Eugene Chen was an eminent leader of the Kuomintang, and his children must be spared the fate of Fanny Borodin. Borodin thought they were zeroing in on him and his Chinese communist comrades.

"They have formed a Holy Alliance against me." There was something grandiose in his bitter voice, as if to imply that only a remarkable enemy warranted this scheme of Machiavellian proportions.

Borodin was so distressed that Jack felt sorry for him. Borodin was the first real-life communist Jack had come to know intimately. Far from being uncouth, Borodin was one of the most cultivated men Jack had ever met. Mr. Bee, the nickname the Chen siblings gave the Russian, seemed to feel at home with them, and they with him. They played records the Chens had brought with them from London. They preferred jazz. Gershwin was then the jazz-maker par excellence for them. They also played Stravinsky, who, at that time, represented the classical avant-garde. Borodin enjoyed Western music and literature, but loved the Russian arts more. It was he who initiated Jack into the magic world of Pushkin, Gogol, Dostoyevski, and Gorky. But in appearance, Borodin was the stereotypical Bolshevik, an easy target for caricature in the British press. He wore a thick, dark walrus mustache, the kind seen on sinister cartoon characters. His rumpled tunic and baggy trousers made him look even more ungainly.

Borodin's lips quivered with agitation. Jack thought a tirade would issue from his mouth, but the voice coming out was more sad than angry.

"Jack, what would you advise me to do? Pray?" Borodin made a face.

"Reading sometimes is a good sedative."

"The Holy Bible?"

"I won't exclude that," Jack answered seriously, "especially not the New Testament."

"No, of course not," Borodin said with a faint grin. "I am not unfamiliar with the New Testament."

Then he launched into a discussion Jack did not expect. Borodin said that his last assignment before the China mission had been in England. He was arrested there and had a sojourn in British prisons, at Duke Street and then at Barlinnie in Glasgow. When he was locked in Barlinnie Prison, he asked the warden to give him books to read. The warden gave him the Holy Bible. He had studied the Old Testament when he had shed the orthodox dogma of Judaism. But he had never had so much time to reflect on the Bible as he did in that prison. The result was that he had found similarities between Marxism and Christianity.

Reading the New Testament got him interested in the life of Jesus. Jesus Christ, Borodin ruminated, preached a God who loved all the peoples in the world, not only the chosen one, and the early Christians were the first communists. They shared everything with each other. They lived in brotherhood. Their basic tenets were not so different from those of Marxism: "To each, according to his needs; from each, according to his abilities."

Jesus was a threat to the establishment, Borodin noted, and had to be silenced.

"You know why the mob cried out for Christ's crucifixion and for Barabbas's exoneration?" Borodin asked, stabbing the air with a cigarette. Without waiting for Jack's reply, he continued, "For the most humanly comprehensible reason. Barabbas was their mirror; the mob saw themselves in him, a narrow-minded, shortsighted, hard-boiled petty crook. Jesus, on the other hand, was different and therefore suspect. Jesus' promise to give them a new Jerusalem cleansed of corruption, oppression, and inequity perturbed them, and they returned death for love."

This was the first—but not the last—time Jack heard Borodin quote Jesus' life to allude to his own sorrow. Listening, Jack had an inkling of his own involuntary involvement in a cause too large and too complex for him to comprehend. Nevertheless, he felt compelled to plunge deeper with the conviction of a good Christian. How could he go wrong under the guidance of Jesus?

Jack's first cartoon was published on March 12, 1927. His father and Rayna had chosen this day to begin the *People's Tribune* of Wuhan because it was Sun Yatsen's birthday. The picture was of a coolie carrying a pole across his shoulders, a basket on each end. One was marked "wage," the other "work." The hopeful caption read: "It balances better now the Kuomintang has come."

In 1927, Jack and growing millions of Chinese believed in the truth of that drawing. They believed they would be able to add ten cents (Chinese) to the coolies' daily wage of twenty-five cents for sixteen hours' work. This was no more than a first, minuscule attempt to alleviate the suffering of the working poor, but it was reviled by the colonialists as a Red plot. Why? Jack was at once confused and disturbed.

The day his first cartoon was published, Rayna congratulated him. "Do you feel great? You are the first Chinese artist recording in cartoons a glorious revolutionary period!"

★17★

THE ERA OF CHEN YOUREN

The seven-and-a-half-month Wuhan regime, beginning on December 10, 1926, and ending on July 27, 1927, is described by some Chinese historians as the "Era of Chen Youren."[1] When I first read of it, that sounded a little cynical. Usually historians name an era after a hero because on his watch things were flourishing. From day one, the Wuhan regime was struggling on the brink of collapse, and after late March 1927 it went straight downhill. The fact that it had not collapsed sooner was due, for the most part, to Eugene's efforts. The most outstanding accomplishments of this period were achieved on the diplomatic front.

The Northern Expedition came to an abrupt halt in April 1927, but it had actually started lurching three months before. In January, Eugene prepared to hold a celebration to announce the Kuomintang's determination to take back the two British concessions. He and Chingling wrote a joint letter inviting Chiang Kaishek, as the supreme commander of the Northern Expedition, to take part. Chiang came on January 9, 1927. Wuhan held several mass meetings to welcome him. One was ostensibly organized by Borodin and the Chinese communists. Chiang's speech fit the occasion. He came to congratulate the people of Wuhan on the successful return of the British concessions; he came to support the people of Wuhan in their diplomatic victory and in their regaining their rights. After he had complimented his audience and Eugene, Chiang turned to compliment himself on leading his soldiers from victory to victory. At this point, there were signs of impatience—low jeers and snorts—among certain groups. Chiang was aware of them and, at the end of his speech, he went back to his crowd-pleasing tactics, shouting slogans for unity. In the midst of Chiang's pretentious exhibition of goodwill, Li Lisan, the communist firebrand, stood up and questioned Chiang's sincerity. If Chiang really meant what he said, Li Lisan demanded, why didn't he obey the government and move his headquarters to its new capital, Wuhan? All this created an uproar in the audience. Chiang Kaishek remained impassive. But after the meeting was indefinitely adjourned, he requested an explanation from Borodin.

"If you think you can silence the people, you had better think again," Borodin retorted irascibly. "Let me tell you a story. In ancient times, there was a king in the West who became nettled by the different opinions from his ministers. One day he said to them: 'You all talk too much. I don't like it.' They replied: 'Dogs cannot talk back. If Your Majesty does not like to hear us talk, then go find dogs.'"[2]

Borodin could not have found a worse insult to throw in Chiang Kaishek's face. In this instance, Borodin's lack of knowledge of Chinese culture was thoroughly exposed. In the West, a dog is man's best friend; but in China, dogs are abject creatures. In Chinese, no idiomatic expression was more demeaning than the term "running dogs." It was said that after this exchange of violent words, Chiang made up his mind to expel Borodin from China. Chiang stayed in Hankou a short while, in order to drive wedges between Borodin and the leading Kuomintang members. His overture to Eugene was most obvious. Chiang, a total stranger to Western culture, went to a dance concert organized and showcased by Silan. Though bored, he sat through the entire performance and flattered her on her choreography.

Chiang returned to his headquarters at Nanchang. A month later, Chiang received, with Zhang Jingjiang, the Curio, the delegates of the Chinese Chamber of Commerce of Shanghai. The Curio was their intermediary. Chiang Kaishek was their hired gun. A conspiracy against the communists was in the making, whose ranks would swell with the rulers of the International Settlement, the French concession, and the Green Gang.

Shortly after that, the Northern Expedition troops swept down the lower reaches of the Yangzi River and reached Nanjing. On March 19, between the pullout of warlord troops and the entry of the Kuomintang soldiers, confusion ensued. Men wearing Kuomintang military uniforms stormed the British and Japanese consulates, killing seven people—two British, one Japanese, and four other foreign nationals—and wounding more than a few others. When they got onto the campus of Nanjing (Jinling) University, they murdered the vice president, Dr. Williams, an American missionary educator. The Americans and British evacuated to Socony House on Standard Oil Hill above the city walls. When the Chinese began attacking Socony House, the American and British marines opened fire—or the other way around, depending on whose version you believed. According to some Chinese sources, the mutual shooting killed more than thirty Chinese and wounded several hundred.

Recriminations abounded. Chiang Kaishek pointed his finger at the communists. The communists accused him of framing them. But there were things the communists could not deny. The chief communist commissar of the occupying Kuomintang army at Nanjing was Lin Zuhan, known for his radicalism when he and Li Lisan had urged the unionists and propagandists to raise hell on Wuhan's streets and campuses. The communists and the missionaries chose the campuses as the battleground. Both knew that how the young mind was shaped would determine the prospect of each party. What happened on the campus of Nanjing University was so similar to what had happened in the missionary schools at Wuhan that Chiang Kaishek seemed vindicated in his charges against the communists.

This was the first time Chiang used the foreign newspapers to separate himself from Borodin and the Chinese communists. And yet he told the press that he had confidence in Eugene's investigation of the matter. This was more than an overture to Eugene. He believed in the integrity of Eugene's office, even while he discredited the Wuhan government in which Eugene served. Eugene had won this reputation even from people who did not like him very much.

Nanjing was about a two-hour train ride from Shanghai, and the bloody confrontation there heightened the foreign powers' fear that Shanghai would be next. They declared that they would retaliate, march on Wuhan, and root out the troublemakers once and for all.

Their war cry rose to a crescendo when, a week after the Nanjing Incident, another crisis blew up on April 3. This time it struck right in Hankou. A dispute over a fare between a Japanese marine and a ricksha puller mushroomed into the killing of dozens of Chinese civilians. It started when the Japanese marine accused the ricksha puller of overcharging him. They scuffled, and the ricksha puller was badly wounded. When another coolie rushed to intervene, the marine stabbed him in the heart with his sword. Rather than punishing the marine, the Japanese naval commander ordered a detachment of marines to fire their machine guns upon the Chinese pedestrians on the bank. The stage had been set for war.

That night was noisy. There was the spurting *bang-bang* of guns mixed with the thunder of wheels rumbling. On a few nights after the incident, Eugene took it on himself to walk incognito on the streets in the vicinity of the Japanese concession, so he could see for himself that security was maintained. He asked only a secretary to accompany him, but Jack insisted on going and sharing the danger.

People were fleeing the city. A stream of carts, piled high with boxes and suitcases, was pulled by humans or donkeys through the streets. Suddenly one cart darted out, hit a lamp pole, and overturned. Crying, screaming, and bawling ensued. Above the din came loud mixed sounds of fire crackling and machines screeching from the foreign gunboats. The sky was half lit. A donkey, frightened, leaped into the air and then fell. The whole train of carts broke down. Everyone ran without knowing why or where. The Chinese soldiers guarding the border of the Japanese concession pushed them back while the Japanese marines on the other side shot warning bullets into the air.

Jack felt his father's body grow rigid with tension, but Eugene refused to turn back. It would take only one hothead to plunge the whole of Wuhan into a sea of fire. Eugene feared that the enraged Chinese might overrun the Japanese concession. One more crisis could precipitate a war that would only hasten the Wuhan government's demise, along with the peasant and labor unions under its protection. Next day, Eugene called an emergency council in Borodin's apartment and asked the union leaders not to get emotional and to contain their anger. He noticed, to his misgiving, the absence of Gregory Voitinsky and Li Lisan. Borodin told him that they had gone to Shanghai.

Eugene quickly grasped what Borodin had kept mum about. The communist firebrands had sped off to conquer Shanghai. It was no secret that they were not satisfied to merely orchestrate the Kuomintang troops. They aspired to revive the Paris Commune in Shanghai. They wanted no less than to take the driver's seat from the Kuomintang and do what the Kuomintang dared not do: charge into the International Settlement. This idea, mimicking the French proletariat's attempt at leading a coalition government in 1871 Paris, was lofty and romantic, but utterly unrealistic.

The armed uprising was led by the Party's star strategist, Zhou Enlai. Zhou was a brilliant but still green twenty-nine-year-old military novice. He went to the front line on March 22 and fought alongside five thousand labor militiamen, armed with knives, axes, clubs, and a hundred and fifty guns. Despite their gallantry, they were overcome by the combined forces of Chiang Kaishek's tens of thousands of soldiers, the deep pockets of the Shanghai moneymen, the underworld thugs of the Green Gang, and the unlimited resources of the foreign powers. Zhou and his comrades, having used all their ammunition, were trapped by enemy fire with only fists to fight back with, and their last stand became a slaughter. On the evening of April 12 and in the following days, it was said, the rain poured, and water mixed with blood streamed red down the streets. Zhou made a narrow escape and would reach Wuhan a month later.

The massacre set off a chain reaction among other Kuomintang militarists who also found the communists intractable. They carried out their own purges of peasant and labor unionists. The labor leaders, in particular the level-headed Liu Shaoqi, knew their self-preservation depended on cooperation with Kuomintang members like Eugene. Under the circumstances, they gave and kept their word to Eugene. They "supported the Nationalist government's diplomatic policy and trusted the government to head off the quarrel with Japan about the April 3 Incident in whatever way it saw fit. . . ."[3]

Assured by the union leadership, Eugene persuaded Japan that it was of mutual benefit to resolve the dispute. The Western powers had suspended doing business with Wuhan because of the Nanjing Incident. That would give Japan a long-coveted opportunity to expand trade in the middle reaches of the Yangzi, the area of British influence. Convinced, the Japanese government accepted Eugene's terms without much fuss. They withdrew their marines and compensated the workers in the factories for wages lost when the Japanese owners fled.

There was still, however, the Nanjing Incident to deal with. In order to fend off the possible criticism that the information he had was one-sided, Eugene sent Bill Prohme to Nanjing and Shanghai to hold an inquiry on the spot. Prohme would gather facts from the Western press corps, diplomats, and missionaries.

Based on Bill Prohme's report, Eugene wrote the diplomatic note. Demagogic speeches and rash actions from both sides, Eugene said, created a climate conducive to crime. No eyewitness could say for absolutely certain who the marauders had been—the Kuomintang regulars instigated by their communist commissars' xenophobia, or the defeated warlord's soldiers in disguise, or the local riffraff in a spree of plundering. The note was fair and balanced.

The historian J. A. Rogers described Eugene's contribution during this perilous time in this way:

In 1927, while Foreign Minister, he [Eugene] was instrumental in preventing war between China on one hand and Britain and the United States on the other. White people had been mobbed by Chinese in Nanking [Nanjing]...President Coolidge had already dispatched American marines to the scene but Chen stepped into the breach and in an eloquent note to the white powers expressed China's willingness for peace. He said that he was willing to have the disturbances thoroughly investigated, asking only that the verdict, whether it be for or against China, be just. This frankness had such an effect on President Coolidge that he recalled the marines and in a public address declared for peace, to the great discontent of the interests who wanted war in order to gain greater power in China.[4]

Inside Wuhan the dust had settled somewhat, but in the rural areas, dust storms blasted incessantly. The phenomenal growth of the peasant movement gave rise to stupendous problems. In many places, the peasant unions reigned supreme under the communists' tutelage. The peasant cadres, with no training, experience, or expertise for governing, followed the only precedent they knew. They modeled their rule and justice on the misrule and injustice they had suffered from the landowners. Violence was rife and indiscriminate.

Of the fifty-six generals of the Northern Expedition armies, fifty-one were bigger landlords.[5] The uninitiated peasant cadres turned the Nationalist revolution into an insurrection against their own Nationalist (Kuomintang) allies. For example, the father-in-law of General He Jian, a rich landowner in Hunan Province, was publicly humiliated and beaten. The angry general declared that he would reject any land policy that hurt the interests of his officers and soldiers. These were smaller landowners whose families were being persecuted by the peasant unions. In the chaos of violence or out of greed, the peasant cadres often seized land from small landowners and appropriated small remittances sent by officers and soldiers to their families. The peasant cadres were not above playing favorites and picked on whomever they disliked.

Of all the rural areas, the peasant movement in Hunan, Mao Zedong's home province, was the most troubling. In May, the generals from the Hunan military clique showed alarming signs of unrest. Two mutinied. They made out as though they would do the communist-cleansing if the Wuhan government did not take drastic measures to bridle what they viewed as the mania of the rabble.

The civilian cabinet members were faltering under pressure from the generals. They held Borodin and the Chinese communists accountable for upsetting the overall scheme of things. They blamed the peasant activists for Wuhan's woes. They echoed the military men's call for a reversal of fortune, letting the landowners take back their land confiscated by the peasant unions.

In the midst of this furor, Eugene was the lone voice protesting against any rash decision from the right or the left. While conceding that the Hunan peasant movement, led by Mao Zedong, was overheated, Eugene put it down to experiment. "As for the poor peasants in Hunan, they have already re-distributed the land confiscated from the landowners and they should be allowed to keep it . . ."[6]

Eugene backed the argument with his vision when he explained to Western journalists why he supported the peasant movement. "In Hunan, it is true we have tried the experiment of dividing up land. A man will be a better citizen if he is a land owner. He will fight for his land. Hence, we are trying it out to see how it works. That, no doubt, is where these rumors about our Communistic principles originate."[7]

But an experiment like this could not be labeled as communistic, for it was based on a very English idea. Eugene believed in English parliamentary democracy, and his idea of bettering the peasants' life evolved from the conceptions of the Magna Carta. This document, which limited the king's power to raise taxes and to make arbitrary arrests, helped the feudal lords, but also, later, the farmers. The British and the Americans, whose democracy was founded on the British model, could not deny that the English farmers had benefited from their experiment centuries ago. Why did they deny it to China, which was just trying to catch up?

Eugene's reasoning won sympathy from quite a few Western journalists stationed in Wuhan, among them Arthur Ransome of the *Manchester Guardian,* Henry Francis Misselwitz of the *New York Times,* Anna Louise Strong freelancing from the United States, Von Salzman of the *Vossische Zeitung,* Nordahl Grieg from Norway, and so on. Their reports had an impact on Western readers.

While Eugene pleaded for sanity among the foreign powers, the entire Wuhan administration fell silent. However, they heeded some of Eugene's urgings and decided to send a delegation of officials to the provincial capital, Changsha, promising the mutinous generals that they would exert a tighter rein on Hunan's peasant movement. Eugene insisted that Borodin go too and make a gesture of conciliation. Borodin reluctantly consented and said that the effectiveness of this trip required the cooperation of Mao Zedong, who was, after all, at the head of the Hunan peasant movement.

At the time, the communists were not exactly underground, but they kept a much lower profile. Eugene told Jack to escort Mao. If they were detained, Jack's interpreter could explain it was an interview appointment. Always looking forward to new adventures, Jack's face was aglow with excitement.

He and his interpreter got off a ferryboat outside the city of Wuchang and entered through the ancient thick walls that surrounded the sprawling city. Inside, the streets were narrow. They walked into an alley, where the Peasant Training Institute was located in an old house. Its courtyard had originally been•paved with flagstones, which had been mostly eaten away by the ravages of rain and wind, and the soil underneath was exposed. It certainly did not look like an important sector of the government.

A small group of men came to listen to Mao Zedong, a lanky man in his mid-thirties with disheveled black hair. The rural audience blended perfectly with the earth they sat on. The air was suffused with heat and odors from their bodies, not unlike the earth on a warm spring day, Jack thought, as it suggested hopeful renewal.

The return trip to Hankou, accompanied by the distant booming of sporadic gunfire, was more hazardous. Thinking he was more familiar with the local geography, Mao led Jack and his interpreter to a small ferry landing on the edge of a wide lake. It was used by many fewer passengers, so the ferryboat ran less frequently too. They were clearly in for a long wait, so they stripped to their underwear and jumped into the lake. It was a moment of delightful calm. Above was the cloudless blue sky. The water shimmered and glittered in the sunshine. The gunfire had either receded or ceased. Nothing seemed farther away than mutiny or war. Jack turned on his back, spread out his arms and legs, and simply allowed his body to float motionlessly on the cool water. He raised his head to hear better what the interpreter was saying: "I think we had better get out of this water."

"Why?"

In answer to his query, the interpreter pointed at something floating nearby. It was a formless mass of rags with a pale, bloated hand visible, stained with red streaks of blood like dried tomato sauce. A victim of the mutinous generals, or of the radical peasant unionists?

The stillness was abruptly broken by the buzz of insects. Then they heard the sound of gunfire more clearly. It seemed that they were actually near a killing field.

About two hundred yards away, there was a sign of possible shelter, and they ran for it. Panic lent wings to Jack's feet. He covered the first hundred yards like an Olympic runner, his heart pumping hard and painfully. The next hundred yards was agony. With a gasp, Jack threw himself into a dry ditch overgrown with tall grass. A moment later, a shattering explosion rent his ears and the ground heaved beneath him.

"Dear God," he muttered to himself, cradling his head in his arms. "What am I doing here?"

"Your father is thoughtful, asking you to accompany me, and in return I'll bring you back safely to him," Mao said, panting. Without a hint of self-consciousness, he took command.

Once back, Mao went into Borodin's conference room by himself. He gave a deliberately amusing narrative of his little adventure with Jack, and then got down to business, discussing whether there was any way to sustain the Wuhan government.

The reply Eugene gave was oblique, as he would not allow himself to raise false hopes. He felt responsible for the safety of his allies, so he said the best route for the Wuhan government was to retreat with as little loss as possible. Talk of reconciliation would not move the generals of the Hunan military clique who had not yet succumbed to Chiang Kaishek. Perhaps Mao Zedong and his peasant unionists still had time to demonstrate more substantial goodwill.

His peasant unions, Mao said, now guarded the granary of Hunan Province. He could send grain to feed the generals' soldiers, but how could he be sure that they would not bite the hand that fed them?

"If you reject their demand, they would bite you right now," Eugene said simply.

Mao was too clever to miss the point of buying time. He promised cooperation and said he would repair the harm done. For his part, Borodin went with the government delegation to hold out the olive branch to the rebellious officers. But it was too late. Borodin's train was stopped and his life threatened. He and the rest of the Wuhan delegates were hounded back by the unforgiving generals. Borodin had a nervous breakdown, as he realized that he would soon be expelled from China.

One afternoon, Milly Bennett, Jack's colleague at the *People's Tribune*, staggered into the office and said breathlessly that Borodin was very ill. Borodin spoke incoherently, jumping from subject to subject, all unrelated. In the middle of his tirade against the Hunan generals, he suddenly asked in a soft voice what was the name of those little pink flowers blossoming in snow on Mount Shasta, California? He seemed in better humor, but then he grimaced and harangued at the air: "Our [Russian] revolution was big, big, but nothing compared to this [Chinese revolution]. We work blindly, we lift the curtain and are frightened by the immensity of the scene. This revolution will kill many a Borodin."[8]

Borodin's health worsened as Wuhan kept disintegrating. One minute, there were rumors that Chiang Kaishek or his allies were attacking. The next minute, it was the generals of the Hunan military clique, garrisoned inside and around Wuhan, in revolt. The following minute, it was the foreign powers, sending more gunboats to reinforce the blockade or initiating an all-out military intervention.

On one evening in late May, Jack stayed late in the *People's Tribune*. He was about to leave when he heard the unmistakable crackle of rifle and revolver fire. He hurried to the window and, looking out, saw what seemed to be a badly directed sequence in a Hollywood thriller. Men were scaling the outside wall of his building. The first thing that flashed into his mind was that the enemy had captured Wuhan in a surprise move. But who was the enemy? He then saw a crowd of what appeared to be waterfront stevedores gathered at a street corner.

Those workers, many of whom had probably welcomed Borodin with open arms five months ago, were turning on him as more and more of them lost their jobs due to the endless strikes, the blockade of foreign powers, the devaluation of the yuan (Chinese dollar), inflation, and the threat of war.

Some of them, armed with poles, darted across the road and began scaling the wall of the *People's Tribune* building. As they reached the top, shots rang out. This sent them scrambling back down. Borodin's guard of armed, well-trained worker-volunteers were firing at them from the windows and from inside the yard. Several of them, shooting into the air, rushed out the front gate in a sally to cut off the attacking vanguards from the rest. When the assailants saw this, they slithered off the wall, took to their heels, and ran away, yelling obscenities. The rest scattered in all directions toward the labyrinth of streets and alleys in the Chinese City of Hankou.

As Jack walked toward the door, he heard the sound of scurrying feet coming down the stairs. He recognized Zhou Enlai. Zhou had had a hair-breadth escape from the Shanghai massacre in April. He and Jack had become acquainted by running into each other a few times in the vestibule when Zhou went upstairs to Borodin's apartment.

Inside Wuhan, the generals marked time. The arrest of communists was by no means on a large scale, but it was catching on. It was dangerous for Zhou to go back to his place. Thinking for a moment, Jack took him across the road to the foreign ministry building. Zhou, of course, could not stay long in Eugene's official residence on the top floor, but a quiet break would help them come up with a better idea.

Eugene was reading beside his coffee table piled with papers. After hearing Jack out, he said, somewhat regretfully, "This incident is a none-too-subtle hint from the generals. Borodin should know it was merely a warmup."

Quietly holding up the paper, Eugene asked what Zhou thought about the cartoon in it. The cartoon had been drawn by Jack and published on the International Labor Day, May 1, 1927. It showed how the United States could be lulled into a mistake by Britain if Lady Liberty dropped her torch and wielded the sword at the behest of John Bull. The caption read: "John Bull rages at America: 'You are young at this game! Can't you see it's time for another tactic?'"

Surprised by what he thought were Eugene's naïve sentiments, Zhou Enlai demurred: "They are supporting Chiang Kaishek."

Eugene nodded. He knew the United States was replacing Britain as the main opponent to the Chinese revolution, but he still differentiated between them. The United States was a much younger nation and hadn't stifled all its people's best instincts. He wanted the Americans to see that the Chinese were determined to overthrow colonialism in their country, just as American patriots had in theirs. The diplomat in him must appeal to what he called Americans' best instincts.

"Will they respond?" Zhou asked with doubt.

"Eventually. Anyway, we cannot avoid dealing with them, as they are growing more and more visible," Eugene said point-blank.

Jack interposed, asking if Zhou minded spending a night in the residence of Bishop Logan Roots, an Episcopal Church dignitary. Zhou answered with a smile that he had read Victor Hugo's *Les Miserables* and knew that compassion existed among true believers. They got up to leave.

"Why do you think your father gave me that little lecture?" Zhou asked while walking out the back door of the garden.

Jack darted him a glance and thought Zhou knew the answer, but wanted it anyway to confirm his own speculation. "My father thinks you and your comrades are courageous, but act ahead of the time."

"He meant our Shanghai uprisings?" Zhou looked suddenly very keen.

"I don't know which event he meant exactly," Jack replied as diplomatically as he could. Then he switched the subject and told Zhou something about his future host.

Bishop Logan Roots was an exception to Wuhan's indifferent Christian community. He cared for the wounded and sheltered the needy, regardless of their beliefs. Because of this, he was unpopular among his fellow Christians, who nicknamed him the "Pink Bishop." He and Jack worked together on the Relief Committee and met socially at Rayna Prohme's parties. His house was in the former German concession. The wind chimes hanging from the eaves of front porches there made an enchanting chattering, orchestrated with crickets' singing in unison.

Bishop Roots put his guest in an attic room connected with the rest of the house by a movable ladder. He left them after he had told Zhou to sleep in peace; he would tell a servant to remove the ladder later at night. Zhou thanked the older man and said he liked the attic room, which brought back memories of Paris.

"I have a view," Zhou exclaimed pleasantly, looking out a window.

In the gathering gloom, a corner of an ancient pavilion could be seen through the foliage. Not far from it was a modern building much taller than the one-storied houses close by, the light glinting off its glass. Zhou turned to Jack and said it had suddenly occurred to him that someday many such buildings would replace those pavilions. That would be the modernization previous generations had given their lives for, and that they, themselves, were prepared to die for.

There was an attachment growing between them. They were both young, Jack eighteen years of age, Zhou twenty-nine. They were drawn to each other when they pondered their futures in connection with the lives of their people. They groped for their places in a confusing, turbulent world, and they forged a spirit of camaraderie.

Seeing that he had found probably the safest place in Wuhan for his new friend, Jack headed for home. Out of nowhere, a stone hit him on his forehead. He swerved off the road and into a back alley. Hidden behind a large piece of rock, he stared into the night. Two carts rattled by, carrying the casualties of the shoot-out, with their waxlike feet sticking out. So near to death, Jack shivered from head to foot. He looked around helplessly. The earth was shrouded in a sinister darkness, and for a moment his courage deserted him.

Silence resumed. He dashed up and down street after street and finally reached home.

"What happened to your head?" Eugene asked.

For the first time, Jack saw his father visibly perturbed. "A bruise," he answered lightly.

"Let me clean and bandage it," Eugene said, fetching the first-aid box.

Without looking up, Jack could feel his father wince at his bloodied flesh wound.

"Father, it's really nothing," Jack said in a consoling voice, and then recounted what he had run into.

"Time to get moving," Eugene said vaguely.

His face had aged dramatically. Jack could not tell how much was due to the shadows from the small desk light, how much from the strain of the last three months. Jack's heart ached for him.

Indeed, Eugene was faced with a chilling prospect: what he had spent years building up was beginning to come apart. The possibility of losing all that he had won for the revolution and for himself was a bitter pill to swallow. Since Chiang Kaishek's violent purge of the communists in mid-April, Eugene was waiting for something to turn up at the last minute to salvage what remained of the United Front.

A week or so before Chiang Kaishek started his purge, Wang Jingwei came to Shanghai from Paris. The Chinese Byron, who had been forced into exile by Chiang in 1926, had been recalled by the Wuhan government. He was a weakling, but he had seniority over Chiang in the Kuomintang hierarchy and might be useful as a sort of civilian check on the budding military dictator. During his three-day stay in Shanghai, Wang met T. V. Soong and Daddy Kong, whom the Wuhan government had dispatched to care for its interests in Shanghai. Both men threw their hands up when they briefed the Chinese Byron on the happenings during his absence. Wuhan was sinking. It was time to jump ship. They got Wang's acquiescence and began to bargain with Chiang Kaishek over terms to join the separatist Nanjing government he was establishing.

By June, the duo wrested a promise from Chiang that high positions would be given to the Wuhan cabinet members who agreed to send Borodin packing. Should Eugene go along with this, his vested interests would be secured. The temptation was great. But he finally came to the conclusion that breaking up the United Front, throwing out the communists, and liquidating the peasant and labor unions would reduce the revolution to a fake. That was not acceptable to him.

Before presenting his argument to his fellow cabinet members, Eugene gave it to Chingling, Sun Yatsen's widow, and to Sun Ke, Sun Yatsen's son, for their review, because his argument was an extension of Sun's English will. Borodin had been invited there by Sun Yatsen; it was not appropriate for Sun's disciples to chase the Soviet High Adviser from the city as if he was a common criminal. The Wuhan government must find a way of showing that their approach was different from Chiang Kaishek's. A small delegation should be appointed to escort Borodin home and explain to Moscow why Wuhan had decided to split with—but not to purge—the communists.

Eugene volunteered to go. He hoped Chingling and Sun Ke would go too. Chingling consented. Sun Ke supported Eugene's proposal, but refused to be one of the escorts. Sun Ke's refusal posed a problem for Eugene and Chingling. There were whispers behind their backs that they were lovers. Their trip to Moscow without a political chaperone would be viewed as a confirmation of the rumor, spread by the British press. Because the British press linked Chingling romantically with Eugene, Milly Bennett claimed that "in the end this campaign of vilification had the effect that was intended: It forced Mrs. Sun Yat-sen into practical retirement from political activity."[9]

Surprisingly, Chingling showed steel behind her fragile exterior. She would ignore the rumors and go with Eugene. Backed up by Sun Yatsen's closest family members, Eugene further strengthened his argument with a point that the rest of his colleagues had to take into consideration: he believed that they did not want to look as if they were groveling to Nanjing and doing Chiang Kaishek's bidding to kill the communists. That would decrease their bargaining chips when they haggled with him.

On July 27th, 1927, a grand farewell to Borodin at Wuhan's train station. From left: a Chinese official, Borodin, Eugene Chen, T. V. Soong, Wang Jingwei, (the "Chinese Byron"), Kong Xiangxi (Daddy Kong), Sun Ke (Sun Fo, only son of Sun Yatsen), and a Russian official.

Eugene took the plan of visiting Moscow to Wang Jingwei. Wang knew how fickle political partners could be. Yesterday it was the Soviet Union and the Chinese communists. Today it seemed to be Chiang Kaishek. Tomorrow it might be someone else, or perhaps the Bolsheviks again. He had better not burn that bridge. On July 15, 1927, Wang, as the chairman of the Kuomintang, called for a meeting to discuss Eugene's proposal. "Comrade Borodin will be leaving soon. The Kuomintang ought to send very responsible and very important envoys to escort him. They will reiterate to Moscow the meaning of our policy of allying with Russia, which had been decided by our revered leader [Sun Yatsen]."[10]

In other words, if Stalin would agree to this as Lenin had, there might be room for further dialogue. The Central Executive Committee endorsed the proposal and added another Kuomintang left-winger, Deng Yanda, the director of the Political Department of the Whampoa Military Academy, to the delegation.

In the last days of the Wuhan regime, there were only three Kuomintang members on the Central Executive Committee: Eugene; Chingling, who had given her proxy vote to Eugene; and Madame Liao, widow of the leftist Liao Zhongkai, who opposed the split with the Communist Party.[11]

The two ladies offered Eugene much-needed moral support, but the burden of actually putting off the purge fell on his shoulders. For more than three or four months, Wuhan was the only safe haven in which the revolutionaries, including Mao Zedong, Zhou Enlai, Liu Shaoqi, Deng Xiaoping, and many others, could get their breath back, lick their wounds, and retreat in a relatively more orderly way.

★18★

FLEEING CHINA AND CROSSING
THE GOBI DESERT

At the end of June 1927, Eugene called a family meeting. He told his children that the Central Executive Committee of the Kuomintang had authorized him and Chingling to visit the Soviet Union. They would go to Shanghai, along with Silan and Yolanda, where they would take the boat to Vladivostok. Chiang Kaishek's men, as well as the British and French police in Shanghai, might harass them, but would probably not go so far as to detain or arrest them. But it was dangerous for Borodin to take the same route. His wife, Fanny, was still in the prison of Zhang Zuolin, the Manchurian Tiger.

Jack would accompany Borodin out the "back door," traveling along the northwestern part of the Great Wall. This vast area made up what was described as the Cradle of the Chinese Civilization. They would then exit through the last gate of the Great Wall and cross the Gobi Desert, an area measuring about five hundred miles from north to south and a thousand miles from west to east, nothing but sand, pebbles, and gravel. After surviving that, they would take the Trans-Siberian railroad to Moscow.

Jack left Wuhan with Borodin on July 27, 1927. The group going the Gobi route was composed of twenty-nine travelers. The four Chinese were Jack; Zhang Ke, a secretary from the foreign office; Percy, who got Eugene's permission to join this group only when he had promised to go back to Trinidad via Moscow; and their soldier bodyguard. Jack's other fellow travelers were a motley collection of characters. Among them were Saifoolin, a military adviser to the Christian General, and Feng Yuxiang, who blamed Borodin for letting the peasant movement get out of hand. There was a mystery man named Petrov, whom Percy suspected to be an agent of the Cheka (Russian secret police) who might make an attempt on Borodin's life, because Borodin knew too much about Stalin's bumbling with his China policy. And finally there was the American journalist Anna Louise Strong. Next to Borodin, she was by far the most colorful character in the caravan.

Leaving doomed Wuhan, Borodin and his entourage went north by train with the vehicles they would need when the tracks ended. He chose this route not for the sake of sightseeing, although he had read about its geography and encouraged Jack to read the same books as part of his preparation for the journey, but because this part of China was controlled by warlords who did not like Chiang Kaishek and were therefore less hostile to the people whom Chiang disliked. Their first stop was the city of Zhengzhou in Henan Province, the seat of the Christian General, Feng Yuxiang. Merely a month earlier, Feng had double-crossed Borodin and voted for his expulsion to win a big award in cash from Chiang Kaishek. But Feng thought he was worth more. Now he coyly posed as a neutral, as if saying he was still available to a higher bidder. He swore to heaven that he would allow Borodin safe passage.

The Great Wall.

"That means he'll let us pass through quietly. I only hope he is sincere," Borodin said to Jack.

When Jack alighted from the train, he saw that the platform was thronged with soldiers, tidily uniformed and each carrying on his back a huge, gleaming scimitar with a red tassel. It was a lethal-looking weapon, a sword broader than its Western equivalent, with one very sharp edge. It was usually used by executioners to cut off heads with a single swish.

Percy (front row left) and Jack (back row left) with warlord Feng Yuxiang (back row right), after negotiating safe passage from China to Russia for Mikhail Borodin, August 1927.

"Feng has made this place look like a makeshift mass execution ground," Borodin muttered nervously.

A faintly disdainful smile appeared on Jack's face, his chin up and nose in the air. This was the Chens' manner. They refused to whine. They would meet death with dignity.

A shout, and all the scimitars shot up. Following the thunderous roar, Jack saw a hulk of a man wearing a faded khaki uniform, with shoes of black cotton, the kind worn by peasants. The Christian General liked to present himself to the world as an early Christian, a man of great simplicity.

One by one, the Christian General shook the visitors' hands, a magnanimous smile on his face. Nearly as large as Feng, Anna Louise Strong approached him with an ingratiating grin. Then, to everybody's shock, she whipped out a small, sharp pair of nail scissors from her breast pocket, seized Feng's left arm, and snipped off the army insignia near his shoulder. The prank was done before a single one of the bodyguards realized what was happening. Feng fell back clumsily. For him, to compete for attention with a woman was bad enough; but, worse, this was a foreign devil of a woman.

"My God," muttered Feng's adjutant, a Harvard man if Jack remembered correctly. Grasping his trousers tightly with both hands in mock dread, he added, "I only have one pair of pants."

It was hilarious. With one snip, Anna Louise had exposed the medieval buffoon beneath the pompous self-appointed marshal. Jack silently applauded her.

Feng and Borodin were in conference for a few days. Feng tried to extract from the Russian the promise of military aid, while Borodin attempted to talk his way out of Zhengzhou. The rest of the travelers had time to explore the city. Jack seized the chance to discover a part of China he had not seen. In Wuhan, Jack had experienced the squalor of poverty, but it was, to some extent, hidden away in the back alleys and suburbs. In Zhengzhou it was right in downtown and in full view. The once-great metropolis, fabled in countless travelers' tales, was now a rambling town of one-story wood or adobe shacks, leaning drunkenly in all directions. Everything looked as if it had been built to be abandoned at a moment's notice, but had remained perpetually temporary. Zhengzhou looked like what it was, a town that had been burned, looted, robbed, and overrun dozens of times by marauding soldiers careless of its fate.

About a week after the travelers had arrived, Jack and Percy walked back from downtown one early evening. Through the faint twilight, they saw Daddy Kong, his hands clasped at his back, strolling in an orchard opposite the railway station; but this apparition vanished before Percy had had time to walk up to him. The Chen brothers did not know much about Chinese politics and thought little of Kong's sudden appearance in Zhengzhou. They presumed he was just passing through, en route to his hometown in neighboring Shanxi.

That evening, Jack casually mentioned Daddy Kong's visit to Borodin.

"Are you sure it was him?" Borodin asked, as a dull brown light suddenly flickered in the depths of his pupils. It came and went within a fraction of a second, but it had a disconcerting effect on Jack.

"It was getting dark and the light was not good," Jack answered uncertainly.

"I think you were right. You saw him." Borodin answered his own question with suppressed anxiety. He lowered his head, pondering.

Jack did not want to interfere with Borodin's thought processes, so he kept silent. He listened uneasily to the low rustling as he resettled himself in the chair.

Borodin quickly looked up and around, his face taut with nervous tension. He leaned toward Jack and said: "This is serious. I think Wang Jingwei sent Kong. Probably a huge bounty has been placed on my head. It is too tempting for our host not to consider it."

"Wang Jingwei?" Jack exclaimed, confused. The Chinese Byron had given Borodin a grand sendoff and had even said that he looked forward to welcoming the Russian back. "He could have killed you in Wuhan."

"Not convenient for him. Here he can use Feng's hands to kill me."

"Why?"

"If the relationship between Russia and China gets worse, he is afraid of being blamed for letting me go," Borodin explained. Turning his eyes fully on Jack, he added, "Kong's secret visit to Feng does not bode well for me. I need your help."

"Tell me what you want me to do," Jack said without hesitation.

"Watch out for me," Borodin said.

Jack seldom left Borodin's side as Feng Yuxiang haggled with Daddy Kong. Wang Jingwei's offer was a lucrative one, but the Christian General was reluctant to do the killing for the Chinese Byron and create an international incident. "If you [Wang] want to kill him [Borodin], why didn't you kill him in Wuhan?"[1] Feng was shy of mentioning Wang's envoy, Daddy Kong of the highhanded Soong clan. Anyway, Feng kept Borodin on edge while he was making up his mind. Finally he released Borodin and his entourage. The decisive factor, according to Borodin, was that, ensconced in China's impoverished northwest, Feng's rear was wide open to Russian pressures.

Feng, however, made another theatrical gesture. He asked if Saifoolin could remain with his army as a consultant. His plea was touching. Saifoolin, a great hulk of a man, was brought to tears. Unmoved, Borodin said no. They had a fierce quarrel. It was not clear to Jack if Borodin told his subordinate the home truth: he did not want to leave a hostage in Feng's hands. When Saifoolin stormed out of Borodin's room, his large face was flushed red and bore an expression of hatred.

In the first week of August, Borodin and his entourage departed from Zhengzhou on a decrepit train, carrying them west. They passed the city of Loyang and reached the terminal at Lingbao County, where they packed their five cars and three trucks with food, guns, ammunition, trunks, documents, and medical supplies. Borodin; Borodin's personal doctor, Orloff; his Russian chauffeur; and his bodyguard were in the huge Buick. Anna Louise, Madame Orloff, and Jack rode in the Dodge sedan that Percy drove. In the early morning, the travelers began the long drive through the three remaining northwestern provinces of Shenxi, Gansu, and Ningxia.

The roads were merely dirt tracks, narrow and rutted, with no room to drive outside the ruts. The peasants' irrigation caused another problem. The peasants opened the irrigation ditches without much planning. All they cared about was that the water could flow from one side of the road to the other, where their fields were. Pools of water turned the track into a yellow, oozing morass, and the liquid mud buried the road several inches deep underneath. The cars got stuck and had to be manhandled. All the passengers jumped out and waded in the mire, pushing the vehicles. It took three hours to cover the first nine miles. Some days were even worse. If the wheels sank into crevices covered by drifting dust, they had to do much more work with spades and shovels to extricate them. The worst record was four miles in an entire day.

"At this pace, the Christian General can catch up with us any minute," Borodin whispered to Jack.

"You think he'll stop and arrest us?"

"If the price is right."

As they drove close to the western end of the Great Wall and into Shenxi Province, Jack could not help but marvel at those majestic, ancient gates, barriers built two thousand years ago to stop the invading Huns, Tartars, and other tribes. After they had been on the road two days, they found themselves at the foot of a hill. They drove up a steep slope alongside the Great Wall as the outline of a massive fortress emerged, silhouetted against the evening sky. A ray of the rising moon touched its thick walls and lofty watchtowers, and they could see the imposing roofs of temples and pavilions above the battlement. These were the reputedly impregnable Gates of Tongguan. Tongguan had the proud reputation of being "the burial ground of invaders."

When they drove slowly toward the main gate, Jack looked up at it—a magnificent complex of solid wood, bricks, and stones, studded with iron plates and hard spikes, all crowned by an overhanging drum tower.

"Gates of Tongguan!" someone shouted, followed by a muffled crack.

A huge mass, about the size of a corpse, bounced out of the car in front, and then immediately came back to life. Two arms shot up and waved wildly to stop the caravan. Jack leaped out of his car and ran ahead. He had an awful feeling that something had happened to Borodin. A man reclined in the car seat, his bleeding arm dangling.

"An accident." It was Borodin's voice speaking.

Borodin dropped his admirable mask of composure when he confided to Jack later. He had been half-dozing and had started at the loud, joyous exclamation, and he inadvertently jolted a rifle, which he thought unloaded. But it went off, and the bullet pierced the left arm of his bodyguard. The rifle probably would have gone off anyway due to the violent jolting on the bumpy track, Borodin added with a deadpan expression; then *he* would have been the one to get hit.

It might have been an accident, and it might not, Borodin muttered under his breath. Anyway, he did not want to take chances, and he took precautions to protect himself. He knew Jack was the friendliest among his entourage, so he kept the lad at his side whenever he could. They often shared a room or a tent.

At the town of Tongguan, a local army surgeon operated on the bodyguard's arm and removed the bullet. When it was done, it was too late to continue the journey, so they stayed overnight.

Borodin had with him several boxes of silver dollars, which would be used to pay their way through to Moscow. Every night the boxes were placed at the head of his bed for safekeeping. The mountainous area was bandit country. Traveling at night was not wise. One hot August night, Jack rose to respond to nature's call. He crept gingerly across the floor and out the door. Some of his fellow travelers were sleeping in the open air. Someone had his cot placed next to the room Jack shared with Borodin. The large, tanned face half-buried in the pillow was Petrov's. The secret police agent's close presence made Jack apprehensive. Jack hurried to the latrine and back. Before he got onto his bedding, he heard a terrifying scream, followed by unintelligible babbling, muttering, and howling. In the midst of this medieval pandemonium, the Russians spiced it up with a touch of modernity: they set up their machine gun and opened fire into the sky.

Borodin jumped up. He jerked his hand from a pocket and snatched out his indispensable revolver. His eyes pierced the shadows and fixed on the door. A noise came from the lock. It was turning, and the door opened with a slight whine. But it sounded frighteningly loud to Jack. Voroshin, Borodin's secretary, put his half-bald head in and told Borodin it was a false alarm, nothing more than an old wolf that had invaded the town through a breach in the walls. These were the once-invincible walls that had seen the defeat of the Huns, who were driven westward to the border of the Roman Empire, where their most famous descendant, Attila, was feared as the "Scourge" that God had sent to punish the Romans for their sins. But now Tongguan had failed to halt even a decrepit, shriveled wolf at its gate.

On this trip, Jack got to know more about his fellow revolutionaries. There was much unpleasantness to cope with, including inconsiderateness among comrades who should have known better. The Dodge sedan in which Jack rode was evidently too small for both Percy and Anna Louise. Since it was overloaded and traveling on a bad road, it constantly threatened to overturn. This worried Anna Louise. She then appointed herself the back-seat driver and took over. With wounded pride, Percy smoldered. One morning at a small walled medieval town, Percy decided he had had enough and, without warning, switched cars with Borodin's driver and drove the Buick away before the Russians had loaded it. Anna Louise stood by with mounting dismay as she watched the Russian comrades pile the additional baggage left by the Buick higher and higher on the teetering Dodge.

"Tell me what it's like sitting inside," she bellowed, shoving Jack into the car.

Jack felt the springs burdened to the maximum. They had to give, and a mere jolt would snap them. He told her so.

"Why don't you put some baggage in your larger trucks?" she asked.

Her Russian comrades ignored her. When the stack of suitcases and sacks lashed to the roof reached an even more precarious height, Anna Louise exploded. She stomped up to them and planted herself like a massive rock between them and the Dodge.

"I won't let this car move," she screamed, like a little girl throwing a tantrum.

At that moment, Anna Louise did seem to be indulging in a fit of childish temper. She had a round, baby face under bobbed hair, on top of an incongruously elephantine mass of flesh. Without wasting another breath, she turned, marched to the gate, and laid herself down athwart the entryway. Her huge bulk filled the entire space. Awestricken, the Russians realized that she meant what she said: over her dead body. No cars and no trucks could leave the beleaguered town.

Soon, peasant carts bringing in the morning's vegetables began to line up outside the gate. A large crowd began to gather, watching the giant, middle-aged foreign woman who was immovable and closing the town. The not-so-comradely Soviet Russians had to give in, and they lightened the load on the Dodge. And, thanks to Anna Louise, the Russians could not send the Dodge first over any difficult stretch of road.

From that moment on, she looked with the deepest suspicion at anyone who might play tricks on her. Her fellow travelers tried to keep their distance, but were not always able to. One night they had to share a *kang*—a brick bed, popularly used in the northwest—with her. Large enough for eight people, it took up almost the whole room. Anna Louise was given the first opportunity to choose which side of the *kang* she would like to sleep on. Her tremendous physique needed more than the space allotted to one person, and no man desired to lay next to her. Jack, ever so gallant, was the only one who let himself be persuaded to occupy the narrow strip left. When he agreed, the other men were visibly relieved.

"Good, you are the youngest," Anna Louise quipped.

Pretending not to be intimidated, Jack, a thin and small-boned teenager, bragged: "Ah, but I am the most experienced." At that, everybody roared with laughter.

When all the men lay down, Anna Louise was still sitting up in the dim light of the oil lamp, wrapped in a blanket. The weather was treacherous in that mountainous area; between midnight and daybreak, the temperature could drop precipitously. In the freezing cold, Anna Louise had to rub her hands until her fingers were warm enough to hold a pen, so she could jot down notes of that day's happenings. Jack learned a lot from her on that journey.

Anna Louise worked in the best tradition of American reporting. She went down to places, no matter how difficult, and collected the facts, though her interpretation of them was open to debate. While other foreign reporters were content to remain in Wuhan and get secondhand news in bars, casinos, hotel lounges, or interviews, and while they accordingly described the atrocities committed by the peasants, Anna Louise told of the background of oppression and exploitation of the peasants. Consequently, she made their fierce retaliation understandable.

Anna Louise became Jack's professional role model. Every evening, no matter what hardships he had suffered in the day, he got out his pen and paper and drew the people and things and places he had seen that day. When he recorded what he had witnessed, it was a moment of exultation. He took his art and memory with him.

Poor Borodin did not have this good fortune, Jack sighed. When Borodin lost his position, he lost everything, even memories. He had to adjust his memories to political pressures. With each passing day, he seemed less like the man he had been. His oratory had moved multitudes of people to make sacrifices for the revolution, but now he was utterly speechless before his thirsty entourage, bickering over things as trivial as an orange. Water was scarce. The closer they drove to the desert, the bigger the problem.

When the motor caravan arrived in the city of Pingliang, they reached the gateway to Gansu, the province between Tibet, Inner Mongolia, and Xinjiang. The Yellow River, China's equivalent of the Euphrates, the Tigris, or the Nile, came into sight. The landscape changed into something awesome. Out of the muddy banks soared steep cliffs with dark rocks protruding, hanging precariously over the brown waters swirling furiously over the rapids. Primitive rafts made of inflated ox skin were the only ferries.

The Dodge sedan needed some repairing. While waiting, Jack chatted with a boatman, Zhang Ke interpreting, of course. Making ox-skin rafts dated back more than five thousand years, when the legendary Yellow Emperor defeated his enemies with two great military inventions, the raft and the double-wheeled chariot. With the transport facilities of the unrivaled armada and the two-wheeled tanks, the soldiers sped to the front line so incredibly swiftly that their enemies mistook them for the hosts of heaven. This was how the Yellow Emperor put the Chinese nation on the world map.

Jack had read about the Yellow Emperor, a tribal chief who had conquered other tribes scattered along the Yellow River to become the first national icon. Such reading had left Jack sort of indifferent. It was too distant, too remote, too irrelevant. But now he was at the spot where the Yellow Emperor was supposed to have crossed and fought the decisive battle. His heart was so full that the most natural thing to do was leap onto a raft. As the raft rushed down the stream, Jack had the feeling that the water rose, splashed over, and embraced him, balmy and comforting to his tired, sweating body. Something in the depths of his being was touched, and it connected him to this land. He knew he would return one day.

Crossing the Gobi Desert in 1927. From left to right: Borodin, Percy, Jack (with shovel), Mrs. Orloff, Zhang Ke, and Anna Louise Strong.

On August 24, nearly a month after they had left Wuhan, they reached Yinchuan, the outpost of the western part of the Great Wall and the provincial capital of Ningxia. It was the crossroad between central China and its western regions, a walled city that contained the government and public buildings. These one- or two-story houses had gables with deep eaves and horned projections. During the two weeks Borodin and his entourage stayed in Ningxia, they got recharged and refurnished in preparation for traversing the Gobi Desert. On September 10, they set off, following an invisible trail across the desert. It was an old camel route, running from northwest China to Karakorum, the ancient capital of Genghis Khan. The locals warned them that no motor caravan had ever traveled that way before. Borodin decided nevertheless to take the chance, to avoid a greater danger: enemy warlords.

For the first few days, they saw little hint of life, driving across a desolation of sand or gravel dotted with the skeletons of humans and animals. There was no flowing water or vegetation at all. Above them the sky was blue, pure blue, not a single patch of cloud. The sun was brilliant, the heat intense. They drove, nonstop, for hours in the yellow-sand furnace without drinking a drop of water, which was strictly rationed. They drank only when necessary. Necessary meant when a person was on the verge of collapsing of dehydration. Jack tried to bring up a little saliva. No saliva.

In the rising heat, the light played tricks to lure the travelers on. The air above the seething earth shimmered as if it was a screen of quivering silver wires. Jack, to his great joy, suddenly glimpsed cold streams cascading down a hill into indigo pools, creating curtains of rainbows. It looked like Trinidad! But when the car drove near the heavenly scene, it vanished, leaving nothing but empty sky and earth. "Mirage," Jack muttered bitterly, and his face turned pale. A mirage had lured the Dodge away from the main track, and they were not able to reach their destination before nightfall, and now they had to cope with the treacherous changes in the desert weather.

The wind rose suddenly. The blue sky instantly darkened with yellow and gray dust. A freezing blast roared down upon them, shifting whole mountains of sand so that places they had thought were level gravel were found to be rolling sand dunes, dozens of feet high, which could bury them alive. That was how whole villages or towns had been wiped from the face of the earth. There was nothing they could do but sit through the storm on the most sheltered spot they could find, against the side of their vehicles.

Then the howling of the wind stopped as suddenly as it started. Disbelieving his ears, Jack lifted his face, which had been buried in his arms. The wind had dropped completely. The evening stars appeared. One by one they came out and hung like tiny golden and silver lanterns in the dark blue canopy of the sky. A light haze on the horizon showed that the moon would be rising soon. A phantom was emerging as Jack's car drove on; it was a deserted hamlet. They would spend the night in this place, in the middle of nowhere. Jack got out of the Dodge, stretching his aching and cramped limbs. He walked around the wall and found an opening which could have once been the gate. Walking through it, he saw in the clear soft starlight a street filled with debris and lined with ruined houses. The place was as dead as a graveyard. He got a weird feeling that the phantom town was still inhabited by its former ghost-residents.

Then he found that he was right: it *was* still inhabited. He gaped at faint light exuding from several dilapidated cottages huddled together. There behind the crumpled walls, people had hidden for years—or centuries. By using sign language, he found out that they were the remaining desert dwellers, and that they could put the travelers up for the night. Their hosts cooked a meal for the guests. The stove was three holes dug in the ground. Deeper down, under them, was a tunnel connecting them. The hosts put the pot in the middle hole. They lit and fed the fire by thrusting firewood into the right hole. The smaller left hole functioned as chimney. One Russian quipped that Eve must have cooked food on such a stove for Adam.

Amused, Jack said to Borodin that he felt that as they traveled forward on the road, they moved simultaneously backward in time, from modern Wuhan to medieval times, then antiquity, and now genesis. Soon they would see the super-advanced society, the first socialist nation. Borodin shrugged lamely. He was not optimistic about the assessment that Moscow would give of his work in China.

After the dinner, Jack and Borodin took a stroll among the dunes. The moon was half covered by clouds, and its hazy light softened the outlines of the desolate landscape. The desert took on a dreamy appearance, and the ghost town was shrouded in mist. Borodin halted at the edge of a sand hollow as though transported by the timeless beauty of the Gobi.

"The bewitched castle of the Sleeping Beauty!" Jack exclaimed, gazing at the phantom town.

"You'll soon see the best Bolshoi production of that ballet," Borodin said with a grin. Chatting about art put him in a better humor. He cleared his throat as if he was going to continue his favorite subject. Strange to say, he began to orate in Russian, a language he knew Jack did not understand.

Jack, however, understood his body language, his arm-sweeping gestures, and his legs standing spread-eagled. Borodin was rehearsing his victorious speech for his arrival in Moscow. He concluded his oratory in English: "Comrades, we must hail the heroic Chinese people!"

He grinned and moved his feverish eyes from left to right, up and down, as if seeing a vast crowd of silently cheering ghosts.

The following day was the hardest they experienced. They were to cross the Sand Mountain, piled up by sand blizzards of past millennia. It was high, steep, and surrounded by its vast attendant sea of sand. The surface sand shifted even in the softest breeze. Tired of tortuous traveling, Borodin was in no mood to spend days trying to find a way around it. The longer the journey, the longer he was in agonies of doubt. He was in favor of the decision to barge straight across the Sand Mountain, although it was so steep that it was impossible for them to drive uphill.

All the trucks and cars had to be unloaded. All the passengers had to scramble out. Stationed at various levels up the mountain, they pushed and shoved the trucks and cars up to the next contingent higher up. Then they passed the vehicles from hand to hand further up to the top of the ridge where the wind raised a plume of sand, whirled it into the sky, and tinged it a dull yellow. When the burning sand fell, it blurred their sight and stung their faces and limbs. As each vehicle reached the peak, the driver stopped and left it there and went back down the slope to lend a hand with the next in line. In this way, one by one, all the vehicles were pushed to the summit of the Sand Mountain. Then each piece of equipment, each bit of luggage, and all the supplies were toted up, and all the vehicles were reloaded.

After this toughest hurdle, the going was easier, though far from easy. There were more sand hills ahead, though much smaller. At times they drove by places that were nothing but moonscapes of sand and wind-eroded clay. It was a relief when a few small desert animals flashed by. Then a lone plant appeared, dancing in the breeze, and then more. All of a sudden the place came to life, with flocks of white sheep and black goats sauntering out of the azure sky where it was edged with an undulating green ribbon. A pasture! Farther on, spreading before Jack glittered a gemlike blue brook, flanked by flower trees and fields with golden crops laid out on its bank. Oases offered these dramatic contrasts in countless surprising variations.

No beauty, though, could divert Borodin from what he saw in his tormented mind's eye. His heart grew heavier as they traveled on. On September 16, their caravan was approaching Ulan Bator, capital of the Mongolian

People's Republic, or, as China and most of the rest of the world knew it then, Outer Mongolia. They were at the border of the Soviet Union.

Several days later, as if anxious to get it over with, Borodin angled for a plane to fly him to Verkhneudinsk, the nearest big town on the Trans-Siberian Railroad, a twelve-day journey from Moscow. The rest would stay a little longer and then leave by road for Verkhneudinsk, where they also would board a train to the Russian capital.

The ancient plane wheezed down, small, battered, devoid of any passenger comforts. Its open cockpits could hold only a pilot and two passengers. Seemingly on the spur of the moment, Borodin decided to take Jack with him.

"Jack will come with me. He is the lightest in our group." He made it sound like a joke. Jack's weight had been reduced through the Gobi purgatory, he added, and he was now the exact size to fit into the narrow seat beside Borodin.

★ 19 ★

STALIN'S BETRAYAL

Borodin and Jack shared a Pullman international two-berth compartment, the best on the train, and settled down for the long trip ahead. Holding on strenuously to the vision of a hero's homecoming, Borodin whispered into Jack's ear: "I want the welcoming crowd to see that I have brought the young future of China with me."

Jack was flattered. He liked the feel of living history and the role of representing the youth of China. He wanted to look good to the Muscovites. But the mirror told him otherwise. He was always skinny, and crossing the Gobi Desert had whittled him down by more than one size. He looked small for a young man of nineteen; he needed to put on a few pounds. The restaurant car took care of that. The cooking was excellent, and food was plentiful. There were Wiener schnitzel, smoked Baikal fish, fresh milk and sour cream, autumn fruit and berries. Jack filled out a bit, though was far from being impressive.

In the first week of October 1927, after twelve days on the road, the train pulled into the Moscow station. The engine, panting smoke and steam like a dragon, finally came to rest. Jack looked out the window. There was a crowd of people on the platform, but no banners, no band playing music, no honor guard. In a word, no festivities to welcome a hero home. Borodin set his jaws stolidly.

As soon as the train came to a halt, their compartment was filled with a wave of men, all well dressed and all officials of some kind or other. The new arrivals' bags were seized by several minor officials, and they were swept to the door of the train. Borodin stood for a brief moment on the top step surveying the not-too-large and not-too-rejoicing crowd. Jack peered out from behind him and saw their upturned faces. A murmuring crowd, no cheers, no hand-clapping. The security man gave Jack a polite push from behind. Jack, all keyed up, nearly lost his balance. With heroic determination, he straightened and squared his shoulders, a posture he imagined fit for the young future of

China. But nobody seemed to take note of him. Still, he was more alert than Borodin, who seemed to feel numb. His Party saw him as a failure, an embarrassment. For the first few minutes, Jack had to nudge him forward.

A narrow lane opened before them. They got into a vintage Rolls-Royce, one of the few in Moscow. They rattled through the narrow cobblestone streets, hooting aside horse-driven droshkies. There were few buildings over four stories high. Everyone wore dark clothes and was in a hurry. How different this was compared to London or downtown Shanghai!

Their car stopped at the ornate entrance to the Metropole Hotel, one of the grandest in Europe. A uniformed concierge opened the car door for them and bowed. They might have been at the Ritz in Paris or the Savoy in London. They walked in. The interior was ornate too. They were ushered through the hotel's red-carpeted vestibule, up by elevator to the second floor, and deposited in a large corner room. This was the hotel's Ambassadorial Suite, the finest suite in all Moscow, with a magnificent view of Theater Square. Jack caught his breath at the sight of the shimmering Bolshoi Theater, its white walls shining like a beautiful woman in a crowded thoroughfare. On the farther side was the red-brick Historical Museum and, beyond that, the great red walls and golden domes of the Kremlin.

Standing entranced at the window, Jack did not hear the door open when Silan burst in. She and Yolanda shared a room, and their father had a suite on the same floor. Silan could not wait to hear about Jack's adventures crossing the Gobi and regretted she had missed out on it. Compared to Jack's, her journey to Moscow had been much less interesting. On August 22, 1927, she, along with her father, Yolanda, Chingling, and Rayna Prohme, had boarded a Russian ship. At Vladivostok a special train waited, which the Soviet leaders had sent to take them to Moscow. At every stop on the way, a delegation of Soviets was sent to greet them. Reaching Moscow on September 6, the reception they got was very different from Borodin's. There was a brass band playing loudly in a sea of Chinese and Soviet flags, and movie cameras rolled. The whole place was swamped by reporters—Russian and foreign—who were eager for a revealing word from Eugene Chen and Madame Sun Yatsen.

Their first Soviet banquet was given at the Sugar Palace that night; their host was Chicherin, the commissar of foreign affairs, and among the guests were Mr. and Mrs. Litvinov and Henri Barbusse. Their food was served on gold plates, with silver cutlery.

"You'll have your share of partying," Silan said.

The Chen siblings in Moscow, 1927. From left to right: Percy, Yolanda, a Russian friend, Silan, Nadia, who took the Chen brothers to Bukharin's parties, Jack, and a Russian friend.

Indeed, invitations poured in. Jack spent quite a bit of time sorting them out, with Silan or Percy, who had arrived in Moscow about three weeks later than Jack. They were instant celebrities. Anybody who was somebody wanted to be seen with them.

Jack went once or twice to visit the apartment of Bukharin, then Stalin's right-hand man. His host was refined and looked comfortable in the aristocratic world described in books by Pushkin, Lermontov, and Tolstoy. The vodka and champagne flowed. Jack was no drinker, and as he tried to dodge the sparkling glass, his new friend, Nadia, dolled up in an elegant outfit, came up. A mysterious woman, Jack never figured out who she really was. She took him to a corner where Bukharin sat.

Bukharin wore a Russian blouse and a short leather coat that had been more or less the uniform of the famous political commissars during the revolution and civil war. Jack remembered his attire because the color of his blouse was a subdued green, Jack's favorite color. Bukharin was good at making his guests feel at home. He asked what had impressed the teenager the most on the long journey from China to Moscow. Jack, cautiously keeping any political topic at bay, answered that it was the high mountains, so awesome, so inaccessible. He was pleased with his own repartee. Nothing was more neutral than nature.

"Masada," Bukharin murmured while turning his face slightly to a liveried servant who held a tray with two glasses of vodka on it.

Jack stared blankly at his host. He did not know what Masada was, but somehow he had the feeling that he had underestimated a mountain's political potential. He was, of course, not aware that Mao Zedong, with his peasant militia, had disappeared into a mountainous fortress, and the Russians were trying to track him down and bring him to court-martial for disobeying orders from Moscow.

Nervous nevertheless, Jack raised his glass as Bukharin did and drained it. The effect was instant: he passed out. When he regained consciousness, he found himself reclining against the door frame of the drawing room. Nobody fussed over him, acting as if he was just passing through a natural phase into manhood. When he managed to stagger to his feet, nobody was so inconsiderate as to come to his aid, or to make him feel any lack of virility.

With Silan, it was dancing. Jack was her escort and partner. Their new friend, Nadia, could sometimes let her zeal run away with her. Without telling Jack and Silan, she put their names down to enter the all-Russia Charleston competition, the event of that evening. They won, of course: Nadia saw to that. It was late when Jack and Silan returned to the Metropole. At the door of Suite 108, he fumbled with his key. Noises, though muted, could be heard. He got the key in finally and, slowly turning it so as not to wake Borodin, opened the door to find himself staring down the barrel of a revolver. Back of that was Borodin. When he saw that it was only Jack, he lowered his gun. He said not a word. Neither did Jack, beyond a very British "Sorry to disturb you."

They sat silently, each on the edge of his own bed. In the midst of the silence, Borodin got up and went to the door, putting his ear against it, and then returned to sit beside Jack. Jack sensed that things were not going well for him in the conferences held at the headquarters of the Comintern.

"Do you know that Bukharin's private quarters are in the same building that also houses the headquarters of the Comintern, where I am grilled?"

"No," Jack answered, hanging his head low. While he was being soaked in champagne, Borodin was fighting for his life. He was too ashamed to confess that he had made a mockery of his friend by turning his vision of the Young Future of China into a lousy drunkard.

He felt a hand pressing his shoulder, and he sat straighter, facing another round of music.

"Do me a favor," Borodin entreated instead of reprimanding him. "At the moment, it is not convenient for me to communicate with your father directly. Please pass on this message to him. I am in a nearly hopeless situation. Debates at the Comintern hinge on the outcome of the bitter and still unresolved struggle between Stalin and Trotsky, though Stalin is getting the upper hand. The China debacle is a blunt instrument that the Trotsky clique uses to hit Stalin. The Stalin clique makes desperate attempts to whitewash their boss by shifting the heavy load of responsibility onto me."

Jack relayed this message faithfully to his father. Eugene took it in rather calmly. "I had the first inkling of trouble when Adolf Joffe did not show up at the welcome banquet."

There were rumors about Joffe. Some said he had committed suicide. Others said he had attempted to, or that he had been locked away or had been done away with. The Sun Yatsen–Joffe joint agreement, which had officially sanctioned the alliance of the Kuomintang and the Bolsheviks, had preceded Borodin's coming to China. Would Joffe's fate foreshadow Borodin's?

A few days after October 23, 1927, the day Borodin concluded his debate at the Comintern, he did not come back to the hotel. Jack expected the worst. When a waiter gave him a message from Borodin, he moaned. He read it quickly. Then he read every word slowly, carefully, so as not to mistake one word.

The first Jack heard of the exoneration of Borodin was from this phone message. Borodin said that evening that he was going to take the whole Wuhan delegation to the premiere of the new Bolshoi Theater ballet, *The Red Poppy*.

"Mr. Bee has won!" Jack cried with joy.

"Not so fast," Eugene cautioned. "In any event, there will be a celebration, the kind of grand occasion only the Russians know how to stage. We must look our very best."

When Jack finished his toilet, he went to his father's suite. Eugene was trimming his moustache fastidiously.

"Ready to go?" Jack asked.

"We'll be driven over there."

"Why? The Bolshoi Theater is within shouting distance of the Metropole. It won't take two minutes to walk there." Jack raised his eyebrows in question.

"Diplomatic etiquette," Eugene winked.

When Borodin came around to pick them up, they were all ready, dressed in their best. Borodin, too, looked his part. He wore something like a red rosette in his lapel; it was the medal of a Hero of the Socialist Revolution. He seemed to glow with pleasure. They were driven over to the theater's majestic entrance in the only Rolls-Royce the foreign office had. They were led through a colonnaded portico and into the former czars' salon, all crimson brocade and gilt to the left of the stage. The director or manager bowed so low over Madame Sun's hand that he postured as if making obeisance. When everyone was seated and the ceremony was over, they were ushered into their box—the old imperial box framed in red plush curtains with enormous gilt tassels—at the center of the second-floor horseshoe. The welcome from the audience was something that Jack had never known and would never know again. Everyone stood up, and every eye in the huge theater was upon them. The applause was deafening. The Russians were demonstrative, and they wanted to show how much they admired the Chinese people in their long struggle for freedom. It was fully a fifteen-minute ovation.

The red velvet curtains quivered and then parted, presaging entry into the grandest of shows. The new ballet, *The Red Poppy,* had been composed for the occasion under the supervision of Party bigwigs. The plot goes like this: a Soviet ship docks at a Chinese port, bringing goods for trade. In contrast to the haughty antics of the white capitalist hobnobbing with the warlord who rules the port, the Soviets, all smiling comrades, drive away the bad guys and join the throng of Chinese dockhands.

It was such a letdown when the story unfolded that it reminded Jack of some cheap Hollywood movies, picturing the good white southern landowners and their darkies. If the audience believed the story, Jack grumbled to himself, they would believe that it was the destiny of the great Russian people to lead the benighted Chinese masses to the back-door entrance of the great house of all-embracing Soviet communism.

Incredible though it was, *The Red Poppy* did reflect Stalin's understanding of the Chinese revolution, something he could twist around his little finger. He did not wait long to reveal to the three members of the Wuhan delegation—Eugene, Chingling, and Deng Yanda—what roles were intended for them. The first to be enlightened was Deng Yanda, a man in his thirties. For some reason, the Soviets had cold-shouldered him. On his arrival in Moscow with Eugene and Chingling, he had been taken aside and put up in a less posh, secondary guesthouse, the National Hotel. The slight made him bitter. One evening in early November, without warning or notice, Stalin summoned Deng to the Kremlin. He went at eight o'clock and didn't come back until after two o'clock in the morning. Eugene was alone, waiting anxiously in the delegation's office, which was in his suite in the Metropole Hotel.

In a state of great agitation, Deng stammered out his recounting of the meeting. He had prepared to tell Stalin some home truths: let the Chinese people run their own revolution. But Stalin interrupted and made a proposal that stunned him. Stalin unilaterally dumped on him the top job in the Chinese Communist Party, secretary general. But he was not a communist, Deng reminded the Russian dictator. That could be arranged, Stalin said peremptorily. Vexed, Deng retorted that he did not believe that communism could be transplanted to China, because China was an agrarian country.

Deng Yanda's defiance instantly made him a "person non grata." He left the Soviet Union, it was said, one step ahead of the Cheka, which came to get him. Eugene was deeply upset by the Soviet attempt to subjugate Deng, which recalled their attempt to undermine him and Chingling. They had arrived in Moscow six or seven weeks earlier than Borodin and, while waiting, had accepted the Soviet government's invitation to take a vacation in the Caucasus. They came back immediately after being informed of Borodin's return. At the station, they were approached by an English journalist who congratulated them on their wedding. The news had been released by the Associated Press on September 28 when they were far away from Moscow.[1]

Eugene suspected that the rumor had more to it than met the eye. He asked Rayna Prohme—who mingled rather freely with the Western journalists stationed in Moscow—about it and got to the bottom of the matter. One day, Rayna recounted, when the journalists chitchatted about the coming wedding of Chiang Kaishek and Mayling Soong, a reporter from *Pravda,* the Soviet Party's most important organ, said he had a scoop for them: Eugene Chen and Madame Sun Yatsen were honeymooning in the Caucasus.

Now, in the light of Deng Yanda's banishment, the rumor of Eugene's marriage to Chingling took on a vaguely ominous quality. He called in Silan, who, footloose and lighthearted, had asked if she could go on the Caucasus vacation with him and Chingling. Eugene had told her to ask for Chingling's permission. Now he wanted to know exactly why Chingling had not assented.

Eugene Chen and Soong Chingling (the widow of Sun Yatsen) at Sun Yatsen University in Moscow.

"I thought Madame Sun would have jumped at my offer. She always took a chaperone, either Rayna or me or Yolanda, with her. She was not unaware of the existence of Western journalists in Moscow, nor was she unaware of their eagerness to rehash the old elopement rumor if she went off to the Caucasus with you without a chaperone. But she made the decision to travel alone with you." Lowering her eyes, with a barely suppressed knowing smile, Silan added, "Probably on an intermittent romantic impulse."

"I hope you won't contribute your speculation to the professional gossips," Eugene scolded his daughter. "Madame Sun is a guest here, and she probably did not feel it appropriate to ask the Soviet government to extend an invitation to you or to Rayna."

Temporarily acquitted, Borodin was allowed to see Eugene. In a hushed voice, Borodin recounted his argument at the Comintern. He had given a comprehensive picture of what he viewed as the political and economic situation of contemporary China, defending his work there and enumerating his accomplishments. While doing so, Borodin credited Eugene for his share of successes. Altogether, he brought up the names of three Kuomintang members who had been consistently cooperative: they were Sun Yatsen, Liao Zhongkai, and Eugene Chen. In two places, Borodin made a special mention of Eugene. In the first, he said that during the Hong Kong–Canton Strike, Eugene had offered the laborers the opportunity "to exercise their rights in governing for the first time in the history of their struggles..."[2] In the second place, he listed "the re-possession of the two British Concessions along the middle reaches of the Yangzi River" as one of the four great victories of the Northern Expedition.[3]

Borodin was to accompany Eugene to a series of conferences with Soviet leaders, and discussed with him what questions they wanted to broach. He trod carefully and said: "I am on parole, for the most part due to you and Madame Sun. It is not convenient to sentence me to death now."

"That was the purpose of our coming here with you," Eugene said.

Eugene, who had spent more than two months in Moscow, had learned not to raise his hopes. As far as the China policy was concerned, Borodin had tipped him off, there was a difference between Lenin and Stalin. Lenin was no altruist, but he was more of an internationalist than Stalin. Stalin was a nationalist in the narrowest sense of the word. He was to change the international slogan of "world revolution" to that of "building up the socialist mother country," meaning the Soviet Union. That was the first and foremost duty of every communist, Russian and non-Russian. At this juncture, to approve of renewing the alliance between the Left Kuomintang and the Chinese Communist Party was tantamount to declaring war on the Nanjing government led by Chiang Kaishek. Soviet Russia was not willing to take on such a task.

Eugene, however, was a man of stable mind and strong conviction. The vision of his ideal was fading, but the determination founded upon that conviction was not shaken. When he was told that Stalin wished to receive him, he used the few days prior to the meeting to think over what points to make.

Eugene wanted to know if Borodin stood any chance of being given a job connected with the Chinese revolution, so they could all go back to China to continue their unfinished work. This proposal was fairly well received by the governmental officials such as Chicherin and Karakhan. But the leadership in the Comintern took a diametrically opposite stand. Stalin, the man who had both the government and the Comintern at his service, hadn't shown his preference yet.

"At one session he [Eugene] met Stalin," recalled Percy in his memoir, "and after this meeting my father described Stalin as a taciturn man. 'He sat all during the evening puffing at his pipe. . . . But when he spoke what he said did not please me. He thought that I should return to China and cooperate with Chiang Kaishek.'"[4]

At this juncture, Stalin's words suddenly clicked with Eugene, linking this proposal to the one he had offered to Deng Yanda. Stalin, like the British imperialists before him, did not want to see China unified. It would suit him perfectly if the Kuomintang and the Chinese Communist Party constantly hampered and warred with one another. Stalin had tried to plant Deng Yanda in the Chinese Communist Party, and now tried to plant Eugene—and Chingling—as a team in the Kuomintang. The marriage rumor! Stalin had approved of it! The rumor was leaked at the time when the news of the upcoming wedding of Chiang Kaishek and Mayling Soong was released. The Western newspapers printed both simultaneously. Stalin himself could not have done better. Curious readers could draw their own conclusion: Stalin had the trump card.

Inflamed by national pride and chivalrous sentiment, Eugene told Stalin firmly, frankly, but in a roundabout, polite way that he would not be his man in Nanjing. "Since I don't speak Chinese, I do not know what really is taking place among the numerous cliques and factions within the Kuomintang. Far less do I know of the goings-on among the cliques and factions in Peking and in the various provinces of China. They are myriad."[5]

That night, Eugene reviewed the day's happenings. He was sure now that Stalin thought it was in Russia's best interests to take steps to recognize Chiang Kaishek's government. These two dictators would play diplomatic chess. He refused to be a pawn, but could the Chinese communists do the same? He felt deeply for them. He had worked with Mao Zedong, Zhou Enlai, and Liu Shaoqi. These were highly intelligent and efficient young men with whom he could reason. Sometimes he had heated debates with them, but at the end of the day they had struggled to come to a true understanding, without pretense or forced acquiescence. Their problem was that they had to take orders from the Bolsheviks. When Moscow had helped establish their party back in 1921, the party constitution had specified that the Moscow-dominated Comintern was their superior. He hoped they could someday shake off this political shackle.

Eugene had made the case for taking this Moscow trip. He had taken a great risk, not only to his political career but also in his personal life. If he succeeded in persuading Stalin to revive the United Front between the Left Kuomintang and the Chinese Communist Party, he and Chingling could go back to China together and work out a new lease on the revolution. Failing that, they had to go into exile, and then they had better go separately in order to quell the slander. Suddenly he felt sick at heart. He did not show up at teatime. Jack went to his study to see if he wanted to order a light meal.

Sitting in his chair in the bedroom, Eugene was listlessly turning the pages of newspapers. Jack took a seat, resting his right elbow beside a vase of fading flowers on a table.

"Father, you haven't eaten since breakfast."

"I am not hungry."

Jack had the impression that his father wished to remain silent for a short time. He listened uneasily to the low rustling as Eugene resettled himself in his chair. After a few minutes, he heard his father speak in a weary voice.

"Come with me to the Sugar Palace. I'll break the bad news to Madame Sun."

The Chens' old friend Rayna Prohme led them to Chingling's room, which was crammed with furniture in the old czarist style, with fringed lampshades, heavy plush tablecloths, and fringed velvet drapes. The current tenant looked even more frail in the midst of these heavy pieces.

"So this is it," she murmured.

Eugene said that he would continue trying to work with the Chinese communists in spite of Stalin's objection.

"I will too."

"They are patriots and they will realize that what is best for Stalin is not best for the Chinese revolution," Eugene said positively.

Several thousand miles away, on a late July night, a middle-aged man was painstakingly drawing a map indicating the deployment of the Kuomintang troops, checkpoints, and weapon depots of Nanchang, former headquarters of Chiang Kaishek and a conservative citadel. As the police chief of the city, Zhu De, also known as Chu Teh, marked all the possible targets of the communist insurgents. Rumors had it that they were preparing for an armed uprising, led by the wily Zhou Enlai. Zhu De's superiors and peers counted on him to secure the city. Zhu De appeared to be dependable. He had a brawny, weather-beaten face with a flat, distended nose, wide mouth, thick lips, and two small eyes sunk in wrinkled skin that told how much hot sun and cold wind its owner had weathered. Zhu was the man whose name could make the communist insurgents nervous, but he was acting a little awkward tonight. He pricked his ears, jerked his head, and now and then craned his neck at the faintest sound.

When his orderly announced that a guest was waiting for him in the reception room, Zhu De's face suddenly became alert, and it instantly broke into a broad smile when he saw who it was. Uttering a low cry of relief, he stretched out both hands to hold Zhou Enlai's, a gesture that spoke highly of his trust and affection for the man who was at the top of his most-wanted list.

Although Zhu De was Zhou's senior by twelve years, he had respected the younger man as his mentor from the day they had first met in Berlin five years previously. In Zhu's youth, he had harbored two ambitions: to make a fortune for his poor peasant family, and to serve his country as a soldier. By skillfully playing the field with the other militarists of Sichuan, his home province, and of other southwestern regions, he got promoted and rich. He bought several large houses and possessed quite a few fat bank accounts. He indulged in sumptuous dinner parties, replete with entertaining singsong girls. He played nepotism and stuffed his brigades with relatives. Before long, he became the kind of man he had hated and despised, a warlord, and, for that matter, a small-time one.

Behind the façade of a jolly good fellow, Zhu De was a frightened man, struggling not to drown in the cesspool. Weighed down by self-loathing, he could not bear looking himself in the eye. To escape, he started smoking opium and let his mind be numbed in the fog of the drug. As he was sinking lower and lower into hell, a hand stretched out to him from a woman he loved dearly. His second marriage had not been arranged by his parents; he had been introduced to his wife by friends. He did not find her pretty, but congenial. Both liked reading, music, and gardening. The happiest moment he had in that period was to come home and find her playing hide-and-seek with his son from his first marriage, among the orchids they had planted together. Up to his death, Zhu De, the Father of the Red Army, took care of the orchids himself in his Beijing garden. The sweet scent brought back the memory of the woman who had gone through the darkest phase of his life by his side.

She tried in every way possible to get him away from the opium couch. She played lute to accompany his flute. She discussed with him the books, magazines, and newspapers they had read. New Youth, the first Marxist magazine published in China, caught their notice. She persuaded him to give up opium smoking, grasp a new lease on life, and seek a new road to fulfill his destiny.

He listened, and then heard from friends that the French hospital in Shanghai had a rehabilitation program. He told his wife that he would go to Shanghai, come clean about the addiction, and from there he probably would go to Europe where the socialist movement was strong and find out firsthand what he could do to make his motherland as advanced as France or Germany.

In mid-1922, Zhu De walked out of the French hospital a healthy man physically and turned his mind to find a cure for his spiritual disease. He went to visit Chen Duxiu, secretary general of the Communist Party and editor in chief of the Marxist magazine New Youth, which Zhu De had read with admiration. He expressed his wish to join the Communist Party; but his enthusiasm was immediately dampened by his host, who told him cuttingly that the Party would not accept a warlord as a member.

The future slammed its door shut in Zhu's face. Was he to return to the past? This thought plummeted him into the deepest depression. He was thirty-six years of age and in his prime, but he felt old, gray, and unwanted. Burdened and disillusioned, he boarded a French ship sailing for Marseilles in early September 1922. He rented a room in a Chinese merchant's house and heard accidentally from the landlord about a group of Chinese students who had recently set up a branch of the Chinese Communist Party. The chief organizer was a young man named Zhou Enlai.

The information instantly swung Zhu De into action. He got Zhou's address in Berlin from an acquaintance of his landlord. Without delay, Zhu took the train to Berlin and went directly from the station to find Zhou at a house on Kant Street. Zhou responded with compassion to Zhu's confession of past sins. He recalled to Zhu his own fumbling in the dark, and how that made him understand others' frailties. The exchange of experiences went so well that they forgot time until they felt very hungry. They dined in a restaurant and ate with gusto, then returned to Zhou's apartment together and continued in conversation that night and for a few days after.

Zhou Enlai told Zhu De that he had established a communist cell in Berlin and agreed to sponsor Zhu for Party membership. While he sent Zhu's application to the Party headquarters in China to be processed, he allowed Zhu to take part in the activity of the group as a candidate. But Zhu must keep this a secret, Zhou cautioned; Zhu would remain a Kuomintang member publicly, so he could do work that a communist was not able to. All of a sudden Zhu realized that his old connections with the militarists were no longer liabilities: they were weapons to defeat them.

Now, five years later, Zhou Enlai would tell him what role was assigned to him in the impending Nanchang Uprising. Zhu De would throw a party, or more frankly an orgy, for the Kuomintang officers when his fellow communists advanced on the city. On August 1, 1927, the uprising began, and a few days later it collapsed in failure. The defeat was partly caused by the fact that on the eve of the uprising, Moscow suddenly reneged and informed their Chinese comrades not to expect any assistance from them. Zhou Enlai couldn't believe his ears, because it was Moscow that had issued the order to launch the three armed uprisings to take back the cities—Nanchang, Changsha, and Canton—from Chiang Kaishek's allies, so as to prove that the communist revolution, directed by Moscow, was not ebbing away. Then, probably realizing that the uprising would become another disaster and cause Stalin to lose more face, Moscow, at the last minute, gave confusing, contradictory orders to halt it. But Zhou and his comrades were too far gone in the plans to turn back.

While Zhou Enlai, though angry and "threatening to resign,"[6] endured Moscow's treacherous reverse of policy, Mao Zedong reacted in a devious way, surpassing his Russian comrades. Mao was assigned to lead the uprising in his home province of Hunan, targeting the city of Changsha. A few days before the uprising, Mao was arrested and escorted to the enemy headquarters. On the way, Mao deliberately let dozens of silver dollars fall out of his pockets. While the enemy escorts scrambled for them, he slipped away, jumped into a dirty pond, and hid behind tall weeds, getting out only after they left. He lost his shoes in the dirty water and walked barefoot for miles. Enduring the excruciating pain in his injured and festering feet, he reached his destination, the town of Bronze Drum, a day afterward.

The uprising was launched on September 10, 1927. Mao's wounds grew worse, and he was carried by his soldiers to take the command at the front. He had counted on his troops to capture the cities surrounding Changsha at their first onslaught, but had underestimated his enemies. Mao's troops fell back. As soon as they gave ground, the enemies pressed all the harder. On the fourth day, Mao lost two thirds of his forces. He sank into a pessimistic mood and told his lieutenants that he doubted they should march on Changsha as planned by their Russian comrades: to go on fighting amounted to suicide, and he had absolutely no intention of dying for Stalin. On the other hand, he dared not drastically reduce the scope of the operation without getting his bosses' approval. The Soviet Russian consul at Changsha, Mayir (Chinese transliteration), was waiting for Mao to coordinate this most crucial battle. Mayir would attack from within, and Mao from without.

At the time that Mao was faced with this dilemma, one of his lieutenants, Wang Xinya, was familiar with the mountainous area and the two outlaw leaders who controlled the fortress at the Jinggang Mountain. They were "Green Forest Heroes," the Chinese equivalents of Robin Hoods. They robbed the rich and powerful; they protected the poor and persecuted. A number of local communists had already found refuge there.

The lieutenant continued spinning yarns that made Mao think of an ancient parallel, the one hundred and eight Chinese Robin Hoods in his favorite classic novel, *Water Margin,* also translated as *All Men Were Brothers* or *Outlaws of the Marsh*. If they, from their mountain fortress, carried on a long struggle with the emperor of the Song dynasty, why couldn't he with the Bolshevik czar? To hell with Moscow's command; he would take to the mountains. Knowing very well that he was going to violate party discipline and commit insubordination, he had to make sure that Moscow would not be able to locate or reach him. Jinggang Mountain seemed perfect for this purpose.

Hitting the ceiling, Stalin wanted both Mao Zedong and Zhu De to be sent to Moscow. They refused. In face of such defiance, the Soviet Russian leadership smoldered with impotent anger. When Bukharin likened a Chinese mountain fortress to Masada in his conversation with Jack, he unwittingly exposed Moscow's ignorance about China. That ignorance would cost them a lot.

★ 20 ★

ART FOR REVOLUTION

Eugene would exile himself to Paris while Chingling would go to Berlin, so as to preempt the recycling of the elopement rumor. Eugene asked his friend Arthur Ransome, the English journalist who happened to be in Moscow, to take Yolanda, about fourteen years old, back to England to finish her English education at the school on the Isle of Wight where Silan had studied. He told Jack and Silan that if they wanted to remain, they would get the schooling they wished. Karakhan, the former Soviet ambassador to China and now deputy commissar of foreign affairs, had promised to help them. Silan said that she wanted to enroll in the Bolshoi Ballet School.

Then it was Jack's turn to say what his plan was. He had carefully considered what he would do, giving himself an appraisal as objective as a cocksure nineteen-year-old boy could. He knew he had what it took to make a good cartoonist, and he also knew he ought to get more artistic education. Actually, he already had a school in mind.

He had heard from Borodin of a school that sounded like what he was looking for. Before his father's departure, he asked Borodin to arrange for him to visit the director of this extraordinary art school near the Metropole, called VKhUTEMAS (or High Art and Technical Workshops). It was based on Lenin's idea of a work-study program, the world's first college based on such a concept. It taught students not only drawing and painting but also the graphic arts: woodcuts, etching, lithography, photolithography, photography, and even how to print without a printing machine under the most difficult circumstances, such as clandestine printing of leaflets or newspapers. It was a school to train revolutionary artists who would use their art to serve the struggle. It sounded just right for Jack. He packed a selection of his cartoons, drawn for the *People's Tribune* at Wuhan, in a folder and went to the college.

The director was Pavel Novitsky, the ugly, shock-headed, and brilliant theoretician of the ultraleft October Group, a veteran revolutionary who looked it. He had the lined face of a man who had lived a hard life. Glancing through Jack's pictures, he said, "Very good!" and the interview concluded. With no further question, the director accepted Jack. Because Jack spoke little Russian, he would be excused from the normal requirements. But at year's end he would be expected to attend theoretical classes and pass examinations.

He was accepted! He was singing in his heart when he heard a laugh behind him, and he knew immediately who it was before turning. He had never heard anybody else laugh like that. It was clear, cheerful, and melodious, like the bubbling sound of a mountain spring. He had to check himself from running to Rayna Prohme like a little boy.

"Tomorrow I'll attend my first class," Jack told her.

"I have found a school too," she said. "It trains revolutionaries to work in foreign countries. We'll go back to China and work together again."

"Bravo!" Jack exclaimed

"But why not start right now?" she added with great gusto.

She suggested that she write what she described as "color stories" about great events, and that Jack do "smashing drawings" to illustrate them.

"Each of us makes a list of topics that we'd like to write and draw. How is that?" she said.

With Rayna by his side, Jack was more confident about finding his way back to China. While sketching his sample "smashing drawings" for her, he felt that his journey home became more real. He was looking forward to meeting her again in a few days.

One afternoon on November 18, Anna Louise Strong, who had a room on the ground floor in the Metropole Hotel, sent for him urgently. Another of her whims, Jack dismissed it. He couldn't think of anything urgent between them. But he would go, so that she would not call down fire and brimstone on him. He puttered about and reached Anna Louise's door at his own pace. Opening it, his eyes fell on a scene that struck such fright in him that he was rooted to the spot. Rayna was in a bed, and her hair fell in a tangle on the pillow. Inexperienced though he was, Jack could see that the waxy pallor of her face presaged death.

Rayna had an inoperable brain tumor and died on November 21, 1927. Three days later, her friends followed her hearse to the new crematory. The funeral was simple. Jack listened half-consciously to people speaking of Rayna's life and her dedication to the Chinese revolution.

A funeral march began. A switch was turned on. Rayna, with her laughter, her dreams, her zeal for life, slowly vanished into a monstrous black hole in the wall that led to the crematorium. When the door of the furnace was clos-ing, it seemed so final. Jack shivered and cried uncontrollably. He literally howled. He had to be dragged out and escorted back to the hotel.

Sobbing into his pillow, Jack went over things in the recent past, dwelling for a long moment on Rayna. She had been a dear friend, but she could not have been dearer to him than his mother; yet he hadn't cried so helplessly at his mother's funeral. He was probably not only crying for Rayna's passing—it was an outburst of emotions, entangled and bottled up for the last eighteen months. Much had happened to him since May 1926: His mother had died. He had left a world he had called home for a strange country, which, he was told, was his real homeland. After he had put down roots in the land of his forebears, he was abruptly cut off from them. His father, a role model, had fallen precipitously from the height of his career. Borodin, his Marxist mentor, had been reduced to a nonentity. The best friend he had made in Wuhan, Rayna Prohme, was gone. The world collapsed around him, and he came apart with it.

When his father came to sit by his bedside, Jack managed a wan smile and said, "I am sorry to make a spectacle of myself."

The fine wrinkles on his father's face softened, and Jack saw sympathy. "I'll set up a small office in Paris. Paris is beautiful, and there are many won-derful museums. Will you come to visit me?"

Jack warned himself not to make another scene. But for all his determi-nation, he was overpowered by the sadness of the past loss and imminent part-ing. A dry retch rose in his throat. He heard a cry escaping his lips: "Father, take me with you."

"Together or separate, we know we are striving for the same goal," Eugene said as he took off his glasses, wiping the lenses and then the corners of his moist eyes.

To pick up the shattered pieces, Jack needed something to hold on to. And he chose the Rev-olutionary Cause, a sort of family heirloom. He would live and fight for a free and prosper-ous China. Everything else was secondary.

Art was for revolution, and for revolution only. Jack's first love was oil painting, but he put that on hold, for he decided that the rev-olution needed an art form more immediately effective. As a cartoonist, he could produce a

A peasant woman mourning her son, a resistance fighter, who was killed by Japanese invaders, circa 1936.

A refugee from Japanese-occupied Manchuria (the northeastern part of China) begging in Peking, circa 1936.

cartoon every day and make constant connections with the masses, who had not been educated to appreciate more sophisticated art forms.

His art school had a system of "Production Practice," meaning that students did not learn to make pictures only in their studios. While still a second-year student, Jack had ample opportunity to try his hand at every process of book and newspaper artwork during practice with one of the leading publishing firms. He chose the Ogonyok Publishing House, after having consulted Borodin.

Borodin, having survived the Comintern's inquisition, was appointed to run factories. Ill-suited to these bureaucratic jobs, he failed again and again. Snubbed and forgotten, he appreciated Jack's loyalty and guided the youth like a substitute uncle. He was protective of Jack. Ironically, it was he who warned Jack off the Bolshevik Party.

"Being a Marxist artist does not mean you have to join a political party," he said. "Jack, politics is not your cup of tea."

"Intrigues disgust me," Jack agreed.

"Jack, when you first came to Wuhan, you had with you a solution to Wuhan's problems and the world's. According to you, it was all quite simple: the human race only needed a change of heart. Then the greedy would become generous, the evil good, and the hostile friendly. I suppose you have grown out of your Charles Dickens–inspired belief," Borodin said, gazing at his friend with a tender look.

"I am still optimistic," Jack said with what he imagined was a sophisticated smile to extenuate a young man's fault, naïveté.

"You know what optimism is? It is invented as a means of deluding fools." Now when Borodin talked about politics or politicians, his voice could not help being tinged with skepticism.

"Not if I have a goal to strive for."

The People Rise, *fighting back against Japanese invaders, 1931.*

"Fine. I suggest that you do some apprentice work at Orgonyok Publishing House, because they will soon publish an English magazine which I may edit some day; and if I get that job, I'll invite American and English writers and artists to help. Such an office is more open and transparent and can help pave your way to China."

In the late spring of 1930, Jack graduated from VKhUTEMAS and accepted an offer to work in a new English-language weekly, *Moscow News*. Anna Louise Strong was the editor in chief. She once had had a crush on Borodin, and of course had known Jack since they had met at Wuhan. She called Jack in, together with an Englishman, Herbert Marshall, secretary of the London

Film Guild, who would manage photographs, and three other Americans: Ed Falkowski, a former coal miner and now journalist; Maxwell Stewart, an ex-correspondent of the magazine *Nation;* and Joshua Kunitz, of *New Masses,* who was in Moscow doing theater. Jack started as cartoonist and lay-out man, and later would branch into writing about current political events, art, theater, and stories on various aspects of life in the Soviet Union.

Jack's drawings began to appear not only in *Moscow News,* but also in other newspapers and magazines. He contributed to *Ogonyok,* a weekly; *Zarubezhom (Abroad),* a current-affairs weekly of international events; *Smena (The New Shift),* a magazine of Soviet Youth; and *Komsomolskaya Pravda,* the daily newspaper of the Young Communist League. He helped organize movie shows and concerts and lectures to raise money for victims of fascism and Nazism. When one of his dancers failed to show up at a concert, he danced himself, with considerable success. He deliberately confined his activity to artistic and humanitarian work. The Soviet Union was not his country, and he would not let any entanglement in its politics hinder him from going back to China.

After work, Borodin's two-bedroom apartment on Granovsky Street (Chinese transliteration) was Jack's home away from home. The apartment building was either in or near the center of Moscow; Jack could not recall precisely where. But he remembered vividly the quiet and green foliage in the courtyard, and also a type of ivy with small lavender-colored flowers, something like wisteria, that covered the front wall and hung over the front gate. In the summer of 1930, the lavender ivy was in full bloom.

Inside the building, the tantalizing, homey smell of well-boiled cabbage grew stronger as Jack ascended the staircase. He smiled to himself in antic-ipation of drinking the delicious borscht, Fanny Borodin's best dish. She had turned up in Moscow in 1928. Her escape from the prison of the Manchurian Tiger was never exactly told, although bribery played a part and also diplomatic finesse and pressure. The story Fanny herself told was a most amusing one. She had passed the security guard, she said, by disguising her-self as a boy wearing a man's overcoat and a slouch hat. It was credible, since the overcoat surely could conceal her vast bosom, and her hair, cut short like a man's, could hide in the slouch hat from the jailers' eyes.

Walking through the short doorway of Borodin's apartment, Jack saw a man sitting in a chair with his back toward him. Hearing the steps, the man rose hastily and turned. Jack uttered an exclamation of joy. He lifted his arms, about to put them around the other visitor's shoulders, but then lowered them quickly as he wondered whether Zhou Enlai still remembered him. Zhou did, and warmly shook hands with him.

Jack couldn't wait to ask about his chances of working for the revolution back in China. Zhou's response was slow and cautious. Jack caught him exchanging glances with Borodin and had the impression that they were continuing a private conversation he had interrupted.

"We have gone underground," Zhou said.

"I can go underground too." The words gushed out.

Zhou Enlai thoughtfully cupped his chin with his hand and fell into silence.

"I have a bottle of champagne. Let us celebrate our reunion," Borodin interposed, veering the conversation around to a lighter subject.

"I'll join you over a glass of water," Jack begged off.

"Not even a sip?" Zhou asked.

"A sip will send me right to sleep. I want to hear your news from China."

"Wine has the opposite effect on me: the more I drink, the more I talk," Zhou said, raising his glass. The wine brought out little twinkling specks in his eyes and made his face less somber. "I'll introduce you to some of our comrades here. They may ask you to draw for the leaflets they distribute to China. Through them, you will be able to keep abreast of what is going on in China and have a better idea of when will be the right time to go back."

That was not the most satisfactory answer to his question, but Jack had the feeling that was all he could obtain at the moment. His speculation was later confirmed by Borodin: Zhou had come to Moscow to receive a reprimand for his straying comrades.

Zhu De was on the run after the defeat of the Nanchang Uprising. He had retreated to Canton, where the uprising, led by Zhou Enlai's close colleague at the Whampoa Military Academy, Ye Jianying, had also failed. Desperate, Zhu De roamed along the road, now and then extracting "contributions" from the landlords he ran into, which kept his hungry rabble going. That was how he earned fame as a bandit. He tried several times to contact Mao Zedong. Mao did not seem to welcome him and his rabble, who carried weapons. Jinggang Mountain was Mao's territory. Given Zhu's bellicose reputation, Mao's concern was understandable. Mao did not succumb until after the Party Center sent a special envoy to pressure him to.

In April 1928, Zhu De, at the head of a column of ragtag soldiers, took a barely discernible path around the foot of Jinggang Mountain. It led them to an even narrower path, snaking up until it was just a foothold on the side of a steep ravine. Down at the bottom lay the carcasses of several mules, still laden with heavy boxes. Ahead, the path disappeared into immense clumps of large boulders, long weeds, and thick bushes. They had to carve out their own trail as they crawled, behind their guide, over seemingly insurmountable hurdles. They clutched at anything—the sharp edge of a stone, weeds, dead roots of trees—so as not to slip into the dark abyss below. Danger also hovered above them. A trickle of small stones from higher up could be the prelude to an avalanche of larger rocks.

Zhu De, a soldier trained in modern warfare and also well-versed in ancient Chinese classics on the art of war, immediately saw that such a mountain stronghold could hold out long and hard. Tanks and airplanes were useless here.

The combined forces and talents of Zhu De and Mao Zedong made for a winning team, though they were not without differences, sometimes sharp differences. Zhu De had seen more battles; Mao was a theorist. Their regular discussions of strategy resulted in Mao's essay on guerrilla warfare. As Zhu De recounted, it boiled down to four parts.

1) When the enemy advances, we retreat. 2) When the enemy halts and encamps, we harass them. 3) When the enemy seeks to avoid battle, we attack. 4) When the enemy retreats, we pursue.[1]

For a troop, small in size, poorly equipped, and lacking resources, these tactics enabled the soldiers to win battles and conquer towns and cities around and near the Jinggang Mountain area. Things were looking up when, as in every successful human endeavor, folly and greed intervened.

Zhu De was what the Chinese describe as a *wenjiang*, which could be roughly translated as an intellectual-general or a militarist who was a learned man. But he remained a peasant soldier, in heart and in appearance, throughout his life. When he got excited while talking, he would roll up his sleeves and his pants legs and bring down his fists on his naked knees for emphasis. His habit of sprinkling soldier's vocabulary in speeches must have jarred on the sensitive ears of Mao Zedong. In cold winter nights, when his soldiers' tattered uniforms and threadbare blankets could not shield them from wind and snow, Zhu De would dream up incentives for them to persevere. One day, he exulted, when they conquered Nanjing, each of them would be given a cozy cottage and sleep in the warm arms of a pretty young wife.

The soldiers loved their earthy commander. He chatted with them, joked with them, did menial work with them, drilled with them, and fought with them. He was one of them. He was the opposite number to Mao Zedong, who held himself aloof and acted like an arbitrary patriarch.

Soon Mao suspected that Zhu De was intent on superseding his leadership. Zhu De insisted that in every jointly signed official document, his name be above Mao's. Mao retaliated ruthlessly and launched his first purge sometime between 1930 and 1932. He put his minions on a rampant search for shadowy enemy spies. They broke into Zhu De's apartment and shoved Madame Zhu aside, hollering at her to hand over her husband's "fifteen-year-old orderly, a peasant lad."[2] Why did they bother to trump up a charge against a young boy who was so obviously innocent? A teenager easily bullied into "confessing"—anything he said would be lifted out of context and blown out of proportion. Mao's minions backed off only when Zhu De himself confronted them. This incident set the pattern of Mao's later purges.

With Zhou Enlai's mediation, Mao and Zhu De declared a truce. Zhou criticized Mao, which Mao never forgot nor forgave, nor did he miss any chance to get back at him. Zhou also criticized Zhu De's remnant warlordism. A communist soldier was a new man, Zhou said, who should never use his military position to seize political power. Zhu De, the founder of the Red Army, had the responsibility to set an example for the men in uniform. Zhu De was so moved and ashamed that he volunteered to demote himself and be Mao's subordinate. From that day on, he put his signature below Mao's in every official document.

While the storm was still brewing, Stalin knew that if he wanted to maintain his control over the Chinese Communist Party, he had to plant his man in it. The new head at the Far East Department of the Comintern, Pavel Mif, was to do the recruiting. Mif, like Stalin, had a predilection for sycophants. Among his young protégés, no one was more eager than Wang Ming to curry favor. But Wang Ming had neither the qualifications nor the experience to take on the job. Before he came to Moscow in 1926, Wang Ming was a college student in Wuhan. His résumé boasted of a few demonstrations he had taken part in. After he came to Moscow, he enrolled at Sun Yatsen University, of which Mif was the president. What he mastered quickly was the art of second-guessing. When Mif parroted Stalin, Wang Ming echoed Mif. It was apparent that a great deal of grooming had to be done before Mif could present Wang Ming as the new leader of the Chinese Communist Party.

In 1930, the Russian leadership summoned Zhou Enlai. They saw in him a perfect kingmaker. Without his assistance, they would not be able to implement their plan quickly and efficiently. Zhou obliged in order to keep his Party, which was already in a shambles, from being torn further asunder by the pro-Moscow and anti-Moscow factions. That, however, was not how some of his peers thought of it. A clever kingmaker, they sneered, knew who would be the king of the moment and take the winner's side. The name of the potential king, Wang Ming, caught Jack's notice through Zhou Enlai.

But they did not meet until the end of 1931, when Jack decided to return to China in spite of the difficulties in store for him. Every day, he read the newspapers that informed him of every disaster that could possibly be conceived of by humans occurring in China: the ravages of an economy gone awry; natural and manmade famines; typhoons; floods, droughts, and the extermination campaigns against the communists, led by Chiang Kaishek.

China, thoroughly exhausted and weakened by the civil war, was too big a temptation for Japan not to take on. It seized Manchuria, the northeastern part of China, in September 1931. Pictures of refugees and corpses strewn across the land haunted Jack. After the Japanese occupation of Manchuria, Chinese students, with other patriots from all walks of life, came together in massive demonstrations, demanding that Chiang Kaishek end the civil war and take action against the Japanese invaders. Chiang countered by proclaiming his policy: first crush the communists, then resist the Japanese.

Chiang hoped that, through secret negotiations and lucrative concessions, he could ask Japan to stop moving southward. He could then concentrate his fire on the communists. Resisting the Japanese would divert his attention and forces from the communists and allow them to regroup, grow, and expand. But the Communist Party refused to die, and the Japanese would not wait. The Japanese army moved from the already-occupied northeastern Manchuria southward, and Peking was actually run by their puppets. The outcry denouncing Chiang grew louder and reverberated even through the Kuomintang government at Nanjing. Chiang stepped down, but he retained control of the army through his generals and the treasury through his brothers-in-law, Daddy Kong and T. V. Soong. Chiang had traded in his third wife for Mayling Soong in December 1927. All in the family.

The Kuomintang asked Sun Ke (Sun Fo), Sun Yatsen's son, to form a new cabinet. Sun offered Eugene the job of heading the foreign office. Eugene accepted the invitation on the condition that they bring in the Cantonese Nineteenth Route Army to replace Chiang Kaishek's troops, which were garrisoning the Shanghai and Nanjing areas, because the commanders of the Nineteenth Route Army opposed Chiang's policy of capitulation to Japan. They would do the fighting that Chiang shirked.

On January 28, 1932, Japanese marines struck the Chinese City of Shanghai, outside the French concession and the International Settlement. They made no bones about moving south to control China's lifeline, the great Yangzi River. The Nineteenth Route Army, supported by Eugene and other patriots, fought back heroically.

On hearing the exciting news, Jack started packing. At this moment by an uncanny coincidence, he received a call from Wang Ming. Wang Ming introduced himself as the representative of the Chinese Communist Party at the Comintern. Jack paused. Wang Ming probably guessed that Jack found his call abrupt and explained in a pleasant voice his purpose in phoning.

"Your fame precedes your good self and spreads to the Chinese community here. We all admire your drawings," Wang Ming complimented him. Before he hung up, he said something about publishing papers in Paris and that he would like Jack to do drawings for them.

"Paris" turned out to be a small, shabby shop, just back of the last remaining corner bastion of the Chinese City at Lubyanka in the vicinity of Stalin's notorious Lubyanka Prison. When Jack arrived at the appointment, there were several Chinese youngsters standing by an ancient printer, surrounding a short young man who was talking in an important way. The young man, probably in his mid-twenties, had the face of a grown, streetwise urchin. Wang Ming, who would be labeled later by Mao Zedong as the evil genius planted by Stalin in the Chinese Communist Party, appeared to be a regular guy. Nothing about him impressed Jack, either favorably or unfavorably.

When Wang Ming led Jack into a back room, he halted for a second at the threshold and looked back over his shoulder as though seeing if anyone was following him. His mysterious air puzzled Jack, who had come to discuss what drawings he wanted. This could not be a secret to his comrades in the process of publishing. They walked through a short, dark doorway. The room behind, cluttered with papers, magazines, and rickety furniture, served as Wang Ming's office. It actually seemed to Jack a shack built haphazardly onto the shop.

Jack put an album of his drawings on his knees, waiting to show it to his host.

"Your father has returned to China. How about you?" Wang Ming began their conversation on a subject that Jack was not prepared to discuss with a stranger.

Jack's guard was up instantly. His experiences had taught him to be careful with people with political affiliations, and especially so with those who pried into his father's affairs.

"I am planning to go back." Then he added in a lighter vein, as if joking, "I am twenty-three, old enough to wean myself from my father. I'll go directly to Shanghai."

Jack was taken aback by the instant trust Wang Ming put in him, but quickly realized why. He asked tentatively: "Has Comrade Zhou Enlai mentioned me to you?"

"He and I worked together in our Party Center at Shanghai. I just came back last month," Wang Ming answered in a roundabout way. "Meeting you, I don't need any recommendation. I know a good comrade when I see one." He was anxious to be his own man.

Wang Ming's proposal sounded very conspiratorial. Jack was to present himself at a certain bookshop in Shanghai, pick up a certain book, and say a certain phrase to the shop attendant, who would ask him a certain question and receive a certain reply. This shop attendant then would tell him how to contact the Party. When Jack recalled this to me thirty-five years later, he could not remember what all the instructions had been, although at that time he memorized them until he was word perfect.

Jack said good-bye to Moscow and to his bride, Lucy Flaxman, whom he had married in 1931. In the same year, his father had remarried, and Georgette Zhang, the fourth daughter of Curio Zhang, was the new Mrs. Eugene Chen. The person who had reconnected them and encouraged them to develop their relationship was Madame Sun Yatsen, who went to Paris especially for their wedding.

Jack told Lucy he would come back to fetch her, and she would have no problem finding a job in cosmopolitan Shanghai. He boarded a train heading toward Berlin and then Venice, where the ship *Conte Rosso,* of the Lloyd Trestino Line, would take him to Shanghai. The last supper he had on board was at a table on the deck, facing the China Sea. Hong Kong was a fairy-tale isle set in a shimmering sea of all shades of turquoise blue and aquamarine. A myriad of lights from fishing boats carpeted the surface of the water, outshining the stars above.

Jack had to check his impulse to kneel down and kiss the land when he went ashore. On the wharf to meet him was Eugene's loyal secretary, Lam Yaukan. In this British colony, the Peninsula Hotel was famous for its English tea. Jack invited Mr. Lam to take it with him.

Jack's Russian family in 2002. Back row: my son, Jay, his Russian brother, Danny, and Danny's wife. Front row: Jay's wife, Chui Inn, Yolanda Sr., and Danny's daughter, Yolanda Jr.

"How is my father?" Jack's words rushed from his lips, filled with expectations.

"You'll hate me for the news I bring," Mr. Lam said. He lapsed into an awkward silence.

Jack sat back and held himself rigidly upright, staring at Mr. Lam.

The bearer of sorry tidings bent his head low: "The resistance is over."

The Nineteenth Route Army was finally defeated, not by Japanese aggressors but by Chiang Kaishek, who ordered his men in the Nanjing government to cut off all reinforcement to the beleaguered soldiers. The surviving troops retreated to the south and Eugene went south too, after the Sun Ke–Eugene Chen cabinet fell. The first decision Chiang Kaishek made after he came back to power was to resume his anticommunist civil war with a vengeance. Through his secretary, Eugene warned Jack that somehow Chiang's secret police knew of his belief in Marxism, and they were watching for him.

Reality, harsh and cold, set in. Jack was nevertheless considering brushing aside his father's warning and going to Shanghai anyway. But what could he do there? Mr. Lam said that Chiang Kaishek had cracked down on all organizations advocating resistance against Japanese aggression. The Communist Party, of course, had not been spared. They had been raided and raided again. Any attempt to contact them would lead Chiang's secret police straight to their remaining underground cells.

There was nothing to do but to return to Moscow. Jack spent his remaining several days in Hong Kong fiercely sketching the downtrodden residents in back alleys, coolies at the waterfront, peddlers in the open-air market. He wanted these Chinese faces to stay in his memory and album. Later, based on these sketches, he would draw some of his best pictures to alert not only the Chinese but the people in America and Europe to Japanese atrocities.

It bothered Jack that Wang Ming had not spoken a word of the extremely dangerous situation in Shanghai, which he surely knew of. Jack complained about his callousness to Borodin and watched a glitter of contempt and bitterness appear in his eyes. Mif, Wang Ming's mentor, was one of the inquisitors who had grilled Borodin in the Comintern after the China debacle. The memory still rankled.

"I don't know how bad the situation is in Shanghai. I have heard a word here and a word there. Piecing them together, I could imagine it is very bad," Borodin said gravely. "The Party's Central Committee is virtually destroyed. Wang Ming, fearing for his life, came running back to Moscow."

"I know I serve the revolution at my own risk, but I refuse to give my life to satisfy Wang Ming's inflated ego," said Jack angrily.

"Then keep away from Wang Ming."

"I can't. Wang Ming's little shop is the chief channel through which my drawings can get to progressive publications in China," Jack said, staring at Borodin in disagreement.

"Then stick to your drawings and leave the intrigues to others," Borodin replied.

Jack nodded to Borodin as well as to himself. That had been the advice he had given to himself ever since he had entered the Soviet Union. He was in Russia to further hone his skills and to learn more about Marxism. Only by setting up such goals could he not only cope with the life of an exile, but also enjoy it sometimes.

"Wang Ming is a thorn in my side; I suppose not only in my side," Jack said. Leaning his head on one side as if pondering some perplexing question, he asked, "Does Stalin really think Wang Ming can direct the Chinese revolution from that dingy shop at Lubyanka?"

He and Borodin looked at each other and burst out laughing.

★ 21 ★

A LONE KNIGHT ON HIS MISSION

When Jack recalled his sojourn in Moscow, that small printing shop at Lubyanka occupied a large place in his memory. Whenever he felt like being back in China, he went there, to draw or deliver a drawing or help run the printer, whatever work needed to be done. Most of the young men and women there were students, learning revolutionary tactics to apply in their own country when they went home. They kept up correspondence with people back in China and were better informed of the goings-on there than Jack. When there was a particularly interesting paragraph in a letter, they would translate it into Russian for him. Here was an eyewitness account of a demonstration against Japanese aggression on the Nanjing Road of Shanghai.

The market was busy, and people went in and came out with their shopping bags. I could see nothing unusual until a stranger, his face in the shadow of a hat, elbowed his way through a gathering crowd and then disappeared into the market. The crowd dispersed furtively onto either side of the road and merged into the anonymity of pedestrians when I heard the sound of a penny whistle. I felt a roll of paper thrust into my hands. Pushed by someone, I found I was in the midst of a handful of people who rushed into the middle of the street, shouted a few slogans and scattered leaflets around. At the sound of another penny whistle a great number of young men and women suddenly collected, some hurrying in from neighboring streets, some coming out from the market. In a second banners were unfurled denouncing the Japanese invaders and calling for a United Front of all patriots. Quickly a column was formed and began to march. In the very front were boys and girls from middle schools. Many of them were mere children.

The column had not marched a couple of blocks before I heard the screeching of police sirens. The British riot police of the International

Settlement swarmed out of the red-painted lorries and barred the roadway. On their heels came a posse of soldiers with drawn bayonets sent by the Chinese mayor whose jurisdiction covered only the Chinese City. He had no business interfering in what took place in the International Settlement, but this was a show co-produced by him and the British authority for the benefit of the Japanese government. It sent a message from Chiang Kaishek's government which preferred to be Japan's friend, and from the British who were hesitant to openly challenge Japan: it was a manifestation of neutrality.

But our spirits prevailed. I hope you can tell your comrade Chen I-fan [Jack] that those leaflets carry his cartoons, which underscore the resistance message and also prove our cause has earned international sympathy. We are not alone.[1]

Reading it, Jack thought if that was the only kind of show the Party Center occasionally managed to put on in Shanghai, the Party was indeed in a very bad way. In the midst of the discussion, a man sidled into the shop and out to the back. Instantly Jack noticed a growing coolness in the young workers. Jack had been curious about this man, who had a Russian name, Alexander, and his odd behavior. Someone told Jack in a hushed voice that he was under investigation. Another said the investigation was over and he was doing penance. What charges? No one seemed to know or dared to know.

Absolved or not, this Chinese Alexander nevertheless acted like a man with a dark cloud permanently hanging over his head. When he saw Jack, he walked away silently, eyes cast downward, in order to avoid greetings. One evening, Jack was walking through the deserted lot and saw the Chinese Alexander standing in the middle of the path, waiting for somebody. When he saw Jack, he hesitated for a second and then walked on, very slowly. Jack slowed down too. But he walked so slowly that Jack had to stop or he would have caught up with him.

Jack sat on the ground, leaning against a tree, and pretended to rest his legs. The Chinese Alexander turned around and smiled at him. For a moment neither of them knew what to do next. Jack did not remember exactly how they approached each other, but they did. Alexander evidently needed someone to talk to.

"You don't recognize me?" Alexander twisted his thick lips into a wider smile. "We first met at Wuhan, you know, on a few public occasions."

Jack stared at him. The pouting mouth with protruding teeth jolted Jack's memory. Alexander was Li Lisan, the super-radical who had confronted Chiang Kaishek in front of a huge audience at a Wuhan mass meeting!

"You are transferred to work here?" Jack asked, pretending not to know his trouble.

"I am being punished for all the defeats of the armed uprisings," Li Lisan groused. "I should have refused to come here like Mao Zedong and Zhu De. The more defiant they grow, the more savagely Wang Ming attacks me, killing the chicken so as to frighten the monkeys into submission."

As part of the penance for his "crimes," Li Lisan edited the publications under Wang Ming's supervision. Wang Ming used his assistant as a punching bag. Li Lisan longed to go back to China, but he had been taken by Stalin, through Wang Ming, as a sort of hostage from the Chinese Party. He had heard of Jack's plan to go back to China and Jack's friendship with Zhou Enlai. He saw in Jack a future messenger who could help him get out of Stalin's clutches.

"The monkeys are too far for Wang Ming to reach," Jack commented rather sanguinely.

"Not really," Li Lisan muttered under his breath. "Wang Ming is a manipulator."

Before Wang Ming left Shanghai for Moscow in November 1931, he planted his men in his Party's Central Committee. They were all returned students from the Soviet Union and approved by Pavel Mif, Wang Ming's immediate boss. The twenty-four-year-old Qing Bangxian, alias Bo Gu, was whisked to the top job of secretary general of the Party. This raw lad particularly lacked knowledge in military affairs, and Moscow provided him a military adviser named Otto Braun, a Soviet-trained German soldier. Although he was totally ignorant of everything about China, he was to direct the war.

By 1933, the Mao-Zhu team had conquered quite a large area below their stronghold on the top of Jinggang Mountain. They owed their victory to what they called mobile warfare. Sometimes they applied hit-and-run guerrilla tactics; other times they lured the enemies into a place geographically disadvantageous to them and beat them up.

It was warfare with imagination, but Otto Braun repudiated it and formed his own team for military operations. It was called the Three-Member Team that included himself, Qing Bangxian, and Zhou Enlai. He chose Zhou for an obvious reason: he needed someone more respected, more seasoned, more senior, and more workable than the greenhorn weakling Qing Bangxian. He wanted to fight what the Chinese described as the frontal war, which allowed Chiang Kaishek plenty of opportunities to showcase his superior modern weaponry. It was predictable that the Red Army would be routed and forced, in the fall of 1934, into a most devastating retreat, which they called the Long March.

The disaster thoroughly discredited Braun, and what authority he still enjoyed was waiting to be toppled. But only Mao was bold enough to strike, making an attempt to free, or at least partially free, his Party from Moscow. Mao secretly courted two of Wang Ming's cronies, Wang Jiaxiang and Zhang Wentian. He frequently bumped into them and confided to them his worry about the Party's future. They strolled together, they chitchatted together, they dined together. Zhang Wentian relished spicy Hunan dishes, which Mao's second wife cooked. Knowing he was attracted to a pretty, young woman from Hunan by the name of Liu Ying, Mao cracked a joke about marrying a Hunan native good at fixing hot stuff. When Zhang shyly acquiesced, Mao immediately transferred the object of his affection to his office, to work as his secretary.

Soon Mao proposed replacing the blundering Qing Bangxian with Zhang Wentian as the new kingpin of the Party, a choice Moscow could tolerate, for Zhang was also among the favorite Chinese of Pavel Mif, who, far away in Moscow, could wish to do no better. Then Mao formed his own Three-Member Team to replace the one created by Otto Braun. Mao's team included himself, Wang Jiaxiang, another favorite student of Mif who also had converted to Mao's side recently, and Zhou Enlai. Mao knew he was too pugnacious for Moscow to consent to the shakeup without a moderating influence such as Zhou. From that day on, Mao, who disliked and distrusted Zhou, could not do without him. Zhou handled Mao like a masterful impresario handling a prima donna, publicly gratifying his ego while quietly taking the edge off him.

A winning partnership developed, and they led their wounded, despairing, exhausted comrades to the northwestern city of Yanan in 1935.

When Jack learned that the Party had narrowly escaped total destruction, he became more hopeful. One day in the mid-autumn of 1935, Li Lisan called. He told Jack that the Party had decided to publish a newspaper, the *National Salvation Times*. Chiang Kaishek had almost destroyed the Party, Li Lisan went on to explain, and the revolution was at its lowest ebb. Defeated and scattered, the revolutionaries looked to whatever little information about the Party they could find to reconnect with it. The newspaper would be printed in "Paris," camouflaging Moscow's sponsorship, and distributed secretly in China.

Jack needed very little persuasion to work longer hours. In a street as desolate as the one at Lubyanka, the single flickering dim light in the printing shop exuded warmth for the revolutionaries lost in the cold. It was a great comfort to know that some comrades were making desperate efforts to keep the tiny light burning.

The year 1935 also saw a series of events that changed the political climate. Chiang Kaishek came under increasingly heavy public censure for his policy of appeasing Japan, which was moving southward down the Yangzi River, threatening the interests of Chiang's American backers. In the meantime, the Soviet Union also felt menaced by Japan's expansion and told its tool, the Comintern, to establish a new line proclaiming a worldwide united front against fascism. The Chinese Communist Party was therefore allowed to resuscitate the United Front with the Kuomintang, which Stalin had objected to.

Percy, Jack's older brother, had divorced his first wife, Carmen Maillard, and married a Russian dancer, Musia (Marie Ivanovna), in 1931. He told Jack that he would go back to China and carry out their father's mission, rallying high-ranking Kuomintang members for the eventual confrontation with Japan.

The conversation with Percy made it clear to Jack that this was the time for him to return to China too. His supposition turned out to be correct when he received a letter from his older sister, Silan, in Shanghai.

Silan had married Jay Leyda, an American pupil and assistant to the great Soviet film director Sergei Eisenstein. In 1935, Leyda contemplated going home; but before that, Silan made a trip to Shanghai, exploring other possibilities for them. As Silan pondered the choices she had, fate intervened. She fell seriously ill and was diagnosed as having cancer. After a few operations, she brooded over whether she would ever dance again. However, she had good news for Jack. She wrote to tell him that he had quite a sizable Chinese audience, familiar with his cartoons.

It seemed his cartoons were reprinted not only in underground communist publications but also in progressive magazines and newspapers. Chiang Kaishek was forced to allow them since anti-Japanese emotions were running higher and higher. Without knowing it, Jack had made a name back home. The news gave him an idea. He would take his drawings and exhibit them in Shanghai. He talked this plan over with Borodin, and Borodin urged him to get in touch with the International Society for Aid to the Victims of Fascism. The society would help pay for part of the travel expenses, and in return asked him to bring back an exhibit of the works of progressive Chinese artists. That sounded perfect to Jack, who planned to come back to fetch his wife, Lucy Flaxman, and their three-year-old son, Danny.

The early spring of 1936 in Shanghai was cold, which did not bother Jack, who was used to Moscow's winter. A group of artists came to meet him at the jetty. The warmth of their welcome made Jack feel at home instantly. "Your fame has preceded your arrival," said Ye Qianyu, a cartoonist, who wore a little mustache and a French beret. Another artist, Zhang Guangyu, concurred with a clap on Jack's back as if they were old friends reunited. A pleasant-looking young man, with his fluffy hair parted in the middle, by the name of Wu Ko spoke English and acted as Jack's guide. He hailed two rickshas and threw in Jack's baggage, and he and Jack each jumped into one.

They got off at a place called Garden Villas. "Villa" was a fancy word for an inelegant place with rows of small houses. Jack did not remember the name of the street. It was in the French concession, and nearly a quarter of the houses inside the Garden Villas were occupied by White Russian refugees. Jack's room was on the third floor, and Wu Ko lived one floor down.

"Here it is," Wu Ko said.

He helped Jack deposit and push his baggage under a single bed, since the room was too small for a closet. Actually, the room was about the size of a walk-in closet. It took only a single bed, a table, and a chair to fill it.

Jack had to make do. He had a thin wallet. Wu Ko told him that he would have no difficulty in getting his cartoons and articles accepted by newspapers and magazines, but their publishers did not pay well.

"Tomorrow we'll throw a party in your honor. You'll meet artists, writers, and editors. I would like to suggest that you take a few drawings with you and show them what you do," Wu Ko said. "Zhou Yang will come too. He is one of the guiding lights in Shanghai's cultural affairs." By so saying, Wu Ko was hinting that Zhou Yang was a Party official.

The café that Jack was taken to looked inexpensive. Judging from its decoration, a large part of its clientele were Shanghai bohemians like Wu Ko. An oil painting of the Mediterranean was hung on the wall directly opposite the entrance hall. The small dining room Jack's host had booked was softly lit by a small Spanish silver chandelier, an imitation piece. The glass vase placed at the center of the table was a noticeably cheap replica of the Venetian original.

Jack passed his drawings around the table. One showed a peasant who had lost his child when Japanese soldiers attacked his village. It made an enormous impression on Zhou Yang, a leader of the Left-wing Writers and Artists Association, who would be labeled twenty years later by Western scholars the Cultural Czar of China. But that was not the Zhou Yang Jack

knew. Zhou Yang was good-looking with a pale, shrewd face and an imposing air, which, however, was somewhat refined by a certain melancholy. His
curiosity about what Jack could do for the resistance movement was the best
compliment Jack received that night. Jack's reply galvanized him into instant
action. He asked Wu Ko to help Jack choose drawings of progressive artists
that Jack could take back to Moscow.

"It is very important to make our people's voice heard outside China, and
to let it be known that they don't approve of Chiang Kaishek's appeasement
policy," Zhou Yang said.

They urged Jack to get an exhibit space in the Lyceum Theater, which
attracted the cultural elite, the influential audience Jack was learning quickly
he should go after for the sake of the revolution. It was they who most
needed to be alerted to the impending war with Japan.

While Jack put on his own exhibit, he was devoting as much time, if not
more, to selecting his peers' work to take back to Moscow. He went to every
exhibition in the city and visited every artist's home he had access to. He was
delighted to discover the rebirth of one of China's oldest arts, the woodcut.
A small number of young artists had made use of the rich artistic material of
the everyday life of the people and treated it in a realistically revolutionary way.

The exhibit of Jack's own work ended in Shanghai in November 1936. He
asked Zhou Yang to arrange a trip to Yanan, where the Communist Party had
headquartered after the Long March.

"I would like to include the work of Yanan artists in my Moscow exhibit,"
Jack explained.

Zhou Yang told him to take a secret route to Yanan, through the Western
Hills outside Peking. In the first week of December, Jack got on the train
heading north. The Peking railway station was to the east of Qianmen, the
majestic Front Gate, the pride of the nation, where Japanese soldiers had
now erected a checkpoint. The Chinese, their heads hanging low, were
herded like cattle to be searched before they were allowed to pass through.
There was no more graphic illustration to describe the humiliation China
suffered. Jack's eyes grew moist with burning tears.

Jack stayed in Peking for a week or so, then had to return to Shanghai.
An incredible event had thwarted his plan to visit Yanan: Chiang Kaishek
was arrested by mutinous northeastern (Manchurian) troops in the city of Xian.
They refused to obey his personal order to attack the Red Army. They were
determined to turn their guns on the Japanese army, who had trampled and
taken away their home provinces in 1931.

The mutinous generals would only release Chiang Kaishek if he agreed to end the civil war, form a second United Front, and fight the Japanese invaders. Chiang surrendered at gunpoint.

In the winter of 1936–1937, when the Japanese learned of this agreement, they decided they had to make a move before the second United Front became a reality. Jack left Shanghai on the last Soviet boat for Vladivostok two or three days after August 13, when Japan launched an all-out attack on China. He saw the first bombs dropped on Shanghai.

In Moscow, the International Society for Aid to the Victims of Fascism arranged an exhibition of the work Jack had brought from Shanghai. In addition to his own work, there was a selection of pieces by Wu Ko, Hsiu Po, Zhang Guangyu, and others. The militant woodcuts and cartoons, prints of social protest and national resurgence, were visual proof of the spirit that animated the Chinese people.

The timing for the exhibit was good. Those were the days when young heroes volunteered for the International Brigades to aid the Spanish Republicans in their battle against Franco, Hitler's ally. People were sensing the menace of fascism and what it would mean for the world. All over the world, there was a popular wave of support for China and denunciation of Japanese aggression. In Europe as well as the United States, small groups were getting together to organize their protests. In London, the China Campaign Committee was the core around which various Aid-China and Boycott Japan groups were uniting. Its chairman was Victor Gollancz, who ran the Left Book Club and was the embodiment of the Popular Front movement.

The rave reviews Jack's Moscow exhibit received spread far and wide. They inspired Jack's friends in the China Campaign Committee to get the exhibit to London. Jack was ready to seize any opportunity to do antifascist propaganda. He wanted to take his wife, Lucy, and their son with him, but Lucy said she needed more time to think this decision over. He also took leave of his younger sister, Yolanda, who was now a camerawoman and married to the famous Soviet cameraman Alexander (Shura) Shelenkov. As a couple, they co-filmed several award-winning movies, of which the most famous was the ballet drama *Romeo and Juliet,* danced by Ulanova.

On his return from Shanghai, Jack had found Moscow a changed land. Stalin had started his great purge in 1934, but the evil hand of suspicion did not stretch out to poison the life in the foreign community until 1937. Like many foreigners who were residents there, Jack was faced with the choice:

"Stay and become a Soviet citizen, or keep your foreign passport and go." Jack chose to go, but he could not convince Lucy.

When his ship pulled into the London docks, he saw the lanky figure of Herbert Marshall, half a head above a couple of other friends. Jack had known Marshall, a pupil of Eisenstein, first through his brother-in-law Jay Leyda, and later as a colleague at the *Moscow News*.

"We are taking you to a meeting," they called, overjoyed to see Jack.

Dropping his trunks at the hotel, they set off immediately. Before his friends could finish briefing him on what the meeting was about, they had arrived in Trafalgar Square. It was a rally organized by the China Campaign Committee, which Jack joined instantly.[2] On the platform, a man in black cloth was speaking, his white hair tossed back and forth with emotion.

"The dean of Canterbury," Herbert Marshall told Jack.

The clapping would not stop for ten minutes after the dean of Canterbury had uttered his last remark: the Chinese would fight to the end, and they would prevail.

Next, a giant of a black man strode onto the stage. Who could that be but the incomparable Paul Robeson? His deep, powerful voice resounded through the square. Like a biblical prophet, he sang out the lines of the "Chinese Army March":

"The enemy will be silent. China will rise again."

The entire audience was electrified. In the midst of thunderous applause and shouts, Victor Gollancz turned to Jack: "Jack, we call upon you to be the witness."

Suddenly all the noise quieted, and a frightening hush fell over the immense crowd. Jack looked from the sea of expectant faces in front of him to the chairman and got cold feet.

"I have never addressed such a huge crowd."

"That's all right," Victor Gollancz said. "Just tell them what is happening and keep your sentences short."

1937: Jack embarks on a world tour exhibiting antifascist drawings.

There was no retreat, Jack told himself, and quickly went over what he could say. The dean of Canterbury and Paul Robeson were hard acts to follow.

Jack started haltingly. "My report will tell you how efficiently the Japanese use the scrap iron that the British government allows the industrialists to sell to them, enabling them to manufacture bombs and bombers.

"I was shaving. I remembered that the razor was my last present from my mother before she died.

"It was almost half past eight in the morning. I heard the familiar *clang* of the air raid warning. The routine began. An occasional low hum from the sky and the dull thudding *boom* of the antiaircraft. Somehow it all seemed far away. By nine o'clock it was over. That was a quiet round as far as I was concerned. I thought that was all for the morning, but I was mistaken. At about half past ten another warning sounded. Two bombers were circling very high above, diving in and out of the clouds. I detected a falling bomb, followed by an explosion. Then another and another and another, mixed with the rattling of machine guns. Then all quiet.... Fifty yards away, around a nearby hospital, lay seventy horribly mangled bodies. Forty-one Japanese bombers took part in this morning carnage, and I saw only one tiny part of it."

Jack was so agitated by his own story that he surprised himself. Like any well-bred English gentleman, he had never become emotional at a public meeting. Whenever he spoke, he tried to be cool and balanced. But with a surge of bitter hatred for fascism, particularly the Japanese brand, he found himself yelling at the tops of his lungs: "Who were these people? Chinese working people and their children, people like those a bomb would kill if it fell over the East End of London!" Then he surprised himself further by shouting slogans through the microphone, slogans that brought an answering roar from ten thousand throats: "Down with Japanese imperialists! Get out of China! Boycott the invaders! No British scrap iron for Japan!"

The reviews on the exhibit were enthusiastic too. The *News Chronicle* said: "All the exhibitors are under 30. They have broken away from the old, dreamy, hill-and-blossom pictures, and now depict realistically—yet with artistic selection—the life of their countrymen.... They wish to make the coolie self-conscious that he lives like a pig."

In the *Spectator* of November 19, 1937, an article, "Art, East and West," said: "Some [drawings] are like stills from the best Russian films [Wu Ko's refugees]; others combine a simple observation of fact with something of the traditional Chinese skill in calligraphy; most impressive of all are certain heads by Jack Chen who seems to have arrived by his own route at the position of artists like Rivera and Orozco, and to be capable not only of realism but of heroic realism, a form of art to which revolutionary movements in Europe have hardly led yet."

The lecture theme Jack had improvised, "Now China, and if you don't do something now, next you!" would be developed at scores of meetings. He spoke on his exhibit tour in Oxford, Cambridge, Dundee, Glasgow, Edinburgh, and Swansea. In Glasgow he made the usual mistake. He said "You, the English people..." and there was an answering correction, "We Scots!"

As Christmas approached, Jack received an invitation from the Writers Congress of America to speak at their next congress in New York. Jack left by boat with the reviews of his British tour in his pocket and a grand total of twenty-four dollars. If this seemed very little as recompense for hours of talking and weeks of traveling, it was because Jack thought very little about money. He had the middle-class intellectual's feeling that money was some-how not a fitting subject for conversation. In discussing a lecture or an article or drawing, the very last thing he would bring up would be "What will be the honorarium?" He would try to avoid the word "money" as if it were the plague. He also felt that to ask for money for doing a revolutionary duty was mean, something that should not be done. It was really by sheer luck that he earned enough to live on in those days. His health was excellent, and as long as he had enough money to go to the next place and a few days' liv-ing expenses in his pocket, he was untroubled about the future.

In the United States, Jack was immediately swept up in the same kind of propaganda activity as he had been in London. A devoted band of people in the Friends of China Society were playing the same role as the China Campaign Committee in England. Under their auspices, Jack put on his show in the ACA Galleries in New York.

The *New York Times* used one of the prints for a cover of its magazine, but the review Jack treasured most was printed in the *New York Journal American,* dated January 18, 1938. It was loud in its praises of his being a son worthy of his father. "Jack Chen is known to both Chinese and Japanese as 'Bitter-Brush,' because he has visually portrayed the fiery anti-Japanese sentiments his father portrayed in words before the ascendancy of General Chiang Kaishek's nationalist government in China. Chen, in one of his draw-ings, pictures the Rising Sun of Japan as a huge skull, coming up over the horizon of China."

Life Magazine sent round a reporter and gave Jack a four-page spread in early 1938. When Jack saw this opulent treatment, he thought his financial

UESDAY, JANUARY 18, 1938   15

China Cartoons Portray Japan As Oppressor

Bitter Satires Exhibited Here Aim to Rouse Public's Wrath

China's bitterest portrayal of Japan as a brutal oppressor of China—a collection of cartoons by contemporary Chinese artists—is in New York today on its 45,000 mile trek around the world to rouse anti-Japanese spirit.

Grouped at the American Contemporary Art gallery at 52 W. 8th st., are scores of vitrolic art works by Jack Chen, son of China's one time Minister of Foreign Affairs, Eugene Chen; by Paddy O'Shea, who, in spite of his Irish name is a Chinese; by Li Hua, Chen Yen-chiao, Li-Chun, Yeh Chen-Yo—and many others.

PORTRAYS SPIRIT.

Jack Chen is known to both Chinese and Japanese as "Bitter-Brush," because he has visually portrayed the fiery anti-Japanese sentiments his father portrayed in words before the ascendency of Gen. Chiang-Kai-Shek's nationalist government in China,

Chen, in one of his drawings, pictures the rising Sun of Japan as a huge skull, coming up over the horizon of China.

"The pieces in the exhibit are not for sale," Chen said. "The exhibit is to focus feeling on the oppression of China by Japan, and to show the rise in Chinese art. Your American critics have been very understanding."

Young China Speaks

ANUARY 15, 1938

JACK CHEN, SHOWING ONE OF HIS DRAWINGS
Leads Chinese Art Exhibit to Rouse Anti-Japanese Movement

China's Ace Contemporary Artist Depicts Fiery Feeling Against

A 1938 newspaper declared Jack Chen "Bitter-Brush, because he has visually portrayed the fiery anti-Japanese sentiments his father portrayed in words before the ascendancy of General Chaing-Kai-Shek's nationalist government in China."

problems would be solved for several months at least. Somewhat timidly he went to ask the magazine what the honorarium would be. The man Jack spoke to looked genuinely taken aback and pained.

"Why, this spread is worth thousands of dollars to you," he said truthfully. "Besides, we gave you a terrific review. We compare your cartoons with those of Daniel R. Fitzpatrick."

It was Jack's turn to be so taken aback by the largeness of this sum that he never said another word. *Life Magazine* did give him a good write-up. "The will to fight is symbolized by Jack Chen, in a peasant squatting beside his dead child, looking into a future in which there is no other course but to take up his gun and fight Japan. The emotion, the pathos and dignity of the figure suggest the best cartoons of Daniel R. Fitzpatrick of the *St. Louis Post-Dispatch.*"

After New York, Jack went on a cross-continental tour that took him and the exhibit to Boston, Detroit, Chicago, Los Angeles, San Francisco, and Berkeley. Everywhere he was overwhelmed by the compassion showed to him and his suffering country. But he also discovered that this tour was different from the last one. There was only the narrow English Channel to hold the Nazis at bay; the British support for China had a note of urgency in it. But for the Americans, the war was a long way away. Jack's lecture theme "Now China, and if you don't do something now, next you" did not seem to sink in, or did not sink in very deep. Jack had the impression that his audience felt their duty done once they had signed a check for a good cause. Many were warmhearted, but their way of life was so far removed from that of the common people of China that it was almost impossible to establish contact.

In Chicago, as soon as Jack walked into the entrance hall of a community center, he felt as if he'd entered the dream world of Chagall. Nothing seemed real, and yet everything was real. He saw the notice of his meeting posted side by side with a notice of another meeting to be held next. It was "The Japanese Tea Ceremony, a Talk with Demonstration by..."—someone from the Japanese consulate.

"That," the organizer of Jack's meeting said apologetically, "will be even better attended."

When Jack arrived in Hollywood, the stars were "taking up China." The Friends of China Society was headed by Sylvia Sidney. Her acting in *An American Tragedy* had left an indelible impression on Jack, and he was thrilled

Life Magazine, *early 1938.*

to meet her in person. She and her friends gave generously to aid China. Jack hated to seem ungrateful, but he couldn't help seeing here too a surreal understanding of the problems. But he was learning that he was there not only to make speeches, but also to hear speeches, and to connect with them in the manner acceptable to them.

Jack remembered that at one elegant cocktail party, he saw Paul Muni, Luise Rainer, Edward G. Robinson, and other stars he greatly admired. Boosted by their attention, Jack gave a great deal of effort to talking about events in

China, with the drawings as illustrations. During the intermission, uniformed servants, holding silver trays of delicacies and wines, gingerly threaded their way among the guests. A lady, standing nearby, arched her well-picked and well-painted eyebrows, asking what Chinese delicacies he would recommend for such a party.

"They drink tea made with water from the melted snow on the petals of winter plum blossoms," Jack deadpanned.

"How very quaint," she said as another question struck her. "The resistance fighters in your drawings are all carrying spears and knives. Is it because you like to draw them that way, you know, dramatically quaint?"

"They don't have anything else to defend themselves with."

"Why don't they ask the government for help?"

"It will take a revolution to get it," Jack answered with a smile, acknowledging the wisdom of her question.

The lady thought it was a repartee. Poking fun at government made for lively conversation. After everyone raved about the refreshment and art, the company enjoyed itself for an hour on the theme that what was needed here in the States was a real revolution to stop buying Japanese silk stockings.

Jack immediately cashed in on the subject and interposed: "And to stop selling scrap iron to Japan."

★ 22 ★

YANAN INTERLUDE

In the summer of 1938, Jack traveled back to Canton and then on to Hankou in the Wuhan area, Chiang Kaishek's temporary wartime capital after Nanjing had fallen to Japan in December 1937. Jack had been to Hankou in 1927 and had been welcomed then as his father's son. This time he returned in triumph, a hero in his own right. His exhibit tour was hailed as a means of pillorying Japanese aggression and praised for winning appreciation and sympathy of a depth never before accorded by the artists in the West to those of the East.

Both Chiang Kaishek and his fourth wife, Mayling Soong, extended an invitation to Jack, as well as Zhou Enlai, whose Party again had come aboveground as an ally in the Second United Front, although there were tough restrictions on its activities. Jack knew that if he wanted to see his communist friends, he had better pay his respects to Chiang Kaishek first.

One morning in July, Jack got a call from Hollington Tong, Chiang's press secretary. "The Generalissimo and Madame Chiang will receive you today."

For security reasons, Jack was not told where the meeting would be, or even exactly when. He was to meet Hollington Tong at the Wuchang Ferry, and be whisked away in a limousine to a villa on the edge of a park overlooking the Yangzi. The house was in the modern style, with well-kept gardens. Mayling's drawing room was elegantly furnished just as she was elegantly garbed, without ostentation or luxury. It fitted the drawing room of the first lady of a great but embattled nation, unwillingly asking its friends for aid against a powerful enemy. She wore a well-fitting black brocade gown, cut in the Chinese style with short sleeves, a modest slit on each side, and a modest collar with a simple gold necklace. Only her wedding ring adorned her fingers.

"Ah, Jack, how good to see you," Mayling said with every sign of joy in her meticulously made-up face. "Take a seat here," she said, indicating a space beside herself on the sofa.

Tea was laid, and Hollington Tong, smiling benignly, departed when Chiang Kaishek walked in. Jack marveled at their skill at synchronizing every step they took.

Both husband and wife were affable. Like old friends, they were eager to do some catching-up, as if the betrayal and massacre had never taken place. How was his father? How was his stepmother, a close friend of Chingling's? And his sisters?

"They are all well and busy. Thank you for asking," Jack answered.

Mayling continued: "I see you are a writer, like your father. We need good writers who can tell the world the truth about China and this war."

"I am trying to do that."

The Generalissimo left after one more sip of tea. Altogether he had graced the small tea party for about ten minutes, a rule set by his handlers.

After another ten minutes, Mayling looked at her watch, a small platinum timepiece on a black moiré ribbon on her wrist. "No more time. What a pity. If you stay on, we must meet again for a longer talk."

She pressed a bell and Hollington Tong appeared, still smiling, to lead Jack out.

Jack seized a moment to ask for a safe-conduct to Yanan.

"Of course," Mayling agreed graciously after an indiscernible pause. "Hollington will see to that."

August in Hankou was sweltering. The Communist Liaison Office was on Middle Street in the former Japanese concession. The place was rather rundown and, because it was poorly ventilated, the air was stuffy, reeking of sweat and tobacco smoke. Jack was not surprised that Chiang Kaishek put his communist friends in an eyesore of a house, tucked away from the public. He climbed a rickety staircase. A small room was partitioned from part of the first landing. The door was half open, and Jack saw a man sitting at a desk. He heard Jack's footsteps and peered out.

"Hello, Comrade Wang Ming," Jack called out.

Wang Ming, Stalin's man, looked abashed, as if he himself had been partitioned off into this narrow corner. He greeted Jack and brought him to a larger, more airy room to meet with Zhou Enlai. Zhou was forty now. He had fine crow's-feet around the corners of his eyes, but his hair was still black without a tinge of gray. He still walked with a spring, light and quick. No sooner had Jack crossed the threshold than the air-raid siren sounded.

"You wait for me downstairs," Zhou said to Jack. "I'll take you out of the city in my car."

The rather decrepit automobile wheezed off. Miraculously, it got them to the air-raid shelter before the bombs were dropped. The shelter was a public place, and it would not be discreet to talk about politics, but Jack did get around to telling Zhou that he was to take his exhibition to Yanan, which Zhou thought a good idea. Jack did not get another chance to see Zhou in Hankou.

On his return to the hotel, Jack received a message from Hollington Tong: the day after next, there would be a convoy of trucks going to Xian, a stopover in the middle of Jack's journey.

"I am ready," Jack responded quickly. "My friend Wu Ko wants to go with me. I need him to act as my interpreter."

As twilight came the next day, Jack went with Wu Ko to the Yangzi pier. They crossed the dark river in a motorboat and on the other side, under the walls of Wuchang, found the convoy of trucks about to start. There was a rush to board the truck.

"Hold on," the driver shouted. "Supplies first, and then passengers. Lend a hand with the gasoline drums and put the bales on top, and then you can get on yourselves."

Under his direction, the heavier drums and boxes were arranged in a solid jigsaw on the floor of the truck, bedding, duffel bags, and baskets spread on them. At last Jack, Wu Ko, and everyone else piled themselves on top.

"I hope our truck won't overturn," Jack groaned.

"Gasoline is as precious as blood. Selling it in the black market will make a lot of money," Wu Ko said in a low voice.

"So blatantly open?"

"Why are you surprised? They are simply following the examples of Madame Chiang Kaishek and her siblings. They are the biggest profiteers, except for Madame Sun Yatsen."

With lights dimmed, they set off, one behind the other.

Jack and Wu Ko departed from the Kuomintang convoy at Xian and got on a truck provided by the Communist Liaison Office. The city was just waking up as Jack's truck lumbered through the gateway and took the road north. By the time it reached the city gate, there were two more trucks to join the convoy. It was then that Jack had a chance to see who his new traveling companions were. There were no more black marketeers, but men and women from various walks of life. These students, actors, artists, scholars, doctors, engineers, philosophers, journalists, and others formed the strangest pilgrimage of modern China, each hopefully seeking in Yanan the answer to their questions.

Jack sat in the front of the truck and had a good view of the road ahead. The scenery was reminiscent of the trip he had made with Borodin eleven years earlier; very little had changed. The ancient loess plateau was still cut by innumerable ravines, carved out over the centuries by the rain-fed rivulets. In some cases, the tops of the plateau islands were joined by narrow land bridges. In other places, the land bridges had eroded completely and collapsed, and the road took the truck laboriously down one side of the ravine and up the other, taking perhaps an hour to travel a couple of hundred yards.

Descending from the plateau into a green wooded valley, Jack heard the word going around that they were approaching Yanan. Soon after that, a big church built by missionaries came into sight. The truck entered the valley of the Fen River. High above appeared the pagoda on the hilltop that marked Yanan, and within a few minutes the truck was rolling up the main street to Jack's destination.

The roadway was only a little wider than the truck. On either side were open-fronted shops on the sidewalk, three steps from the road. Most were one story high, with wood and plaster walls and gray tile roofs. Down the road, one low building stood out by a make-believe lantern of red cotton fringe attached to a hoop hanging from a pole, which denoted Yanan's one and only restaurant. Nearly every shop had blue shutters, now stacked by their open fronts. Apparently the mayor had gotten hold of this blue paint from somewhere and had persuaded the merchants to spruce up their shop fronts with it. Here and there was a two-story building with a fretted balustrade verandah, or a tree-lined narrow alley opening off the main street. Yanan was a very poor northwestern county town. And yet it was not like any other town Jack had passed on the road. The blue shutters made the Red Center unique.

Halfway up the road, Jack's truck neared an odd couple going in the opposite direction. The man, big and tall, wore a blue cotton uniform that was a shade too large for him so that it would shrink comfortably to the right size in the first wash. The trousers were turned up in a generous cuff. His bodyguard was a youngster in his early teens, short and small, dressed in a gray army uniform and carrying an enormous old German Mauser. At the sight of the man in blue, the driver set up a shout: "Chairman Mao, we've come back!"

Jack leaned over and shouted to the driver: "Stop a minute!"

Mao Zedong, like every other pedestrian, stepped from the roadway to let the trucks pass. He saw Jack, who put his head out the side window, and seemed to search in his memory for who the young man was.

"I am the son of Chen Youren," Jack called out his father's name in Chinese, jumping out.

A smile of recognition appeared on Mao's face, and he waved his right arm in a gesture of welcome. "I have been told you were coming. Welcome! You have grown up, not so much taller as broader," he said in a benign manner. "Come to see me this afternoon."

"I will." Jack was pleased with Mao's readiness to receive him.

The trucks swung right, into the gate of the guesthouse compound. It was a simple place, with rows of single rooms on three sides, newly built and whitewashed, each with a brick bed covered with a sorghum mat. Some rooms had rough tables under the windows, which were covered with wooden, papered lattices. No bathrooms. A row of enameled basins in the courtyard constituted the washing arrangements. A bath could be taken in the River Fen, which flowed by the town. That was just what Jack needed.

The river, where young people were bathing and splashing around, was comfortably cool under the August sun. After they had washed off the yellow dust that covered their hair, body, and limbs with a thin film, they put on clean shirts and pants. The next thing they needed was a meal. The hostel provided that. With their stomachs full, they set out for Mao's residence.

Mao Zedong at that time was not living in the cave that would become his home a year later, but in a two-room stone cottage in town. The little bodyguard showed Jack and Wu Ko in. Mao was in shirtsleeves, a rather slight youngish figure. He would be lost in a large crowd, but paradoxically would stand out in a small group in any room. He still wore his hair rather long and disheveled, and still had the slightly frowning expression, and the vertical line between his eyes was deeper than it had been.

Jack draws in front of his room in Yanan's guesthouse, 1938.

The future third Madame Mao Zedong (Jiang Qing) (right), who would run the violent purge—the Cultural Revolution—arrived in Yanan in the summer of 1938, and stayed in the same guesthouse with her mother. Jack took this photo.

The room was austerity itself. It had a couple of benches without backs, an old wicker chair covered with a faded rug, a large desk filled with papers and books, an ink stone, and several brushes in a stand. His bed was in the other room. Between the rooms there was no door but a length of much-washed white cotton held up on a string and drawn half open. On a rickety side table was a thermos bottle and a few enameled bowls. The floor was of flagstone. The central part of the latticed window was covered with glass that let in plenty of light. The rest of the window was covered with paper.

Mao offered his guests tea from the flask, which turned out to be more water than tea. Sipping, they exchanged pleasantries like old friends, happy to see each other after so many tumultuous years.

"Now tell me what you think of Yanan," Mao said, stretching his right hand out to Jack.

"I came up to look around. I hope to draw and write about what I see here," Jack said.

"Excellent!" Mao burst out with a mixture of approbation and delight. "We need journalists and artists like you to tell people who we are and what we are working for. See what you like. Don't hesitate to ask questions or give your suggestions."

"I would like to see as many things as possible," Jack answered.

"I am sure our mutual friend, Zhou Yang, can arrange it for you," Mao said. "He is working in the Lu Xun Art Academy. Just tell him what you wish to see."

Jack expressed regret at not having been able to meet Lu Xun, a pioneer of modern Chinese literature, before his death. He was now glad to visit the academy established in his memory.

The sun was sinking behind the pagoda, and Jack felt that the chat was at an end. He got up from his chair, and so did Mao and Wu Ko.

"We'll have a chat after you get your bearings," Mao said, seeing them to the door where the little bodyguard was sitting on a bench whittling a piece of wood, like a child with no other toys to play with.

Still recovering from the trip, Jack went to bed early and fell soundly asleep. The freshness of the countryside was in the air when Jack woke up the next morning. Brushing his teeth and washing his face in the courtyard, he heard someone asking for him. One of the girl students of the Lu Xun Art Academy had come to fetch him and Wu Ko. They would breakfast with the students. They climbed the mountain behind the town, walking up what looked like a goat path to a level space before a group of a dozen caves. Outside on the ground, bowls and chopsticks had been set out for breakfast, the bowls in sets of five with the chopsticks laid out in a five-pointed star design.

The fair-complected Zhou Yang was brown from the sun, dressed in an army uniform, although he did not look soldierly. He laughingly motioned Jack to take the seat of an honored guest on the ground. Breakfast was Spartan in its simplicity: wheat porridge and pickles. Zhou Yang asked what Jack would like to do after the meal.

"Anything an artist does. The daily routine," Jack answered.

"You want to see our art class?" Zhou Yang asked, and led the two newcomers back down the mountainside.

The valley floor the path ran through was covered with bushes three or four feet tall. As he went, Zhou Yang gave a piercing blast on a whistle, so loud that the bushes suddenly woke up and came alive. A couple of dozen young faces emerged, wreathed in smiles under large peasant cartwheel hats, camouflaged with fronds of greenery.

"They are learning guerrilla warfare tactics," Zhou Yang explained. "This lesson in camouflage is the first lesson for an artist in a guerrilla area. You have to learn it to survive, if you want to draw here."

Women militia of Yanan, 1938.

Jack was asked to give an impromptu lecture on art. He took out some of his own drawings and the drawings of the other artists. The students were curious to know which artists had influenced him the most. When he answered Daumier, they looked at one another in amazement. They had expected him to cite a proletarian Soviet artist. How come it was a French bourgeois artist? Because he strove to draw the Chinese poor as Daumier had drawn the French poor, Jack explained: the washwoman was as regal as a queen, and the shrimp girl was as pretty as a princess. Look at his peasants' portraits, Jack pointed out, they bore suffering with dignity.

Jack made this declaration to a round of cheers. He knew at this moment what he wanted to do. Given the lack of communication with the outside art communities and the lack of funds, these art students knew little about the finest masters of the art world. He could use his knowledge to help enlarge their art vocabulary during his short stay.

On the other hand, he was learning too. The next lesson Zhou Yang urged him to take was a militia drill. The beating of drums and gongs sounded like distant thunder rolling into the glade where he held court, and instantly the students put on their large peasant cartwheel hats camouflaged with leaves and twigs, and vanished into the bushes. In less than half an hour, the hoes, spades, shovels, scythes, and other tools suddenly became weapons, and the whole place was poised for war—the whole of Yanan an armed camp. There was no way to tell the fighters from the general populace.

Then came the most interesting part of the maneuvers. Jack, on Zhou Yang's heels, threaded through a labyrinth of carts, oxen, mules, stretcher-carriers, and propaganda workers who flanked the road, beat drums and gongs, shouted anti-oppression slogans, and sang battle hymns to propel the foot soldiers, among them Zhou Yang's art students, into battle. Finally Jack and Zhou Yang came around to the foot of the hills. A peasant lad riding on a donkey was waiting for them. He was one of the few local guides who knew the trail leading to where Zhou Yang wanted to take Jack.

The donkey trotted at a leisurely pace on a gravel path. At times, while turning a corner, its two front feet poised as if to trot into a deep ravine.

"Watch out!" Jack cried in alarm.

The peasant lad nimbly turned the beast of burden. He laughed and spread his arms like a triumphant magician pulling off a trick. Just when they came to the edge of a cliff and the path seemed lost, a lovely village appeared with rows of willow trees and bright flowers. A detachment of peasant militia men and women had gathered in the village square, training rifles on a bull's-eye.

"This is one of the countless mountain villages where our fighters retreat and get recharged," Zhou Yang explained proudly.

They had to make their way down before dark: it was too perilous to travel on the narrow, rugged path at night. Jack took a last look up the crest as he neared the valley. The thick blanket of trees and shrubs gave no hint that any humans were living there. They were invisible.

Busily occupied, Jack scarcely noticed how swiftly time flew by. Then he was invited to their headquarters by Mao Zedong and Zhou Enlai, who had come from Hankou for some conference. Jack was glad he had put off this interview until he had seen something of the region and its life. Now he had some context in which to understand and check their ideas. Wu Ko went with him. They made their way across the Yan River, up the narrow cliff highway to the platform that fronted the headquarters caves; and here Jack found Mao, Zhou, and some other officials sitting on stools or benches, enjoying the afternoon sunshine. An apparently veteran soldier, in a faded gray uniform with puttees, stood up first, but did not come forward until Mao beckoned him. On hearing his name, Jack was a little taken aback. Could this self-effacing man be the flaming founder of the Red Army? Jack could find no trace of his wild past in the Zhu De who was shaking his hand.

"How do you like Yanan?" Mao asked Jack, while ushering them into one of the caves. "It is quiet here," he explained. "We can talk better." And when they were seated in a square, he added, "Please tell us your impressions."

"Excellent!" Jack enthused.

While talking briefly, Jack at once wondered if he could use this interview to extract more information. Here he was sitting before two inventors of modern guerrilla warfare, who only ten years ago had been two hunted men at the head of a band of a few hundred peasant insurgents. They had hidden out then in a bandits' lair on Jinggang Mountain; now, sitting with their close comrades in this bare cave, they were governing areas containing tens of millions of people and giving both the Japanese and Chiang Kaishek sleepless nights.

"You saw our mountain villages, or shall we say mountain fortresses? Like the Jinggang Mountain, they are our bases to fight the guerrilla war, which is a war we can afford to fight. We have no resources except for the support of the people," Mao said. He had the habit of speaking rapidly as if words crowded his mind and clamored to get out. "Part of the training our soldiers get is working in the fields to get acquainted with the local peasants. This way, we let them get to know us better, and they will see that we come to work with them and for them. Our relationship with the locals is like fish and water. We are the fish, and the locals are the water. Without water, the fish die. Without the cooperation of the locals, there will be no guerrilla war. That is why our enemies cannot prevail, for they are hated by the locals. They are fish out of water. Above all, we don't mobilize the poor people into a poor people's war by going out to press-gang them." A jab at Japan's conscripted army, as well as at Chiang Kaishek's mercenaries.

Zhu De weighed in quietly. They had learned their lesson in 1927: they simply did not have the material resources to fight a conventional war. The alternative was guerrilla warfare. "But at times, frontal combat should not be avoided: for example, the Battle of Pingxinguan Pass is one. We call it mobile guerrilla warfare, a combination of guerrilla and conventional warfare. We don't always hit and run in the hills."

The Battle of Pingxinguan Pass was the first victory over the Japanese, and it showed to the world that the communists were better soldiers than Chiang Kaishek's army. In September 1937, Zhu De's officers enticed their enemies into a narrow valley where they could not use their tanks and artillery, at least not effectively. With the guerrilla fighters reinforcing the rear in the hills, the communist soldiers wiped out a whole enemy division with nothing more than rifles and machine-gun fire.

"Can you think of a parallel to our kind of warfare?" Zhou Enlai asked Jack.

Jack was slightly puzzled by Zhou's interjection. He did not know that, at the time, Mao had been arguing for his mountain guerrilla warfare against the mobile guerrilla warfare favored by both Zhou Enlai and Zhu De.[1] He responded to Zhou's question with a quick search in his mind. Maybe Xenophon's Persian expedition was somewhat comparable, in which ten thousand Greeks, in the late fifth century B.C., first fought under the command of a Persian prince and then fought their way back home. "There is a big difference, though, between our Long March and their Long March. They were mercenaries. We fight for the salvation of our own country," Jack said.

Mao frowned at the tip of a cigarette butt held in his hand, as if something was amiss in Jack's speech. "Our Long March is incomparable."

"Well, anyway, comparison is unfair," Zhu De demurred, darting a sideways glance at Mao.

"What about your long march?" Zhou Enlai asked Jack, changing the subject seamlessly.

Before Jack realized it, an intimate note had crept into the conversation. They listened to him recounting the exhibit tours while looking at the drawings spread on a large table in the middle of the room. His monologue was only punctured by a few questions, questions friends would ask in a reunion gathering.

"What was the most memorable happening?" Zhou asked.

Jack thought for a minute and answered. In San Francisco, his last stop in the United States, he had been the guest of a rich and generous elderly lady who lived on Nob Hill. One day, she took him out for a drive in her large black chauffeured car. It was an open touring car, and the chauffeur threw a rug over their knees. They drove across the Golden Gate Bridge to the sequoias. On the way, Jack saw a bank of grass and flowers and exclaimed his appreciation of their beauty. "Would you like some?" the elderly lady asked. Jack said yes, and she told her chauffeur to stop. The chauffeur braked and got out of the car. Jack thought he was going to open the car door for him, but no, the chauffer went to the bank and picked a handful of flowers, which he gave to his mistress who sat on the side closer to him. When she passed the colorful bunch to Jack, he was so moved by her thoughtfulness that he bent low over her proffering hand and kissed it.

"Rather trivial," Jack said with a self-deprecating grin.

"Not at all. There is nothing more human than enjoying little, fleeting joys when you can. You prove to your generous friend that you are as human as she is. That put some doubt in her mind about the Japanese propaganda that makes us out to be some sort of subhumans who deserve to be conquered," Zhou Enlai said. "Your father once told me that it was important to know the cultural tradition of someone I intended to approach. I think your father must be very pleased with what you have done for the country and the people."

There was no praise that touched Jack more deeply than telling him he was his father's son. Getting into an exalted state of excitement, Jack went on to recount how the British and American artists had rallied magnificently. In exchange for Jack's offering of modern Chinese graphic art, the first in Britain, they collected a fine exhibition of their own work. Pearl Bider, Lord Hastings, John Nash, and others contributed. Jack's speeches appealed most to the American artists of social comment—Rifka Angel, George Biddle, Fred Ellis, Wanda Gag, William Gropper, Rockwell Kent, Max Weber, and others donated their work with the expressed hope that their exhibition on Jack's return to China might contribute toward the medical relief of China's wounded soldiers and bring about a more effective organization among artists in China in a worldwide campaign for peace, democracy, and cultural progress.

"I would like to know if it is possible to move my base and family to Yanan," Jack said.

They all considered. Zhou Enlai was the first to speak: "I would like to add a little bit to your plan. If it is possible, could you live alternately in Yanan and abroad?"

In an earnest voice, Zhou went on with his suggestion: "I have read the clippings about your exhibit tours carefully. I am impressed by the fact that you have reached people that we are not able to. You have a gift for languages, for communicating with Western audiences. Furthermore, you have the universal language of art at your disposal. You will be of great help to us if you can use your talents to bridge the gap.

"There is another reason we would like you to do the go-between work. There are a few American journalists who tell the truth about us to the Western audience, but we need you, a Chinese and the son of a renowned Chinese revolutionary, who, while allying with the Soviet Union, never neglected to reach for the West. There is no one more fit to help us open a window onto the outside world."

"The window I am able to open is very small," Jack said with genuine regret.

"When there is no big window, a small one is of big significance," Zhou said judiciously.

"When you come back, please bring your father with you," Mao Zedong interposed. "We invite him to visit Yanan. The international situation is touch-and-go, and especially so for Mr. Chen, who is in exile."

"Please tell him that he always has a home here. We remember his help in a time of extreme need," Zhu De said. There was an air of simple sincerity about the old soldier that Jack believed.

"We are looking forward to welcoming you back and working with you," Zhou said, rounding off the meeting.

It was not difficult for Jack to figure out why they, all extremely busy men, had received him with such graciousness: he had a hunch that making contact with the West was the topic they wanted very much to discuss with him. But he did not know how much, as he was unaware of a heated debate being carried on inside the Party. On the one side were Mao Zedong, Zhou Enlai, and Zhu De, who, for the most part, advocated guerrilla warfare. The other side was represented by Wang Ming, who argued for Stalin, who was pressuring them to adopt the so-called frontal combat. Stalin's mind was transparent. He knew the regular army led by Mao and Zhu De was undermanned and poorly equipped, but it could be used as cannon fodder to divert Japan's attention from crossing Manchuria's border into the Asian part of the Soviet Union.

A photo of Jack's English family.

Beggars had no choice, Stalin figured. Such being the case, he doled out a pitifully small amount, about three hundred thousand U.S. dollars,[2] as the price for getting his Chinese comrades under his command. Chiang Kaishek was worth much more. In the same year, 1938, Stalin offered one hundred million U.S. dollars to Chiang as his ally in the war of anti-Japanese aggression.[3] Mao, Zhou, and Zhu De endured the humiliation not only of the token financial assistance, but also of the limited recognition Stalin gave. The Chinese Communist Party was ignored and isolated by the entire international community. Breaking through the blockade was a matter of life and death.

When Jack said good-bye to his friends, he promised to come back within six or eight months. He could never have dreamed it would take eight years.

Before he reached London in the spring of 1939, he put on the exhibit in Paris, Bordeaux, and Amsterdam. While waiting for his reentry visa from the Soviet embassy there, the Second World War broke out. During the war, Jack, a British citizen and thirty-one years old, was not permitted to leave England, although he was not drafted. In later years, Jack compressed the next six or seven years into a hodgepodge of disjointed incidents, a few of which stood out in his memory. A divorce from his Russian wife and the loss of custody of his son, Danny; a marriage with an English woman, Betty Aaronson, and the birth of their son, Chenny; the bombing of London and the destruction of his best drawings; joining the war effort to defend England; working with the British Communist Party and the left wing of the Labour Party to push the "other China," the China of the communist-ruled Border Regions, into the public consciousness. Jack was fully aware that his voice was tiny, but he was the only one in London who had observed life in Yanan and the Border Regions at close quarters. The field was so thin that a tiny voice echoed in the virtually empty space.

★23★

How Jack's Path Crossed with Mine

On a March night in 1942, a caravan moved northward from the communist-ruled Border Regions between Jiangsu and Shandong Provinces. Among them a thin, tall middle-aged man huddled in an old cotton-padded jacket, braving the cold wind. Liu Shaoqi, who ran the region, had received a cable from Mao Zedong, asking him to take part in the Seventh Party Congress in early 1943. The journey was long and difficult, traversing four provinces and crossing over or skirting around areas occupied by the Japanese or Chiang Kaishek's troops. Now and then he had to stop over, sometimes for weeks, to avoid being caught and to keep up his administrative work, since there were quite a few pockets of guerrilla resistance scattered along the road.

At every stopover where a cable could reach, there was one awaiting him. Mao Zedong gave detailed instructions for Liu's security and showed a deep concern that he had never shown for his other peers. Mao's affection was, of course, selective. He was planning to make a clean sweep of Stalin's influence in his Party, and he needed a capable, tough, like-minded ally. After the Germans' invasion of Russia in 1941, Stalin's forces were so depleted that he could hardly look after Russia's Asian front. His best bet was to use the combined forces of Mao Zedong and Chiang Kaishek to bog down the Japanese troops in China. But it seemed that Mao and Chiang were more wary of one another than of Japan. Each was more interested in preserving and expanding his territory. Stalin was in no position to give orders to Chiang, but he thought he was fully entitled to push Mao around. He strong-armed the Chinese communists to make almost unconditional concessions to Chiang Kaishek. Many of Mao's colleagues, including Zhou Enlai and Zhu De, advised patience and caution while dealing with the Soviet dictator, but Mao decided otherwise.

Mao's purge was always more than thorough. It hit Wang Ming so hard that he fled to Moscow and never returned. Wang Ming, however, was not the only target Mao had in mind. Mao next turned his guns on Zhou, Zhu De, and others who had put up with Wang Ming. It went without saying that Mao had conveniently forgotten his own compromises with Moscow. The onslaught was most vicious on Zhou Enlai; it wounded him so dreadfully that he could not mention the Yanan Purge even after a long lapse of time. It created permanent bad blood between him and Liu Shaoqi, whom he viewed as Mao's chief abettor.[1] It should be noted that the top activists in the purge were nearly all returned students from the Soviet Union, but converted by Mao. They were men with Stalinist training, and perhaps Stalinist impulses, who did not disagree with Mao as long as he could make use of them.

Mao Zedong took advantage of this turning point in the Party to fill in the ideological void the Soviets had left behind. From now on, they would think and act Chinese. The term "Mao Zedong Thought" came into being, although "Mao Zedong Thought" was the sum total of the Party's theoretical and practical experiences, with contributions by other communist leaders as well. For example, Zhu De contributed to the essay on guerrilla warfare, and Zhou Enlai to the theory of the United Front. But Mao penned the "Thought" and felt justified in claiming it as his own property.

The convulsion was over when Jack finally returned to China in 1946 as a correspondent for the English paper *Reynold's News,* the Sunday paper of the Cooperative Movement. He reached Shanghai just in time for another round of civil war between the Communist Party and Chiang Kaishek. The clash surprised no one. It was bound to happen, as the guerrilla zone had been expanding into what Chiang deemed his territories. China was not big enough for both Chiang and Mao.

Without thinking, Jack decided he was going to cover the civil war with his drawings and writings. He felt he was at the peak of his creative power, and he should dedicate the best years of his life to the cause. He revisited Yanan, where his old friends welcomed him with open arms. A meeting was scheduled. Jack attended it with a big album of his drawings and a letter from the chairman of the British Communist Party, Harry Pollitt. Jack had joined the British Party in 1940 or 1941 for one reason only: the British Communist Party was the only political party in London in which, and with which, Jack could rally support for sending medical supplies to the communist-ruled regions. His relationship with them ended when he returned to China in 1950 for good.

The reception was overwhelming. All the Political Bureau members who were in Yanan came. The interpreter assigned to Jack was Liao Chengzhi, a

Central Committee member and son of Eugene's close comrade-in-arms Liao Zhongkai. Jack was received as an old friend and also an envoy from a fraternal party. When Jack held up his camera to take a picture of them, he noticed Mao turning to beckon a timorous man with a dour face to come forth and stand next to him on his right side. The man was a stranger to Jack, but his name, Liu Shaoqi, rang a vague, distant bell in Jack's head.

Liu shook hands with Jack, a constrained smile crossing his thin face as if he had an aching tooth. His words, though, were warm as he recalled how proud he was when, in 1927, he and numerous others had marched into the newly returned British concession of Hankou with Eugene Chen at their head.

Pollitt's letter had asked what the British Party could do to help. Mao's and the other leaders' reply caught Jack so unaware that he begged for some time to think it over: they asked if he could return to London to start the New China News Agency.[2] This would be the first and only overseas Chinese communist news agency in the Western world. They needed him to tell their version of what was happening in the civil war, because virtually all the overseas news agencies got the story from Chiang Kaishek. Chiang, of course, predicted that his final victory was in sight.

After the official meeting, Zhou Enlai privately asked Jack to deliver a letter[3] and a highly confidential oral message to Soong Chingling, Sun Yatsen's widow. The oral message underscored China's need for reconstruction money from the United States and other Western nations through trade. Zhou thought China was more likely to get them to agree if China formed a multi-party, broad-based coalition government with Soong Chingling as the chief of state. It was a message that would not be taken lightly. Zhou Enlai was responsible for the implementation of his party's United Front policy and was most trusted by the noncommunist personages, so it was appropriate for him to have penned the letter. And it was also appropriate to be delivered by the son of Sun Yatsen's "closest friend" to Sun's widow, the keeper of Sun's legacy.

Zhou Enlai hoped to cultivate a friendly relationship with the Western countries, particularly the United States, in much the same manner that Jack's father, Eugene, had, which instantly struck a sympathetic response in Jack. In the mid-thirties, Eugene had moved to a border town between Canton and the British colony Hong Kong. In early 1942, after the attack on Pearl Harbor, Japanese soldiers marched into and occupied Hong Kong. They arrested Eugene, who was hiding in a hotel there. From Hong Kong, he was moved under armed escort to Shanghai's French concession, where the Japanese army had also taken over. Eugene was put under house arrest, but refused to collaborate with the enemy. In May 1944, the Japanese occupation authority made a last attempt to break Eugene's will. Either he succumb or else, they warned. Eugene ignored their ultimatum. He had a dental problem; the Japanese garrison commander sent a doctor to operate on him, and he died. It was suspected that the occupying Japanese forces had ordered the killing. Eugene had been forced to find refuge in Hong Kong because he was being persecuted by Chiang Kaishek. Thus, Jack held Chiang accountable for his father's death. Jack felt obligated to do everything he could to drive Chiang into exile. He agreed to accept the task entrusted to him. But he wanted to come home to China and settle down as soon as the civil war was won.

Jack returned to Beijing in 1950 with his young son, Chenny, whose mother Betty had died in 1948 or 1949. I arrived in Beijing about the same time, working in the Department of Film Scenario Writing. Far away from my domineering mother, who lived in Shanghai, I felt free seeking a writing career. However, Mother still had a remote control over me. Before I left home, I had promised her that I would choose a suitable husband, that I would not become an old maid and disgrace her. I did not think it would be a difficult task when I looked in the mirror. My eyes, to borrow my mother's words, could do the talking better than my tongue, which, in all modesty, was lively. I had what the Chinese approvingly described as a melon-seed face that accentuated my fine cheekbones and small chin. I was pretty and presentable, and therefore eligible.

But I was young and not in a hurry to get married. Mother had told me that it took time to find the right man. I trusted my network of former schoolmates with the choice of a hunting ground where suitable quarries were waiting to be caught. One of my friends, Dora Zhang, introduced Jack to me at a ball.

I did not like him at first. The narrow space between his thick, graying eyebrows gave the impression of a perpetual scowl. But Dora Zhang was persistent. She knew Jack fairly well; they were colleagues in the Foreign Languages Bureau.

"He wants you to give him a chance to pour out his grand passion." A mischievous smile appeared on Dora's moon-shaped face. "Why don't you try him out?"

One conversation led to another. The more he told me about himself, the more I knew I had found an original. When he came back to Beijing in 1950, he could have chosen any job he wanted. But he chose to edit and draw for *People's China,* the new English-language magazine. His drawings and the articles he edited or wrote were a little too rosy, but he had a legitimate excuse: in the early fifties, right after the victory of the revolution, he was in a state of great elation, even euphoria.

"I have no ambition for myself. I work for the revolution without any intention of grabbing fame or position or money," he said.

I caught a flicker of self-righteous pride in his speech, but because it was expressed in a good-humored, quiet manner, it was not offensive.

I met him in the early 1950s, but I agreed to marry him only in 1958. It was a long courtship, with quite a few twists and turns. The decisive year was 1957. If I'd wanted to chronicle my life since 1950, it would read like this: I survived this purge and that purge and I fared better or worse in between. Purges were a part of our lives. We lived from one purge to the next. Every year, or every other year, we had to cope with a new one. This was billed by Mao Zedong as the interminable class struggle to keep everybody in line. I was the kind of person that Mao Zedong was determined to remold. One way to achieve this was to tear me apart in a purge; and before I had time to patch myself up, another purge was launched. All that was supposed to have the effect Mao desired on my bourgeois soul: after the crucible, a brand-new proletarian was born. This crucible theory wore me out. At the end of the Anti-Rightists' purge of 1957, I was so sick and tired that I was ready to surrender, to stop thinking, to let the purge activists turn me into a robot and to send me to a labor camp.

One day, an office boy came to tell me that I had a visitor waiting at the gate. An uninvited visitor could be a euphemism for the police. A colleague who shared my office had been spirited out this way without warning. He was not even allowed to take a toothbrush. As I walked down the long, dim hall, I told myself I would meet my doom with dignity, chin up, shoulders straight, and all that. My heart missed a beat when the man's features became clearer. Jack and I had had one of our breakups nearly a year previously. I had thought it was final. But here he was, in a dark blue jacket and pants, standing with his back against a gray wall, his head leaning slightly on his left shoulder, his hands clasped at his back. He watched me in intense wonder, as though I had been floating down from outer space.

"You should not be seen in the wrong company. I may soon be headed for a labor camp," I said, elbowing him into an alley.

Jack handed me a small package. "A gift I bought on the Silk Road. Open it."

A green lace head kerchief. "From the Silk Road? That is a long way from here."

"You are constantly in my thoughts, far or near," he said.

I stared at him for a long minute. Trembling slightly, I leaned against the wall of a house for support. "Jack, you are puzzling me. How come?"

"It is a long story. I'll try to make it as short as I can. Thirty years ago—" he stopped and dismissed it with a wave of his right hand. "Too long ago. Let me just put it this way. Someone drew a Magic Circle around me, and all the purges pass me by."

I knew Jack's father had been Eugene Chen, a steadfast ally and friend to the Communist Party. "Does your father's name contribute to the forming of this Magic Circle?"

"I have inherited some goodwill from my old man, but I don't rest on his laurels," he said, hinting that there were other reasons for his privileges.

What he had told me piqued my curiosity, and what he had kept unsaid was titillating, but I didn't push him. I let him take his time accepting me into his confidence.

"So the Party committee in your office gave you a vacation in Xinjiang in the midst of a savage purge they were conducting?" After a moment of musing, I added, "Jack, I think I have a vague idea of what you're saying. Events that happened long ago have something to do with your sightseeing on the Silk Road. Let's leave it at that."

Naturally, I wanted to get into Jack's Magic Circle, and we were married in April 1958. Hiding myself in the Magic Circle after work in my office, I became momentarily oblivious to my surroundings and turned a deaf ear to yet another round of the class war that Mao Zedong was drumming up during the first part of 1958, baptized as the Great Leap Forward. We would leap into instant industrialization by brutally exploiting the peasants. It thoroughly demoralized the peasants. Agricultural production fell sharply. Hunger stalked the land. The economy was on the verge of collapsing.

Mao, with a typical peasant mentality, was inclined to think that the land was the sole source of wealth. This mentality was exacerbated by an American embargo, which provided Mao a perfect pretext to go his way and exact capital from the peasants for industrializing the nation. Zhou Enlai disagreed. He wanted to liberalize the domestic policy, present a better image, and rouse foreign trading interests. Displeased with Zhou's lack of enthusiasm, Mao decided to diminish the prime minister's authority. That suited Liu Shaoqi, although he too had doubts about Mao's new campaign. One year later, catastrophe struck, and tens of millions of people began to die in the mostly man-made famine, or from famine-related causes. Mao was replaced by Liu Shaoqi, his protégé and ally, as chief of state. The changing of guards changed the political landscape that had been in existence since 1949: Liu had been in charge of the Party apparatus, Zhou Enlai the governmental apparatus. Mao Zedong, the chief of state, had divided and ruled them. Now the balance of power was tipped heavily in Liu's favor as he made incursions into both men's territories.

In 1962, Liu slowly and cautiously spearheaded a policy of—to put it simply—undoing Mao's previous policy, lowering the agricultural taxes, enlarging the area of the private plots allocated to peasants, extending the scope of the free markets to sell their products, and so forth.

By that time, I had developed a health problem. My heart beat regularly when I was home, but irregularly as soon as I got near my office. The problem got worse because of my concern for my son Jay's future. His big brother, Chenny, was luckier and had had his primary education in London and then in a less-regimented Beijing. As a college student, he was more able to discriminate between education and indoctrination. But now in Jay's kindergarten, he learned nothing but political slogans, such as "Long live Chairman Mao, may he live ten thousand years." The aim of the indoctrination was to train docile tools of the Party. To offset that, I taught Jay at home with the children's books brought to us by relatives and friends outside China. But a nagging question always preyed on my mind: what if the Magic Circle broke?

The budding change moderating the Party's policy—which I did not believe would last long, given my past experiences—did open a new vista for me.

One mid-afternoon in the spring of 1963, Jack and I went to the railway station

A delightful sketch made by Jack while sight-seeing on the Silk Road, during the savage purge of 1957.

Our wedding photo, 1958.

Jack, me, and our son, Jay, in 1961. The office building behind Jack is the Foreign Language Bureau.

to meet Jack's older brother. Percy had left his post in the Nanjing government of Chiang Kaishek in 1947. He moved to Hong Kong and restarted his law firm. Percy, like many upper-class progressives, did not follow Chiang Kaishek to Taiwan; instead, he reconnected with the Communist Party and became a legal adviser to the new government, looking after some of its interests in the British island colony, the "Display Window of Capitalism."

The train pulled in slowly, ponderously. Percy was disgorged first. There was a family resemblance that I could not miss, although Percy was one size larger and had a paunch. The couple at Percy's heels was unmistakably English and aristocratic, wearing a most gracious smile while bestowing honor upon the natives. They were friends of Sir Victor Sassoon, who had amassed a huge fortune by speculating in Shanghai's real estate before the communist takeover. He had been knighted for his trouble.

We drove them to the Peking Hotel, the best in town, putting up only overseas Chinese and foreign dignitaries. Percy invited Jack and me to have dinner with them the next evening. But at noontime, a telephone call from the hotel summoned me: there was an emergency.

"Is my brother-in-law ill?" I asked. Percy was overweight, but refused to be put on a diet or deny himself a full English breakfast: bacon, eggs, slices of toast spread with butter, Earl Grey tea with cream and sugar. He was a likely candidate for a heart attack.

"Just come immediately," the note of urgency in the hotel man's voice made me nervous.

I raced to the hotel, only to find Percy about to explode with rage.

"They insult my guests," he growled. "I have persuaded them to come to see if there are good business opportunities. In one day, those proletarian comrades have ruined my work of months or even years."

The friend, Lord Something, from his lordly viewpoint had seen the Peking Hotel in better times, when his compatriots owned it. Now the management was running the place as if it were a barracks. The waiters and waitresses served him and his lady in an informal, comradely manner, but his lordship found them carrying the idea of equality and fraternity too far. On his second day, when he heard them giggling and whispering behind his chair at the breakfast table, he could not take it any more. He put down his knife and fork and walked out. He asked Percy if he had been invited to China to be insulted. Percy wanted me to talk to the manager.

The hotel manager, though a staunch communist, must have been instructed by his superiors to court this British imperialist. Britain was the first Western country that had established diplomatic relations and traded openly with China in spite of American sanctions. The government certainly had use for his lordship. So I could imagine how the hotel manager panicked when his lordship raised hell.

I avoided giving this proletarian vanguard a lecture on bourgeois etiquette; that would be imprudent. I had a better alternative. When the cinemas were taken over in 1949, a great number of foreign movies from the United States and other Western countries had been found in the storerooms. These had been put in the Film Bureau's archive until someone had the bright idea of showing them "for critical study purposes." Why didn't I take the hotel manager to see a few Hollywood movies with butlers in them? After a busy day's revolutionary work, some decadent entertainment would be welcomed. The movies would show his youngsters how to serve aristocrats and bourgeoisie. I especially pointed out Greta Garbo's *Camille*, my favorite, in which the servants act like wax statues in that rowdy party. They don't bat an eye or whisper a thing while waiting on tables.

The hotel manager got my message and asked: "How shall we apologize to that imperialist?"

"Give him a box of chocolate." I meant it to be a joke.

Guess what? The next morning, his lordship had a box of chocolate on top of the newspapers; his ladyship found a box of chocolate on her dressing table.

Percy discovered my talent and said in his habitually authoritative voice: "I want you to be our interpreter and tour guide. Tell your office that I'll have you on loan."

My office complied. My work so pleased Percy that he made a proposal to Jack and me. "I am a sort of intermediary between the mainland and the outside world. I am good at giving parties, enlightening my guests on the potential in China trade and other areas. I believe the parties I give can help change the course of history." At this juncture, his manner turned majestic. "The workload is heavy, and I am not getting any younger. Jack, you can do your writing and drawing anywhere. Why don't you and Yuan-tsung come to Hong Kong? Yuan-tsung is good at parties and will find a lot to do over there. Think about it, both of you."

I had a long week of partying with Percy and his friends. Dinner party, lunch party, tea party, garden party, picnic party, dance party. . . . Her ladyship clapped her beautifully manicured hands for joy when I took her to the ballroom downstairs. What fun to watch a proletarian ball! Zhou Enlai came in with his retinue. As he proceeded to the table reserved for him, he stopped frequently to exchange pleasantries with his acquaintances. His table was two tables away from ours to the right, the side he did not have to pass before reaching his own table. But he saw Jack and Percy. He smiled, nodded, and was about to come over when the band started playing. Several young women flocked to his side, all inviting him to dance.

"How bold." Her ladyship raised her eyebrows with disapproval.

She made it clear to me that she thought it unladylike to pursue a man, even if that man was Zhou Enlai. It seemed that I wouldn't have a chance to dance with him. I had heard that the prime minister asked only the matronly wives of his veteran comrades to dance; but as I watched him, he had no time to ask anyone. The fact of the matter was that he really had no time to take any initiative. After every dance, he had barely left one partner's side when another woman would seize him by the arm.

Jack must have noticed my desperation. When another tune began, he whirled me around. Before I knew it, he waltzed me to the prime minister's side, and when the music stopped, I was face-to-face with Zhou Enlai.

We exchanged a few pleasant words with Zhou and had started to walk back when the band struck up a Yangge tune, the folk music peasants loved.

"Would you like to dance with Comrade Premier?" Jack asked. He was a good sport!

I lowered my eyes and smiled demurely. I danced with Zhou Enlai. I rapidly reviewed my repertoire of social skills, hoping to make the most of my few precious minutes.

"How is Mr. Chen [Percy] enjoying Peking?" Zhou asked me.

"Very much." After an uncertain pause, I added, "He is very happy to see my small son, Jay. He said that he was getting on and he would like to have us around."

"Has he convinced I-fan [Jack]?" Zhou asked.

"I-fan only listens to you," I said.

"Tell him that I am convinced by you." He inspected me with mock gravity, under which lurked a suggestion of suppressed laughter. He had seen through me, a young woman who was not able to fit well into the highly regimented society and therefore came into conflict with a more adjustable husband.

Suddenly, my feet began to glide, hardly touching the floor. I moved in a dizzy, dreamy realm in which everything whirled around me in a rosy fog.

Later, outside the hotel and going home, I told Jack, in high good humor, how chatting with Zhou Enlai had raised my hopes about our prospects.

"Do you think he meant what he said?" I asked. "He was convinced by me that we should move to Hong Kong to observe our family obligations."

"Give me some time to chew it over," Jack said.

Jack had been struggling with his problems since the end of the Anti-Rightists' purge in 1957, when he had been transferred to work at the *Peking Review*, an English weekly. The birth of this magazine coincided with the launch of the Great Leap Forward for a reason. Mao prophesied that within ten or fifteen years, things in every field would leap ahead of the richest nation on Earth, namely the United States of America. With economic rebirth came cultural renaissance. In the city of Tianjin, one dance troupe put its girls in ballet shoes and had them doing pirouettes to enormous fanfare. This example proved that China under Chairman Mao's leadership could do what the West deemed impossible. It took seven years to train a ballerina in the West, but we Chinese could have done it in seven days! The Party committee of the Foreign Languages Bureau decided that miracles like this required more serious reporting. *Peking Review* was designed to fit the role.

Jack could not deny any longer that his beloved revolution had gone awry. Mao's leadership was isolating China, shutting its door to the outside world. The excesses of the Great Leap Forward were the consequences of a closed society. Jack now felt duty bound to get the revolution back on track.

"I told you how I chose my job when I came back to Beijing in 1950, but I did not tell you the two jobs Premier Zhou would have liked me to take. One was to be his senior adviser in the foreign office.[4] I felt honored, but declined because I was not cut out to be a diplomat. He said that did not matter. He wanted to get me on his team, because I was my father's son, and my father was well known for resolving China's problems with the West through peaceful negotiations."

"What was the other job?"

"In the Beijing branch of the World Peace Committee—something like a folksy diplomat."

"That was a great job! You would get to travel first class, visit magnificent cities, rub shoulders with celebrities like Picasso and Neruda! Why didn't you accept it?"

"A secretary from the foreign office took me to see where my residence and office would be. It was in the compound of the former Italian embassy. The Italians inherited a taste for Roman grandeur. It did not suit me, so I declined again," Jack said, laughing not so much out of self-importance as self-deprecation.

Jack was a modest man. I loved and respected him for that. But I was cursed with an inclination to see both sides of the coin. So I saw the other side of Jack as well. He was not a man who would sit well on a committee and happily raise his hand to pass a collective resolution. What he did best was what he did alone, like the exhibition tours around the world in 1937–1938.

"Jack, you are reaching retirement age. Chenny is British by birth and will soon graduate from college and decide his own future. You can resume your freelance career, writing and lecturing about China as an independent journalist based in Hong Kong. You will, in your way, open a small window to the West and let them see how ordinary people live and work in extraordinary times."

"I don't intend to retire from the revolution."

"You'll continue to serve the revolution in a different city, without Mao's purge looming constantly in front of me," I retorted with what I thought was common sense.

"You want to move to Hong Kong and I don't, but I have to take your wish into consideration. I want this marriage to last. My first marriage was broken, and not only by the complexity of the political circumstances of that time. There were other factors. I was too absorbed in my work, and my wife.... Anyway, for our willfulness our son, Danny, suffered most." It was not his usual happy-go-lucky self speaking, but a world-weary man.

When he spoke again, he put on an assumed show of strength. "I'll conclude my work at the *Peking Review* and find a job teaching English. Working in a school, I'll have summer and winter recesses to be with you and Jay in Hong Kong. In between, you can visit me too. We'll keep each separation as short as possible, so as not to put a strain on our marriage."

In the evening dusk, the fire in our living room was burning low. Gratitude mixed with an unknown melancholy seeped into my heart as I realized that in Jack, I had an emotional anchor in a political sea that would be getting stormier. He had made good his promise to me. When he proposed, he had said: "I don't know a marriage that is free from problems, and so I don't expect ours will be. But I promise you that we'll work through them, because I love you with all that I have learned from loving."

★ 24 ★

THE BREAKING OF THE
MAGIC CIRCLE

In the fall of 1963, Jack and I went on an exploratory trip to Hong Kong, taking our small son, Jay. Hong Kong was something like the old Shanghai before the communist takeover. Forever lit, the city never went to sleep. In Percy's social circle, the etiquette was familiar to me. Nobody called me bourgeois names. All the training I had from St. Mary's Hall, which was frowned on in Mao's Beijing, became an asset again. I felt like a fish returning to water, swimming easily.

Returning to Beijing, I immediately took steps to leave. Usually nobody was allowed to resign from the revolution; but, because of Jack's privileged status, I left my office without much fuss. Jack set his plan in motion. He drafted a letter outlining what he would do to continue serving the revolution in a different capacity.

"I owe the prime minister this explanation. When I came back in 1950, I handed my British passport to him and said that I had decided to live and work here for good. He waved no and said that I might use it again. Now I will, and need to explain why."

In late autumn of 1964, we discussed Jack's letter with our friend, whom we nicknamed Comrade X, for her last name began with the letter X. She had the kind of good looks drawn by nature with bold broad strokes and warm hues. Her mother was a veteran revolutionary and a friend to Marshal Chen Yi, the foreign minister and Zhou Enlai's right-hand man.

"The Foreign Languages Bureau is the turf of Chen Yi, and the Foreign Languages Schools are also within his province. I can ask my mother to deliver Jack's letter to him."

Chen Yi's open-mindedness was well known, but he was a busy man. I assumed that his secretary would file Jack's letter and forget it. That did not bother me. I was looking forward to celebrating the Christmas of 1965 in Hong Kong. I was more assured of that when Chen Yi responded in a friendly

Jack, me, and Jay in front of a Hong Kong resort hotel, 1963.

manner. He invited Jack to his office for a chat.

The rotund marshal listened to Jack with an intense gaze in his small eyes sunk under heavy lids.

"I always regretted that I did not study French diligently when I was on a work-study program in France," he said with disarming candor. "As foreign minister, I deeply feel the need of mastering at least a second language. I sincerely hope our future foreign ministers will do better. They should be trained in the second or third language early in school. Be assured that you have a teaching job waiting for you in one of our Foreign Languages Schools."

So far, so good; then Jack brought up something as a gesture of thanks at the end of the meeting. "I am encouraged to include in the future curriculum some selected publications from English-speaking countries, in spite of their bourgeois content. I honestly think the English staff of my office would work better if they got some retraining in my future class."

"Why don't you give it a try now?" Chen Yi asked genially.

Backed up by Chen Yi, Jack set out to put his plan of retraining the staff in place, thus putting off our departure. Instead of leaving in 1965, we would leave a year later.

"What if we stumble into another purge?" My objection fell on deaf ears.

Alas, my premonition was confirmed by the Cultural Revolution. It broke out in June 1966. It did not follow the usual pattern of purges that Mao had initiated. In the past, Mao had conducted purges through Party and governmental functionaries. He and his two top lieutenants—Zhou Enlai, the prime minister, and Liu Shaoqi, the senior vice-chairman in charge of the Party apparatus—had glossed over their differences and appeared to act as one, as though they knew where they were going. Therefore we knew, more or less, what to expect. But this time, Mao skipped over them and used his new creation, the Red Guards, as the hit men. When they singled out Zhou,

The slum house at Sheep Market Street, Beijing, 1968. The one room allotted to us was in the rear right-hand corner, in front of a garbage dump.

Liu, and their close aides and accused them of standing in Mao's way, all hell broke loose.

One night in mid-October, my brooding was interrupted by the ringing of the telephone. I picked up the receiver from the night table beside my bed and listened. The line crackled. Silence. Well, not really silence, but an ominous humming.

"Yuan-tsung?"

"Yes."

"This is your Comrade X. I have something to tell you and Jack."

She came to the house, wearing a gauze mask. Beijing in autumn was windy and dusty, and it was customary for people to wear masks. But Comrade X had an added reason. She wanted to avoid being seen visiting us. When she took off the mask, I noticed that the perpetual hint of a smile around her lightly made-up lips had disappeared. She had a message from Chen Yi: the foreign minister would grant us exit visas if Jack applied for them, visas that would help us leave China.

"Why do you think the foreign minister wants to do me this favor?" Jack asked.

"Given the havoc the Red Guards have made, you'll work more effectively abroad than here," Comrade X said.

"Do you think Yuan-tsung and Jay will have enough time to go through the bureaucratic procedure of getting exit visas?" Jack asked.

I turned to him sharply. "You won't come with us?"

Comrade X let several seconds pass. "I cannot tell if they'll have enough time to get their exit visas. The Red Guards in the foreign office are running amok too. They are clamoring to remove Chen Yi from office."

"What if we wait for the situation to clear up a bit?" Jack asked.

"Premier Zhou, it is said, is trying to rein in the Red Guards and end their rampage in three months. . . . It is hard to say what will happen next. . . . Who knows? . . . It is late. I must get moving."

She told us not to walk down the stairs with her. She said good-bye to us at the front door.

For the next few days, Jack puttered around, staring, poking, touching, and smelling the plants here and there in our apartment. Alternately smiling and frowning, nodding and shaking his head, and muttering to himself, at last he stopped at the back of a chair. Leaning over it, he looked intently into my eyes and said:

"I am not leaving, but you have two choices. You can apply for exit visas, but if you cannot get them in time, that will spell trouble, big trouble. Or you can wait until the dust settles somewhat. You heard Comrade X? It is possible that Zhou Enlai may bring some order into this chaotic situation within three months. Three months is not too long a time to wait."

I agonized over my decision for days. Should I leave or stay? Jack had made the right decision, and I wanted to do the same. But I feared it was foolhardy, and I was scared, like a small animal on the eve of an earthquake, sensing warning tremors and dying to run for cover. And there was Jay to think of. Would I lose my son if I stayed and let the Red Guards ruin him? Or would I lose him if I left, because he would hate me for abandoning his father and making him grow up fatherless? I was troubled by either possibility.

Taking a morning walk to clear my mind was part of my daily routine. Along the road, I stopped now and then to read the big-character posters pasted on walls all over the city. They were the tabloid specially invented by Mao for his Red Guards. They used them to slander and attack whomever Mao did not like. Since every organization and every field of work was caught up in the purge, Red Guards from each school, college or research institute, theater or film studio, hospital, office, factory, and farm were engaged in the war of words. They were important clues as to the direction and development of the Cultural Revolution.

In one poster, the Red Guards from the foreign office denounced Chen Yi for having betrayed Mao's foreign policy and colluded with the imperialists. The proof was a cartoon based on a photo in which Chen Yi shook hands with Averell Harriman during the Geneva Conference to settle the civil war in Laos in 1961.

I immediately realized that my exit was blocked! As a rule, during a purge no one was allowed to move from one place to another inside the country without special permission, much less move out of the country. Chen Yi had given us that special permission, but it was useless now. I felt the full impact of the blow. I must get home before I fainted.

"Are you all right?" Jack asked, alarmed. Judging from his expression, I could guess that my face must be ashen with fright.

I gasped out what I had gleaned from the wall posters. "The Red Guards know how to connect the dots. They know why Chen Yi supports your plan, because it, in return, supports his diplomatic agenda, seeking some understanding with the West. The Red Guards will soon call us in for interrogation." I tried to say something to make light of my fear, but I halted and felt the muscles around my mouth twitch.

A few days later, a Red Guard came to escort Jack to be interrogated. Because Jack spoke very little Chinese, he insisted that I be allowed to accompany him. We were hustled into a corner room by the staircase in the office of one of the chief interrogators, waiting with other suspects to be questioned. It seemed a long time before the Red Guards called Jack's name. The chief interrogator, named Sha, had an official title, the Military Representative. Exactly which military faction he belonged to was top secret, or so claimed the Red Guards. In fact, nobody really knew. To my relief, however, Sha was polite and had a melting look in his melancholy eyes. He asked Jack to write something like an autobiography, including the important events and people he had been involved with in his life, so as to let them understand him better.

The request of the Military Representative was standard in a purge. Suspects were asked to write about themselves, their parents, and their grandparents. A phrase was specially coined for it: "probe into three generations." As a veteran of purges, I knew the Military Representative was not interested in Jack's pedigree. To run the purge, he must have the right qualifications for the job. He must be a superb political sleuth. He must have developed special talents in reading between totally innocuous lines and in deciphering clues revealing his victim's engagement in subversive activities. Whatever Jack wrote would be distorted to provide his persecutors with ammunition to attack him.

"I have nothing to hide," Jack protested.

I said, with what I thought was justifiable impatience, "I didn't say you have. All I say is that we have to play their game according to their rules. At the request of the Military Representative, we'll write the biography of three generations of men in your family. Let's start with your grandfather's life. It is a safe bet. All the people associated with him are long dead and buried. His and his wife's graves were too far away for the Red Guards to open and rummage. Whatever we write won't hurt anybody. With a stretch of imagination, I am sure we can write a few volumes about the old warrior. We'll make sure it will drag on. If we are lucky, there may come a turn of events and the Military Representative may drop the whole subject."

"You are invited by the Military Representative and his Red Guards to sit in the front row and watch the show at close range. What a privilege!" Jack said and encouraged me to record my thoughts in a notebook, which I did and hid at the bottom of a coal box in the kitchen. It was then that he and I decided to write the family history.

Strange to say, despite the terror, the Cultural Revolution turned out to be one of the finest moments in our married life. The Red Guards now kept Jack under surveillance. He was cut off, with no recourse to get help, and became incapacitated. But he did not despair. With me as his female Sancho Panza, he continued to tilt at evil windmills. He mapped out a plan to fight back, with some input from me. As the only foot soldier under his command, I did all the things that he could not do, not only because of the restrictions imposed on his movement but also because of the language barrier. Most important, I managed to scout around collecting information. Reading Red Guard wall papers, reading history books recounting the past that had led Jack to the present, all enabled us to see the present more clearly and to know better when to do what. Furthermore, I learned to read between the lines in newspaper and magazine articles, which were sprinkled with quotes, allusions, implications, and innuendos from Chinese classics. For readers who were not familiar with Chinese classics, they would disregard them as gibberish. We simply could not afford such a luxury. One wrong move would send us skidding into the Nether Regions.

Whenever it was possible, I sneaked out and met surreptitiously with friends to exchange "intelligence." The back door I knocked on most frequently was Comrade X's. In one of our sessions, we reviewed the situation and the three top protagonists in this purge: Mao Zedong, Zhou Enlai, and Liu Shaoqi.

"There is a fourth one." A suspenseful pause; then she added, "Zhu De, though not so much in the spotlight as the other three."

China altogether had ten marshals. One died before the Cultural Revolution. Out of the remaining nine, only one, Lin Biao, sided with Mao. Of the other eight, two were Zhou Enlai's Paris alumni, Chen Yi and Nie Rongzhen, who actually spent more time in Belgium; two were his Berlin alumni, Zhu De and Liu Bocheng; one was his loyal subordinate in the Whampoa Military Academy, Ye Jianying; one was his faithful pupil in the same academy, Xu Xiangqian; one, He Long, was a participant in the Nanchang Uprising that he led; and the last one was Zhu De's longtime deputy, Peng Dehuai. In the spring of 1967, the military lineup behind Zhou Enlai became manifest in confronting Mao Zedong. On February 16, 1967, three marshals, Ye Jianying, Chen Yi, and Xu Xiangqian, with the acquiescence of Zhou, openly attacked the Cultural Revolution in a conference held in the Great Benevolence Hall—Huai Ren Tang. Marshal Xu warned that the mistakes of the Cultural Revolution were "destabilizing the army."[1] Unrest in the army was spreading, and signs of mutiny loomed. The troops in the Wuhan area troubled Mao most.

While Comrade X and I were playing amateur analysts, Mao, way out there in Wuhan, was playing demigod. He decided to tackle the problem himself.

Mao occupied the best suite in the luxury East Lake Guesthouse, overlooking a pretty, quiet lake, beyond which the scene became magnificent—the three cities, Hankou, Wuchang, and Hanyang, rising majestically from the converging waters, turbulent and thundering, of the Yangzi and Han rivers. Feeling a divine spark within him, Mao thought of swimming against this backdrop. What a sight! It had been reported the previous year by his propaganda machine that, at the age of seventy-three, he had swum nearly ten miles in just over sixty minutes, or four times as fast as the Olympic record for ten miles.

Not long after he lay down that night, Mao started at a deafening noise. He leaped out of bed and went to the window. Shafts of headlights flashed menacingly from he did not know how many trucks breaking through the gate and into the courtyard. Droves of people jumped out, footsteps hurrying, weapons clanging.

A telephone was ringing insistently. Mao picked it up. A voice filled with dread stammered that there was a coup d'état. Before Mao had time to ask the name of the caller, the line went dead. Mao, incredulous, enraged, mortified, and confused, lost his head. One minute, he ordered the bodyguard to open the door wide: he would dare the mutineers to lay their hands on him. The next minute, he asked his orderly in a teary voice, "Where can I hide?...Where can I run to?"[2]

It was his young bodyguard who had the presence of mind to take the distraught man, in his pajamas, by the hand to a small woodland. Staggering along, Mao nearly fell as a sharp pain shot up from his feet. Then he realized in a panic that he had not changed into leather shoes. The slippers he wore in his comfortably carpeted room could not protect his feet from the thorny thicket. Limping through a back door, he escaped. With nowhere to turn, Mao hid himself on a train, waiting and hoping he could dash away. Marshal Lin Biao, his newly handpicked successor and minister of defense, embarked on a naval vessel and sailed up the Yangzi to Wuhan, but the commanders blocked his entrance.[3] They would accept only Zhou Enlai's mediation. Zhou flew to Wuhan and saved Mao. The crisis was over. The conflict, however, was not resolved.

The strong backing of the military men that Zhou Enlai had always had was a constant thorn in Mao's side: a thorn, to his frustration, that he was unable to do without. After all, it was he who had said that political power came from the barrel of a gun. By inference, it was almost impossible to do away with Zhou. The next best thing at the moment was to finish off Liu Shaoqi. Even that he could do only if Zhou consented to collaborate. Zhou did. Since the Yanan Purge in 1943, there had been no love lost between Zhou and Liu, who had been one of Zhou's fiercest opponents.

Late in 1967, Liu Shaoqi was forced out by the combined duo of Mao Zedong and Zhou Enlai. Now the remaining two contenders focused more intensely on one another. A shift of wind at the top blew up a hurricane underneath. The Red Guards of the Foreign Languages Bureau went on another round of rampaging. They looked under every bed for "counter-revolutionaries." The yells and shouts of the searchers could be heard all over the compound. They broke into our apartment.

The Red Guards shoved Jack and me into Jay's bedroom while they ransacked the other rooms. They filled a big basket and a suitcase with their loot: books, papers, toys, not a single thing that could by any stretch of the imagination be called incriminating.

"You two come with me," a Red Guard bellowed, brandishing Jack's British passport.

"Put that back," I shouted in a voice he could not ignore. "If you want to take it away, you must first ask for the premier's permission."

"Big deal," he said, tossing the passport into the hand of another Red Guard whom I had never seen before.

The new Red Guard asked us to follow him to our bedroom and dropped the passport back in a drawer. Then he smiled a dopey smile and bared his long teeth.

"You can win merit if you help us expose a traitor more dangerous than Liu Shaoqi," he coaxed. "That man started working for the CIA in 1927 when you were in Wuhan."

"There was no CIA in 1927. It was established, I think, during the Second World War," Jack retorted.

Long Teeth did not seem to hear Jack. Maybe he was not sure when the Second World War had erupted. "If you come clean, you will be leniently dealt with, and you will spare your family a lot of trouble," he argued, looking sympathetically at me.

"I have nothing to confess," Jack said without hesitation.

"If you don't feel like talking with our Military Representative, he will understand and introduce you to Qi Benyu," Long Teeth said, rising to leave with his gang.

Dumbfounded, Jack and I sat side by side for a long, silent moment. When Mao Zedong launched the Cultural Revolution, he did not have much support from the Party, or the government or the army. He had to depend on a group of his closest aides to do the dirty work for him. It was baptized as the Cultural Revolution Unit, accountable only to Mao. The director of the group was Chen Boda, Mao's longtime, confidential chief secretary, and the deputy director was Jiang Qing, Mao's third wife. Under them, one of the most prominent members was Qi Benyu, who, it was said, was the object of affection of Jiang Qing's only daughter and only child sired by Mao. The frontrunner for the hand of the princess was eager to meet Jack. Evidently there was something that they desperately wanted to extract from Jack's "confession"!

I immediately associated this with the case of Wu Hao. Wu Hao was the alias of Zhou Enlai, and in the early thirties Chiang Kaishek's secret police concocted a false document in the name of Wu Hao. During the Cultural Revolution, Mao used it to trash Zhou as he had done with Liu Shaoqi. One charge against Liu was that he was linked with the CIA through his fourth wife, a graduate from a missionary college and once a translator for Marshal Ye Jianying's team when he held peace talks with General George Marshall who, in the mid-forties, was trying to mediate between the Communist Party and Chiang Kaishek's Kuomintang.

Mao only pulled on the leash restraining his Red Guards when Marshal Chen Yi, the foreign minister whom the Red Guards had "pushed aside," speaking for his seven fellow marshals and their supporters, warned Mao: "We all have come to the conclusion that if we cannot protect Comrade Premier from attack, then your prestige as the Chairman of the Party will be undermined..."[4]

"What a windfall for our Military Representative if he could pressure you to bring a fresh false charge against Zhou Enlai, since Mao failed to resuscitate the old case of Wu Hao," I said.

"I don't think they know it was I who brought Zhou Enlai to meet Bishop Logan Roots. Probably they don't even know Zhou sought shelter in the bishop's house.[5] But they know the fact that both Zhou and I were in Wuhan, and I had American friends. They are trying to browbeat me into making false accusations against Zhou. I have categorically refused. What then?" Jack wondered aloud; his hands, clenched together, were braced tensely between his knees.

"You are doing the right thing," I said.

"I know that when I reject their proposition, they will strike back and strike where it will hurt me most," Jack mused.

I nodded absently, my mind straying for a second. I was conscious that he was saying something important, but I could not grasp its meaning. Frustrated and confused, I killed time by doing what was least necessary—I polished the furniture and the floor. The floor shone—it could have been a dance floor. One foot slowly slid out onto the polished surface, and I found myself waltzing around the room. Suddenly I felt dizzy and my waltz stopped. I buried my face in my hands, shuddering.

The veil over Jack's remark—"They will strike where it will hurt me most"—fell away, and its meaning was clear, too clear. Our little son would become a huge target for the Red Guards. They were capable of torturing children for their ends.

If I had had my way, I would never have let Jay out of my sight. But he was eight years old and a healthy child. Like his father, grandfather, and great-grandfather, he was slightly built, but his legs were long for his body. He could run faster than I. His quick, darting eyes were sharp. More often than not, he saw me before I could spot him. How could I stop him from going out to play with the other children?

During the Cultural Revolution, Jack and I were concerned about how the violence would affect our son. We wanted him to be careful, but we did not want to frighten him. There were children so scared of the cruelties of the world that they withdrew into themselves. We wanted to teach our son how to seize and enjoy the good moments that came his way. Whenever he could slip away, Jack took Jay to Purple Bamboo Park, to fish or wade in the pond. One Sunday, they came home with a small turtle. It became Jay's pet, and he liked to show it off to his friends. For no reason at all, one child threw a stone at it and killed it. Jack happened to be returning home at that time, saw the dead turtle, and blamed Jay. He reprimanded his son, as some children taunted Jay to take the blame and others urged him not to. The two sides scuffled as Jay, who had never seen his father so angry, swallowed his tears in silence. The shouts of the children attracted the attention of a passing Red Guard, nicknamed Crooked Nose.

"What are you yelling your head off for?" he snapped at Jack. On hearing about the incident, he said, "Bravo. How courageous, noble, and kind you are. What are you trying to say? That we take innocent lives? You think counter-revolutionaries' lives are innocent? Then say it outright."

The next thing we knew, he was planted in front of Jay, hollering: "Your father is a big son of a bitch, and you are a small son of a bitch!"

Jay did not hesitate, his large, dark eyes flashing with fury. "Don't you dare call my papa names!"

Crooked Nose twisted Jay's arms backward, and he cried out in pain. Simultaneously a swarm of Red Guards swirled around Jack and hung the dead turtle from his neck. They paraded him about the compound with a hastily scrawled sign pinned to his back: "Defender of counterrevolutionary turtle."

"Why are you so foolhardy?" I whined to Jack when he entered our apartment. "Why?"

"No matter what happens to us, we'll win if Jay grows up to be a compassionate, decent, hardworking man. Otherwise we lose, even if we survive and succeed in other aspects," Jack answered.

That night, Jay, feeling guilty about getting his father into trouble, went to bed early. Jack, however, pretended that nothing unusual had occurred. He breezily walked into Jay's room and exclaimed: "Time for a story! Want to hear another episode of *A Man with a Free Spirit?*"

The story was filled with adventures. Nobody except Jack knew how to tell it, for he made it up as he went along. It was from this bedtime story that Jay learned about the many beautiful places in the world and the good people who lived there. The story was also meant as an antidote to the xenophobia that came with the purge. There had even been a journey to the Moon, where the space aliens lived, and even there Man had found friends and taken part in a struggle between two armies of Moon People. When the good army was victorious—that was the side Man joined—he returned to Earth.

That night, I could tell how much Jay loved to watch his father tell the story. Jack would become so amused by his own storytelling that he would spontaneously burst into laughter.

The room was warm and cozy. The furniture gleamed in the small desk light. The fishbowl was in its place; the wakened fish flicked their tails gently amid the delicate water plants. The flowering bulbs on the side table were as neat and lovely as ever. And Jay slept peacefully. Jack, with his clasped hands resting on his knees, bent lovingly toward his son.

"Jack, let's go to the living room," I said.

The face turned to me amazed me. It was darkened with so much agony and fear that I hardly believed my eyes.

"You know how I felt when I watched Jay suffer? I have failed my firstborn, and now..." He withdrew into himself. He was seeing things that he had never told anyone, perhaps not even himself.

"Jack," I called softly, and went up to hug him to prevent him from slipping further away from me.

He stood stock-still, neither advancing to meet me nor stepping back.

"Jack!"

Hesitation flickered in his eyes. Slowly he came out of himself and into my open arms. With our arms tightly around each other, I had the feeling that we were alone, facing the world.

A long series of incidents ensued. The Red Guards ransacked our home again, took Jack from his job, made him clean lavatories, shaved his head, forced indigestible buns made of chaff down his throat, which made him sick. He had two breakdowns. I nursed him back to health, strong enough to stand on his feet in a huge struggle meeting of 3,000 participants denouncing him.

Finally it was over. Jack's two guards gripped his hair and yanked his arms up behind him so that he was bent nearly double, with his head sticking out in front of him. He was frog-marched into the dormitory at the back of the courtyard, and upstairs to the third floor. They opened a door with a key and shoved him into a room, an improvised cell, bare except for a wooden bed with uncovered boards.

"We'll get your bedding and other things. You stay here until you confess to your crime." They closed and locked the door.

Jack brooded. The excitement had been intense, and now he felt tired, as tired as if he had been running a long-distance race. He fell asleep.

When he woke up, it was evening. Still drowsy, he staggered to the window, opened it, leaned into the darkness, and saw shadows passing through the darkened compound. He moved his eyes to his apartment building. His kitchen was lit. His wife was cooking, waiting for him to eat dinner. His small son was doing his routine chore, laying the table, and anticipating the bedtime story, another episode in *A Man with a Free Spirit.*

Suddenly a desire to be with them gripped Jack. He tiptoed to the door and listened intently, with his ear to the crack. He could hear nothing. With a small coin he had found in his pocket, he unscrewed a metal bracket from the bed, and, using this as a lever, he split the decrepit door frame where it held the lock and then broke the lock itself from the wood. He was moving automatically now, without thought. He went cautiously down the stairs, and it was only when he emerged from the door into the courtyard that he was spotted. Someone shouted.

Jack leaped forward, scrambled up the back wall of the courtyard, and slithered over to the other side. It was useless running to either end of the narrow lane. He could be cut off there. He made a leap up the other wall and clawed his way to the top. But the eyes of one of his pursuers caught sight of his vanishing body. In a moment he seemed to be surrounded. He saw the tall smokestack of a furnace room before him and the rungs of the metal ladder that ran up its side. Another desperate leap, and he was on his way up. He did not look down but climbed steadily. As he emerged out of the shadow of the surrounding buildings, the world seemed lighter. A cool breeze stirred his sweat-drenched hair. He sat astride the top of the chimney. Down below, he could see the small figures scurrying about and hear the confused voices. He felt free.

"Don't you dare touch me!" Jack shouted and shook his fist. After a pause he shouted again: "I am innocent!"

He closed his eyes. They were shouting something to him through a bullhorn. He did not hear what it was they said, but he knew what they were saying. He gestured with a hand, pointing at his apartment building, using sign language to say he would come down if he was allowed to go home. Two young men began clambering up the rungs. They carried a rope.

"Okay, okay, no harm," they agreed in broken English and a deceptively mild voice. "The noose under your arms. Let you down."

Jack shook his head forcefully. He would rather come down by himself. They threw him the rope.

Jack put on a dramatic swagger while meeting his small son in the doorway. He was acting out the victorious Man with a Free Spirit. Jay grinned ear-to-ear, running into his open arms.

While Jack was putting on his spectacular show, I went directly up to the Military Representative. "Let him be," I demanded.

"It is no light thing to be singled out at the direct orders of a higher-up," Sha said in a stilted, long-rehearsed sentence that was addressed not so much *to* me as *for* me. He wanted to make it quite clear that it was not he who had engineered the struggle meeting attacking Jack, but the "higher-up."

"Let him be," I repeated and walked out.

We had another tenuous truce with the Military Representative and his Red Guards. Jack thought I had the right to know what had been going on in the struggle meeting.

"My mind worked like a telegraph." Jack described his ordeal with great gusto mixed with great agitation. "It was as clear as the day outside. The thoughts passed through my brain with staccato precision. I told myself that it's a struggle meeting and the final sentence would be announced. But no, this could not really happen. At the last minute, a message would come that said: 'Let that man out!'"

"What made you think that? Jack, you must know something about the purges from me, your friends, and colleagues. Once the Red Guards sink their teeth into you, they won't stop until they tear you apart."

"How dare they?" he suddenly raved wildly, releasing pent-up anger.

For a second, I thought he was shocked out of his mind and waited help-lessly for him to come to his senses.

"I serve the revolution absolutely without self-interest," he said, resuming his normally quiet manner. "I don't deserve this sort of shabby treatment."

This statement sobered me up and made me think. I stared at him for a long minute as if he were a stranger. "So you think somehow we deserve to be kicked around in a purge, because we are not as virtuous as you are? You are the paradigm of virtue and above any suspicion. Was that why you did not mind delaying our departure for Hong Kong? A purge was nothing to you. It meant taking a trip to the Silk Road. You were sure that whatever happened, they would let you go on a pleasure tour to Hong Kong. What arrogance, what naïveté, what stupidity! Oh God, how little I know you! If you had got away free in the past, it was due to good luck. Don't mistake it for virtue. Now, wake up!"

He had to. In the late fall of 1968, we were thrown out of our home. All our belongings, or what the Red Guards permitted us to take, were piled on a couple of two-wheeled farm carts. Our new home was in a slum house at Sheep Market Street in the western part of Beijing. It had seen better, much better days. It had been one of those Beijing mansions with interlinked com-pounds and courtyards. Now the whole place had fallen into near ruin.

The one room allotted to us was in a desolate courtyard used as a garbage dump. The accumulated trash there, right in front of our room, had been doused with dirty water, slops left from washing clothes or greasy bowls and saucepans. It had all frozen into a solid mass of filth, sprinkled with coal dust. Appalled, I retreated to our cubbyhole of a room. Shivering with cold and fear, I huddled on the bed, looked at the patch of blue sky framed by the one small window, and wondered whether I would ever escape from this madness.

Jack's life was saved, but mine was in jeopardy. I substituted for him to clean the lavatories of his office building. Physical abuse, mental torture, psychological terror, undernourishment all bore down on me. I worked myself to exhaustion, and one evening, returning home, I tripped over the doorsill of the gate to our slum house and broke a bone in my left foot. The fall caused me to hemorrhage, which led to a swollen tumor between my thighs. I fell severely ill. I was on the verge of death, but no doctor dared operate: I was the wife of a "counterrevolutionary," and the Red Guards declared that I should die like a stray dog. A neighbor got some cheap herbs, which poor peasants used to break tumors. They worked slowly. The pain was nearly more than I could endure. I often prayed to God to release me. My belief would not permit me to take my own life, but I would not have minded being killed by my enemies, the Red Guards.

"Don't talk nonsense. You'll get better," Jack said as he comforted me and fed me, spoon by spoon, the soup he had cooked.

"I cannot eat any more," I moaned, pushing the bowl away.

Squinting down his nose and frowning, Jack seemed to be pondering how to snap me out this state.

Half teasing and half critical, he began: "You know everything, and you know best. Maybe you can answer this question. Why does the Military Representative not put you away? He can easily do it."

It was a mystery to me. I had been labeled an inveterate bourgeois and the evil influence on a henpecked husband. And yet I escaped. Not only did the Red Guards not restrict my movements, they did not even tail me. And even more befuddling, they had refused to throw me to the possibly worse wolves—the Red Guards in my former office who had demanded extradition. Why?

"Our Military Representative is a double-dealer," Jack said. "To satisfy his 'higher-up,' he pushes me whenever he can without leaving his fingerprints, or as little as possible. On the other hand, he has some vague idea that some-one will hold him accountable if I die on his watch. Without you, I would die. That's the reason he lets you roam around. How long he will look the other way, I don't know. While he still does, you should make the most of it. Our survival hinges on what you can do for us. You don't have time to indulge in self-pity."

A week later, the pain from the tumor grew increasingly excruciating. I thought I was dying. Then, in a wink, the pain was gone. I asked Jack to look between my thighs. He said blood was oozing; the tumor had broken. Still weak, I resumed my duties nevertheless, starting to read newspapers. The big news was the fall of Qi Benyu, Mao Zedong's would-be son-in-law, and two other prominent members of the Cultural Revolution Unit, Wang Li and Guan Feng. They were the scapegoats for Mao; they were blamed for trying to usurp diplomatic authority from Zhou Enlai and military authority from the marshals and generals.

And then Jack explained to me, "When I made that spectacular home-coming, you and many others thought I had gone off my head. But, you see, ever since the Wuhan Incident, I had a hunch that we were entering a new stage of the purge. By defying my jailers, I cried out, loud and clear, that I would not collaborate with them. I decided that this was the time when I had to stand up and be counted. I did not clearly visualize what would hap-pen, but I did realize that in a battle I have to fight for that bit of ground that has been allotted me to defend. If I go down, then at least I have held up the enemy at that point, if only for a time. That gives my fellow fighters so much more time to strengthen their defenses and counterattack. The fall of Qi Benyu, Wang Li, and Guan Feng shows my side is counterattacking, and I cannot stand by. Getting information is crucial in deciding our next step."

But as the reign of Red terror went on, the few friends whom I trusted to be pro–Zhou Enlai vanished or lost touch with me. Comrade X was locked in a makeshift prison cell in her office.

I despaired of the dire peril we were in. I thought of running away from it all. One morning, I carried a shopping basket on my arm and went to the food market as usual. The unusual thing was the thought that flashed through my mind: take a bus to the railway station. But then where would I go? I didn't know and I didn't care, as long as it was away from that slum house.

The day before, I had finished the wash and mended my husband's and my son's socks. I had left everything in good order, except for a small package of peanuts, which I had put away as a special treat for Jack and Jay. I had waited hours for them in a long queue. Peanuts were an exported item and sold abroad for desirable foreign currency. Ordinary people in China had nearly forgotten what they tasted like. Anyway, as I thought about running away, I worried about whether my husband and son would find those peanuts. I wanted to use the public phone at the railway station to tell them where I had put them. Imagine, I was about to destroy their lives and all I could think about was saving that small package of peanuts.

If the Red Guards found me missing, they would accuse my husband of assisting me to escape. They would decide he was guilty, and they might kill him. Our son would be left an orphan. Loveless and homeless, he would drift into a life of crime, like many youngsters. How could I do this to them? I still had time to turn back. Nobody knew yet that I was trying to run away. Nevertheless, I did not turn back. I took the bus to the railway station. I felt I no longer had control over my actions.

The railway station bustled with people. The train's whistle blew. I rushed with the crowd to the platform. At the entrance of one compartment, I halted. I didn't have a ticket to board. I rushed to buy one. On the way I saw a telephone booth and called home. As we had no private telephone in our Beijing slum, I called the number of a public phone in a small, less than 300-square-foot grocery shop next to our slum house. Fortunately, the owner in this semi-private and semi-governmental venture, now labeled a "capitalist," happened to be in an amiable mood and he fetched my son. Jay answered. Hearing his voice, I broke down. I couldn't bring myself to tell him why I was calling. So, I went home instead of catching the next train.

That was a moment of weakness, and not my only one. I had many. I was constantly wavering, faltering, falling. Every time, I managed to hobble on: not out of courage, but out of desperation. There was no better alternative.

★ 25 ★

FROM BEIJING TO UPPER FELICITY AND BACK

I had learned in previous purges how casual conversation might reveal what was lurking beneath the surface and how big schemes were played out in small ways. My main purpose at the moment was to make new friends in this unfamiliar environment. I started with my immediate neighbor, Mrs. Han, a short woman with a face like a dried tomato, round and flat and of warm pinkish color. She had a larger room next to ours, on the right side of the courtyard. Her husband, a sturdy man, walked with the gait of a samurai that I recognized from Japanese films. He was an overseas Chinese who had lived and worked for many years in Japan, where he had acquired a few virtues from the native men. For one, his wife was a bag to punch around. For reasons unknown to himself or her, he was accused of being a spy sent by Japan's CIA. In the eyes of the Red Guards, all spies were on the CIA's payroll.

Under the kind guidance of Mrs. Han, I eased into the collective's daily routine. Every day, the Red Guard ringleader, Crooked Nose, supervised us, an all-woman work team, as we dug for a few hours.

Crooked Nose thrust a small shovel into my hands and said, "You are all skin and bones. Take this."

We were digging something like an underground tunnel. Some said it would be a cellar for keeping cabbages. Nobody knew for certain.

The work was not heavy. More often than not, Crooked Nose did not bother us. He had better things to do, he told us. His lunch break could last three hours. Nine months later, he would present a sun child, whom he had sired in broad daylight, to his barren wife.

Discipline was lax. We just went through the motions of digging and shoveling. Most of the time, we chatted, gossiped, and bickered. We were a mixed group, consisting mostly of homemakers with husbands in trouble; sprinkled in were women from what could be described as the lower depths, including a former prostitute, a semi-reformed thief, a laundress who doubled as a bed playmate to her employer, and an old witch who practiced black magic.

They were wonderful company and purveyors of all the latest gossip. Some of what they said was speculation, a little bit was fantasy, but all of it was absorbingly interesting to me. As I expected, they became new sources of information.

Of all my new friends, Spring Swallow, the laundress/playmate, operated by far the best grapevine. Her chief source was her lover, a rather important official. She had a face neither plain nor attractive. The man chose her for her body, especially for her high breasts and wide hips. She exuded sex.

"I can make him tell me anything," she boasted, giggling. To prove it, she spoke in a confidential undertone: "Do you know for whom we are digging? For Chairman Mao."

She went on with her scoop. Chairman Mao was preparing to fight a tunnel war with the Soviet Union if they dared to escalate the skirmish along our northeastern border and threaten us with their nuclear weapons. For the security of the capital, all alleged suspects would be removed from Beijing.

"He—you know who I mean—" she said, smiling coyly, "is Chairman Mao's man. He will keep me in the city."

Jack was also a suspect—for that matter, a prime suspect—and he would, no doubt, also be removed from Beijing. I gave him the tip.

"Our Military Representative must know more confidential information than the laundress's lover, and he's scheduled the struggle meeting against me in time to put me away," Jack mused.

Of course, if Jack and I were exiled to a rural village in the back country, we would be isolated and, in effect, buried alive there. Finally the Military Representative had found a pretext to dispose of us. He was in Beijing, and his Red Guard watchdogs would be with us, far away from the capital. His leash was not long enough to restrain them. A plausible excuse for his role in murder. The Red Guards could easily make us die in an "accident."

"It is clear to me now that he has a final solution for us. I thought he might not go that far."

The vicious plot being hatched by the Military Representative put us on our mettle. I went to work more diligently. Digging with the other women, I would not miss any news on the grapevine. Sometimes even Crooked Nose unwittingly divulged things I looked for.

"I bring in people outside our courtyard to dig, so we may finish our tunnel as a tribute to the coming Ninth Party Congress," he blabbed.

While he led us in making obeisance to a portrait of Mao, the demigod himself was squirming on his pedestal. He frowned at the list that Zhou Enlai had carefully hammered out. On the platform of the Ninth Party Congress, Mao would sit in the middle, Zhou suggested; and on his left side would sit his handpicked successor, Lin Biao, and all the upstarts of the Cultural Revolution; and on his right side would sit Zhou Enlai and, among others, the six living marshals who had openly and furiously opposed the Cultural Revolution. The fact that he was unable to throw out his most formidable detractors diminished Mao. His pedestal most likely would be chipped away, bit by bit.

When Mao fumed over the list, Crooked Nose, like us ordinary mortals, had no idea what was going on in the demigod's head. He went on blabbing: "We'll demonstrate our love and loyalty to our Great Leader and our determination to defeat his enemies, foreign or domestic."

Domestic? So our tunnel was also designed to trap enemy soldiers in a possible civil war.

On April 1, the Ninth Party Congress opened and the most important Party organ, the *People's Daily*, printed a photo of the major players on the platform, and the seating was exactly what my grapevine had predicted.

Less noticeable was the lack of news about Deng Xiaoping, the party secretary general and deputy premier, Zhou Enlai's Paris alumnus and "kid brother." Deng had been vilified along with Liu Shaoqi as the two top traitors hidden inside the Party.

"Deng is working in the premier's office, filing documents," Mrs. Han told me. "The premier put his foot down. He would not sign the documents to formally seal Liu Shaoqi's fate if the chairman did not let Deng off the hook."

Whether that was true or not, I did not know. But Zhou Enlai had certainly taken Deng off Mao's hit list. After the Ninth Party Congress, Deng's name simply disappeared from the Red Guards' abusive tongues. The salvaging of Deng Xiaoping proved to Jack and me Zhou's determination to pursue his open-door policy, which Deng would carry out vigorously in the early 1980s.

"I think it's time for us to apply for our exit visas," Jack said.

I fell back in my chair, astounded. The place to go to apply for an exit visa was the district police station, a place the residents had been afraid of entering even before the Cultural Revolution. Now it had become part and parcel of the Red Guards' justice system.

"They cannot take away my birthright," Jack said. "Anyway, I won't go to them; I'll hand in my application to Premier Zhou, through Qiao Guanhua, the deputy minister of the foreign office. When I came back to Beijing in 1950, Premier Zhou told me if I wanted to contact him, I could do so through Qiao."

"Who knows what may happen to Qiao tomorrow?"

Then Jack told me his reason. He knew that the Red Guards and their backers would rather see us dead than let us go. He knew we would be taking a risk, but he felt that not taking it was even riskier. By taking this chance, he would give Zhou a signal that he would fight on in a way he knew best. He could explain, in writing and speech, to the Western world what the power struggle was all about: whether China would enter the modern world and be a member of the international community, or stay isolated and languish. In other words, Jack was ready to go on the long-overdue lecture tour.

"We probably will make several drafts, so we had better start writing the letter now," Jack said.

I made the first draft, because I knew more about the current situation from reading the Chinese papers. But I wrote in English for Jack to read, to edit, and to add his input. English was my second language, and sometimes the things I composed in my mind were very lively; but as soon as I transferred them onto paper, they sounded dull and even not quite intelligible. There were gaps of silence, sighs of indignation and protest, that I felt incapable of rendering into words. I turned the draft over to Jack. At night, alone in bed, we conversed intimately. We got our notebooks and a flashlight from the bedside table and brought them under the quilt. We used all the information we had collected to analyze our situation and formulate a strategy. We would discuss and debate and come to agree what should be kept in the draft, what should be cut, and what should be strengthened. Then he would work on it. With a little rearranging of words here and there, the draft would become more coherent and comprehensible.

It was not possible to write lying down. Jack and I alternately squatted in the space between the legs of the large desk, with an old dark green tablecloth hanging around the desk so that the tiny desk light we used while writing the letter would not be seen by busybodies. After several drafts, we got the letter ready in both English and Chinese; both copies would be presented to the premier's office.

During the process of writing this letter, I learned from Jack not only how to write better English, but, more important, how to fight better. Jack had grown up in a culture where the rulers were supposed to rule by law, although there were many who had made—and were making—a mockery of the law. I had grown up in a culture where the rulers ruled by their own judgment of right and wrong. I would never have dreamed of taking legal issue with the lawless Red Guards, backed up by the infallible emperor. But for us, seizing the moment to act would be the most important turning point—for better or for worse—in our struggle for survival.

Before we went to the foreign office, I needed to do some solid homework to ensure success. Two days after the opening of the Ninth Party Congress, Zhang Zhizhong, the father of our matchmaker, Dora, died. General Zhang and Zhou Enlai had worked together in the Whampoa Military Academy in the mid-1920s. Zhang was a true patriot and had decided not to leave China in 1949. He was one of the noncommunist, high-ranking officials in the Beijing government. I figured Zhou would take part in the funeral ceremony.

I hesitated to go to Dora Zhang's office in the Foreign Languages Bureau for obvious reasons. Her father-in-law was a Christian theologian and was in hot water up to his chin. To call on her might be to fall into the Red Guards' dragnet. Her father's residence had been carefully guarded even before the Cultural Revolution. Visitors had been asked to fill out a small form: name, profession, address, purpose of visit, and so forth. I could not rush there by myself. For two days I walked back and forth between her office, her house, and her father's residence, hoping to run into her.

On the third day, I was so tired due to lack of sleep that my head was splitting. I went to Crooked Nose to ask for a day off. A large crowd began to gather. I scanned the faces through the morning mist, trying to find him in the midst. Suddenly the familiar face of a young woman came into focus. Her gaze, wavering for a split second, settled on me. I saw her leaning toward the back of another woman and whispering something. Dora Zhang walked toward me. She looked a little haggard and asked if she could lie down for a minute. I took her to my room.

"How have you been?" she asked, lying down on my bed.

Gazing at two rats scurrying around, I answered: "I have a phobia about rats. Otherwise, so-so. And you?"

"My father has passed away. I'll leave the digging early to be with my mother."

"Dora, could I attend your father's funeral? I want to pay my last respects to him. He was always kind to Jack and me."

"I don't see any problem, but go with me. You can take care of my baby. You don't mind playing her nanny?"

Up to the day of the funeral, I did not know if I would have an occasion to exchange words with Zhou Enlai, or what I would say if I did.

"Seeing you is a reminder to him," Jack said.

Probably that would be it. Mentally and emotionally, I was so drained that I could not worry any more. I was not well, but I told myself I could not afford to fall ill.

At the Eight-Treasure Hill Cemetery, I could see Zhou Enlai standing between two large trees. He was grayer, and his face was gaunt. I was overcome by an indefinable melancholy. With his eyes gazing at the flowering shrub and his chin cupped in his hand, he was exchanging greetings with other attendees. He was not doing anything extraordinary. But what was extraordinary was the mood he projected, at once so full of serenity and so full of foreboding. Having known about the violence and turmoil and danger the prime minister faced, I found a certain pathos in this tranquility.

At long last, he came into the hall. Someone beside me murmured something. I turned to ask: "What did you say?" without seeing who it was. When I opened my mouth, I suddenly found my voice faltering, my breath short, my heart racing with a vague fear. I stared helplessly at Dora's baby daughter in my arms as a chill crept over me.

"Your daughter?" Zhou asked.

"No, my son is ten years old and his uncle Percy hopes that he will attend school in Hong Kong," I answered on the spur of the moment.

"Very good." A faint smile appeared around his thin sensitive lips. It was an expression that I could not define. It contained a bit of sorrow, a little compassion, some hurt, a little bit of shame from a man who apparently felt guilty for not being able to shield from harm the people who looked to him for protection, and a shade of encouragement of the kind extended from one survivor to another.

The final decision to evict Jack from Beijing came down, but it did not take us unaware. One morning in early October 1969, Jack, taking his British passport and me, went to the foreign office. At the reception room, we handed in a copy of the letter to the prime minister to a secretary of Qiao Guanhua. Qiao was one of the deputy foreign ministers still functioning. He would lead the first People's Republic delegation to the United Nations after the ouster of Chiang Kaishek's Taiwan delegation in 1971.

That evening, I went to a small diner down the street, a few blocks from our slum house. When I came back with a pot of meat dumplings, I saw Crooked Nose hanging around the gate. He saw me before I had time to go to another entrance at the back. He turned off his swagger, drew his neck into his collar, and furtively vanished. It was so out of character for this bully that I guessed Jack's formal application for exit visas had taken effect.

But about ten minutes later, a bigger surprise was in store for me when I opened the door, answering someone's knock. There in front of me stood Military Representative Sha, with a shy half-smile on his face. He was not sure if I would let him cross the threshold. I decided not to help him.

"Could I come in?" he asked after a moment of dead silence.

"What can we do for you?" I asked, not budging an inch.

"We need to talk."

"You mean you need to talk," I said.

He nodded, and I stepped aside to let him in.

"Comrade Chen, your application for exit visas has been granted by the prime minister himself," the Military Representative addressed Jack directly in Chinese. Then turning to me, he asked, "Would you please interpret for me?"

So, in a wink he reversed the verdict on Jack. Jack was a comrade again.

"Military Representative, finish what you want to say." Jack intentionally avoided using the usual epithet "Comrade Military Representative."

"There is a message from Comrade Premier." The Military Representative took out a piece of paper from his jacket pocket and read: "Chen I-fan [Jack] and his father Chen Youren [Eugene] were our friends since the early twenties, a very difficult time for our Party. Ever since, they have served the cause of the Chinese people with perseverance. We shall never forget them. We shall always welcome Chen I-fan back, should he wish" to return.

"When shall we receive the exit visas?" I asked the Military Representative.

A slight frown, a slow pause before he answered. "We are very concerned about Comrade Chen's health. A vacation in the countryside will help. There the air is fresh and the diet is adequate, with a lot of vegetables and fruit," he said with solicitude and without the faintest hint of his own contribution to Jack's health problems.

"You are sending us to the May 7 Cadre Retraining School?" I asked. The May 7 Cadre Retraining School had been invented as a kind of labor camp annexed to each organization.

"No, of course not. Comrade Chen will be allocated to an Old, Sick, and Disabled Team. He could do some light manual labor, you know, like exercises, but it will not be mandatory," the Military Representative hastened to pacify me.

Jack and I were fully aware of his changed strategy. He would detain us, on behalf of his backers who were running the show for Mao Zedong, as long as he could, and in another reverse of fortune he would put us back on his death row.

Jack, however, agreed to go to the countryside first, because a cooling-off period was a required condition from them, and under the circumstances Jack felt a truce might be in order. In such a pandemonium as this most violent purge, Zhou Enlai had already done all he could manage to do at the moment. The rest of the battle, we had to fight on our own. It was the last round and also the hardest because, once exiled to the backwoods, we would be cut off from all the recourses we had in Beijing. That was not where I wanted Jay to be.

My mother, an elderly widow, was evidently not thought much of by the Red Guards. She was left alone to live in relative peace. Jay would be safer with her. I wrote to ask if she could take care of him in her Shanghai home. She was ill and could not come then, but promised to come later to wherever we would be and fetch Jay.

Our train trotted southward to our destination in Henan Province, literally meaning the province on the south of the Yellow River. Two days later, we clambered out at the station in Ji County in late November 1969. A truck from the county town picked us up and deposited us at the big gate of the Great Felicity Commune. A handcart waited there. After a quick look around, we piled our belongings onto the handcart and, with a cadre from the commune pulling and Jack and I pushing, trundled it up the road. Jay walked with two bundles in his arms.

A man in black trousers and jacket came running to us.

"Lao Man, your host," the commune cadre said.

Seeing us, Lao Man broke into an enormous, good-natured smile of welcome that creased his sunburned face in wrinkles. Hardly waiting for the introductions to be over, he seized our biggest bag, slung it on his shoulder, and was off with a long stride, with us trailing after.

Our hostess, a middle-aged woman with a light, rosy complexion and a finely shaped nose and mouth, stood at the gate.

"Mother of my children, here are our—we are all one family," Lao Man grinned, showing all his teeth and gums.

"Da Sao, thanks for your trouble." I held both her hands with mine. Da Sao meant older sister-in-law, a traditional courtesy title for an older woman addressed by a younger one, a mark of respect and affection.

The Man family in their courtyard in the Upper Felicity Village, where we lived between 1969 and 1970. We stayed in the room next to the latrine, which you can just barely see at the right edge of this photo.

Virtuous Beloved, Lao Man's wife, had a quiet way of going about her business. She lit and started a fire in our cold, obstreperous stove. Having it purring under her hands made us feel at home. The unassuming, unaffected goodness of this couple was balm to the soul. I did not expect the same kindness from the other six couples who arrived with us from Beijing. All six men worked in the Foreign Languages Bureau. The three noncommunist couples resided at the far end of the village. The other three couples' cottages formed an arc encompassing our bungalow. Lao Bai, a veteran Party member and our team leader, occupied with his wife a cottage, separated from us by a small pond. Young Cai and his wife had their cottage right beside ours. Mrs. Cai, a fragile-looking woman, was a Party member and took her responsibilities very seriously. Without doubt, she would conscientiously report her observations of us to her Party unit. Young Cai, a tall, lanky, bespectacled man, was applying for Party membership, naturally eager to show his worthiness as a candidate. Behind our cottage resided Lao Yang, a veteran communist who spoke fluent English, and his wife. Eavesdropping was easy, as his cottage was next door.

According to the rules and regulations of the Party, three members could form a unit. So there was a whole unit functioning to stake us out. The Military Representative certainly had made meticulous arrangements to block us off. I did not know what he had told Lao Bai, the team leader, about Jack's status. I suspected his instruction was vague. I could tell that from the

Jack's American brother-in-law, Jay Leyda, mid-1970. Jay was arranging a speaking tour for Jack in Canada and the United States while we were still in Upper Felicity Village.

alternately mild and grumpy manner in which Lao Bai spoke to us, as if he was not sure who we were, comrades or class enemies.

Within our courtyard and with the Man family about, we felt safer. We had two rooms. The smaller one was our bedroom; the larger one was kitchen, living room, dining room, and studio combined. The centerpiece was the clay stove. Except for that, it did not look quite like a peasant's home. We had the same cheap rustic furniture and bed, but in arranging them to our taste they became different. By the time we tacked Jack's drawings on the walls, the cottage looked just like what it was—that of an artist, a townsman come to live in the countryside for a year or so.

Our peasant neighbors liked our place and were quite at home when they visited. The stories they told us would be included in a future book, *A Year in Upper Felicity*. I did the interpreting and also translated and wrote related materials. The work was good practice for my English.

"Your mother will see for herself that we are living pretty well," Jack said.

Mother's coming lifted my spirits, but also threw me into a tumult of conflicting feelings. I did not blame our incompatible temperaments on Mother alone. I had not been an easy child to raise, and I was a rebellious teenager. We had quite a few shouting matches. The worst one was over my decision to go to Beijing in 1950 when she wanted me to go to Hong Kong with her cousin, my aunt Duan.

"One day you will regret this," she said with the authority of a great prophetess.

Now Mother would claim that her words were vindicated. Had she not told me so? I anticipated her onset and prepared to swallow my pride. I desperately needed her assistance to break the Red Guards' blockade and reconnect us with the outside world. Who else would be willing to oblige me now?

She arrived quietly three months after I had settled in Upper Felicity Village. She had aged. Her sagging upper lids drooped over eyes that now looked smaller, dimmer, sadder.

"Mother, sit down. You must be tired," I said, taking a small bag from Jay, who had gone to the bus stop with his father to meet his granny.

"Yuan-tsung has prepared a few northern dishes, but I am afraid she is not as good a cook as you are," Jack said, paying her an appropriate compliment. My mother was an excellent cook.

A quick repartee followed. "I did not bring up my daughter to toil in the kitchen," Mother said. Glancing around, she added unhappily, "You don't have a kitchen. You only have a stove."

After the opening jibe, my mother got the floor. Jack and I fell silent guiltily, and Jay was bewildered. They were glad that the meal was finally over and left me alone to deal with her.

"Mother, I have a little confession to make," I began tentatively. "I always want to live up to your expectations for me. I want to pursue a career, which I thought I could only do here. Artists and writers should not be uprooted from their native soil, otherwise they will wither."

Mother showed no response. Her eyes moved from one side of the sparsely furnished room to another, as if to ask: "Is this all you have achieved, and you want me to be proud of it?"

Mother shrugged with an air of regret and interjected: "Yuan-tsung, your problem is your stubbornness, refusing to admit mistakes. Do you now wish that you were in Hong Kong?"

At this moment, I hated her. I wished she would just go away.

"What mistakes? I am living a life I want to live." I raised my voice. "Marrying Jack was my best decision. When I lie in bed, staring up at the ceiling, thinking what he has told me about his grandfather, his father, and himself—you know what I see? I see them filing by with their comrades. Then this vision merges into the scenes of the purge, and I see myself marching with them. It is impossible to see these scenes as unrelated. Mother, I am in the continuum of a grand, grand struggle. It is the opportunity of my life. . . ."

"You see all that on the ceiling?" she asked.

"Yes."

"You don't have a ceiling," Mother retorted, shaking her head. "You have a roof supported by termite-eaten beams."

I slumped in my chair, punctured by Mother's sharp tongue. As if I did not have enough trouble coping with her, Da Sao's little pig entered the fray. Tacked onto the east side of our wall was the pigsty. This was its home. It was an unsavory-looking creature, probably the ugliest in our village. At the best of times, it was not the sort of pet I would introduce into my living room and kitchen, but it pushed its way in regardless. Its eating habits were most disconcerting. It was an indiscriminate eater of unconsidered trifles. To put it brusquely, it ate *shit*.

Mother recoiled when the little pig, covered with feces, waddled in. I drove it out.

"Mother, why don't you try to understand me?" I tried to continue our interrupted conversation.

"What do you want me to understand? I saw a dirty pig, your immediate neighbor. It is not difficult to understand. Or you could enlighten me with the profound meaning behind what I saw?"

"All right, you win. I was stupid and did not listen to you. Now I am press-ganged and trapped, but somehow I have become a reluctant fighter. How is that? Satisfied?"

"Why do you want to hurt yourself and me?" Mother's short chin quivered, and her voice suddenly cracked.

"Mother, let me come to the point. I want to fight my way out. Would you help me?" My attempt at a conciliatory tone calmed her.

Then I laid out my strategy in detail. I needed her to forward Jack's letter to Jay Leyda, Silan's husband, who was teaching in Canada, and one to his brother, Percy, in Hong Kong. A letter sent from Shanghai to Hong Kong would not attract much attention, as many Shanghai residents had relatives and friends in Hong Kong. Our letter to Jay Leyda should be mailed to Hong Kong first, then Percy would forward it to Canada. Then Leyda and Percy should send a letter to Qiao Guanhua, inquiring after Jack.

Mother stayed two or three days. No sooner had our team members—the six couples from Beijing—learned of my mother's visit than she left, taking our son, Jay, with her.

Jack and I went back to our daily routine. From time to time, I went to the county town to mail a letter for Mother to forward to Percy. I took Da Sao along when she wanted to see a doctor or buy prescription medicine, making the trip look more for her than for myself.

One day at the bus stop in the county town, a woman sitting opposite Da Sao and me roused my curiosity. She sat timidly on the edge of a bench as if she would jump off at the slightest sign from her Red Guard escort, who stood, with arms akimbo, beside her. His face looked familiar to me. I had probably run into him in the compound of the Foreign Languages Bureau. But I did not know the woman. She looked poorly, and she was clearly frightened.

"Why are you here?" the Red Guard asked me in a peevish voice, staring at me as if his prominent eyes were about to pop out of their sockets.

"Do you have an objection to my caring for a poor peasant woman?" I snapped back at him. "Da Sao needs a pair of glasses."

He was a little embarrassed and sauntered out of the waiting room. The woman squinted uncertainly in my direction. I guessed she wanted to talk. I smiled at her.

"I don't know where he'll take me," the woman leaned her puffy face toward me and whispered.

"I'll find out where you'll be sent, and I'll wheedle your escort into giving you a break," I promised.

We all boarded the same bus and got off at the same stop. I invited both of them to have a cup of tea at my nearby cottage.

"I am busy. I have no time to waste," the Red Guard grumbled.

"All the more reason you should come to my cottage. You need a bicycle to run around doing your business. I could let you use mine," I cajoled.

Now, a new bicycle was a luxury at that time. The Red Guard's face lit up like that of an American teenager who has been given the keys to a new sports car. He took off on a long joyride and left his charge with us overnight.

Our guest, who spoke good English, told Jack and me of her misfortune. Her name was Bao. Her husband had been arrested because he was a former banker. Her two teenage daughters, as children of a counterrevolutionary, had been exiled to a border town in the Northeast. The younger one had been burned badly in a forest fire and forever disfigured.

She wept. I softly adjusted her blue head kerchief, blown awry during a truck ride, which held her mane of gray hair in place. Jack used milk powder, an egg, and a spoonful of rum to whip up a cup of eggnog for her.

"I am all alone, and I have heart trouble," she murmured, bowing her head as if submitting to her harsh fate.

"I may be able to find out where your escort is to place you—" I halted as I attempted a consoling smile through tears.

"He only told me that I was under his watch," Mrs. Bao said.

When the Red Guard returned the bicycle next morning, I spoke to him in a confidential voice: "If you live in a nearby village, you can use the bicycle any time you need it. But don't tell anybody else. I'll only loan it to you."

"That's neat. My village is not far from here, about two *li* [one kilometer]," the Red Guard said with a wide grin, caressing the bike's handlebars.

Mrs. Bao went into the cottage with me to get her traveling bag.

"It seems you won't be far away. Let's meet at the supply and marketing cooperative when you want to buy groceries," I said to her before parting.

nphasizes understanding   1971 mid-December   *no. 14*

Chinese journalist visits SIU

By Chuck Hutchcraft
Daily Egyptian Staff Writer

...idence that the distance of the ...ionship between the People's ...blic of China and the United ...s is lessening was shown ...day when a journalist from ...ng came to SIU to visit an old ...d. ...ter being separated for 22 years

by the bamboo curtain, Jack Chen met with his friend of some 41 years, Herbert Marshall, a theater professor and director of the Center for Soviet and East European Studies.

Chen, a friendly man who wears a Chairman Mao tunic with the top lapel button unbuttoned so he won't look "square," jokingly told Marshall that his visit was part of the "ping-pong diplomacy."

This reunion of friends ironically reflected the relationship between the two peoples on a national scale.

Marshall says he received Chen's letter from Peking at about the same time that it was announced that Henry Kissinger had made his secret trip to Peking to set up a trip to there by President Nixon.

Speaking seriously, Chen says that his trip to the United States is one of diplomacy as well as to see Marshall. "I want to try in my little way to develop an understanding between the two countries."

Chen and Marshall have known each other since 1930 when they met while studying in Moscow. Their reunion meant recollections of their past experiences in such places as

India, Russia and Great Britain.

Chen spent a few years in the United States just before World War II, so this country is not completely strange to him.

To make his trip more worthwhile, Marshall has set up a nationwide lecture tour of several major universities. Chen will return here in January.

For the last year or so Chen has spent a great deal of time traveling and collecting information about his own country. He ·is currently working on two books, one about the cultural revolution in his country and another on communal life in China.

"After I have looked at my country and now at yours," he said, "I see many similarities."

Both countries are seeking an understanding of each other, he sa...

Professor Herbert Marshall says he "received Jack's letter from Peking at about the same time that it was announced that Henry Kissinger had made his secret trip to Peking to set up a trip to there by President Nixon."

As if carrying out some sort of clandestine plot, we did not even nod at each other in the shop. She and I slipped out separately and climbed up a sharp slope. On top of it, we stood on the sizable remains of the tamped-earth wall that had once surrounded a neighboring village. Alongside the wall ran an old moat, now dried up and partly overgrown with grass and planted with saplings. We sat down in the moat, chatting or doing nothing, just watching the sky change color at sunset or the horizon blend into the earth in the evening twilight.

She fumbled in her shopping bag for something and took out a slip of paper. She fell into silence for a few minutes before she smiled tremulously and spoke again: "I read a letter that was sent to Jack. It was written in English by a man named Jay Leyda. I know it's not right to read a stolen letter, but the Red Guards forced me to translate it for them."

She paused, her eyes appealing for my understanding and forgiveness. The intensity in my gaze probably startled her, and she muttered with chagrin: "I know I should not have done it, but—"

"No, no, you did right. Do you remember the content of the letter?"

"Here." She gave me the slip. "I noted down the names and the places, and I memorized what I thought was important to you. Jay Leyda said that he was arranging a speaking tour for Jack. Two universities show interest. One is York University in Canada, where Leyda is a professor in the fine arts department; the other is Southern Illinois University, where Jack's old friend Herbert Marshall is teaching."[1]

"This message is very important to us. I cannot thank you enough," I said. "But don't put down anything in writing again."

"I am getting on and becoming forgetful—wait, I know I have forgotten something. Jay Leyda also said that he hadn't received any letter from Jack for quite a while, so he wrote to the foreign office to inquire about his whereabouts."

The soft clarity of June merged with the brilliant sunshine of July. It was harvest time. As the wheat ripened, its color changed from green to brown and finally billowed gold. As we worked in the fields, I heard a familiar voice calling me gently. I turned around. A face, beaded with sweat, gleamed pink in the sun. It was a face as bright, warm, and vital as the sunlight playing on it.

"How come you are here?" I asked Mrs. Han, my lost friend from the slum house.

"Can we find a place to talk?"

"Hold on."

Something moved hesitantly in a clump of weeds. A pair of long ears appeared over the tips of the low thistles and moved very fast. A small brown animal scurried across a bare patch.

"Rabbit!" a child playing nearby shouted with surprise and joy. Several men and women ran after him, threw their tools at it and, when these missed, snatched up stones for another try. The vision of a dish of rabbit meat cooked with spices must have made their mouths water.

Mrs. Han and I joined the chase, and then made a sudden swerve off a path when nobody was looking. I headed to the moat, with Mrs. Han on my heels. The brush there had grown in profusion, with the help of the spring rain. Very secluded. The moment we leaped into the moat, Mrs. Han started firing her words like machine-gun bullets. Her right hand tapped her thigh in the same quick rhythm of her words:

"I have been looking for you, Yuan-tsung. How I have missed you! When I found out you were in Upper Felicity, I volunteered to do the cutting. You see, my village plants sweet potato, no harvest as yet."

"Who told you I am here?"

"Our mutual friend, Mrs. Bao."

She had a lot to tell me. The Red Guards and the people who lived and worked with her in the same village did not isolate them as my team did Jack and me.

"They think and see nothing of us; they couldn't care less for small fries."

The big news was that Premier Zhou himself had gone to the Foreign Languages Bureau, asking the ringleaders of the Red Guards what the charges were against Jack. They implied that Jack was a CIA agent who had worked in collusion with Liu Shaoqi. Their proof was an old album of cartoons that Jack had drawn when he was in his teens. The prime minister refuted them. He said that the cartoons were immature, but hardly criminal. What he said next dealt the Red Guards a heavy blow. "I know why you are attacking Chen I-fan, because you aim to attack me through him."

"Good news first, and then bad news," Mrs. Han said in a worried undertone. Rumors, in the meantime, started buzzing that Jack would be transferred to the May Seventh Cadre Retraining School, where the local headquarters of Red Guards was. Once there, he would be run over with a tractor in an "accident."

When Jack and I studied the two pieces of contradictory information, he explained to me that we had two options. One, we wait for the premier's order to work its way through various bureaucratic hands. The downside was that the bureaucrats would process the order as slowly as possible. That's their way of working, because they knew that when the wind shifted again, they would bear the brunt of the counterattack from the premier's opponents.

The second option was: we just pack and leave. But Jack worried about his being derailed and forced out of China with Jay only. What finally made us decide on throwing down the gauntlet was another piece of confidential information that Mrs. Han brought to me: the downfall of the director of Mao's Cultural Revolution Unit, Chen Boda.

Mao had used him to float the idea of "pulling out" and "knocking down" the intractable marshals and their generals two years previously. When that failed, the hapless Chen Boda became the scapegoat. This was not the only reason Mao was forced to sacrifice him, but it was, nevertheless, one of the reasons. Faced with this blow falling so close to home, the Great Leader was shrinking, and it seemed that he would keep shrinking until he could fit into the niche of a figurehead, provided by his opponents.

"Military Representative Sha is here, holding confidential meetings with Party members and preparing them for the news that will soon break out," Mrs. Han said.

As Jack and I anticipated, he would come to discuss with the three communists in the Old, Sick, and Disabled Team what to do about us. I kept a close watch on Lao Bai's cottage. I pushed aside a curtain and looked out the window, so that I could see into the dim haziness of the road. I saw a man in uniform appearing from the edge of the path, where it fell away from the field. Sha was coming. I put a letter I had written in my pocket and headed to their closed-door gathering.

"What a convenient coincidence, Military Representative! I come to tell Lao Bai that we are packing and leaving," I announced, sitting down.

Lao Bai gaped at my challenge. "You cannot leave without my permission. I am the team leader, and I demand that you observe discipline."

"What discipline?" I asked defiantly and turned to Sha. "Military Representative, why don't you tell them that Jack came here for a rest cure? After eight months, Jack has recovered fully, and he is strong enough to take a long trip. We will return to Beijing soon."

The Military Representative stared at me as if seeing a ghost. His uniform hung loose on his body; he had lost quite a few pounds, probably from fear of the looming day of reckoning.

"Chen Yuan-tsung, your husband holds a British passport, but you do not. You are in our hands," he upbraided me to assert himself.

Those words unleashed in me the fury of a tormented and caged animal. "You are threatening my life, but you know you cannot threaten a person's life when she is sick and tired of living under your thumb." And I took out the farewell letter to Jay and read it to them.

"I hope I am doing the right thing for you, encouraging you to go with your father. You must move on to new things. I wish that bit by bit you will move away from the sad life and sad past we have shared. There will come a day when that past will seem distant and hazy. You have your whole life ahead of you, and that is what you ought to look forward to. That is the way it should be, but then how sad it is for me." I closed my eyes and choked back my tears. I grabbed the front of my jacket, as if my heart were contracting with the pain I was trying to suppress.

Then I addressed the Military Representative directly: "This is my decision, and now you know it. I am your hostage, but I won't ask my husband to pay ransom. You can hold me as long as you can. You even can run into me with a tractor."

Time was getting on. Autumn began. The leaves were turning red, brown, and yellow, and scampering away in the wind. The day we left Upper Felicity was quite an occasion. A stream of friends came to help. With all these willing hands, we cleared the cottage and put everything on the truck in less than half an hour. Da Sao and I embraced each other, and our eyes were wet.

"We must be off!" called the driver.

Jack and I clambered up among the beds and chairs, boxes and easels, suitcases and quilts. Everybody shouted good-bye and waved. The motor roared, and we were off with a jerk and a bump.

We waved and waved until we turned the corner at the end of the lane. We shouted our last good-byes as we lurched up the narrow lane and met some neighbors coming belatedly home for their morning meal.

EPILOGUE

We returned to Beijing. For several weeks, Jack, taking Jay and me with him, visited factories, schools, universities, and other institutions in Beijing, Shanghai, Suzhou, and Canton, so he could have a broader view of the current situation. On May 1, 1971, we arrived in Hong Kong.

The British-instigated Opium War of 1839 caused, though not solely, the eruption of the Taiping Rebellion. After the war, Hong Kong was ceded to Britain. The Brits had a long memory and were bent on making me pay for what the three men in my family had done to them. After Jack left on the lecture tour in the fall of 1971, I was left alone in Hong Kong with our small son, Jay, to cope with them. They harassed my family and me with ingenuity: for example, they took back Jack's reentry visa and blocked his way home.

The hostility of the Brits compelled me to consider further the three Chen men's careers in retrospect. Their story had its roots in the overseas Chinese communities. There were many others who had come back from the United States, Canada, England, and other parts of the world to fight for the

With the help of our friends, I prevailed over the Brits and got Jack back into Hong Kong after his speaking tour in Canada and the United States, 1972. Pictured here, from left to right: a friend, me, Mr. Wang, who was the chairman of the Chinese Chamber of Commerce of Hong Kong, and Jack.

liberation of their homeland. But that was not the only thing they had been fighting for. What they had inherited and learned from the Western democratic cultures had a positive effect on the Chinese revolution. Although, up to now, much has been written about the Chinese revolution, not much room, either in Chinese or in English, has been devoted to an appraisal of the role played by the overseas Chinese, and to the appreciation of the democratic Western ideas they brought back in their minds. This family history tries to emphasize this aspect of their contribution. Modern China is as much the creation of the overseas Chinese as of the indigenous population.

As for myself, the Hong Kong sojourn gave me a taste of capitalistic shenanigans and prepared me for the journey ahead. It would be, I had a hunch, as arduous, hazardous, and unpredictable as the road I had left behind, but in a different landscape.[1] But that is another story.

Acknowledgments

Writing this family saga was like running a long-distance race, not knowing where the finish line was. But I was fortunate to have four friends cheering me on. I wish to thank them in the order of their appearances on that lonely road: my son, Jay, for his consistent support; my former neighbor Linda Yoshikawa, who smoothed most of the first draft; my literary agent, Regina Ryan, who took on a difficult book project and guided me, with acuity and patience, to its completion; my editor, Michael Denneny, who coached me with understanding, skill, and imagination.

This book made a stopover at Carroll & Graf. I wish to thank the people there, in particular the editor-in-chief, Bill Strachan, and Assistant Editor Adelaide Docx, for their help and graciousness. And then it traveled on and reached its destination, Union Square Press. I wish to thank Philip Turner, editorial director, for his insight and enthusiasm, and Editorial Assistant Iris Blasi, for her kind attention.

Notes

Prologue

1. The statement, made in an interview, was published throughout Asia on February 5, 1967. Sources: interviews with Percy Chen in 1972 and with Lee Seng-Gee, a well-known Singapore financier, in January 2000.

Chapter 1: Fight for God's Kingdom on Earth

1. Wang Binyi, "Diplomat of the Early Republic, Chen Youren," Taipei, Taiwan: *Biographical Literature Magazine,* vol. 67, no. 2, p. 43, 1995.
2. The History Departments of Futan University and Shanghai Teacher's University, *The Taiping Revolution* (Peking: Foreign Languages Press, 1976), p. 36.
3. Wang Binyi, ibid., p. 44.
4. Ibid.
5. When Jack and I drafted the story of Grandmother Chen's childhood and sent it to Angela Cheyne for her comments, she wrote her version, with corrections and amplifications after she responded. That version is included in a book, *Essays on the Chinese Diaspora in the Caribbean,* edited by Walton Look Lai, and published by History Department, University of the West Indies, St. Augustine, Trinidad and Tobago, in 2006.

Chapter 3: The Return of the Native

1. Public Record Office, London, Reference no. F0371/12473/08314, Registry no. F1651/1398/10, dated February 18, 1927, received in Registry February 21, 1927.
2. Ibid.

Chapter 4: The Maelstrom of Peking Politics

1. *China Year Book for 1913,* ed. Bell and Woodhead (Shanghai), p. 487, as quoted by Lyon Sharman in *Sun Yat-sen, His Life and Its Meaning* (Palo Alto: Stanford University Press, 1934), p. 138.
2. "China Is United, Declares Dr. Sun," *The Sun* (New York), September 24, 1912, p. l, as quoted by Lyon Sharman in *Sun Yat-sen, His Life and Its Meaning,* p.149.

3. H. G. W. Woodhead, *A Journalist in China* (London: Hurst & Blackett, 1934), p.59.

Chapter 5: Battling the Warlords

1. Tang Degang, *Under the Reign of Yuan Shikai* (Yuan Shi Dang Guo) (Guangxi Normal University Press: City of Guilin, 2005), p. 165.
2. Wu Jiaxun and Li Huaxing, *Selected Works of Liang Qichao* (Liang Qichao Xuan Ji) (Shanghai: Shanghai People's Publishing House, November 1984), pp. 682–683. Qian Yuli: *The Biography of Chen Youren* (City of Shijiazhuang: Hebei People's Publishing House, 1999), p. 22. According to this source, Eugene published the whole of Liang Qichao's manifesto in the *Peking Gazette*.
3. Public Record Office, London, Reference no. F0371/12473/08314, Registry no. F5758/1397/10, from Sir M. Lampson to Sir V. Wellesley, dated April 29, 1927, received in Registry on June 24, 1927. F: China. The article written by W. Sheldon Ridge in the Far Eastern Times of the 16 instant: "Eugene Chen, A Character Sketch, by One Who Knows Him," was enclosed in a diplomatic dispatch by Sir M. Lampson, the Minister in Peking, to Sir V. Wellesley of the foreign office.

Chapter 6: From Shanghai to Versailles

1. Sharman, *Sun Yat-sen, His Life and Its Meaning*, p. 241.
2. Shi Yuanhua, *Ten Diplomats of China* (Zhong Guo Shi Wai Jiao Jia), (Shanghai People's Publishing House, 1999), p. 168.
3. Xin Ziling, *The Comprehensive Biography of Mao Zedong* (Mao Zedong Quan Zhuan), vol. 1 (Hong Kong: Li Wen Publishing House, 1993), p. 103.
4. J. A. Rogers, *World's Great Men of Color,* vol. 1 (New York: Touchstone, 1996), p. 180.
5. Ye Yonglie, *The Beginning of the Chinese Communist Party* (Zhong Gong Zhi Chu) (Hong Kong: Cosmos Books Ltd., 1991), p.87.
6. *Selected Works of Mao Tse-Tung* (Mao Zedong), vol. 2 (Peking: Foreign Languages Press, 1965), p. 373.
7. Robert Payne, *Mao Tse-Tung* (New York: Pyramid Books, 1967), p. 73.
8. Shi Yuanhua, *Ten Diplomats of China,* p. 304.
9. Silan Chen Leyda, *Footnote to History* (New York: Dance Horizons, 1984), p. 20.
10. Ibid., pp. 20–21.

11. Qian Yuli, *The Biography of Chen Youren* (Chen Youren Zhuan) (City of Shijiazhuang: Hebei People's Publishing House, 1999), p. 34.
12. John B. Powell, *My Twenty-five Years in China*, reprint (New York: Da Capo Press, 1976), pp. 48–49, 71–72.

Chapter 7: Blending Confucius, Lincoln, and Marx

1. Harry Schwartz, *Tsars, Mandarins and Commissars*, (Anchor Books, 1973), p. 98.
2. Translation by Dr. Willard Lyon, cf. *The World Mission of Christianity*, vol. 1 (New York, 1928), p.80, as quoted by Sharman, *Sun Yat-sen, His Life and Its Meaning*, p. 269.
3. Marie-Claire Bergere, *Sun Yat-sen*, trans. Janet Lloyd (Palo Alto: Stanford University Press, 1998), pp. 13, 64.
4. Sun Yat-sen, *San Aim Chu I*, trans. Price (Shanghai, 1927), pp. 428–429, 440, 444, as quoted by Sharman, *Sun Yat-sen*, pp. 279–280.
5. *China Year Book for 1923*, ed. Bell and Woodhead (Shanghai), p. 863, as quoted by Sharman, *Sun Yat-sen*, p. 248.
6. Dan N. Jacobs, *Borodin, Stalin's Man in China* (Cambridge: Harvard University Press, 1981), pp. 19–20.

Chapter 8: The Merger of the Kuomintang and the Communist Party

1. Public Record Office, London, W. Sheldon Ridge, "Eugene Chen, A Character Sketch, By One Who Knows Him."
2. Guo Hengyu, *The Secret Files of the Russian Communist Party Regarding the Chinese Revolution, 1920–1925* (E Gong Zhong Guo Ge Ming Mi Tang, 1920–1925) (Taipei, Taiwan: Dong Da Books, Ltd., 1996), p. 99.
3. H. G. W. Woodhead, *A Journalist in China*, p. 196.
4. Li Xin, Xiao Chaoran, et al., *The Rise of the Nationalist Revolution* (Guo Min Ge Ming Di Xing Qi) (Shanghai: Shanghai People's Publishing House, 1991), p. 288.
5. Yan Kuisong, *Breaking Up, The Ups and Downs in the Relationship Between Mao Zedong and Moscow* (Zou Xiang Po Lie, Mao Zedong Yu Mosike Di En En Yuan Yuan) (Hong Kong: Joint Publishing Co., Ltd., 1999), p. 7.
6. Leonard S. Hsu, *Sun Yat-sen, His Political and Social Ideas* (Los Angeles, 1933), pp. 130–132, as quoted by Sharman, *Sun Yat-sen, His Life and Its Meaning*, pp. 264–265.

Chapter 9: From Drawing Room to Firing Wall

1. Zhou Xingliang, *Liao Zhongkai and He Xiangning* (Liao Zhongkai He He Xiangning) (Henan: Henan People's Publishing House, 1991), p. 185.
2. Li Xin, Xiao Chaoran, et al., *The Rise of the Nationalist Revolution,* p. 330.
3. Department of Documents Studies of the Central Committee of the Chinese Communist Party (Zhong Gong Zhong Yang Wen Xian Yan Jiu Shi), *The Biography of Zhou Enlai* (Zhou Enlai Zhuan), vol. 1 (Beijing: Zhong Yang Wen Xian Publishing House, 1998), p. 35. No individual author is credited.
4. Dick Wilson, *Zhou Enlai* (New York: Viking Penguin, 1984), p. 58.
5. Department of Documents Studies, *The Biography of Zhou Enlai,* vol. l, pp. 97–98.
6. Li Xin, Xiao Chaoran, et al., *The Rise of the Nationalist Revolution,* p. 334.

Chapter 10: Maneuvering Around Sun Yatsen's Deathbed

1. Feng Yuxiang, *My Life* (Wo Di Sheng Huo) (Changsha: Yuelu Books, 1999), pp. 389–390. Originally published by Shanghai Education Book Shop (Jiao Yu Shu Dian) in 1947.
2. Ibid., p. 392.
3. Milly Bennett, *On Her Own,* edited and annotated by A. Tom Grunfeld (Armonk, NY: M. E. Sharpe, Inc., 1993), pp. 149 (note), 156.
4. Jin Kangzhong, *To the Abyss—Number One Traitor Wang Jingwei* (Zou Xiang Shen Yuan—Tou Hao Han Jian Wang Jingwei), vol. 1 (Beijing: International Culture Publishing House [Guo Ji Wen Hua Chu Pan Gong Shi], 1991), pp. 123–124.
5. Sterling Seagrave, *The Soong Dynasty* (New York: Perennial Library, 1986), p. 201.
6. Ibid., p. 202.
7. Li Enhan, *New Studies of the Diplomatic History of Modern China* (Jin Dai Zhong Guo Wai Jiao Shi Shi Xin Yan) (Taipei: Commercial Press, 2004), p. 242.

Chapter 11: From Firing Squad to Canton

1. *The Biography of Chen Youren,* p. 80.

Chapter 12: Coup d'État and Counter–Coup d'État

1. Xie Youtian, *The Alliance of the Kuomintang, Russian and Chinese Communist Parties Versus the West Hills Conference Faction: The History*

of the Origin of China's Anti- and Preempt Leftist Campaign (Lian E Rong Gong Yu Xi Shan Hui Yi: Zhong Guo Fan Zuo Fang Zuo Yun Dong Di Li Shi Geng Yuan), vol. 2 (Kowloon, Hong Kong: Ji Cheng Books, Ltd., 2001), p. 317.

2. *The Secret Files of the Russian Communist Party Regarding the Chinese Revolution*, 1920–1925, pp. 2, 144.

3. Chen Jieru (the third Madame Chiang Kaishek), *Chen Jieru's Memoirs*, trans. Wang Lingshi (Taipei, Taiwan: New News Cultural Enterprise Company, Ltd. (Xin Xin Wen Wen Hua Shi Ye Gu Fen You Xian Gong Shi), 1992), pp. 155–167.

4. Harold R. Isaacs, *The Tragedy of the Chinese Revolution*, 2nd rev. ed. (Palo Alto: Stanford University Press, 1961), p. 107.

Chapter 13: The Strike and the Northern Expedition

1. Lowell Dittner, *Liu Shao-chi and the Chinese Cultural Revolution: The Politics of Mass Criticism* (Berkeley: University of California Press, 1974), p. 13.

2. *Footnote to History*, p. 40.

3. *The Rise of the Nationalist Revolution*, p. 273.

4. Enhan Lee, *The Nationalist China's "Revolutionary Diplomacy,"* 1925–1931 (Taipei, Taiwan: Institute of Modern History, Academia Sinica, 1993), p. 43.

Chapter 14: March with the Northern Expedition Army

1. *Footnote to History*, p. 63.

2. Ibid., p. 65.

3. Ibid., p. 64.

Chapter 15: Twisting the Tail of the British Lion

1. Percy Chen, *China Called Me* (Boston: Little, Brown, 1979), pp. 90–91.

2. Ibid., p. 91.

3. Ibid., pp. 95–96.

4. *My Twenty-five Years in China*, p. 138.

5. Arthur M. Guttery, *Arthur M. Guttery in China, 1915–1928* (excerpts from reports and letters by Arthur M. Guttery) (New York: YMCA Historical Library, National Board of YMCAs, 1975), pp. 41–42.

6. *The Nationalist China's "Revolutionary Diplomacy"* 1925–1931, p. 67.

7. Sha Benren and Pan Xingming, *China's Relations with Britain in the Twentieth Century* (Er Shi Shi Ji Zhong Ying Guan Xi) (Shanghai: Shanghai People's Publishing House, 1996), p. 159.

Chapter 17: The Era of Chen Youren

1. *The Biography of Chen Youren*, p. 104; Shi Yuanhua, *Ten Diplomats of China*, p. 349.
2. N. Lee, W. S. K. Waung, and L. Y. Chiu, eds., *Bitter Smile: Memoirs of Chen Kungpo*, 1925–1936 (Hong Kong: University of Hong Kong, 1979), p. 104.
3. Department of Documents Studies of the Central Committee of The Chinese Communist Party (Zhong Gong Zhong Yang Wen Xian Yan Jiu Shi), *The Biography of Liu Shaoqi* (Liu Shaoqi Zhuan), vol. 1 (Beijing: Zhong Yang Wen Xian Publishing House, 1998), p. 100. No individual author is credited.
4. Rogers, *World's Great Men of Color*, vol. 1, pp. 180–181.
5. Jacobs, Borodin, *Stalin's Man in China*, p. 216.
6. Li Xin, Chen Tiejian, and Zhang Jingru (editors-in-chief), *The Northern Expedition, 1926–1927* (Bei Fa Zhan Zheng, 1926–1927) (Shanghai: Shanghai People's Publishing House, 1994), p. 716.
7. Henry Francis Misselwitz, *The Dragon Stirs: An Intimate Sketch-Book of China's Kuomintang Revolution, 1927–1929* (New York: Harbinger House, 1941), p. 95.
8. Bennett, *On Her Own*, p. 243.
9. Ibid., pp. 191–192.
10. Li Xin, Chen Tiejian, and Zhang Jingru, *The Northern Expedition*, p. 800.
11. Xin Ziling, *The Comprehensive Biography of Mao Zedong*, vol. 1, p. 298.

Chapter 18: Fleeing China and Crossing the Gobi Desert

1. Feng Yuxiang: *My Life*, p. 524.

Chapter 19: Stalin's Betrayal

1. Israel Epstein, *Woman in World History, Soong Ching Ling* (Madame Sun Yatsen) (Beijing: New World Press, 1993), p. 207.
2. Guo Hengyu, *The Secret Files of the Russian Communist Party Regarding the Chinese Revolution* (1926) (Hong Kong: Roaring Sea Publishing Company [Hai Xiao Chu Pan Shi Ye You Xian Gong Shi], 1997), p. 238.

3. Ibid., pp. 251–252.
4. *China Called Me*, p. 186.
5. Ibid., p. 186.
6. Zhang Guotao, *My Memoir* (Wo De Hui Yi), vol. 2 (Beijing: The East Publishing House [Dong Fang Chu Pan She], 2004), p. 8.

Chapter 20: Art for Revolution

1. Agnes Smedley, *The Great Road, The Life and Times of Chu Teh* (Zhu De) (New York: Monthly Review Press, 1972), p. 229.
2. Kang Keqing (Madame Zhu De), *Kang Keqing's Memoir* (Beijing: People's Liberation Army Publishing House, 1993), p. 70.

Chapter 21: A Lone Knight on His Mission

1. Jack and I wrote this episode from his memory, and also from his own experience of taking part in similar demonstrations later in Shanghai in 1936.
2. Arthur Clegg, *Aid China, 1937–1949, A Memoir of a Forgotten Campaign* (Beijing: New World Press, 1989), p. 32.

Chapter 22: Yanan Interlude

1. Feng Zhijun, *Zhou Enlai and Mao Zedong* (Kowloon, Hong Kong: Huang Fu Books and Huang Fu International Company Ltd., 1998), pp. 230–233.
2. Xin Ziling, *The Comprehensive Biography of Mao Zedong*, vol. 2, p. 311.
3. Ibid., vol. 2, p. 276.

Chapter 23: How Jack's Path Crossed with Mine

1. Feng Zhijun, *Liu Shaoqi and Mao Zedong* (Kowloon, Hong Kong: Huang Fu Books and Huang Fu International Company Ltd., 1998), pp. 118–119.
2. Arthur Clegg, *Aid China, 1937–1949*, p. 171.
3. [Beijing]. *People's Daily* (Ren Min Ri Bao), March 2, 1983, p. 2.
4. Beijing. *China Daily*, April 27, 1996, p. 5.

Chapter 24: The Breaking of the Magic Circle

1. Shi Dongbing, *Storm and Reverse of Stream* (Feng Bao Yu Ni Liu, the third volume in the Series of the Record of the Cultural Revolution) (Hong Kong: Fan Rong [Prosperity] Publishing House, 1992), p. 180.

2. Shi Dongbing, *Wuhan, Tiao Yu Tai, Mao Jia Wan* (the fifth volume in the Series of the Record of the Cultural Revolution) (Hong Kong: Fan Rong [Prosperity] Publishing House, 1992) p. 233.

3. Jack Chen, *Inside the Cultural Revolution* (London: Sheldon Press, 1976), p. 279.

4. Shi Dongbing, *Prelude at the Fishing Terrace* (Xu Mu Cong Diao Yu Tai La Kai, the fourth volume in the Series of the Record of the Cultural Revolution) (Hong Kong: Fan Rong [Prosperity] Publishing House, 1992), p. 73.

5. Dick Wilson, *Zhou Enlai*, p. 148.

Chapter 25: From Beijing to Upper Felicity and Back

1. Ben Gelman, "Mainland Journalist Visits SIU [Southern Illinois University], Chinese Welcomed in U.S.," *Southern Illinoisan*, December 14, 1971; Chuck Hutchcraft, "Emphasize Understanding, Chinese Journalist Visits SIU," *The Daily Egyptian*, December 13, 14, or 15, 1971. In this article, Marshall (professor at South Illinois University) says he received Chen's letter from Peking at about the same time that it was announced that Henry Kissinger had made his secret trip to Peking to set up a visit there by President Nixon.

Epilogue

1. Richard L. Madden, "Buckley Questions China-Studies Plan," *New York Times*, January 14, 1973; Governor Nelson A. Rockefeller's replies on February 2, 1973 to Mr. Robert Y. Lee, president of the Republican Club of Chinatown, New York; and Mr. Stephen Pan of the East Asian Research Institute at 86 Riverside Drive, New York; and Mr. Henry Chung, president of the Chinese Consolidated Benevolent Association at 62 Mott Street, New York. In the letters, the governor explained why the State Education Department employed Jack as a consultant. "Mr. Chen's work with the State Education Department is one step toward enlarging our knowledge and understanding of modern China and therefore of fulfilling one of the goals of the communiqué jointly issued by the President [Nixon] and the Chinese Premier Chou Enlai [Zhou Enlai]." Jack received copies of the letters through Mr. Ward Morehouse, from the office of the State Commissioner of Education, Ewald B. Nyquist.

SELECTED BIBLIOGRAPHY

The selected bibliography includes a large part of my research material, and the books and articles I mention in the notes.

Feng Zhijun. *Lin Biao and Mao Zedong*. Kowloon, Hong Kong: Huang Fu Books, 1998.

———. *Deng Xiaoping and Mao Zedong*. Kowloon, Hong Kong: Huang Fu Books, 2001.

Hu Shiyan, Wu Kebin, et al. *The Biography of Chen Yi*. In the series The Biographies of Contemporary Historical Figures of China (Dang Dai Zhong Guo Ren Wu Zhuan Ji Cong Shu). Beijing: Contemporary China Publishing House, 1991.

Kai-yu Hsu. *Chou Enlai, China's Gray Eminence*. New York: Anchor Books, 1969.

Low, C. C., and Associates. *Modern History of China*. Singapore: Canfonian PTE Ltd., 1999.

Rice, Edward E. *Mao's Way*. Berkeley: University of California Press, 1974.

Shen Chuanbao. *Deng Xiaoping's Stories*. Zhong Guo (China): Changan Publishing House, Beijing, 2004.

Shi Dongbing. *Series of the Records of the Cultural Revolution* (Wen Hua Da Ge Ming Ji Shi Xi Lie), 13 vols. Hong Kong: Fan Rong (Prosperity) Publishing House, 1992–1994.

Spence, Jonathan D. *God's Chinese Son*. New York: W. W. Norton & Company, 1996.

Strong, Anna Louise. *China's Millions*. New York: Knight Publishing Company, 1935.

———. *I Change Worlds*. New York: Garden City Publishing Comapany, 1937.

Tang Chunliang. *The Comprehensive Biography of Li Lisan*. City of Hefei: Anhui People's Publishing House, 1999.

Vishnyakova-Akimora, Vera Vladimirovna. *Two Years in Revolutionary China, 1925–1927*, translated by Steven I. Levine. Cambridge: East Asian Research Center of Harvard University, 1971.

Wan Yan Shao Yuan. *The Biography of Wang Zhengting (Thomas C. T. Wang)*. City of Shijiazhuang: Hebei People's Publishing House, 1999.

Wang Yongqin. *Zhou Enlai in Purgatory*. Guangzhou (Canton): Guangdong People's Publishing House, 2002.

Yin Jiamin. *Zhou Enlai and the Kuomintang Generals*. Beijing: People's Liberation Army Publishing House, 1998.

INDEX